UNDER THE STARRY FLAG

Under the Starry Flag

How a Band of Irish Americans

Joined the Fenian Revolt and

Sparked a Crisis over Citizenship

LUCY E. SALYER

THE BELKNAP PRESS OF

HARVARD UNIVERSITY PRESS

Cambridge, Massachusetts

London, England

2018

First printing

Library of Congress Cataloging-in-Publication Data

Names: Salyer, Lucy E., author.

Title: Under the starry flag : how a band of Irish Americans joined the Fenian revolt and sparked a crisis over citizenship / Lucy E. Salyer.

Description: Cambridge, Massachusetts : The Belknap Press of Harvard University Press, 2018. | Includes bibliographical references and index.

Identifiers: LCCN 2018015222 | ISBN 9780674057630 (cloth)

Subjects: LCSH: Citizenship—United States—History—19th century. | Expatriation—United States—History—19th century. | Expatriation—Great Britain—History—19th century. | Irish Americans—History—19th century. | Fenians. | United States—Foreign relations—1865–1898. | United States—Foreign relations—Great Britain. | Great Britain—Foreign relations—United States.

Classification: LCC JF801 .S277 2018 | DDC 342.4108 / 3—dc23

LC record available at https://lccn.loc.gov/2018015222

For my mother,
Frances Helen Pyeatt Salyer,
and my daughter,
Naomi Helen Salyer Rubin

Contents

UNDER THE STARRY FLAG

Prologue

Erin's Hope and the Forgotten Right of Expatriation

FORTY MEN straggled out of a house on East Broadway in New York City one April day in 1867, leaving in small groups to blend into the city's busiest and unruliest neighborhood. Look casual, carry no baggage, they had been told. They sauntered down Canal Street to the Hudson River and climbed aboard a steamer, posing, perhaps, as day-trippers out for a springtime boat ride. But once they reached the outer harbor at Sandy Hook, the men dropped anchor and waited. They had almost given up hope when the brigantine *Jacmel* showed up the next day, with a skeleton crew of five commanded by Captain John F. Kavanagh, a U.S. Navy captain during the Civil War. A cache of weapons and ammunition, packed in piano boxes, sewing machine cases, and wine casks, with Spanish labels affixed to fool the casual observer, lay in *Jacmel*'s hold. In 1880 one newspaper article would exaggerate wildly that the ship had over 25,000 stands of arms, six batteries of artillery, and 20 million rounds of ammunition, but the testimony of one of the participants in 1867 is closer to the truth. He claimed there were at least 5,000 stands of arms, including Spencer repeating rifles, Enfield rifles, a few Austrian rifles, and Sharp breech-loading rifles; a number of revolvers; three pieces of artillery, capable of firing three-pound shot or shell; and 1.5 million rounds of ammunition. Without clearance papers and flying no flag, *Jacmel* slipped out of the harbor with all the men aboard and headed toward Cuba, but after a day changed course for its true destination: Ireland.[1]

The ship sailed without incident for a week, evading detection when necessary by flying the Union Jack, until on Easter Sunday, April 21, the men on board stopped to dedicate their mission. Before noon, the crew hoisted the ship's true colors, a green flag with a yellow sunburst, and honored it with a thirty-two-gun salute, one blast for each county of Ireland. Captain Kavanagh proceeded to read the orders he had been given in New York. Colonel James E. Kelly, head of the Fenian Brotherhood's Military Council, directed the men to land their arms at Sligo, on the northwest coast of Ireland, or elsewhere if that proved impossible. On the day of the Christian celebration of resurrection and rebirth, the captain rechristened *Jacmel*. The ship became *Erin's Hope*. Its broader purpose, according to one of the men: to "revolutionize Ireland."[2]

The men on board were a diverse lot in terms of their day jobs in the United States, including among their ranks a tailor, carpenter, bricklayer, glasscutter, cooper, shoemaker, "bar boy," actor, jeweler, newspaper reporter, and customs house clerk.[3] But on *Erin's Hope,* they became "bold Fenian men," Irish soldiers in the tradition of the Fianna, legendary ancient warriors who had protected Ireland from outside aggressors.[4] Many, including one of the leaders, Colonel John Warren, had crossed the same ocean years earlier as immigrants to the United States, but now the "fierce Exile[s] of Erin" were "coming back with a vengeance."[5] Most, if not all, of the men on board were veterans of the recent American Civil War, several having served as officers in the Union Army's Irish Brigade. They were comrades and compatriots, joined together by their common Irish heritage, their American citizenship, their bitter hatred of England, and their determination, as part of the Irish nationalist Fenian Brotherhood, to liberate Ireland from British rule. They sailed to aid the Rising of March 1867, the day of reckoning long anticipated by Fenians in Ireland and the United States, when the Irish, aided by their Irish American kin with their American military know-how and weapons, would "crush the hand clutching our Country's throat" and "hurl the usurper from his throne."[6]

Despite the ship's name, the daring men aboard *Erin's Hope* had little chance of success. The mission of *Erin's Hope* ran aground as the promised Rising faltered, tempers on board ship frayed, and water and food stores grew dangerously low. Forced to land on the southern coast of Ireland, thirty-two of the *Jacmel* men were arrested by the vigilant Irish Coast Guard within hours and thrown into prison.[7] Their capture came as little surprise to most at the time. More puzzling, even to sympathetic observers, was how forty men expected to "revolutionize" Ireland with their expedition.

The *Jacmel* voyage, like the other ventures of the Fenians, was a dismal failure militarily, but it would lead to one of the most successful Fenian challenges to British authority. If the men of the *Jacmel* failed to liberate Ireland as a nation, they would succeed in provoking an international crisis that many feared would bring the United States and England to the brink of war—and over what? The right of expatriation.

EXPATRIATION, explained historian and diplomat George Bancroft in 1869, is the "right of an individual to choose his home, & with it the right to change his country."[8] When arrested and tried by the British for treason, the Fenians demanded to be recognized as American citizens. Having left Ireland, they had escaped British rule and pledged their allegiance to the United States, becoming naturalized Americans, which freed them from the "shackles of British slavery." The British breezily dismissed their claims with a phrase that never failed to infuriate Americans: "Once a subject, always a subject." The Irish might pack up and leave Erin's shores, but along with their trunks, they carried their status as British subjects for the rest of their lives. Their allegiance to the king was permanent, "written by the finger of the law in their hearts," as Sir Edward Coke so eloquently put it, and no oath they took in America could erase that obligation.[9]

Americans had been resisting the doctrine of perpetual allegiance since the American Revolution, when they threw off the yoke of British rule and boldly declared their right to form their own political allegiance to the sovereign of their choice. But it was only during Reconstruction, in the wake of the Civil War, that the revolutionary right of expatriation gained explicit recognition. Within days of the ratification of the Fourteenth Amendment, Congress passed the Expatriation Act of 1868, declaring for the first time what had long been assumed: Individuals had the inherent right to change their political allegiance, and the government had the obligation to protect its adopted as well as native citizens when they traveled outside of the United States. The United States signed a dozen treaties between 1868 and 1872, beginning with a landmark agreement that Bancroft signed with the Prussian government in 1868, that enshrined the principle of choice in political membership. Americans gloated that the "young republics" had finally gained sway over "ancient monarchies" in breaking the sovereign's stranglehold over the individual's allegiance. They were witnessing the fulfillment of revolutionary principles and "one of the greatest and most important triumphs of American diplomacy."[10] If the Fourteenth Amendment marked the victory of Union over the states, the naturalization treaties bore witness to the newfound respect for the United States, which had emerged from its most serious national trial intact and was ready to take its place on the world stage.[11]

Yet expatriation has been the forgotten child of Reconstruction citizenship policies, curiously absent or sidelined in the many histories of the so-called civil rights revolution wrought by Reconstruction.[12] Nor does the right of expatriation have much presence in contemporary discussions of civil rights, despite the fact that every year hundreds of thousands of individuals in the United States exercise that right by becoming naturalized citizens.[13] The right of expatriation may seem unfamiliar or quaint to twenty-first-century observers. It lacks the heft or thrill of other well-known rights—the freedom of speech, freedom of religion, the right to a fair trial, the right to vote. Asked about what rights we have by virtue of being free human beings, few people would likely mention the right to change one's citizenship or allegiance.

To the extent that expatriation rings any bells of recognition, it conjures up examples of *losing* rather than *choosing* citizenship.[14] The United Nations Declaration of Rights in 1948 declared that "everyone has a right to a nationality" and that no one "should be denied the right to change his nationality." Such rights seem obvious, perhaps, and uncontroversial, but the United Nations felt compelled to declare them forcefully precisely because so many individuals had lost their citizenship involuntarily in the 1930s at the hands of totalitarian regimes, the most notorious example being the denationalization of Jews in Hitler's regime, which, as Hannah Arendt revealed so powerfully, led to the loss of fundamental rights and protection.[15] More recently, in the fall of 2011 politicians introduced to the U.S. Congress a new "expatriation act"—originally entitled the Terrorist Expatriation Act but later repackaged as the Enemy Expatriation Act—that lashed out at Americans believed to be supporting terrorist activities, such as Faisal Shahzad, the Pakistani American arrested for the attempted car bombing of Times Square in May 2010. The bill proposed to strip citizenship from any American "engaging in, or purposefully and materially supporting, hostilities against the United States."[16]

Involuntary expatriation has a long history. Expelling disloyal or unwelcome subjects from the realm had been a favorite punishment of European sovereigns, who defined expatriation as "banishment."[17] In the depths of the American Civil War, Americans eagerly read Edward Everett Hale's wildly popular cautionary tale, "The Man without a Country," many taking as fact the fictional story of Lt. Philip Nolan, condemned to loss of citizenship and lifetime exile at sea for uttering the words, "Damn the United States! I wish I may never hear of the United States again!" Still, while Hale's story of the stateless Nolan provided a powerful allegory of the dire consequences of disloyalty, many Americans in the nineteenth century faced a quite different problem: having too many countries. As individuals joined the "exit revolution" of the nineteenth century, leaving their homes by the millions to populate New World countries—Australia, New Zealand, Canada, South American nations, and especially the United States—they became caught in a jurisdictional tangle, especially when they pledged allegiance to their new homes.[18]

In the twenty-first century, governments guard their borders primarily to keep people out, but at the beginning of the nineteenth century, leaving one's country often proved more daunting than entering a new one, as governments deployed exit rules to control their populations and ensure the long-term strategic interests of the state. For European states, bursting with ambition in the sixteenth and seventeenth centuries to expand their power and wealth, people were as important a natural resource as timber or fish, to be harvested and employed in the task of building empire. Subjects provided the laborers in the fields, the skilled artisans for early manufactures, and, perhaps most important, the soldiers and sailors for the military arm of empire building. In the eighteenth century, most European states viewed emigrants who left without permission, especially seamen and artisans, as deserters and tried to stem their departure with stern laws threatening fines, imprisonment, impressment, loss of property, and even death to disloyal subjects who ignored their obligations to the motherland. Migration for the purpose of populating the colonial outposts of the empire was fine; leaving to become part of a competing state's enterprise was not. Undeterred, millions of migrants left anyway, often at great cost and personal risk.[19]

As migrants traveled back and forth across national boundaries, they called into question the "borders of belonging" in the Atlantic World.[20] The constant flow of people created a crisis for both the migrants and the nation-states that laid claim to them. Emerging nation-states in the nineteenth century worked hard to define and control their territorial boundaries, asserting their exclusive sovereign power to govern everything and everybody that fell within their physical borders. But conflicting rules of membership threw that project into question, as claims by the home countries to the allegiance of their native subjects threatened to plant "alien colonies" within "settler societies" such as the United States—foreigners who lived within the country but who would never be fully subject to its authority. In turn, America's liberal naturalization policies (for white men) posed challenges for European countries, which viewed the laws as predatory. The naturalization laws enticed subjects to escape the onerous obligations of the homeland, only to return to their native land armed with American citizenship as a shield against further demands of their natural sovereign. Nothing less than the definition of national sovereignty was at stake.[21]

Immigrants saw the problem differently. Often they thought strategically and pragmatically: how could they best secure their lives and the future of their families from the demands of sovereigns to whom they might have little attachment? But they also articulated a vision of citizenship that seems strikingly modern and radical in its emphasis on the right of individuals to determine their own fate and choose their political home. They declared expatriation a "natural right bestowed on man by his Creator," as "sacred a right, as inalienable, as the rights of persons and of property, the liberty of speech and religion."[22] It was "a right indispensable to liberty, and . . . ought never be surrendered"—a right so precious that many Americans, native-born as well as naturalized, willingly went to war in 1812 against Britain, in part, to defend the "American doctrine" of expatriation.[23] Clearly, the right of expatriation, so unfamiliar to us today, had a different resonance in the mid-nineteenth century.

This book seeks to recover the history of the forgotten right of expatriation. Why the right of expatriation mattered in the nineteenth century and why its meaning remains obscure and elusive today are the puzzles it aims to solve. The Fenians on *Erin's Hope* prove to be surprisingly important in unraveling that mystery, as they stepped into an international controversy that had been brewing for years. Bent on freeing Ireland, the Fenians sparked a revolution in the law of citizenship instead.

ONE

The Fenians and the
Making of a Crisis

I

Clonakilty, God Help Us!

WHAT DID John Warren think as he gazed at the Irish shore from the deck of *Jacmel* in the spring of 1867? He had not seen his native land for fourteen years, not since 1853, when at the age of nineteen he had fled from the southern coastal town of Clonakilty in County Cork, escaping the disastrous Great Famine, which had killed over 1 million Irish since 1845. Warren had joined the flood of his countrymen—2.1 million over eleven years—who left for the United States and other destinations in the wake of the catastrophe, hoping to find refuge for themselves and their families. A once lively market town, Clonakilty by 1853 had increasingly little to offer Warren, an energetic young man of the artisan class. Even before the Famine spread its deadly reach, those with any skills or economic means had been tempted to leave for fairer horizons as Ireland's meager industry deteriorated and farming became less profitable. The Famine had been the last straw. Warren left a ravaged country, which journalists struggled to find words to describe.[1]

When he returned in 1867, both Warren and Ireland had changed. Now thirty-three, a family man and business owner, catering to the Irish immigrant community in Charlestown, Massachusetts, Warren had survived the Civil War as an officer in the Irish Brigade and wanted "to revisit old and dear scenes." The Ireland he returned to seemed on the rebound. Telegraph lines and railways had begun to link isolated counties, creating paths to communicate news and carry new manufactured goods to hinterlands. Livestock, one of Ireland's most successful exports after the Famine, covered the green hills of new, larger Irish farms. The Guinness family had transformed its "small, poky brewhouse" in Dublin into the United Kingdom's largest brewery, gaining international fame for its dark, bitter stout. Yet neither Warren nor Ireland was at peace, and neither was content.[2]

As Warren gazed on Ireland from *Jacmel*, he may have contemplated how far he had traveled over the years between Clonakilty and Boston, but it may have seemed as though he had never left.

THERE WAS something about Clonakilty that seemed to breed rebels, a historical trait that might seem at odds with its image today. Now Clonakilty enjoys a reputation as a lively but laid-back town in West Cork, nestled at the mouth of a shallow harbor that stretches out a third of a mile to Inchydoney Beach, a popular surfing spot with spectacular sea cliffs and broad sandy shores. Clonakilty regularly earns recognition as one of Ireland's "tidy towns." The European Union named Clonakilty a top tourist destination in 2007, and in 2011 it became the first Irish town to receive the international Cittaslow ("slow city") award in honor of its preservation of "traditional values" and dedication to a "slower way of life." Clonakilty hardly seems a troublesome place—and is certainly a nice place to visit.[3]

Yet the town embraces a history of rebellion as part of its "traditional" way of life. Walking through the town, you encounter its rebellious past everywhere, written into the townscape in street names, public plazas, historical markers, and shop displays. A monument to Tadhg O'Donovan Asna, the leader of Clonakilty's part in the 1798 rising against British forces, stands in the center of town; follow Asna Street west out to the wharves and you can see Croppy Quay, where British troops tossed the bodies of the slain Asna and his followers into the harbor. Or turn south from the Asna monument onto Rossa Street, named for Jeremiah O'Donovan Rossa, the flamboyant Fenian leader famous for organizing the "dynamite campaign" of English cities in the 1880s. Nearby stands the family home of Mary Jane Irwin, wife of Rossa and cousin of John Warren, but remembered in the marker on the house as a "poetess" and "Fenian" in her own right. Turn the opposite direction and you reach a square named after another national hero (though not of Clonakilty origin), Robert Emmet, executed in 1803. Ringed around the square are trim, elegant Georgian houses, one especially prized as the onetime home of Michael Collins, otherwise known as the "big fella," the leader of the Irish Republican Army who played a central role in the Irish War of Independence between 1919 and 1921 before he was assassinated not far from Clonakilty during the Irish Civil War in 1922. The controversial architect of modern Ireland is everywhere in Clonakilty: as a statue adjacent to Emmet Square, in photographs lining the walls of the old O'Donovan Hotel in the town center, in the tourist literature highlighting Clonakilty's claims to fame, in posters peering out of shop windows at passersby.[4]

What you won't find in Clonakilty are any historical plaques commemorating John Warren, the Fenian who shared the command of *Jacmel*. If there were a marker, it would probably be on Rossa Street, where Warren's family lived when he was baptized by the local Catholic priest, though it was called Main Street then. The association of Warren's birthplace with Jeremiah O'Donovan Rossa is fitting. Born only three years and seven and a half miles apart, and loosely linked through family intermarriage, they both became ardent Fenians and even spent time together at Chatham Prison. Yet Rossa secured a historical fame that eluded Warren, becoming part of the pantheon of Irish nationalist heroes and freedom fighters. Warren has disappeared from Clonakilty's history, perhaps because, like so many Irish, his family emigrated from the town during the Famine and eventually faded from local memory. Warren did have his time in the international spotlight and would even be included in John Savage's tribute, *Fenian Heroes and Martyrs*, but Warren remained a midlevel leader rather than part of the Fenian elite. Born to a family of artisans, Warren did not represent the average Irish man of the 1840s any more than Clonakilty, as a large market town, encapsulated the typical Irish community. Most Irish—70 percent of County Cork's inhabitants—lived in the country, working on farms and enjoying few of the advantages of town life. Yet Irish nationalist movements, especially the Fenian Brotherhood, drew their strongest support from towns like Clonakilty and men like Warren.[5]

PERHAPS Clonakilty's nationalist fervor stemmed from the fact that it was born through conquest, becoming an official town only when ambitious English Protestant colonizers—the "New English"—arrived in the province of Munster in the late 1500s to settle on confiscated "plantations" with the express aim to reap profits and, more broadly, to "make Ireland British." Richard Boyle purchased 42,000 acres of land in Munster—land confiscated from native Irish and "old" English Norman owners—from Sir Walter Raleigh in 1601 and became the first Earl of Cork. From his luxurious seat of power at Lismore Castle, Boyle devoted great energy to developing the economic potential of his new fiefdom. He carved out towns and villages, with markets, schools, almshouses, courthouses, and jails. He launched new commercial enterprises—mines, marble quarries, fish-curing operations, ironworks, the manufacturing of barrel staves—anything that might yield profitable exports. And, of course, Boyle collected rents from tenants on his extensive land holdings across the southern coast of Ireland, a lucrative business that earned him £50 a day and made him one of the richest landowners in Ireland. Boyle lured a hundred English settlers to populate his new town, the Borough of Cloghnikilty, seeding the town with English woolen weavers in his effort to foster new local textile industries. By 1641, Boyle, as "Lord of the Town," had turned Clonakilty into a thriving market town and a political borough, allowing the corporation governing the town to send two (English Protestant) representatives to the Irish Parliament. Little wonder that when Boyle became the first Earl of Cork, he chose as his family motto "God's Providence is mine inheritance."[6]

By the mid-1600s, Boyle and other English colonizers could note with smug satisfaction that Munster had become increasingly more "English," both literally, with 22,000 English Protestants settled in the province by 1641, and culturally, as more inhabitants spoke English, adopted English styles of clothing, and pursued "English" occupations.[7] Yet the Great Rebellion of 1641 abruptly checked any assumptions that the Anglicization of Ireland would continue without opposition, as many Irish joined forces with their fellow Catholic Old English neighbors to rise up against the New English in a bloody war that would last until 1652. Clonakilty became the "scene of sad carnage," one account noted primly, as Irish insurgents stormed the town, stripped English residents of their clothes, imprisoned them in the market house, and nearly burned the town to the ground.[8] In their deadliest attack, Irish killed two companies of English and Scottish soldiers, sent to subdue the rebellion, in the streets of Clonakilty; in furious retaliation, the English militia struck back, driving the rebels to the sea where as many as 600 drowned, trapped by the surging tide.[9]

The battles festered long after in local memories. George Bennett of nearby Bandon, who was of Anglo-Irish descent, would recall in 1869 the shocking attack of the "Amazon" women, Joan Barry and her force of 300 Irish women, who ransacked and pillaged the houses of Clonakilty "like a swarm of locusts." These "unwomanly women" swept through the town "with one weapon in their fist, and another between their teeth," terrorizing the inhabitants and stuffing "everything in their bottomless wallets."[10] The Irish would remember the Rebellion of 1641 differently. Oliver Cromwell and his New Model Army, having beheaded Charles I in England and secured the victory of Parliament over the monarchy, marched into Ireland in 1649 and, with legendary brutality, defeated Catholic rebels in bloody battles that, in conjunction with famine and plague, killed as much as one-third of the Irish Catholic population. Jeremiah

O'Donovan Rossa recalled "fireside stories" he heard growing up near Clonakilty in the 1830s of English soldiers who "used to kill the women, and take the young children, born and unborn, on the points of their bayonets, and dash them against the walls."[11]

Such origin stories, and how they were remembered, mattered to men such as John Warren, who was born almost 200 years after the Great Rebellion but who carefully preserved the dramatic tales in his Irish American newspaper. For Irish nationalists, intent on securing Ireland's liberation from England, the history of Ireland's unjust conquest and rule by foreigners became an oft-told saga, in poetry, song, speeches, and pamphlets, used to rally Irish to the cause of freedom. Irish nationalists were avid historians but hardly impartial ones. They told tales of a glorious Irish civilization that had been tragically derailed by English predators. They exposed patterns of exploitation that reached across the centuries and legitimized revolution. So too, the past provided models of heroic resistance that should be emulated.[12] More Joan Barrys, please.

Modern Irish historians have often been uncomfortable with the partisan, passionate tone of the nationalist histories, striving for more objective analyses. Ireland was often depicted in the English press as Britannia's younger and less experienced sister Hibernia, in need of guidance, and its position in the empire remained ambiguous. Recognized as a separate kingdom and governed by its own Parliament until 1801, Ireland appeared, at a glance, to have considerable constitutional autonomy. Yet from the time of the Irish Rebellion of 1641 to the Act of Union of 1801, the Irish had watched their independence slip away.[13]

After Cromwell's reconquest of Ireland, England handed the Irish government, and much of Irish wealth, over to Protestants, particularly Anglicans, a distinct minority in Ireland. Under the "Protestant Ascendancy," Catholics lost much of their land, Catholic-owned property falling from 59 percent of the total in 1641 to a mere 5 percent in 1774. They lost their political voice, as the Penal Laws prevented them from voting, holding office, or serving in the militia. They lost access to the professions and education, as laws restricted their occupations and forbade Catholic schools. And they lost the freedom to practice their faith openly, as the Protestant Irish Parliament, in its zeal to "prevent the growth of Popery," passed laws forbidding "popish masses."[14] Their faith criminalized, Catholics suffered the further insult of having to pay mandatory tithes, or taxes, to support the state-sanctioned Anglican Church of Ireland. Never fully enforced, the Penal Laws nonetheless declared loudly and clearly that Irish Catholics—who constituted the vast majority of the population, 80 percent by 1834—were second-class subjects.[15]

Finally, in 1801, Ireland lost its last shred of independence in the wake of the bloody Irish Rebellion of 1798. The United Irishmen began as a small elite movement in 1789 to obtain moderate democratic reforms but by the mid-1790s had flowered into a radical mass movement, inspired by the French and American revolutions. Catholics, Presbyterians, and radical Anglo-Irish joined together to demand Ireland's complete independence. Clonakilty again distinguished itself as a site of insurrection with its Battle of the Big Cross in June 1798. Tadhg O'Donovan Asna led several hundred rebels in an ambush of the Westmeath militia, but the British army delivered swift and brutal retribution, as it had throughout Ireland. The Caithness Fencibles killed Asna and dozens of his followers, displaying their bloodied bodies in front of the Market House for several days before dumping them off Croppy Quay.[16] Those rebels who survived had to endure a scolding by the Reverend Horatio Townsend, serving as sovereign and chief magistrate of Clonakilty, the following Sunday at the Roman Catholic chapel. "Surely you are not foolish enough to think that society could exist without Landlords and Magistrates," he cautioned. "Be persuaded that it is quite out of the sphere of country farmers and tradesmen to set up as politicians, reformers and lawmakers."[17]

The rebellion repressed, Britain tightened its grasp over Ireland. With the Protestant Ascendancy no longer trusted to govern Ireland on its own, the 1801 Act of Union abolished the Irish Parliament and created the United Kingdom of Great Britain and Ireland. Pro-Union advocates hastened to reassure Irish doubters that the new Union would "be neither British nor Irish" but a co-governing enterprise, as the Irish received 100 seats in the British Parliament. Together, all would profit in the glorious cause of building and sustaining the British Empire. Some did indeed profit from Union. The English government paid the Anglo-Irish handsomely for their support with titles of nobility and money, leading critics to charge that the Union had been bought through bribery. The Anglo-Irish retained their economic and political power, but many Irish, Protestant and Catholic alike, found the new Union a sharp break from the past, sweeping away even the pretense of Irish self-government with strong-arm tactics.[18] Coming on the heels of the rebellion, the Union created new breeding grounds for resistance, especially among Irish Catholics and especially among the "aspiring" classes—people like the Warrens of Clonakilty.

As the only boy of five children, John Warren probably received a warm welcome from his parents, Timothy and Mary Warren, when he was born on

May 14, 1834. Here was the son to carry on Timothy's trade as a wool comber, an ancient and noble craft typically passed down from father to son. In the 1700s, County Cork had been famous for its worsted woolen fabrics, encouraged, no doubt, by Boyle's importation of English woolen workers. When the woolen industry was at its height in the mid-eighteenth century, master wool combers—dubbed the "aristocracy of the worsted workers"—earned high wages by purchasing raw wool and preparing it to be spun and woven. But English wool manufacturers had always kept a jealous eye on their markets, securing high tariffs on Irish woolens. Between 1825 and 1838, Irish woolen manufacturing plummeted 85 percent after English manufacturers flooded the Irish market with woolen items in the 1820s, selling them so cheaply that even peasants began to wear imported wool clothing rather than making their own.[19] The prospects for the Warren family—and the town of Clonakilty—looked bleak.

Just ten years earlier, Clonakilty had been a "considerable market town," typical of the new Irish economy of the late eighteenth and early nineteenth centuries. England's incessant demands for Irish beef, pork, butter, wheat, and linen during the long Napoleonic Wars between 1793 and 1815 had kept Ireland's towns and farms humming. Cork merchants traveled to Clonakilty's weekly Friday markets and its four annual fairs to buy its famed poultry, hogs, sheep, cattle, and farm produce. Farmers came to town to sell their produce but also to spend the growing contents of their pocketbooks on an ever-expanding array of "cheap and good provisions" in town shops and, perhaps, a "Clonakilty Stout" from the local Deasy Brewery.[20]

The town supported numerous artisans and shopkeepers, but beginning in 1790, the booming linen industry dominated the town's economy. Clonakilty's linen market thrived in part because the British Parliament encouraged its production, allowing Irish linen to be sold duty-free in England. As many as 10,000 people in Clonakilty and the surrounding countryside worked at producing linen in 1824. For many rural families, linen manufacturing made all the difference between thriving and merely surviving, as the wages women and children made spinning and weaving became crucial to family incomes. Clonakilty's linen market became "the best frequented in the district," ringing up weekly sales that could reach £1,000 and an annual income of £30,000. By 1824, Clonakilty could boast that the town of 4,138 inhabitants was "rapidly improving," with "several spacious and handsome private residences" in Shannon Square.[21]

But the linen industry slumped in the late 1820s after Parliament embraced "free trade" policies, no longer guaranteeing Irish linen a reliable market as it competed with foreign countries. The remaining linen production moved to large factories in Ulster, and thousands of workers, both in towns and in the countryside, lost what had been a major source of income. Weavers in nearby Bandon complained they were "reduced to a state of beggary," blaming greedy English merchants and officials for their economic woes.

By 1834, Clonakilty's fortunes were declining rapidly, and by 1846, the town had little bustle left in it, taking on "an appearance of desertion, decay, and coming misery." Clonakilty shrank in size, its population dropping 5 percent between 1821 and 1831 as residents abandoned the town searching for work, several no doubt joining the surge of almost 1 million emigrants who left declining market towns and commercial centers for North America between 1815 and 1844. Towns like Clonakilty and Bandon, which had been the harbingers of Irish prosperity, became by the 1830s symbols of a new economic phase: the deindustrialization of Ireland.[22]

Left with dwindling industrial opportunities, the Irish could—and did— turn to farming to eke out a living, but Irish agriculture also was in crisis by the end of the Napoleonic Wars, when demand for Irish crops dropped and prices plunged. Farmers' incomes fell, but expenses remained high. The population of Ireland exploded in the late eighteenth century, jumping from 2.6 million in 1750 to an astounding 8.5 million in 1845, putting more pressure on available land. Land values spiked, as did rents, enticing landlords and tenants to subdivide their land into ever smaller plots to maximize their rental income. Over half of all Irish farmers had meager one- to two-acre plots of land by 1841. The vast majority of rural Irish—about 75 percent—lived in dire poverty.[23]

Landlords, especially the "improving" types infected by the free trade fever of the day, looked at their estates, crowded with huts and crawling with tenants on ever smaller plots, and envisioned a different sort of agricultural empire, one that used the most modern farming techniques, which would yield more efficient and more profitable farms, and perhaps even turning to grazing animals rather than growing crops. But that meant major changes in landholding and in ways of thinking. Just as linen production had shifted from cottage industry to factory, the Irish farm imagined by modernizing landlords would gather all of the small plots together and reconstitute them into large commercial agricultural ventures that would run with more factory-like efficiency and profitability. But of course, consolidating the land meant figuring out what to do with the thousands of tenants clinging to whatever land they had managed to claim. The British Parliament made it easier for landlords to evict tenants and also forbade tenants from subdividing land, all at the behest of landlords seeking to consolidate their lands. Well before the Famine, evictions of peasants from their homes became all too common, and even those who remained received leases on much less favorable terms.[24]

Why did Ireland suffer so? Looking back through the lens of an economic historian, the struggles of artisans in Clonakilty and the farmers of the surrounding Irish countryside hardly seem unique. Throughout the industrializing world, machines edged out the skilled artisan and large commercialized farms uprooted peasant farmers, creating an ever-growing pool of landless wage earners and tenant farmers. Advocates of the new order, at the time, saw progress at work—the unfolding of natural economic principles that would increase production and the "wealth of nations." If anyone was to blame, it was the greedy or profligate Irish worker. Irish children attending the new National Schools, set up by England in 1830, learned in their textbooks that Dublin businessmen "took their money and machinery elsewhere" because stubborn workers "refused to work at a lower price." And workers suffered "great want" because they failed to think about tomorrow, spending all they had on alcohol.[25]

John Warren may have heard such lessons in school, for he certainly received a formal education somewhere in Clonakilty—a distinctive achievement, as nearly 48 percent of the town's residents could neither read nor write in 1841.[26] But his education outside of the classroom was just as crucial for the budding nationalist. Explaining his political awakening as a youth in Clonakilty, Warren said simply, "I observed, I read." His "patriotic parents" taught him "by example and instruction" about his proud Irish heritage, lessons reinforced by the swirl of political activity in the 1830s and 1840s.[27] Secret societies, bound by oath, sprang up in troubled regions to carry out their own brand of vigilante justice. They tore down fences on new "grazing farms"; maimed and killed livestock; beat, threatened, and even assassinated land agents and tax collectors; and violently resisted eviction. They launched rent strikes and refused to pay tithes to the Anglican Church. Nor were cities peaceful. Artisans in trade unions—weavers, wool combers, carpenters—desperately sought to stem their declining economic status through petitions, violent strikes, and intimidation.[28]

It was also the era of Daniel O'Connell, the "Liberator" of Ireland, so called because he waged a successful campaign to emancipate Catholics from their political bondage, securing passage of the parliamentary act of 1829 that allowed Catholics to vote and hold limited offices. Success bred hope for more far-reaching change. O'Connell stirred the masses with his ongoing battle to repeal the Act of Union and restore the Irish Parliament, thousands thronging to his "monster rallies" to cheer his speeches and contributing hard-earned shillings to the campaign. People flocked to the "Repeal reading rooms" that popped up throughout Ireland, where they pored over the *Nation* and other new nationalist newspapers or browsed pamphlets published by the Library of Ireland in 1845 on Irish history and literature.[29] "Educate that you may be free," preached new nationalist heroes such as Thomas Davis, the editor of the *Nation* and the leader of the "Young Ireland" movement of the late 1840s.[30]

Perhaps John Warren learned something of his craft as a writer in one of the three newsrooms in Clonakilty or in its lending library for the poor. He certainly soaked up the nationalists' message: politics—not greedy Irish artisans or lazy peasants—accounted for the sorry state of the Irish economy. "We are oppressed by the tyrannical laws of the English government, which we can endure no longer," declared the proto-nationalist Rockites, an "exceptionally violent agrarian rebellion" that erupted in Munster (including Clonakilty) in the 1820s. "They crowd us up with rents, tythes, and taxes."[31] English laws made it easier for landlords to evict tenants, burdened small potato farmers with church tithes while exempting new "grazing farmers," and favored English manufacturers at the expense of Irish.[32] Subservient to English parliamentary control, the Irish suffered because they had little say over their governance and had been turned into "aliens in their own country."[33] Warren, an adolescent at the time, likely responded especially to the Young Irelanders, the passionate young men who grew increasingly impatient with O'Connell's insistence on peaceful, constitutional change. Repealing the Act of Union was not enough, they insisted. Only complete independence, by force if necessary, could rescue Ireland from its wretched state.[34]

The Great Famine drove that political lesson home.

No one knew why potato plants turned black and shriveled into a stinky mush in Ireland beginning in the fall of 1845. Scientific commissions created throughout western Europe and Britain offered a host of explanations for the potato blight that spread with ferocious speed through the Continent, destroying apparently "healthy and vigorous Potato-fields" almost overnight. Insects, worms, parasitical fungi, night frosts, or "vegetable cholera" might be to blame. Some believed "electrical agency" played a hand, reporting "blue lights seen at night playing over the doomed Potato grounds." Or perhaps it was just a bad season for potatoes. But the next year was no better. Almost the entire potato crop withered in 1846, and again in 1848, the blight not ending until 1850. In the face of such devastation, people could only guess that Providence, the inscrutable will of God, was at play. It was probably for the best, commented the *Illustrated London News* in August 1846. While the "calamity" produced "very great distress," the blight would eliminate "a curse to Ireland," as the potato "plant . . . is one of the most worthless of all known food."[35]

The London newspaper could not have been more wrong. The lowly potato packs a powerful nutritional punch, rich in carbohydrates, minerals, and vitamins, particularly vitamin C. In the early nineteenth century, the "potato people" of Ireland—40 percent of the population—relied almost solely upon potatoes for their food, each consuming five to twelve pounds of potatoes a day. They ate potatoes for breakfast, lunch, and dinner, sometimes augmented with a little buttermilk or water flavored with pepper, or perhaps herring for those living near the seacoast. Potatoes thrived in the cool, damp Irish climate and needed very little space to grow, less than one acre of land yielding six to eight tons of potatoes—enough to feed a family of nine for a year. The diet may have been monotonous, but it allowed the Irish to thrive, spurring the spectacular population explosion of the eighteenth and nineteenth centuries. Without potatoes, many Irish could not survive.[36]

Statistics paint a grim picture of the "Great Hunger" that decimated the Irish in the wake of the potato blight. Between 1 and 1.5 million Irish—one-eighth of the entire Irish population—died of starvation or related diseases, while another 2.1 million escaped Ireland to find refuge elsewhere. Weakened by hunger and crowded into poorhouses and hospitals, many fell prey to measles, typhus, consumption, and, in 1849, the dreaded cholera epidemic that swept regions already devastated by the Famine. The poorest, especially in the west and south, died in the greatest numbers, but few escaped the trauma of the Famine, telling tales of "the horrors of meeting living walking ghosts, or stumbling upon the dead" on Irish roads and abandoned cottages. County Cork, home to Clonakilty, lost 40 percent of its population to death and emigration in less than twenty years. Almost overnight, much of Ireland emptied out, leaving behind ghost towns.[37]

Clonakilty once again became the "scene of sad carnage," though this time hunger, rather than Cromwell's armies, stalked the town. James Mahony traveled to West Cork in February 1847 to investigate "famine country" and first encountered the "horrors" of the Famine in Clonakilty, where his carriage stopped for breakfast. "A vast number of famished poor . . . flocked around the coach to beg alms," he reported, including the most "horrible spectacle" of "a

"Woman Begging at Clonakilty." Irish artist James Mahony first encountered the horrors of the Irish famine in West Cork when he stopped for breakfast in Clonakilty. He drew this "horrible spectacle" of a woman "carrying in her arms the corpse of a fine child" and begging for money to bury him.

woman carrying in her arms the corpse of a fine child." She begged the passengers for money to buy a coffin to "bury her dear little baby." Every day, he discovered, dozens of desperate people streamed into Clonakilty, seeking help. Desperation turned to rage only a few months later as starving mobs broke into storehouses and bread shops in Clonakilty, demanding food. A saying born of the Famine—"Clonakilty, God help us!"—survives to this day, a stark reminder of the dark period that changed the town, and all of Ireland.[38]

The cause of the blight remained a mystery, the fungus *phytopthora infestans* fingered as the culprit years later. But John Mitchel, the fiery Young

Ireland nationalist, knew what caused the Famine: "The almighty indeed sent the potato blight, but the English created the famine." Many at the time—and since—agreed with Mitchel's terse summary that "Ireland died of political economy."[39]

The British were sympathetic, to a point. Few could read the shocking stories of children "worn to skeletons, their features sharpened with hunger, and their limbs wasted almost to the bone," without feeling some compassion.[40] But leading economists, championing the classical liberal economics of the day, warned policymakers not to let their hearts govern their heads, seeing the Famine as a necessary, though unfortunate, adjustment to correct the population explosion in Ireland by "thinning out" the stock. Rebuffing pleas for more government aid, Treasury Undersecretary Charles Trevelyan insisted that Ireland—and England—would be better off in the end if the Irish learned to "depend upon themselves" instead of asking the government for help. If the government stepped in, it would upset the "natural law of distribution," shifting resources from the most worthy to the least worthy and insulating the Irish from learning from their mistakes. After all, argued many, the Irish were to blame for the Famine, "idly and stupidly" putting all their faith in a single crop.[41]

Seeing "handouts" as economically inefficient and morally repugnant, government relief programs insisted that famine victims work to earn their food, either in grim workhouses set up under the poor law regime or on public works projects. Irish workers, weakened by hunger and disease, made a pitiful spectacle as they struggled with their assigned tasks. In Skibbereen, not far from Clonakilty, "a gang of about 150, composed principally of old men, *women*, and little boys," headed out in the bitter cold, with snow on the ground, to build roads and clear ditches. Scantily clad, "the women and children were crying out from the severity of the cold," reported T. H. Marmion to the *Cork Constitution*, and struggled to grasp their tools. Soon "an old man" had to be carried away "on a man's back dying." Paid a measly sum for their work, even those who survived could not buy enough to eat. Surely there must be a better solution, Marmion concluded, than asking people "to sacrifice their lives to carry out a miserable project of political economy."[42]

The widespread evictions of Irish from their land as part of government "relief" efforts became the most hated and condemned of the policies. Evictions, already common and bitterly resisted before the Famine, rose sharply, as the "Gregory Clause" of the Irish Relief Act of 1847 required relief applicants holding more than one-quarter of an acre of land to give up their property if they wanted aid. Some landlords offered "lucky" families passage to America in exchange for their land. It was still a stark choice: your home or your life. Some chose to stay and take their chances even if it meant dying in their homes, but others eventually gave in. Poignant eviction stories filled newspapers and lingered long after in popular memory. Sheriffs and constables turned people out in operations "conducted like a military raid," confiscating any food or animals farmers had managed to hold on to and burning their houses to the ground.[43]

British commentators saw emigration and evictions as the "silver lining" to the wretched cloud of the Famine, the emptying of Ireland paving the way for a brighter economic future. Finally the land would be cleared of the cottiers who had clung to their minuscule plots, allowing larger, more modern farms to be built in their place. "It is good" for the emigrant "that he should go," *Blackwood's Edinburgh Magazine* said reassuringly, and just as "good for those he leaves behind."[44] But survivors remained unconvinced, emigration often feeling more like a mass eviction by the foreign English "sassenach." The shadow of the Famine haunted them, even as they made their way to America.[45]

2

Exiles and Expatriates

"I HOPE YOU never will be an exile," John Warren wrote in 1867 to Fernando Wood, Democratic congressional representative from New York City. Warren painted a sorrowful scene of his decision to leave his beloved Ireland. Either he could remain an Irish slave of England, an alien in his native land, or he could "cast off the allegiance imposed on me by my birth" and become a free man in America. Warren opted for freedom under "the glorious Stars and Stripes" of America, but it was a bitter break: "A happy home is broken up; a disconsolate mother, weeping sisters, relatives and friends . . . ; another exile expatriated." America held a powerful hold on emigrants' imaginations, as did its promised riches. But even as they settled into American cities and towns, becoming American citizens at a rapid rate, Irish Americans did not always feel at home.[1]

Men and women poured out of Ireland in the Famine years, over 2.1 million—one-fourth of the entire population—leaving within eleven years for England, Australia, Canada, and particularly the United States. Irish had been leaving in droves since 1815 as the economy worsened. But the unprecedented exodus in the wake of the Famine astounded observers. Before, more-Anglicized Irish with some resources, often artisans like the Warrens living in market towns, provided the bulk of emigrants. The Famine unleashed a broader array of migrants, especially from the hardest-hit regions in the west and south. Some traveled with the assistance of landlords and local governments, others clutched prepaid tickets sent by family already in America, and still others scraped together what they could to pay their passage. Emigrant ships struggled to keep up with the demand of "increasing swarms of Irish." Overwhelmed and unprepared for the thousands of sick and malnourished passengers, some ships suffered terrible fates, from deadly fires and shipwrecks to rampant death from "ship fever" and other diseases, the mortality rate on board reaching as high as 20 to 30 percent in 1847.[2]

John Warren joined the "great stream" of immigrants in 1853, leaving Clonakilty in the spring, the peak season for emigrants. The Warrens, as town artisans with some means, were in no danger of starving but faced a grim future in Ireland, especially after the death of John's father left his mother to head the household. John may have sailed directly to the United States from Queenstown, Cork's large seaport, but he probably left, as did most Irish emigrants, from Liverpool, England's bustling emigration port. Perhaps Warren picked up a copy of Vere Foster's *Penny Emigrant's Guide,* full of helpful advice. "Ask no questions in the street, pay no attention to the offers of service of any one you meet," Foster cautioned, to avoid unscrupulous "man-catchers." "Choose a ship that is well ventilated," he advised. The dark, airless steerage decks were famous for a stench so powerful that one government inspector said he could smell an emigrant ship arriving. "Bring some epsom salts" to calm the stomach and relieve constipation due to the rolling sea and lack of exercise. Pack extra food and tin cooking utensils. *"Remember,* that you cannot, when at sea, run to a shop to get what you want," nor could one count on receiving one's allotment of food from the ship's cook. Finally, choose a route carefully. While the vast majority of ships sailed to New York, Enoch Train's White Diamond Line to Boston provided "by far the best" ships, even if passage was a little more expensive. For £3 to £5 (about $20), Warren could reach Boston in about forty-one days; for a pound less, he could arrive in New York a few days sooner.[3]

Warren was just one of millions of immigrants from Europe who joined the "exit revolution" of the nineteenth century, leaving their native lands in search of economic stability, adventure, and political freedom. Between 1815 and 1924, an astounding 55 million Europeans emigrated, the "unsettling of Europe" dovetailing with increasing immigration from Asia as individuals and families hoped that moving on would mean moving up the economic and social ladder— or at least would increase their chances of surviving economic and political turmoil. Old World residents traveled to several New World countries— Canada, Australia, New Zealand, South American nations—but the United States was the destination of three-fifths of immigrants during the era of mass migration.[4]

Irish stood at the forefront of the first era of mass migration in the 1840s and 1850s, which dramatically reshaped the United States. Between 1840 and 1860, more than 4.5 million immigrants—over 70 percent of them from Ireland

and Germany—arrived in the United States, at a time when the national population reached 31 million. The *rate* of immigration—that is, the ratio of immigrants to the host population—was substantial, making the impact of immigrants keenly felt, especially as cities mushroomed with new foreign residents.[5] New York City was the ultimate immigrant city, with half of its population foreign-born. German immigrants fanned out across the "German belt" in the Midwest, making up a third of the population of Milwaukee, St. Louis, and Cincinnati, while Irish favored cities along the Atlantic seaboard, though they also headed west to Chicago and San Francisco.[6] Warren ended up in Boston, the "Dublin of America"; by 1855 the city was home to over 68,000 Irish, one-fourth of the city's total population.[7]

Why Warren chose Boston is unclear, but it comes as no surprise. The city was the third-most-popular destination for Irish, after New York and Philadelphia. Perhaps, like most Irish migrants, Warren joined family and friends already there, counting on them to provide housing, jobs, and a touch of familiarity to cushion the transition of moving from his hometown of 3,297 to a foreign city of over 260,000.[8] Irish immigrants needed all the help they could get. Foster's *Penny Emigrant's Guide* promised emigrants better wages and brighter futures in the United States, drawing pictures of destitute, ragged Irish peasants exchanging desolate hovels in Ireland for middle-class parlors in America, complete with their own servants. The reality was much bleaker. Irish immigrants crammed into overpriced, dilapidated tenements in Boston slums, "huddled together like brutes" without even the basic necessities of fresh water and adequate sewage systems. Nor were well-paying jobs easy to find. The vast majority of Irish worked as unskilled laborers doing the "grunt work" of the city, hauling, digging, dredging, scrubbing, nursing, and building.[9]

As the son of artisans, Warren was more fortunate than most Irish immigrants, arriving with some financial resources and skills. He had all the marks of a young man on the rise, eager to make his way in America, but not through his parents' Old World trade as woolcombers. Warren enrolled at Comer's Commercial College in Boston, a pioneer in offering flexible education to ambitious young working-class men and women. While Boston's elite sent their sons to Harvard to study the classics, Comer's focused on practical studies—penmanship, bookkeeping, and banking—provided by tutors so that busy working students did not have to attend class at set times. "FOREIGNERS, and persons whose early education has been neglected, have special attention," the college advertised.[10] By 1864, Warren was the proud owner of a liquor and grocery store—the most common business for immigrant entrepreneurs—located in Charlestown, across the river from Boston and home to the Charlestown Navy Yard and a rapidly increasing number of Irish immigrants. He also pursued his avocation as a newspaperman, writing for various Boston and New York newspapers.[11]

John seemed to be settling into his life in America. The family, broken apart by emigration, regrouped quickly. His two sisters and mother soon all lived in the Boston area, and John began his own family, marrying Joanna Madigan, another Irish exile, shortly after his arrival, a fruitful marriage that by 1865 resulted in five children, all American citizens by birth.[12] And when his new homeland dissolved into the "awful" civil war that shook "the government of this great Republic to its centre," John's ties to his new "national family" deepened as well. John was one of 150,000 Irish Americans who served in the Union Army, raising his own company of 101 men in Boston to join Thomas Francis Meagher's "Irish Brigade" in New York. Though most Irish Americans cared little for the abolitionist cause, they cared deeply about preserving the American republic, the asylum for "the unfortunate exile who is driven in despair from his fatherland by oppression."[13]

After the war, John cemented his relationship with his chosen homeland, taking the final steps to become a naturalized citizen of the United States on December 12, 1866. Becoming a citizen in the 1860s was a relatively easy process, at least for white men—too easy, in the eyes of some American critics and foreign governments. Warren could apply for citizenship before any state or federal court of record, but he went to the Massachusetts Superior Court for Suffolk County, declaring he had met all the necessary requirements for naturalization under United States law: he was a free white person, had lived in the United States for at least five years, and had filed the necessary declaration of intent to become a citizen at least three years earlier. He had never held a title of nobility; if he had, he would have had to renounce it to become a citizen of the American republic. Two witnesses, Patrick Cahalin, a cabinetmaker in Somerville, and James A. McCool, a lithographer from Boston, swore they had known Warren for at least five years and that he "has conducted himself and behaved as a man of good moral character, attached to the principles of the Constitution of the United States, and well disposed toward the good order and happiness of the same." Finally, in the last, clinching act of the naturalization process, Warren "absolutely and entirely" renounced "all allegiance and fidelity" to "every foreign Prince" and "particularly to Victoria, Queen of Great Britain and Ireland." Swearing to "support the Constitution of the United States," John Warren was now an American citizen.[14]

"I AM AN American citizen," Warren declared in 1867, but also "I am an unmitigated Irishman, and love every blade of grass that grows on her soil."[15] Becoming American did not mean leaving Ireland behind—far from it. Sometime between 1858 and 1862, Warren took another oath of allegiance, solemnly swearing "by all the wrongs inflicted on Ireland and on my Irish Ancestors, that I will labor while life is left, to rid Ireland of English Government" and to "aid the men at home to put themselves in a state of preparation to fight England."[16] With this oath, Warren joined the newest Irish secret society, the Fenian Brotherhood, the American counterpart to the Irish Republican Brotherhood, which sprang up among artisans and shop boys in 1858 and spread through Warren's native southwestern Cork.[17] One of approximately 250,000 Irish Americans who joined the Fenian Brotherhood, Warren threw himself into the cause, even as he fought in the American Union Army. He served as the "head centre" from Massachusetts for the brotherhood in 1863, naming his son born that year Robert Emmett after the famous Irish nationalist martyr. In perhaps his proudest business venture, Warren cofounded with Peter O'Neill Larkin the fiery though short-lived newspaper *The Fenian Spirit* in 1864. Its objective: "to perpetuate our undying hatred of English oppression" and to free Ireland from its "accursed tyranny under which she has so long suffered." The masthead, featuring a rising phoenix, a harp, and a cannon, promised Ireland's rebirth through armed force.[18]

The British claimed to be baffled by Fenianism. Perhaps the Irish had reason to complain of injuries done them in the distant past, but why now, in the 1860s, when conditions had so improved and administration of Irish government had become so much better?[19] Americans, Canadians, and Europeans, according to the *New York Herald*, shared the British fascination and confusion about the rapid spread of "Fenian fever." "The more the people hear about Fenianism," remarked the *Herald*, "the less they appear to understand it."[20] The British and the Americans blamed each other for fostering Fenianism. "There can be no doubt that this disease has been imported from the West," declared the *Illustrated London News*, carried over by swaggering "Yankee-Irish" from America who infected "the lowest class of the [Irish] community."[21] But the United States disowned Fenianism, too. Secretary of State William Henry

Seward emphatically declared, "The Fenian agitation is a British and not an American movement."[22]

In truth, the Fenian movement sprang from the soil of both Ireland and the United States, the political expression of a new hybrid: the Irish American. Fenianism thrived among expatriates like Warren who left Ireland "with a vengeance," viewing themselves as exiles from their beloved land, "driven away" by oppressive British policies.[23] It was a vengeance that their American lives did little to ease, as the majority of Irish immigrants struggled to make a living in crowded and often inhospitable cities.

Warren, at first glance, seemed a moderate American success story, but consider this: of his five children born between 1856 and 1865, only one survived into adulthood. Eliza Jane died of consumption at seven years of age, Robert Emmett of "convulsing" at age one, and John junior of "scrofula" (tuberculosis) at age seven—all diseases that plagued densely packed immigrant neighborhoods. Ironically, Warren's family in Ireland had fared better in terms of longevity, even during the Famine, than had his own children in America. The Boston Board of Health offered grieving parents like the Warrens cold comfort, blaming Massachusetts's high infant mortality rate on Irish "ignorance" and "lack of moral sense" and charging Irish parents with "wilful, and even criminal neglect" of their children.[24] And as Irish—the poorest and sickest of European immigrants in the United States—filled public hospitals, insane asylums, and poorhouses, their new American countrymen responded with increasing hostility. "There . . . are limits to our national hospitality," cautioned the Reverend W. H. Lord.[25]

GOVERNOR Henry D. Gardner, newly elected in the American Party's stunning political upset in Massachusetts in 1854, began his inaugural address by reciting statistics—not always the catchiest ploy in political speeches, but they served his purpose. The immigrant population in the United States had increased at an "alarming" rate, doubling between 1840 and 1850, and the astonishing "flood" of immigrants—many destined to end up as paupers, beggars, and criminals—showed no signs of stopping. The fate of the nation hung in the balance, for newcomers threatened to demolish all that was "American" about the United States. Immigrants spoke different languages, clung to their native customs, and lounged in beer gardens and saloons—even on the Sabbath. With their "cheap labor," they made it impossible for "honest American mechanics" to earn a living wage. And citizenship, too, was "becoming cheap," as foreign-born Americans glibly took their naturalization oaths with little understanding of what true American citizenship entailed and sold their votes to the highest bidders. Too often they remained bound, in heart if not in law, to their homeland or, more insidiously, to the Catholic Church, which, Gardner insisted, held that the alien's "duty to his church is higher than his duty to the state." The governor's speech before the state legislature surely fell on receptive ears. The American Party—the political arm of the Know-Nothing movement—won all eleven of the congressional challenges in Massachusetts and all but three of the open seats in the state legislature in the 1854 election, but its message appealed far beyond the state of Massachusetts as the nation fastened on immigration as its most pressing problem, second only, perhaps, to the growing conflict over slavery.[26]

Not all jumped on the nativists' bandwagon. William Henry Seward, as governor of New York in the 1850s, could not afford to ignore the foreign-born, who made up a quarter of the state's population and half of New York City's, but immigrants were more than just potential votes to Seward. They remained as critical to the country's development and to America's commercial empire as bankers, ships, and coaling stations. Where would the United States be without immigrant labor? That was the question Seward asked legislators in 1854, at the height of the nativist movement. Immigrants provided the labor to build the canals and railroads that knit the nation together, the skilled artisans necessary to launch fledgling industries, the unskilled workers to operate increasingly mechanized factories, and the farmers that would turn America's western prairie and plains into the breadbasket of the world. Immigration not only made good economic sense for the growing nation, argued Seward, but also was inevitable, as Irish, Germans, and even Chinese left their native lands in obedience to "natural laws" of supply and demand. Since nothing could be done to stop the flow of people, it was unjust, impolitic, and even "un-American," suggested Seward, to make a "distinction of whatever kind in this country between the native-born American" and the foreign-born who "renounces his allegiance to a foreign land" and swears loyalty "to the country which adopts him."[27]

But *had* naturalized Americans renounced their allegiances to other causes and lands? Know-Nothings doubted their loyalty, tapping into a long-standing ambivalence about the place of naturalized citizens in the United States. From the nation's beginning, Americans had questioned how the nation would incorporate an increasing number of immigrants who might have different religions, values, languages, and experiences. Thomas Paine, himself an immigrant, assured skeptics that "people of different nations" would be held together by common political principles, including the bold notion arising with the American Revolution that individuals could choose their political allegiances. Who better represented the republican notion of voluntary citizenship than naturalized Americans? They made a deliberate decision to become Americans, while native-born Americans became citizens by the "accident" of their birth, something entirely beyond their control. Still, many could not shake the belief that birth in the United States made one more "American" in outlook and allegiance. The Constitution of 1789 said little about citizenship but did specify that only native-born Americans could serve as president. Congress debated just how long it would take for foreigners to learn republican ways, changing residency requirements for naturalization—from two to fourteen to five years—as fears of foreign influence rose and fell between 1790 and 1802.[28] In the 1850s, as thousands of Irish and German men became naturalized Americans—and voters—native-born Americans once again demanded a slower path to citizenship. We must "nationalize before we naturalize," cried Governor Gardner.[29]

The political stakes were simply too high, argued many. In 1854, in a preview of the Civil War, pro- and antislavery forces battled in "Bleeding Kansas" over whether the American West would be free or slave. Closer to Warren's home, violence broke out in Boston when federal authorities ordered the return of escaped slave Anthony Burns to his master in Virginia. As abolitionists rallied their forces to resist the enforcement of the fugitive slave law, with force if need be, a militia of Irish Americans, who typically aligned with the proslavery Democrats, came to the aid of the federal government, conducting Burns under armed guard past thousands of booing and hissing Bostonians to the ship waiting to return him to slavery. Antislavery advocates could not fathom why the Irish, who professed to love liberty, could support slavery. But many Irish Americans could not understand why crazy abolitionists would put the nation's future in jeopardy over the question of slavery, adopting the stance of Catholic archbishop John Hughes that slavery was God's will and not to be questioned.[30]

Enraged by seeing Burns escorted by the Irish American militia in "the vile procession" through the streets of Boston—the "cradle of liberty"—Know-Nothings fastened their fury on the twin evils of slavery and immigration.[31] The Irish, no less than Africans, were enslaved, shackled to their religion and national character. Oppressed by the British for centuries and bound to the Catholic Pope, the Irish were "the most helpless race in the world" and did the bidding of others, whether it be the pope or Tammany Hall's corrupt Demo-

"Irish Whiskey, Lager Bier." This cartoon taps into anti-immigrant sentiment in the 1840s and 1850s, accusing Irish and Germans of corrupting American politics through election fraud, fighting, and alcohol.

cratic Party. And the hold of the Catholic Church and the Democratic Party only seemed to be expanding. The number of Catholics exploded from 663,000 in 1840 to over 3.1 million in 1860, fueling deep-rooted fears of sinister Catholic plots aimed at destroying Protestant America and undermining republican government.[32] The Democratic Party's "naturalization mill" churned out new citizens with alarming speed, and the number of naturalized voters in Boston and New York City tripled between 1850 and 1855.[33]

Such newly minted citizens, having little understanding of the "genius of our institutions" or capacity for self-government, could not be turned loose in the American political system, warned the Know-Nothings. The American Party unleashed a bevy of new laws to protect America from Catholic immigrants. Even as the Massachusetts legislature passed "personal liberty" laws to protect fugitive slaves from recapture in the state, it stepped up the expulsion of immigrant paupers, the state deporting 15,000 paupers—almost all Irish—to other states, Canada, and England by 1863.[34] While Protestant street preachers roused angry mobs in their fiery denunciations of the "Catholic harlot church,"

"Naturalization of Foreigners, Scene in Tammany Hall" (1856) portrays the naturalization process as a casual affair, under the control of political bosses. Such scenes fueled
demands to tighten and centralize the naturalization process.

often leading to violence between Catholics and Protestants and the burning
of over a dozen Catholic churches, the Massachusetts legislature created a
"nunnery committee" to ensure that nuns were not being held against their will
by "lewd priests." But, above all, legislatures tried to insulate the American
political system from the "insidious foreign influx" and to reserve the "sacred
right of citizenship" to those who could be fully entrusted with it. "Every
additional naturalization tends to denationalize, to Europeanize, America,"
warned Governor Gardner. Massachusetts lawmakers instructed state judges to
stop issuing naturalization certificates and imposed a twenty-one year "waiting
period" before naturalized Americans could vote.[35] Cooler heads intervened,
with politicians from the new Republican Party whittling down the waiting
period to two years in the hopes of appeasing Know-Nothings and refocusing
the nation's attention on the core issue at hand—slavery.[36]

The Massachusetts "Two-Year Amendment" of 1859 enraged Irish and
German Americans, the up-and-coming German American political leader Carl
Schurz traveling to Boston's Faneuil Hall to urge Massachusetts Republicans

not to approve the amendment. "True Americanism" rested on "equality of rights" for all, including those "who come to you from foreign lands," Schurz urged. But nativists pressed for ever more stringent national restrictions on immigration and foreign-born political participation. America for Americans! Otherwise, the American republic, like the republics of the ancient world, would perish "under a horde of foreign barbarians."[37]

This was not the warm welcome Warren and many other Irish had hoped for from the "Great Western Republic." They saw Ireland and America as kindred republican spirits, yoked together by their struggle for independence from their common British enemy. Warren remembered "it was a proud, a glorious day, when my foot touched the sacred land of Washington, the land of freedom."[38] Naturalization fraud might be rampant, many immigrants becoming citizens well before the five-year waiting period had passed and relying on witnesses who may have been paid for their efforts. But that did not necessarily mean they had little regard for their American citizenship. Warren described his naturalization as liberating: "One stroke of the pen . . . and I who had entered that court shackled, degraded, and branded as a British slave, came [forth] . . . elevated and adorned with the insignia of freemen."[39] Surely no one renounced his allegiance to the queen of England, or embraced the right of expatriation, with greater enthusiasm than Warren.

For Irish nationalists, expatriation had a complicated meaning. It spoke, on the one hand, to their sense of loss—of being involuntarily thrust from their homeland by the cruel English.[40] But the *right* of expatriation—the ability to choose one's nationality—meant something altogether different, made all the more powerful by the experience of exile. For Irish nationalists, fighting to free Ireland from Britain, it could be a thrilling individual declaration of independence to be able to renounce allegiance to the queen of England and say, "I am an American citizen." If Ireland's independence still waited to be won, Irish could emancipate themselves by going to the local court and swearing allegiance to the United States. Naturalization transformed the abject subject into a proud republican citizen. Yet the foreign-born were often treated as "pariahs" by the nativists, driven into a "second exile" within the United States.[41]

THE AMERICAN Civil War promised to redraw the "borders of belonging" for the foreign-born in the United States. While some "skedaddled," fleeing the United States to avoid military service, other foreign-born Americans volunteered with enthusiasm. First- and second-generation Americans made up

40 percent of the Union Army. Irish Americans fought to preserve the Union, the most successful republic in the world, which provided them asylum, but many also linked the cause to their long-cherished hope of achieving independence in Ireland. Fenians saw their military service in the Union Army as excellent training for the coming war with England. Irish Americans left for battle carrying flags from both of their beloved countries, the green Irish flag, emblazoned with the golden harp, and the "starry flag" of the United States.[42] While a few years earlier Boston crowds had booed the Irish militia, in 1861 they lined the streets to cheer the Irish Brigade leaving for battle and praised the loyalty of their "adopted sons." "Know-Nothingism is dead!" crowed General Thomas Meagher, a former Young Irelander and the commander of the Irish Brigade, in a speech at Boston. The war "has silenced forever the charges against the naturalized citizen and the Catholic, as being unworthy of citizenship," declared William E. Robinson, an Irish-born lawyer in New York, in a speech before Warren's regiment.[43]

Know-Nothingism did die down, squelched by the need to unify all Americans to preserve the Union, but the war did not vanquish all tensions between native-born and naturalized citizens. As the war dragged on, resentment rose on both sides. The foreign-born were not doing their share, grumbled governors of immigrant-rich states that struggled to recruit more men for depleted armies but encountered a mountain of petitions by noncitizens for exemption from military service. The country's first mandatory draft law, adopted in 1863, targeted aliens, requiring all who had filed their declaration of intent to become a citizen, had voted, or had held office to register for the draft. Why shouldn't men who, by their actions and declarations, had cast their lot with America be called upon to serve in the nation's army "when the aid of every hand, the strength of every arm is needed to save the ship of State from destruction"?[44]

But Irish Americans' frustration grew as well, exploding in the violent New York draft riot of July 1863. Over five days, New York City mobs, heavily but not exclusively Irish American, unleashed their fury against everything associated with the Republican administration and its war effort—draft offices, police, and especially African Americans—leaving a path of destruction and death that ended only after Union troops, just released from the devastating battle at Gettysburg, arrived to quell another domestic rebellion. Appalled by the "hideous barbarism" of the raging rioters, spectators blamed the "brutal, base, cruel" Irish as the culprits. Here was fresh proof of Irish savagery and their complete disregard for republican government.[45] Irish Americans, even those who condemned the riot, insisted it had not occurred in a vacuum. "We have poured out our best blood," insisted M. Keane in a letter to Warren's *Fenian Spirit,* but "our people are looked down upon by all others, scoffed, sneered, and jibed at—the butt of ridicule."[46]

The riot came on the heels of a very bloody year, one that devastated the Irish Brigade. At Antietam in September 1862, in the deadliest battle of the Civil War, the Irish Brigade lost 60 percent of its men, and at Fredericksburg in December it lost another 45 percent in a particularly fruitless and ill-considered campaign. "Oh, it was a terrible day," wrote Captain William J. Nagle, Warren's future co-commander on *Erin's Hope,* to his father. "We are slaughtered like sheep, and no result but defeat." The Irish seemed little more than cannon fodder to President Abraham Lincoln and Secretary of War Henry Stanton, Irish American critics charged, with the administration leaving the Irish American units undermanned, neglected, and disrespected. General Meagher's repeated requests for a leave for his exhausted brigade went unanswered, pushing men like Warren to desperate measures. An illness in the family prompted Warren to leave his regiment to obtain his division commander's signature on his application for leave. Unsuccessful, he rejoined his regiment the next day, only to face a court-martial that ended with his dishonorable discharge for being absent without leave, despite his impassioned pleas of "honorable and faithful service . . . in every battle from Fair Oaks to Antietam."[47]

The Irish Brigade depleted, the foreign-born then faced the new Conscription Act of 1863, which, in their opinion, unfairly targeted aliens and allowed the rich to pay substitutes to serve in their place. "Substitutes!" advertised the *Boston Herald.* "Aliens furnished here!" The *Fenian Spirit* published a warning that "so long as they can get cheap Irishmen—so long as Irishmen can be kidnapped, drugged, and cheated out of their liberties," the law would not "waste the lives of American citizens."[48] And what were they fighting for? President Lincoln's Emancipation Proclamation of 1863 changed the stakes of the war, alienating many Irish Americans who had willingly joined to preserve the Union but bitterly resisted fighting to free African Americans. By 1863, even the popular General Meagher found it difficult to rouse new Irish American recruits for the Irish Brigade. And native-born Americans no longer threw lavish going-away celebrations for their adopted sons.[49]

IRISH AMERICANS emerged from the war emboldened but also embittered. Having "shared the dangers" of the war, they insisted, they should also "share the honors" with their fellow citizens. William Nagle remarked in anger that "in any other country the brigade which had fought and suffered as [the Irish Brigade] has would be gratefully and proudly cherished, its ranks kept full, its deed of heroism acknowledged and rewarded." Instead, "the Irish Brigade is blotted out of the army of the Union."[50] John Warren returned to his grocery store in Boston after his dishonorable discharge in 1863, still believing in the United States as a refuge for the oppressed of the world. But republicanism, at home for Irish Americans and abroad in Ireland, still needed to be secured.

Released from the bloody American Civil War, Irish American nationalists armed for their next conflict: battling England for the independence of Ireland. In August 1864, even before the Civil War was over, John Warren urged in the *Fenian Spirit*, "Irishmen throughout the world! The day of our Country's trial is at hand; assist us in the work of regeneration. The morning approaches, the hour is near—PREPARE—PREPARE!" As Fenians stepped onto the international stage, they entered a world shaken by the American Civil War. British-American relations had been stretched almost to the breaking point. With some help from the Fenians, perhaps Anglo-American ties might snap altogether, untethering Ireland from England in the process.[51]

3

The Fenian Pest

THE FENIANS initially seemed harmless enough, at least as covered in the press. "We have become a Nation of Pic-Nickians," declared the *New York Times,* and the Fenian Brotherhood's "pic-nic" in Jones Woods in New York in July 1865 seemed little different from the annual gatherings of a host of groups and associations—"Sunday schools, target companies, brothers of every name and degree, Germans, Irishmen, Frenchmen, and colored persons"—who, "one and all, spread themselves and their table cloths . . . in the open air." The Fenian "monster gathering" was noteworthy, perhaps, for the size of the crowd, estimated at 30,000, and for the lengthy, passionate speeches exhorting the revelers that "the time has come when every Irishman who loves his country and believes in the ultimate independence of his native land must take his place beside the Fenian Brotherhood" and free Ireland by armed force. While dutifully reprinting the speech of the featured Fenian spokesman, the *Times* devoted more attention to the carnival-like atmosphere of the gathering, the headline focusing on the "thirty thousand men and women dancing in the woods and shouting for Ireland," plus "a six-legged curiosity," worthy of Barnum, which "drew the largest crowd" at ten cents a viewing.[1]

The humorist Charles F. Brown, an early inspiration for Mark Twain, poked fun at the Fenians' love of gatherings and fiery speeches, reporting in the unique dialect of his character Artemus Ward that at the "Finian meeting" he attended, the crowd "took steps toord freein Ireland . . . The enthusiasm was immense. They cheer'd everybody and everything." Artemus Ward later claimed to spot the "Head Centres" of the Fenian group dining at the best restaurants in New York, "but bemoaning, 'I am miserable-miserable! The wrongs we Irish suffer! . . . Must we be for ever ground under by the iron heel of despotic Briton?'"[2] In

"Freedom to Ireland," Currier and Ives, 1866. "Erin" calls her "Fenian sons" to take arms for "the Freedom of your Native land."

Ireland, too, young Irish artisans, constituting almost half of the Fenian membership, flocked to pubs, rallies, military drilling exercises, parades, and cricket games sponsored by the Irish Republican Brotherhood, prompting some to conclude that Fenianism was perhaps more about male social bonding—"patriotism as pastime"—than it was a serious revolutionary movement.[3]

The British government did not find the Fenians a laughing matter, and it did not underestimate their political objectives. Nor should they have. The Fenians were on the march. Throughout 1865 and 1866, Fenian men turned up in Ireland, wearing their telltale "Yankee" square-toed boots and slouchy American hats and carrying valises packed with revolvers and gold coins. Fenian troops drilled on the border of Canada, creating fears of an invasion into the British-controlled provinces. It was a bewildering and ominous movement, these men who heartily proclaimed their American citizenship but left their new homes to strike a blow for Irish independence. Just where did their allegiance lie? British officials cared little about any oaths of allegiance to the United States Irish emigrants might have taken. Only one thing mattered: anyone—whether American citizen or British subject—who came into British territory, hell-bent on rebellion, was subject to British control and would face the mighty force of British law.

THE BRITISH government had many eyes and ears on the ground in the United States as well as in Ireland, England, and Canada. British consulates in the United States combed the local newspapers, studied political debates and speeches, vetted the stories brought to them by informants, and watched the passenger traffic on Atlantic steamers for any increased travel to Ireland by young men. Following the Fenians was not difficult, as they often operated in the open, their conventions, rallies, and speeches covered in depth by both mainstream and small newspapers. Not all of the Fenian activities could be discerned so easily, however, particularly their specific plans for attacking Britain. Informants arrived periodically at the British consulate to offer details about the secret dealings of the Brotherhood, usually for a price.[4]

What they had to report was not encouraging. As early as October 1864, the British consul in New York, Sir Edward Mortimer Archibald, sent alarming reports of the mounting threat posed by the Fenian organization, enclosing copies of John Warren's newspaper, *The Fenian Spirit*, as evidence of "their design to bring about a revolution and to establish a democratic Republic in Ireland."[5] Increasing numbers of Irish American men were leaving on steamers bound for Ireland, reported the British consulate, claiming that they were going to visit relatives, recuperate from the rigors of the war, or attend the Dublin International Exhibition.[6] Daniel Ryan, superintendent of police at Dublin, noted with alarm the growing numbers of "idle strangers" congregating in Dublin's lodging houses, pubs, and streets throughout the fall of 1865 and winter of 1866.

Fenians had even infiltrated the British Army, recruiting soldiers in public houses, he warned in February 1866, and had attracted converts among dockworkers at Liverpool, a crucial port of entry for Fenian men and arms coming both to Ireland and to England.[7] Magistrates and landlords throughout Ireland sent anxious petitions to the Lord Lieutenant, the king's representative in Ireland, reporting a "general feeling of uneasiness as to the Peace of the Country."[8] When Irish authorities raided the Dublin offices of the Fenian newspaper the *Irish People,* arresting the key leaders Thomas Clarke Luby and Jeremiah O'Donovan Rossa and capturing a treasure trove of incriminating documents, the British government hoped it had nipped the rebellion in the bud. But the "Fenian fever" only seemed to increase.[9]

The reports, though exaggerated, accurately captured the growing determination of the Fenians. As the Civil War came to a close, the Fenian Brotherhood in the United States, under the leadership of John O'Mahony, collaborated with its sister organization in Ireland, the Irish Republican Brotherhood, led by James Stephens, to plot a rebellion in Ireland, declaring 1865 to be the "year of action." The Americans were to provide money, arms, and military leaders, fresh from their commands in the Civil War; the Irish were to be ready to carry the rebellion forth.[10] Paid organizers swept American towns and cities, from Maine to California, creating new circles and registering a growing number of Irish freedom fighters whose initiation fees of one dollar and weekly dues of ten cents helped to swell the American organization's coffers. In August 1864, John Warren, appointed the "Central Organizer" of New England, triumphantly reported to Fenian Brotherhood president John O'Mahony that "our cause never was in a better condition than it is at the present time."[11]

The Fenian Brotherhood at its third annual convention, held in Philadelphia in October 1865, began to assume the powers of an independent state, choosing as its headquarters the Moffatt Mansion in a "very fashionable" and very visible location on Union Square in New York City. The Fenians adopted a constitution with a preamble that had a familiar ring, beginning, "We, the Fenians of America, in order to form a more perfect union . . ." It provided for a bicameral legislature and for a president who had the power to make treaties, appoint ambassadors, and create a cabinet. President John O'Mahony soon appointed a secretary of war, Brigadier General Thomas W. Sweeny, to organize and prepare the Fenian Army for battle.[12] Soon, promised the Fenian leader William Randall Roberts, the rising Irish Republic would have a fleet of cruisers, capable of exacting revenge on England for her crimes against Ireland as well as her perfidy during the Civil War.[13]

Canadians eyed their southern border nervously, as the Fenian faction led by Roberts noisily declared its intention to invade British Canada. Canadians had long feared attacks from their American neighbors, and for good reason. "Filibuster fever" gripped the American nation before the Civil War, driving thousands of young men to join private "filibustering" expeditions into Mexico, Nicaragua, Cuba, Ecuador, Honduras, and Hawaii, loudly proclaiming America's destiny to control the Western Hemisphere.[14] The annexation of Canada, in particular, had been a recurring objective of American expansionists since the American Revolution, though many—including Secretary of State William Henry Seward—believed the political consolidation of North America under American rule would come about peacefully and naturally. Canadians would surely recognize their common economic and cultural ties with the United States and became disenchanted with British imperial rule. That time had come by the mid-1860s, thought some Americans, as Britain relaxed its hold on Canada, preparing the way for the British North American Act of 1867, which would allow the Dominion of Canada control over domestic affairs while the British retained control over its foreign affairs.[15]

But the Civil War drove Canada and the United States further apart. As diplomatic ties between England and the United States soured during the war, so too did relations between Canada and America, especially after Confederate Army soldiers launched a raid from Canada into St. Albans, Vermont, robbing local banks and setting several houses on fire before they escaped back into Canada. Howls of outrage from Americans, already embittered by what they saw as British support of the Confederate cause, gave rise to calls for retribution in the American press. The Roberts wing of the Fenians fixed its sights on Canada in 1866, declaring that "if we can get a foothold on which to raise the Irish flag," then "we will have a base of operations from which we can not only emancipate Ireland, but also annihilate England." If the invasion failed, Fenian organizers thought, at least it might provoke a diplomatic rupture between the United States and England, and perhaps it would even spark a war that would ultimately result in Ireland's independence.[16]

By March 1866, preparations were picking up pace. British consul Charles E. K. Kortright at Philadelphia wrote one of several warnings to Lord Clarendon, the British foreign minister, that "this wicked organisation has assumed formidable proportions" as men joined the "Fenian Army" and prepared to leave their homes, "singly or in small squads," to rendezvous near the border.[17] Armed with a medley of retired Union Army weapons and decades of bitter resentment at English tyranny, the Fenians waited and planned, girding themselves for battle with blustery rhetoric and rousing tunes. The 69th Regiment's Irish Brigade war song became the Fenians' battle hymn, pledging: "We'll march into the battle-field, / At the word of command; / And we'll die or gain the Freedom, / In our own Native Land!"[18]

THE BRITISH government did not wait for the Fenians to strike before taking action. It had learned to regard talk of colonial insurrection seriously, especially after the Indian Rebellion of 1857. The mutiny by sepoys, soldiers of the East India Company, whom the British had supposed to be loyal and committed to imperial goals, came as a rude awakening, and the bloody revolt that spread across India had been brutally suppressed with martial law, swift executions, and a take-no-prisoners policy. By 1865, as the Fenians lay in wait, the vast British Empire faced rebellion by the Maoris in New Zealand and emancipated slaves in Jamaica; since 1860, other regions crucial to British imperial interests—China, Syria, Nigeria, South Africa—had witnessed wars and revolts sparked by resistance to Western Christian powers. What was needed, urged British conservatives, was a stronger hand in colonial governance, one that would quickly bring native dissidents in line by force, if not by persuasion.[19] "Erin's little difficulty," portrayed in a *Punch* cartoon as a naughty simian-faced boy, beating his drum and waving a flag with the slogan "Fenianism For Ever," could best be handled with a firm thrashing, overseen by a smug Britannia.[20]

Ireland did not quite fit the colonial mold of Jamaica and India. It was part of the United Kingdom, though not by choice, and sent a hundred representatives to Parliament. Nor would British responses to Fenianism be as bloody or as ruthless as they were to rebellion in its Southeast Asian and Caribbean colonies. Yet Ireland remained too important to British strategic interests to be allowed independence, its physical proximity to England providing a potential inroad for foreign enemies.[21] The British did not trust the Irish to rule themselves, nor to handle the "Fenian pest" on their own, especially with the lessons of Jamaica and India hovering in the background. In one *Punch* cartoon, Erin brings a glowering miniature Fenian to an English doctor, who reassures her: "I treated a somewhat similar case to this very successfully in India. Leave him to me."[22]

British officials never expressed any doubt that they would defeat the Fenians. Britain was, after all, the world's largest empire, with considerable resources at its command. The only questions were how, and at what cost? On these questions, Conservatives and Liberals in Parliament and in the cabinet

THE FENIAN-PEST.

Hibernia. "O MY DEAR SISTER, WHAT *ARE* WE TO DO WITH THESE TROUBLESOME PEOPLE?"
Britannia. "TRY ISOLATION FIRST, MY DEAR, AND THEN——"

"The Fenian-Pest" (1866) depicts Britain ready to stomp on the Fenians, portrayed, as usual, as ape-men. Hibernia (Ireland) asks: "O my dear sister, what *are* we to do with these troublesome people?" Britannia responds ominously: "Try isolation first, my dear, and then—."

often differed. Obviously, the government needed to nip the Fenian rebellion in the bud before it spread too widely, but brute force would only create martyrs and generate popular support for Fenians. The few members of Parliament who had actually been in Ireland warned of widespread disaffection with British rule, making it fertile ground for Fenian recruiters. "Had there been peace or contentment in Ireland," argued John Francis Maguire from Cork, "we never should have heard of Fenianism."[23] Rather than alienate the Irish further by repressive tactics, some Liberals urged, steps needed to be taken to isolate dangerous Fenians while trying to foster allegiance among "respectable" Irish.

And Britain had its image to consider, an image that had been considerably tarnished by its brutal handling of the Indian and Jamaican insurrections. British politicians spoke eloquently about the many virtues of the British constitution as the safeguard of individual liberty and the importance of the rule of law as the bedrock for any legitimate government. But British reliance on martial law and military tribunals—and, indeed, the absence of any legal authority for the wanton killing of rebellious colonials—made appeals to the superiority of British constitutionalism seem hollow. Liberals such as John Stuart Mill protested against British responses to colonial insurrections and became critics of the government's policies regarding the Fenians.[24]

Finally, British officials had to take the thin-skinned Americans into consideration. They were already spoiling for a fight over perceived British violations of neutrality during the Civil War, and the British minister in Washington, D.C., Sir Frederick Bruce, repeatedly warned that the volatile Fenian issue could easily spin out of control, driving the two countries to the brink of war. The British government, then, walked a thin line between coercion and conciliation, determined to meet the impudent Fenians with all necessary force while taking care not to spark further national and international disputes that could undermine its ultimate objectives. It would be a difficult balancing act, as imperial officials on the ground in Ireland and Canada soon discovered.

THE IMPERIAL command center in Ireland was Dublin Castle, the site of power for centuries of invaders. First the Vikings and then the conquering Normans built the mighty fortress at the highest point of Dublin, near the banks of the Liffey River, which runs through the city. They encircled the large castle with formidable stone walls and wide ditches and built high round towers for lookouts above and prisoners below.[25] Dublin Castle was more than just an ancient fortress, the home of successive generations of invaders. It was the linchpin of the British Empire in Ireland, fastening London's hold over the Irish capital and spreading its reach to disparate counties through its army of officials. While the Lord Lieutenant served as the premier imperial officer in Ireland, the task of managing the Fenian crisis fell to a handful of men at the top: Lord Naas (later Earl of Mayo), who served as chief secretary during the critical years, 1866–1868; Undersecretary Thomas Larcom, the workhorse at Dublin Castle; and Dublin police superintendent Daniel Ryan.[26]

The castle loomed large in the political imagination, its vast size and enclosed courtyards imparting an unnerving sense of a "veiled, anonymous, and all powerful institution."[27] But those who worked within the heavily fortified castle walls did not always feel powerful nor all-knowing. The Irish executive was "over worked, under financed, under staffed, and under continuous unsympathetic sniping."[28] The Fenian rebellion especially taxed the patience and stamina of Dublin Castle. Larcom would despair at one point that, in regard to Fenianism, "one does not see how it is to end, or what means to use."[29] Still, the Irish government had formidable resources at hand, which it marshaled to defend the empire from the Fenian threat.

The first imperative was to restore law and order and reduce public panic. In the fall of 1865, British troops filled garrisons in "nearly all the larger towns" in the south and west of Ireland, the regions viewed as most supportive of the Fenian movement, and armed vessels patrolled the western coast on the watch for possible attacks from the sea.[30] Irish officials in Queenstown in County Cork and in Dublin met incoming ships from America, questioning passengers and searching their baggage in their efforts to identify and track potential troublemakers. Once landed, travelers remained under the eagle eye of the Irish constabulary, one of the most comprehensive and centralized police forces in the British Empire, developed to respond quickly and decisively to any potential rebellion. In counties that were particularly vulnerable to unrest, the Irish executive employed its power under the Peace Preservation Act to proclaim the district "disturbed," making it illegal to carry any weapons in the area without a special license and establishing curfews.[31] With reports of American Fenians bringing arms to Ireland to aid in the rebellion, the act made it easier to arrest any travelers found with weapons in their baggage before they could do any harm.[32] In Dublin, Superintendent Ryan created an impressive system of surveillance, employing plainclothes detectives and well-paid informants to monitor the growing number of strangers in the city who seemed to have "no occupation but walking about, and to be waiting for some event." John

Whitehead Byron arrived in Ireland on August 2, 1865, and from the time he landed, he was watched: "My 'slouched' hat and 'square toes,' as I very soon learned drew upon me wherever I went, the attention of the local authorities; I was arrested, searched, and liberated on four different occasions."[33]

The Irish legal system provided rapid recourse if evidence of wrongdoing could be found. In 1848, when the Young Irelanders had mounted an earlier rebellion against British rule, Parliament had devised innovative legal means to prosecute them, expanding the old law of treason, which made any act or conspiracy to deprive the queen of her crown, levy war against her, or encourage foreigners to invade the United Kingdom punishable by death, and a gruesome death at that. Traditionally, those convicted of high treason were hanged and, after death, beheaded, their bodies quartered, and their severed body parts displayed as a warning to other potential traitors. But the sentence was so harsh that juries often failed to convict defendants of high treason. Nor did the act clearly apply to Ireland. The Treason-Felony Act of 1848 extended the government's reach, allowing it to punish not only overt acts and conspiracies against the queen but also seditious speech, either printed or spoken, that incited subjects to oppose "all legitimate authority in the country" or encouraged outsiders to invade the queen's realm. Rather than death, the sentence for treason-felony was imprisonment or, for more extreme cases, transportation to a penal colony outside Britain for at least seven years—a change that prosecutors hoped would make juries more likely to convict offenders.[34]

Treason-felony became the charge of choice during the Fenian crisis, allowing the Irish attorney general considerable leeway to prosecute Fenians for a wide range of activities, both acts and speech. The Fenian Brotherhood was quite vocal at rallies about its objectives and plans, its newspaper, the *Irish People,* unabashedly urging its readers to agitate and revolt. It was easy to slap the Fenians with the new charge of treason-felony. Rather than wait for the regular court sessions, the government could convene courts in "special commissions" to try the Fenian cases, a tactic that not only allowed speedy justice but also afforded the attorney general the opportunity to choose the presiding judge. Convictions came readily, and the act provided an efficient way to pack the leaders off to jail or out of the country.[35]

But many Fenians remained at large by the winter of 1866, and the government's case against them rested on suspicion rather than hard evidence. Even if apprehended, Fenian suspects usually carried no documents and confessed to nothing, saying only that they were visiting friends or family. Legally, the police had no grounds to hold them. The lord lieutenant and chief secretary informed the home secretary, Lord Russell, in the winter of 1866 that Ireland was "in a most perilous position," as the "Fenian spirit . . . continues unsubdued." The "peace of Ireland" could not be guaranteed "unless the Irish government are armed with greater powers." The Irish government asked Parliament to equip them with "the most stringent measures of repression": a bill suspending the writ of habeas corpus in Ireland, freeing the police to make arrests without warrants and to detain prisoners indefinitely without charge. Parliament readily complied, as it had in earlier Irish rebellions. The House of Lords approved the bill on February 17, 1866, without debate, and in the House of Commons only eight members, all from Ireland, opposed the measure. All hoped that "when the Fenian emissaries find that they are exposed to summary arrest and imprisonment," they might think twice before venturing to Ireland and disturbing its "deluded people."[36]

As Fenians were quick to point out, Parliament particularly targeted Americans in the suspension of habeas corpus, seeing them as the prime troublemakers in Ireland. Most British government officials refused to believe that Fenianism would have taken root in Ireland without the Americans' influence and saw the Civil War as particularly to blame for creating a more martial spirit and fanning the anti-British sentiment that Fenians manipulated so well.[37] The British government and the loyal press depicted Fenians as a group of "restless adventurers whom the close of the American war has let loose upon the world."[38] The Irish who left for the United States became, as one commentator said sneeringly, "Irish Americans," who had imbibed too liberally of republican ideology and the anti-British sentiment that simmered in American political culture.[39] Irish Americans provided the money, the men, the organizational structure, and the energy behind Fenianism in America; the only thing "Irish" about the movement, concluded the London *Times,* was the craziness of the scheme.[40] Eradicating Fenianism, then, meant purging Ireland of corrupt American influences.

Superintendent Ryan wasted no time in exercising his new powers. Even before members of Parliament finished casting their votes to suspend habeas corpus, Ryan launched a raid of suspected Fenian gathering spots on Saturday, February 17. Taking advantage of his opportunity to "pounce, without a moment's warning," Ryan gathered his men at the Detectives' Office at six o'clock in the morning, divided the list of suspects and their dwelling places among small squads, and dispatched them quickly in the hopes of catching the suspects unaware while they lay in bed. The raid was a rousing success, as the police swooped in and rounded up ninety-one men by noon. "Some of them were in bed, others were dressing, and some were at breakfast when the police came on them by surprise," a newspaper reported. By evening, 250 men had been arrested, "marched in batches through the streets" to various police stations, and conveyed in police vans under "strong escort" to Dublin's two main jails, Kilmainham Gaol and Mountjoy Prison, cheered only by a "number of ragged boys" who followed their carts. The men, including many Irish Americans, were great catches, crowed Ryan: "They were all without exception fine athletic men" wearing "very fashionable" clothing, and were believed to be key players in forthcoming Fenian plots.[41] They were "much surprised and annoyed," and threatened that their treatment "would cause a bloody fine row when the intelligence would reach their Government (the American Government) as they would not submit to John Bull."[42]

CANADIAN authorities took an even harder line against Americans when the long-anticipated raids finally occurred in the early summer of 1866. Under the command of General Sweeny, the Roberts wing mounted three ill-fated attacks on Canada in the early summer of 1866. The first was a particularly ineffectual attempt of a few hundred disorganized Fenians to invade New Brunswick through Eastport, Maine.[43] The second attack, on the Niagara frontier on June 1, 1866, known as the Battle of Ridgway, was the Fenians' most successful military venture, as a force of at least 1,000 men under the command of John O'Neill crossed the Niagara River from Buffalo, New York, before dawn. Despite Fenian assurances that they had "no issue with the People of these Provinces" but sought only to extend to Irish Canadians "the hand of brotherhood" and "to smite the tyrant where we can," Canadian volunteers united to rebuff the Fenian incursion.[44]

The Battle of Ridgway, as imagined in a colorful lithograph, entailed orderly young Fenians, smartly attired in green coats, gray pants, and gray caps, each equipped with a rifle and bayonet and under the command of officers on horseback, carrying their green banner adorned with the harp and the initials "I.R.A." In the romanticized image, they confronted in line formation the equally well-dressed British Canadian redcoats, who were clearly panicking and losing the battle, struggling to reload and falling before the "charge of the Fenians."[45] The real battle looked different. At later trials, Canadian farmers testified that the Fenians were a diverse lot, from the very young to the old, some dressed in Union uniforms, some wearing green coats, and others in civilian clothing.[46] The Canadian troops included some of the regular army, "the

"Battle of Ridgeway." A highly romanticized and inaccurate portrayal of the actual battle. The caption reads: "Desperate charge of the Fenians, under Co. O'Neill, near Ridgeway Station, June 2, 1866, and total route [*sic*] of the British troops including the Queen's own regiment under command of Col. Booker."

Queen's Own," but relied heavily upon ill-trained volunteers, including two companies of university students called up in the middle of their exams. Far from a decisive line-formation battle, the Fenians engaged in skirmishes with the Canadian militia over two days, some in thick woods and others in open fields, with some success. But by the early morning of June 3, the Fenian forces were tired and hungry, and they appeared cornered by Canadian troops approaching their camp at Fort Erie. They made the prudent choice to leave on canal boats on the Niagara River but made little progress before U.S. military officials, under orders of General George Meade, intercepted and arrested over 700 of the Fenian fighters for violating American neutrality laws.[47]

The arrests came as a rude surprise to Fenian leaders, who believed that both Secretary of State William Henry Seward and President Andrew Johnson supported their Canadian campaign. While Seward and Johnson had never explicitly promised to lend aid and had rejected requests from leaders for money, they had never forbidden or disavowed the Fenian project either.[48] The armed invasion forced the hand of President Johnson, caught between the popular Fenian upswell during a crucial election year and the indignation of British authorities about the government's failure to curb the "marauders." Johnson finally issued the Proclamation of Neutrality, though it did not become public until a full week after the Battle of Ridgway. By that point the Brotherhood had launched its final unsuccessful invasion on June 7, when an inadequately armed force of less than 1,000 Fenians left St. Albans, Vermont, and crossed into Quebec, only to be easily repelled by Canadian forces.[49]

The Fenians who did not manage to escape back across the border faced the wrath of Canadians who saw little connection between Irish grievances and the unprovoked attack by a group of marauders on a peaceful people. Thousands of Canadians had rushed to answer the call of Governor-General Charles Monck on June 1, 1866, to defend "their altars, their homes, and their property, from desecration, pillage and spoliation" by "a lawless and piratical band, in defiance of all moral right." Nine Canadians died and twelve more were seriously wounded defending the country from the Fenian attacks, and the fifty-six Fenian prisoners facing trial in Canada found little sympathy for their cause.[50] "This Fenian filibustering was murder, not war," declared Canadian politician, Thomas D'Arcy McGee. McGee had fled Ireland in 1848 to escape prosecution for his participation in the Young Ireland nationalist movement, but he was no fan of Fenianism in 1866. "What had Canada or Canadians done to deserve such an assault?" asked McGee.[51]

Canadians howled for retribution, demanding court-martial trials and immediate executions. Canadian officials refused to be rushed but still dealt harshly with the Fenian marauders, charging them under the Lawless Aggressions Act with invading Canada with the intent to "levy war against her Majesty," a charge that carried a mandatory death sentence. Passed during the Canadian Rebellion of 1837–1839, when groups of Americans poured over the border to "free" Canada, the controversial act sought "speedy justice" by sidestepping traditional procedural protections. After the Fenians' arrival in 1866, Canadian officials quickly (and retroactively) expanded the law's geographic reach to cover the regions of the Fenian attacks.[52] By October 1866, crowds thronged to watch the Fenian trials in Toronto, filling the courtrooms and sitting on windowsills, and listened in a quiet hush, "as still as death itself," when the judge announced the "dread sentence of the law"—death by hanging—in the first case to come to trial, that of Robert F. Lynch, an alleged newspaper reporter from Wisconsin, convicted after an hour and a half's deliberation. Next the court condemned to death Father John McMahon, a Catholic priest from Indiana who protested he had been kidnapped by the Fenians while on his way to Quebec and had provided only spiritual aid to the dying and wounded on both sides. Within five months, twenty-five prisoners stood convicted and sentenced to hanging.[53]

IN BOTH Canada and Ireland, then, Britain unleashed its powerful legal system, perfected in earlier rebellions, to corner and subdue the Fenians. Imprisoned, shadowed by police detectives, awaiting death sentences, American Fenians appeared to be no match for England, which could, if need be, "collect the whole strength of the empire to crush" the Fenian campaign.[54] The Fenians in 1866 had achieved none of their military objectives, and the Brotherhood became mired in quarrels over strategies and fund-raising scandals.[55] Yet the Fenians, though outmanned and outmaneuvered, did not yield. While the *New York Times* dismissed the Canadian invasions as the "Fenian fiasco," the Boston *Pilot* concluded that "the lesson of the hour is that the Irish, as a race, are terribly in earnest in their feelings and wishes against the government of Great Britain." Failure would not stop them but only "intensify their feelings against their lifelong oppressors. They will but wait for a more favourable opportunity."[56]

Perhaps Fenian leaders had the British precisely where they wanted them. Rifles, after all, were only one of the Fenians' weapons and, in the end, not their most powerful. "Our PEN is the sword, and our voice is the cannon," declared one Fenian ballad.[57] And, the songwriter might have added, American citizenship was their shield. As the Fenian prisoners awaited their final fates in Ireland and Canada, they and their supporters seized their pens and did what many American citizens did when they ran into trouble in foreign countries: they wrote the local American consulate, demanding protection as American citizens. Soon their pleas piled up on the London desk of Charles Francis Adams, U.S. minister to Great Britain.

4

Civis Americanus Sum

IN THE FALL OF 1864, as John Warren exhorted his Fenian comrades to bloody rebellion, Charles Francis Adams, the U.S. minister to London, gave little thought to Fenians or Irish Americans or to the rights of naturalized citizens. Warren lived only eleven miles from Adams's ancestral home in Quincy, Massachusetts, but they were worlds apart. No one, perhaps, was as secure in his American citizenship as Adams. The son of President John Quincy Adams and the grandson of President John Adams, Adams hailed from one of the country's oldest and most prominent New England family dynasties. Adams shared little with Warren and the Fenians, except, perhaps, a deep-seated belief in republicanism and a dislike of the English that intensified over the course of the Civil War. "Our English friends have succeeded in doing almost everything conceivable to make themselves offensively unpleasant to America," Adams complained in 1865.[1] Yet while Warren wanted nothing more than to provoke a war between the United States and England, in the hopes of securing Ireland's independence, Adams had worked tirelessly to keep the two countries at peace—and to keep England out of the American Civil War. It had not been easy.

Just as the war was coming to an end, the Fenians' arrests promised to undo his painstaking diplomacy by fanning long-simmering international disputes over citizenship. The British imperiously brushed aside the demands of naturalized Irish American Fenians that they be treated as American citizens under international law. "Once a subject, always a subject," insisted British authorities. These had been fighting words between Americans and the British since the American Revolution, when Americans had thrown off their status as British subjects and asserted their right to be "citizens" and to swear allegiance to the sovereign of their choice. But the Fenians' exploits raised perplexing questions in the age of mass migration and the rise of modern nation-states. As they crossed national borders and got into trouble, the Fenians drew into question where one nation's power began and another's ended, not only in controlling territorial boundaries but also in policing membership in the nation-state. How far could nations reach in demanding allegiance from subjects living beyond their borders? How far should the United States go to protect rights of citizens—especially naturalized Americans—against the claims of other states as they traveled abroad?

IN 1864, as the war wore on and the Fenians were just a speck on the horizon, Adams longed to go home.[2] He worried about his children's health in the inhospitable London climate. Nor was he fulfilled individually by his mission as America's chief diplomat to the world's greatest power. "I have utterly lost interest in any thing here," he moaned. "If I remain, it will probably be to spend more time in solitude."[3] As the new year of 1865 dawned, Adams noted with gratitude that the war seemed to have taken a decisive turn and that a Union victory lay at hand. He wrote to Secretary of State William Henry Seward, asking to be released from his position. After weeks of anxious suspense, he received an unwelcome reply. As he noted in his diary, "The President had not thought it for the public interest to take up for consideration my suggestion" at the present time.[4]

Adams took what heart he could from the disappointing answer. He hoped that by spring the war would be at a point that he could be released from the post that increasingly made him so unhappy. Then the terrible news came of the assassination of President Lincoln on Good Friday, April 14, and the attempted assassination of Seward. Seward had sustained serious knife wounds when John Powell, an accomplice of assassin John Wilkes Booth, attacked him in bed.[5] "To the country, the loss of Lincoln is hardly reparable," reflected Adams, but the possible loss of the secretary of state was "infinitely more grave. He has been the guiding principle through this struggle, the balance wheel of the machine of government."[6] Some had thought "the dubious condition of Mr. Seward" might lead to Adams taking over as secretary of state. "There might have been a new shake of the dice," reflected Adams. But "luck would not have it so. Mr. Seward recovered." Seward notified Adams on January 2, 1866, that the new president, Andrew Johnson, "has no desire to provide for any body else. His desire is . . . that I remain." Adams concluded regretfully,

"Of course, after this, and with my notions of public duty, there is nothing left but to stay until I am recalled."[7]

Adams seemed destined for the job as U.S. minister to Great Britain. "For a hundred years," observed his son Henry, "the chief effort of his family had aimed at bringing the Government of England into intelligent cooperation with the objects and interests of America."[8] John Adams had been a key negotiator for the peace treaties between Great Britain and the United States at the end of the American Revolution and became the new nation's first minister to England. John Quincy Adams became as well known as his father for his diplomatic skills, leading the American negotiating team that brought the War of 1812 with Britain to an uneasy end and later serving as U.S. secretary of state. Charles Adams learned diplomacy at his father's knee, spending most of his childhood abroad in Russia and England. With the family's long history of negotiating with Britain, Adams "thought it was natural that the Government should send him out," following in the paternal footsteps and even adhering to the family tradition of bringing his son Henry along as his private secretary and possible apprentice.[9]

Keeping England out of the war had been a challenge. Both Confederate and Union agents lobbied foreign countries for support, and the Confederacy's cotton, so crucial to the booming textile mills of industrializing nations, exerted a powerful pull on France and England. On the day Charles Adams and his family arrived, May 13, 1861, England released the official announcement of Queen Victoria's Proclamation of Neutrality, sparking an outcry among Union supporters. Rather than adopting the U.S. government's view that the secessionists were unlawful rebels, England recognized the Confederacy as a belligerent. American critics denounced the proclamation for its "undue haste," arguing that by acting so soon after the war began, England encouraged the South in its rebellion and gave it hope that England would soon recognize the Confederacy as an independent nation. England declared it acted simply to ensure perfect neutrality.[10]

But English views were not that simple or that neutral. "When I first reached this country in 1861," Adams reflected, "the general impression [was] that the 'bubble of democracy had burst in America'" and that the United States' experiment with republican government had finally come to an end. Some influential British leaders had been predicting the inevitable breakup of the United States since the Revolution, so certain were they of the folly of republicanism and the instability of the fledgling nation. The rapid expansion of the "mammoth" American republic irked naysayers such as Prime Minister

Charles Francis Adams, ca. 1861, U.S. minister to Great Britain. Photographer George Kendall Warren captures Adams's cool demeanor.

Lord Palmerston, who began to worry that England's former colony might thrive after all and encourage other movements for popular government. While Palmerston adopted an official stance of neutrality, Adams believed the belligerent London *Times* became the unofficial voice for Palmerston's views in its critique of the United States. Lord Russell, the British foreign minister and a liberal antislavery advocate, appeared more congenial and trustworthy but, as Henry Adams put it, "Minister Adams had much to learn." Lord Russell, the diplomat's son observed, "set the example. Personally, the Minister was to be kindly treated; politically, he was negligible; . . . All conceived that the

Washington Government would soon crumble and that Minister Adams would vanish with the rest."[11]

By war's end, Adams had not vanished, nor had the United States. Adams gradually became accepted by "London society" because he was "by birth and manners, one of themselves . . . In society few Londoners were so widely at home."[12] He at least knew how to dress, not an easy feat for American diplomats in Europe, whose first task was to negotiate the complex rules of etiquette and protocol. Adams's predecessor had adhered to the secretary of state's instructions that diplomats at official functions should appear "in the simple dress of an American citizen," as befitted representatives of the world's leading republic, and wore a plain black suit when presented to the queen. The queen was not amused. Adams made sure to appear at Court in more traditional finery, prompting the queen to remark, "I am thankful we shall have no more American funerals."[13]

Adams had not only secured entry into the London social set by 1865 but also succeeded in his quiet, controlled way in becoming a strong political force, carefully defusing explosive situations that threatened to push Britain into more explicit support for the Confederacy or draw the United States and England into conflict. Often described as cold and austere, Adams's unflappable personality proved invaluable as a diplomat. "Whatever the Minister thought," observed his son Henry, "he showed no trace of excitement . . . his mind and temper were as perfectly balanced; not a word escaped; not a nerve twitched."[14] His superior, Secretary Seward, was an astute politician and foreign-policy maker who tended to blow hard in his dispatches, taking a tough line, for example, in threatening England with possible war when the queen issued the Proclamation of Neutrality. With his blustery dispatches (often made public), Seward sought to keep Americans at home satisfied and foreign powers on alert. He could count on Adams to soften the blow. Adams proved adept at the special language the best diplomats speak, conveying Seward's forceful and belligerent messages in a more modulated tone that allowed relations to continue.[15]

Such tactics enabled Seward and Adams to help prevent the *Trent* affair from flaring into a more serious battle. In November 1861 the British ship was carrying two Confederate representatives on their way to England to persuade the government to support their cause. Acting on his own initiative but to the great acclaim of the American government and people, a U.S. Navy captain forcibly boarded the ship, arrested the two commissioners, and delivered them to a military prison in Boston. England expressed outrage that a neutral British ship had been violated. War was averted only after America released the prisoners but without extending the official apology demanded by the British.[16]

Soon it was the Americans' turn to express indignation and demands for retribution when the British allowed Confederate commerce raiders to be built in their ports, despite Adams's stern protests. The vessels, especially the notorious *Alabama,* provided a crucial boost to the Confederate navy and left a wake of destruction, crippling the Union navy and Northern commerce. Perhaps most infuriating, the new ships gave the Confederacy confidence and, in the American government's view, allowed the rebels to hold out longer and increase the casualties of the horrific civil war. "This is war," threatened Adams in 1863 when he learned of even more Confederate rams being built in English shipyards. England found a face-saving solution: the government purchased the rams for its own use.[17] But Americans remained deeply bitter over what they saw as English treachery and blatant pro-South policies. "It touched us sorely, that all through our darkest period" the British ministry worked "to aid and comfort a rebellion which was striking at our national life," a *New York Times* editorial bitterly remarked. At the very least, many Americans insisted, England should pay for the damage caused by the *Alabama.*[18]

As the Civil War drew to an end, relations between the United States and England remained tense. When news arrived in London of the passage of the Thirteenth Amendment abolishing slavery and the beginning of peace talks between the North and South, "it was as if a calamity had befallen the good people of England," observed Charles Adams. While "I have had several of our friends to congratulate me on the advance of the good cause," others who had banked on the success of the Confederacy experienced "consternation, disappointment, vexation . . . All stocks but American fell. They rose. Cotton fell."[19]

Rumors that the United States would now take its revenge for British violations of neutrality, possibly ending in war between the two nations, circulated in private correspondence, in dinner conversations, and in the public press. "The Americans are an excitable people," the London *Times* remarked, "thin-skinned beyond the most sensitive European nations."[20] Even the unflappable Adams expressed amazement when Lord Clarendon, after his appointment as British foreign minister, suggested that both sides should forgive and forget. "Americans are asked to bury their resentments against England," but "that we cannot do," said the editor of the *New York Times.*[21]

Still, Adams expressed confidence that the two nations would resolve their differences peacefully. "The position of the country never has been so high before" in England, Adams informed Seward in January 1866, and "the tone of the press towards the United States is gradually improving." He had no doubt that once the dispute over the *Alabama* claims was cleared up, "very soon the business will fall into its normal state." He bowed in January 1866 to Seward's request to remain in his position for the time being, hoping that by April things would have calmed down sufficiently that he could return home after five years' absence.[22]

Then the Fenians came.

CAPTAIN John Fanning had only come to Ireland to visit his relatives and "recruit his health after the hardships of a soldiers life in active service" during the Civil War. At least that's what he wrote in a letter to the American consul in Dublin, William B. West, after his arrest. Traveling with Lieutenant Timothy McNeff, a comrade from the 10th Ohio Volunteers, Fanning arrived in Queenstown, the major port of entry in County Cork, on SS *Louisiana* on September 14, 1865. Before he even disembarked, Fanning attracted the attention of Irish officials, who searched him and his luggage, observing the revolver Fanning had in his trunk but allowing him to land. After a two-week stay in Dublin, Fanning and McNeff departed for Ballinamore in County Leitrim to visit Fanning's relatives but got no farther than Killeshandra, where they were arrested, handcuffed, and thrown into jail by Irish police. The charge: carrying weapons and ammunition in a "proclaimed district," in violation of the Peace Preservation Act. Each man carried a revolver and a "number of percussive caps" in his trunk as well as papers and a substantial number of gold coins, which made police suspicious of their ultimate designs.[23]

Indignant at his treatment, Fanning immediately turned to the "sanctuary" for American citizens abroad, the American consulate, to intervene on his behalf. "When sick or alone, or when grasped by the power of an alien government," the American consul was the "one friend upon whom [the citizen] had a legitimate claim" in a foreign land, observed the essayist and traveler Henry T. Tuckerman in 1868. Especially when the "wanderer" became the victim of another government, his citizenship, as protected by the diplomatic agents abroad, "has a significance never before realized."[24] Fanning and other Irish American prisoners argued their case to the American consul, William West, insisting that they were innocent, targeted only because they were Americans. Demanding rather than asking for help, Fanning and other Irish American Fenians tested the United States' commitment to its adopted citizens, articulating in the process their own theories of citizenship and the obligation of the American government to protect all—whether native-born or naturalized— when abroad and threatened by foreign powers.

In asserting the right to be protected, Irish American prisoners invoked a particularly nineteenth-century understanding of citizenship as nestled within a network of allegiances and obligations—something between the feudal relationship of allegiance to a lord and the modern concept of citizens as autonomous, rights-bearing individuals. Citizens and subjects certainly used "rights talk" in a way that sounds familiar to modern ears, but they spoke with equal ease and fervor about "obligation," "allegiance," and "duty." Reciprocal obligations tied the state and the citizen together, and it was the performance of one's duty and declarations of allegiance that allowed one to assert one's rights and demand protection from one's government.[25] Irish Americans reminded government officials of the sacred oaths they had taken upon becoming naturalized, renouncing their previous sovereign and pledging their allegiance to their adopted land—a promise many had sealed with their blood during the Civil War, when the nation's very survival was in peril. It was now time for the U.S. government to fulfill its end of the bargain. "I have a more than ordinary claim on that Government for the preservation of which I struggled for four years through a bloody war, for protection," wrote Michael Kerwin in a typical letter.[26]

Struggling to keep up with the deluge of prisoner petitions, West steered a tricky course. He condemned Fenianism, denouncing "our citizens who may have been silly enough to have engaged in this vain revolutionary attempt." Yet he protested indignantly about the scores of Irish Americans who landed in Irish jails "on the mere caprice of the Constables . . . without a scintilla of evidence." As arrests of Irish Americans began to mount and prisoners badgered West with letters proclaiming their innocence, West turned often to Adams for guidance about what rights American citizens had when they left their country to venture abroad. "The question is naturally and frequently asked me," reported West, "is there no redress or remedy to be had for such illegal treatment of American citizens[?]"[27]

This was a big question with repercussions not only for Irish American Fenians ensnared by the British authorities in Ireland but for many other American citizens as well. Everywhere, people were on the move, whether as workers, political exiles, adventurers, or tourists. Steamship and railroad travel became faster and cheaper by midcentury, making it possible for even those of modest means to crisscross national boundaries and oceans. Many naturalized

Americans traveled to their homelands after the end of the Civil War for personal and business reasons, and an increasing number of native-born Americans, "drawn by the cheapness of living," lived abroad for years. Citizens abroad often caused headaches for American diplomats. Benjamin Moran, Adams's secretary in London, complained that "Americans are always getting into trouble in Europe" and turning to their government to intervene on their behalf. But how far could the United States reach beyond its borders to protect its citizens?[28]

The answer to that question was complicated, given the unsettled state of international law in the mid-nineteenth century. The "law of nations"—the rules governing the relationships between nations, and between nations and foreigners—was notoriously difficult to define and enforce, leading philosopher John Austin to argue that international law was not "law" in any real sense. There was "no legislature to enact its decrees; no judiciary to interpret its doctrine; no executive to enforce its decrees." Most international law experts believed Austin went too far, but they could not always agree upon the rules that bound nations, especially in a world changing so rapidly. As capitalism spread, global markets and mass migration exploded, propelling people and goods across borders. At the same time, sweeping political changes rocked many countries, as state-builders battled to create new, modern, centralized states and expand their power in the world, often resorting to war and redrawing political and territorial borders in the process. The old international law could not keep up, argued a growing number of international law activists, resulting in "constant conflict and [an] ever widening breach" between new social realities and old maxims of law. Nothing illustrated that better than the diplomatic wrangling over the Fenian arrests.[29]

IF SOME international rules were uncertain and disputed, British and American diplomats readily agreed on the core principle of "territorial sovereignty," a rule they felt was as self-evident as the mathematical fact that two plus two equals four. Absolute control over its territory was the defining mark of a sovereign state—the essential condition which made it a "state." A sovereign state had the power to fashion its own laws and enforce them against all who came within its territorial boundaries—both its nationals and "strangers" who voluntarily entered into its domain. No independent state wanted to be told by other governments how to handle its own domestic affairs. To a significant extent, then, states adopted a hands-off policy when it came to the domestic affairs of other sovereign states, even when a foreign state enforced its law against other states' nationals.[30]

Generations of lawyers and political thinkers in America, as well as Britain, had learned that principle from William Blackstone's *Commentaries on the Law of England,* required reading for most young lawyers in training and often the only legal reference book on their shelves.[31] Blackstone offered a commonly accepted rationale that linked the state's power to exercise control over persons to concepts of allegiance and protection. Allegiance, said Blackstone, came in different forms. Those born in England or its dominions (including Ireland) were natural-born subjects and automatically owed allegiance to the king, even if they swore no oath. In turn, the subject automatically enjoyed the protection of the king. This relationship of obligation provided the rationale for the sovereign's rule and the obedience of his subjects. Aliens also became enfolded in the logic of allegiance. While strangers were in a foreign land, they enjoyed the temporary protection of the sovereign state and thus owed temporary or "local" allegiance to the government and were "bound to obey its laws as native subjects or citizens" until they left. Foreigners could be charged with any crime forbidden by the law of the host state, even treason, as they had an obligation of loyalty under the theory of temporary allegiance. So British officials in Canada and Ireland had no qualms about trying Irish Americans for treason.[32]

But what if a foreign government acted arbitrarily, as West and the Irish American prisoners charged, and denied foreigners basic legal protections and rights? The suspension of habeas corpus in Ireland particularly rankled United States officials, as Irish authorities imprisoned Americans—" innocent and guilty alike"—indefinitely, without pressing charges.[33] Ironically, English authorities provided the American government a justification for intervening in such cases. Blackstone had argued that the sovereign's obligation to protect his subjects did not stop at the border of his realm; rather, "the prince is always under a constant tie to protect his natural-born subjects, at all times and in all countries."[34]

Lord Palmerston, Adams's nemesis during the Civil War negotiations, extended Blackstone's notion of the sovereign's obligation to his far-flung subjects as a useful tool in the age of the modern British Empire to shield British subjects from harm as they traveled to far regions to expand British trade and power. In 1850, Palmerston sent the Royal Navy to blockade the Greek port of Piraeus after the Greek government refused to compensate David Pacifico, born in British Gibraltar and thus a British subject, after an anti-Semitic mob in Athens destroyed his property. Ordinarily, Palmerston conceded, Britain would stay out of the domestic affairs of foreign states, but not in "uncivilized" countries that failed to provide basic security and justice for British subjects. Only countries that belonged to the Western "family of nations"—Christian nations bound by the rule of law—could expect to have their territorial sovereignty respected.[35]

Empire-builders in the nineteenth century liked to compare themselves to what they viewed as the most successful and long-lived imperialists—the ancient Romans, who had such power that few dared to cross them. Palmerston boldly declared in 1851 that just "as the Roman, in days of old, held himself free from indignity, when he could say *civis Romanus sum* [I am a Roman citizen], so also a British subject, in whatever land he may be, shall feel confident that the watchful eye and the strong arm of England, will protect him against injustice and wrong." Palmerston's version of *civis Britannicus* imagined a "portable" British subject who moved throughout the world, rights and allegiance intact.[36] International law scholar Sir William Vernon Harcourt took a more cynical view of his country's stance. "The ordinary Englishman's idea of his rights as a *civis Romanus* are simple enough. He thinks himself entitled, wherever he goes, to trial by jury, to *habeas corpus,* to a Protestant chapel and the Bill of Rights. In short," he concluded, "to do and say what he likes, and make himself as disagreeable as he pleases, with the comfortable confidence that there are any number of ironclads in the background to protect him from being called to account for it."[37]

Americans such as Captain Fanning in his letter to Seward advanced a similar belligerent view of Americans' rights abroad, appealing to the model of *civis Romanus* to prod the U.S. government into action. "Time was when no power on earth dared molest the Roman citizen untainted with crime," declared Fanning, "when the name alone was a sufficient passport through the nations of the earth." Fanning thought of his American citizenship as providing the same sort of armor wherever he traveled in the world, but especially against his former sovereign. He was not alone in urging the United States to extend its reach, to endow American citizens with the ability to declare *civis Americanus sum,* "I am an American citizen," against any who trifled with them when they left the safety of America. "It is a poor justice that is bounded by rivers and mountains," argued George H. Yeaman, the U.S. minister at Copenhagen. "A citizen should be a citizen wherever he goes."[38]

These were brash words—"spread eagle" talk, in the words of Harcourt—that had become all too common since the Mexican-American War of 1848 as Americans thumped their collective chests and declared it their manifest destiny to expand American power throughout the Western Hemisphere and perhaps the world. Harcourt dismissed such talk, whether voiced by Palmerston or American Fenians, as the "language of the bully." British officials bristled at American arrogance in suggesting that Britain needed lessons from America about rights and due process. Britain, after all, had taught its former subjects most of what they knew about constitutional liberty and the rule of law. They rebuffed any suggestion that their legal system was on a par with Greece's, requiring the intervention of the American government. And just what kind of shield did Americans imagine their citizenship provided? Surely Americans packing pistols, invading British territories, and plotting rebellion against the queen could not expect to hide behind their American citizenship when caught. The duty of self-preservation was one of the fundamental rights of nations, according to the father of modern international law, Emer de Vattel, and Britain was entirely justified in telling foreigners, "Obey or begone!"[39] And, obviously, Britain wielded absolute jurisdiction over its own subjects, including Irish who had gone to America, and it would tolerate no meddling by foreign countries.

Here was the nub of the issue that would soon blow up into an international controversy. Many of those arrested, though born in Ireland, claimed to be naturalized American citizens. The British government insisted that naturalized Irish Americans remained British subjects, regardless of any oath they had sworn in the United States or their possession of a "mere ticket of naturalization."[40] The British held fast to the doctrine of perpetual allegiance, as did other European powers.

Blackstone again offered the legal rationale. Subjects born within the sovereign's realm were subjects forever, as their natural allegiance was "intrinsic and primitive," "written by the finger of the law in their hearts." The subject's allegiance could not "be forfeited, cancelled, or altered, by any change of time, place, or circumstance." No matter where the English subject ventured, whether "he removes to France or to China"—or to America—he "owes the same allegiance to the king of England there as at home." Only his "natural prince" could dissolve the tie and release the subject from his obligation of allegiance.[41] Following such logic, Irish judges in the fall 1865 treason trials dismissed defendants' claims to be American citizens, holding that "having returned to their native land their allegiance to the Queen attaches to them as much, and effectually, as if they had never renounced it or become American Citizens," as "a native born subject can never shake off his allegiance."[42]

"My own government will, I trust, entertain a much different opinion," wrote Eneas Dougherty from Mountjoy Prison. "If I remember correctly the doctrine of 'once a subject always a subject' has been done away with."[43] Indeed it had. The American Revolution had been a defiant rejection of the doctrine of perpetual allegiance, declaring it the natural right of individuals to choose their own sovereign. In a mass act of voluntary expatriation, British colonists shed their status as the king's subjects and embraced a new identity as American citizens. The naturalized citizen became the model of the American theory of "volitional allegiance" that lay at the heart of consensual government. The individual willfully and actively decided to join the body politic and swore allegiance to it.[44]

American theories of voluntary allegiance—and its generous naturalization policies—put the United States on a collision course with England and much of Europe, especially as millions of Europeans joined the "exit revolution" and headed to the United States. Even as the United States championed the right of expatriation, using rapid naturalization as a tool to incorporate white immigrants quickly into the growing nation, many sending states refused to relinquish their hold on emigrants. Emigrants leaving German states in the mid-nineteenth century had to obtain emigration permits, a costly and time-consuming process, verifying they had paid all taxes, church tithes, and personal debts, and, most important, that they had fulfilled their compulsory military service. Then they endured a tongue-lashing by an official, bound by law to tell emigrants they were being foolish. Many chose instead to simply slip away, becoming undocumented emigrants, subject to arrest and punishment should they return to their native land. German governments washed their hands of emigrants who left, even those with exit permits, stripping them of citizenship and any rights or protections. But the stateless emigrants still had to fulfill the duties of German citizenship, especially military service, no matter where they roamed.[45]

By 1865 several European states had begun to gradually relax their vigilance over departures, as their populations began to explode and industrial capitalism created both new demands for a mobile labor force and new problems of poverty and social unrest. Perhaps, thought poor-law commissioners in England and elsewhere, siphoning off poor, underemployed, and discontented subjects was not such a bad thing, particularly if they could be encouraged to go to underpopulated colonies. Everywhere, it seemed, freedom of movement was on the rise: serfs released from the land in Europe, slaves freed from bondage in the United States, workers following the supply and demand of labor markets.[46]

European countries still balked, however, when it came to recognizing the absolute right of individuals to choose their nationality, insisting that, at the very least, the government's consent was required. Allegiance was "sacred," not a thing to put on and take off as a man pleased, "to be a Prussian, a Frenchman, or an Englishman, just as it suited his convenience."[47] Irish American Fenians might be ungrateful, even traitorous subjects, but they remained subjects under the complete control of the British, despite their naturalization in America. But in the eyes of the United States government, they were American citizens, entitled to government protection.

Yet what exactly could the government do to protect its citizens abroad? As Harcourt pointed out, it helped if a nation had ironclad warships to back up demands on foreign countries to afford certain rights to its nationals. The ability of a nation to intercede on behalf of its nationals abroad depended not only on legal claims but also on the practical power it wielded in the world and on a delicate political calculus, balancing the advantages of intervening on behalf of a few individuals against the possible social costs.[48] Palmerston could rattle his saber at Greece because he had the Royal Navy at his back. Did the United States have the power and the will to face down the British government over its treatment of Irish Americans and to insist that it recognize the right of expatriation?

It had done so in the past. In 1812, outraged by British raids on American ships and the impressment of British-born American citizens (including many Irish Americans), the United States declared war on Britain. Battling Napoleon and desperately short of sailors, the British saw their seizure of naturalized Americans, born in Britain and thus British subjects under British law, as the exercise of a well-recognized sovereign right to recall all subjects, no matter where they were, to serve the country during times of war. But the United States saw the impressment of an estimated 10,000 Americans as nothing less than an "insolent" assault on its sovereignty. "Our laws are as good as British laws," wrote former president John Adams defiantly, and American naturalization laws had turned British subjects into American citizens, worthy and deserving of the government's full protection.

America's "second war of independence," as many called the War of 1812, once again sought to emancipate British subjects—and affirm American sovereignty—by securing recognition of the right of expatriation, by drastic means if necessary. When Britain seized twenty-three naturalized Irish American soldiers, planning to try them in England as traitors for bearing arms against their native sovereign, Congress empowered the president to retaliate, and the secretary of war took twenty-three British officers hostage. Enraged, the British upped the ante, taking forty-six Americans, which the American government matched, ratcheting up their number of hostages. The hostage standoff escalated, each side holding hundreds of soldiers and threatening retaliatory executions, until the two countries finally backed down.[49]

At war's end, however, nothing had been settled. John Quincy Adams had broken with the Federalist Party to support the war because he felt so strongly about impressment and the "nullification" of America's naturalization laws, but when he led America's negotiating team to Ghent, he made little headway. The British, flush with victory over Napoleon, conceded nothing in the Treaty of Ghent on impressment or expatriation.[50] The battle over expatriation continued to fester, erupting periodically when naturalized Americans ventured to their homelands and landed in trouble. When the Young Ireland rebellion broke out in 1848, the British government suspended habeas corpus in Ireland and ordered the arrest of all Americans who came to the green isle, targeting Irish Americans in particular. U.S. minister George Bancroft protested mightily and shook his literary fists, but Lord Palmerston (who had been secretary of war during the War of 1812) remained unperturbed, turning always to the doctrine of perpetual allegiance.[51]

IT WAS NOT only the British who blocked recognition of the right of expatriation. Diplomats wrestled with an embarrassing truth: the United States had never explicitly recognized the right of expatriation by statute, despite Americans' noisy claims that expatriation was the "American doctrine." In fact, the only existing federal law on expatriation provided for stripping Americans of their citizenship. An act passed on March 3, 1865—only a year before the Fenian crisis erupted—declared that military deserters "shall be deemed to have voluntarily relinquished . . . their rights of citizenship."[52] While Americans trumpeted that citizenship in the young republic rested on the radical doctrine of consent, the United States had never fully embraced the idea of voluntary allegiance, especially for those on the political and social margins of American society. Loyalists in the American Revolution, for example, found they had precious little choice in their political allegiance, the Continental Congress declaring them American citizens against their will. If they insisted on retaining their allegiance to the king, loyalists often had to flee, most leaving the only home they had known, or else face charges of treason. So too, women, Native

Americans, and African Americans (both free and enslaved) seemed more akin to subjects than citizens, their movements and legal status controlled by husbands, masters, or policymakers.[53]

America's naturalization laws certainly implied the right of expatriation, especially since the new citizen had to renounce allegiance to the former sovereign. But in the wake of the War of 1812, a bitterly divided Congress failed to pass a proposed expatriation act. American judges tried to dodge the issue on the rare occasions when it arose, upholding the right of expatriation in theory but—not unlike European countries—usually requiring the explicit permission of the government before an individual could renounce his citizenship. Critics worried especially about Americans who wanted to "quit the country," suspecting them of sloughing off their citizenship to shirk their obligations or to pursue crass moneymaking schemes. A rash of expatriation cases involving Americans who abandoned their citizenship in the 1790s to become French privateers, attacking British ships to line their own pockets, prompted critics to cast expatriation as the refuge of the "traitor and pirate."[54] More pragmatically, America simply could not afford to let its people go, noted Chief Justice Oliver Ellsworth in 1799: "Our country is but sparsely settled, and we have no inhabitants to spare."[55]

Critics had little patience with the naturalized American who declared "he is free to go wherever the winds and the waves may carry him," under the protective eye of the "American Eagle." They blamed naturalized Irish Americans for dragging the nation into the unprofitable war with Britain in 1812, saying they should "keep themselves out of the way of the claims of their former country" and "avoid becoming a curse to the country of their adoption."[56] When Johann Knocke, a naturalized Prussian American, complained that he had been forced into military service upon his return to Prussia in 1840, Henry Wheaton, U.S. minister to Prussia and author of the best-known treatise on international law, said, in essence, Knocke should have stayed home: "Had you remained in the United States, or visited any other foreign country, (except Prussia,) on your lawful business, you would have been protected by the American authorities, at home and abroad." But Knocke chose, unfortunately, to return to his native land, and in doing so, said Wheaton, "*your native domicile and natural character* revert, (so long as you remain in the Prussian dominions,) and you are bound in all respects to obey the laws exactly as if you had never emigrated."[57]

Almost twenty years later, however, the State Department had changed its position, perhaps due to the surge of immigrants and their growing political power, but also reflecting a more robust sense of America's potential power in the world.[58] Many Americans cheered in 1853 when Captain Duncan Ingraham of USS *St. Louis* rescued Martin Koszta from an Austrian ship, heralding it as a "new era" in American foreign affairs. Koszta, a political refugee from the failed Hungarian Revolution of 1848 against the Austrian Empire, had declared his intention to become a United States citizen. When in Turkey on business, Koszta was scooped up by Austrian imperial forces, with the aim of punishing him for political rebellion. Even though Koszta was only a "declarant," not a full-fledged American citizen, Secretary of State William L. Marcy declared he was "clothed with our national character" and deserved the fullest protection from the overreaching Austrians.

Finally, the *New York Times* crowed, the "long period of humiliations" and the "powerlessness of United States Ministers to protect their countrymen in Europe" had come to an end. At last the "cry—'I am an American citizen'" might mean something in the world.[59] As the right of expatriation gathered political steam, Secretary of State Lewis Cass in 1859 struck at Europe's tyrannical hold on its emigrants, especially condemning Prussia's military conscription of naturalized Americans upon their return to their native land. Prussia could claim nothing of its expatriates, said Cass. "The moment a foreigner becomes naturalized, his allegiance to his native country is severed forever. He experiences a new political birth. . . . Should he return to his native country he returns as an American citizen."[60]

Yet on the eve of the Civil War, the United States still hesitated to endorse explicit statutory declarations in favor of expatriation, in part because American law on citizenship was in a state of confusion, and hotly debated. If, internationally, individuals became entangled by nations' different rules on membership, Americans at home also navigated multiple allegiances and overlapping jurisdictions between state and federal governments. With power divided between states and the federal government, Americans were members both of their individual states and of the nation. But to which entity—the states or the federal government—did Americans owe their main loyalty? Was one a citizen of a state first and the nation second, or the other way around?

That seemingly abstract issue divided a nation torn over questions of slavery and states' rights. In the infamous *Dred Scott* decision, Justice Roger Taney exacerbated an already tense situation in ruling that African Americans were not U.S. citizens, even if free and born in the United States. He affirmed the dual sovereignty of federal and state governments to determine independently who was a citizen of their jurisdiction, but he denied that state law could make free blacks national citizens. On the eve of the Civil War, Americans could not agree on their own definition of citizenship or on how the rights of citizens were to be determined and protected in the domestic sphere; it is little wonder, then, that the United States failed to articulate a consistent, clear vision of the rights of American citizens abroad. The growing threat of Southern secession and civil war made expatriation—or any acknowledgment of a right to leave—a volatile topic, best avoided. It was only after the war and the Union's victory over secessionist ideology that expatriation became a viable political issue in the United States.[61]

The victory of the Union in 1865 swept aside state sovereignty and divided citizenship in the United States. Congress turned to redefining national citizenship, clarifying that American citizens had only one allegiance: to the government of the United States. That notion of a singular, indivisible allegiance also fueled the movement toward recognition of expatriation at home and abroad. It was time, argued the Fenians and other foreign-born Americans, to turn abstract ideals into hard policies, to make naturalization mean something, both at home and abroad.[62]

IRISH AMERICAN prisoners quickly made their citizenship the key issue, pitching their treatment as a test of the United States government's commitment to its adopted citizens. When the raids began on February 17, West reported, "the consulate was . . . invaded by adopted citizens" and their friends, "choking with rage" as they bitterly complained "that we should allow the [British] Government to treat them as British subjects." Any effort to obtain the release of native-born American citizens without a similar attempt being made to free naturalized Americans was sure to create a fuss, West warned. The Fenians' ultimate goal, he predicted, was to push the American government "to adopt decisive measures" to protect the rights of naturalized Americans, and "thus bring about a collision" between Britain and the United States that would lead to "the success of their cause"—war and the subsequent liberation of Ireland.[63]

Adams read West's reports of the arrests under the habeas corpus suspension act with a sense of foreboding.[64] In his earliest reports to Seward on the Fenian movement in Ireland, in late September 1865, Adams confessed he had "not taken much trouble to inform myself . . . of its precise nature" but thought it "scarcely deserves to be regarded as formidable." By February 1866, Adams had learned much more about the Fenians and viewed them as a more serious threat, not to British rule in Ireland but to his diplomatic mission. He expressed little doubt that many of those arrested were "more or less connected" with the Fenian effort to subvert English rule in Ireland, which threatened to sour relations with England just when he hoped tensions were finally easing. The Fenians' decision to ground their new campaign against the British on the question of their American citizenship raised one of the "gravest difficulties" that had "always been a breeder of dissension" between the two countries. It had led to war once, and if not handled carefully, might well spark war again.[65]

News of the arrests quickly grabbed headlines in the United States as the Fenian Brotherhood rushed to make the most of their compatriots' imprisonment. "The Habeas Corpus Act is suspended in Ireland!" shouted a circular issued by the Fenian Brotherhood headquarters on Union Square. "Success depends on immediate Action!" Much-needed money poured into the Fenian treasury, thousands of supporters flocked to "monster meetings" in Boston, New York, and Washington, D.C., and Boston Fenians roused Union Army veterans to take to the "war path." Fenian leaders even asked for a meeting with President Johnson. Nervously eyeing the upcoming elections in November, Seward and Johnson resisted pressure from the cabinet to take a strong stand against the Fenians.[66] Instead, Seward sent a flurry of letters to Adams pressing him to get Britain to back down before the expatriation issue, a "harmless abstraction" until now, spun out of control.[67]

Adams had no intention of letting the Fenians disrupt the fragile peace he had gone to such great lengths to preserve. While Adams shared West's indignation at Britain's arrogant refusal to allow consular intervention, he ordered U.S. consuls in Ireland to speak "quietly and carefully, avoiding all appearance of threat or of emotion," in their dealings with Irish officials as they worked to defuse the explosive situation. Adams declared it his duty to protect all citizens, "whether native or naturalized"—but only if they had done nothing wrong, and only as long as they could prove they were U.S. citizens.[68]

Proving one's citizenship was not easy. Today Americans can present their birth certificates, social security cards, or passports to prove their citizenship. Such documents did not typically exist in the mid-nineteenth century or, in the case of passports, did not necessarily verify one's citizenship. Passports had originally functioned as "letters of introduction," a sort of character reference in which the issuing official gave assurances that the individual was respectable and traveled under the protection of the government. Except in times of war, passports remained optional until the 1930s, and before 1856, might be issued by local officials, rather than the State Department, to resident noncitizens as well as citizens.[69]

In lieu of documents, prisoners laid claims to citizenship in other ways. Many simply declared in affidavits that they were citizens, providing information about their birth or naturalization. Others recounted how they had lived in the United States for years, arriving from Ireland as children. They detailed their participation in military campaigns and listed wounds sustained in battle. They spoke of their passion for American republican principles and admiration for the founding fathers. They submitted letters written by people in their community who knew them to be upstanding and loyal, or they provided evidence that they had voted. Irish American prisoners, in sum, shared an expansive idea of citizenship that rested as much on what one did or believed—one's demonstrated allegiance to the country—as it did on legal documents.[70]

Adams, however, dismissed the prisoners' "very vague ideas . . . of their citizenship," grounded in "residence, military service or a declaration of intention." He insisted that they obtain documentation from the United States of their birth or naturalization, a lengthy and often futile process given the haphazard state of record-keeping in many localities.[71] But not even the most formal legal documents would have made a difference to the British. A small number of prisoners were able to rustle up naturalization certificates, but the British rejected them, insisting that naturalized Americans remained British subjects, beyond the protection of the American government.[72]

Gradually, however, politics and pragmatism, as well as Adams's calm reassurances, wore the British down. Other weighty diplomatic issues divided the two countries—disputes over fisheries, trade, and especially the contentious *Alabama* claims—and these might become inflamed if the naturalization question was allowed to fester, especially during an election year. Get the explosive citizenship issue out of the public eye and keep it from gaining traction in Congress, advised Sir Frederick Bruce, the British minister in Washington. Adams reassured Clarendon that he did not want "to screen offenders" from their just deserts. But wouldn't it be better to "ease . . . off" and come to some sort of compromise? Surely peace was more important than taking a stand over a few scoundrels.[73]

On June 1, 1866, Adams sent a triumphant note to Seward. The British had agreed to "remove all unnecessary distinctions" between native-born and naturalized Americans and had begun to release all prisoners, except those "deeply implicated in the plot," on the condition they leave Ireland immediately.[74] Within days of this compromise, Fenians launched their invasions of Canada. Here, too, British and Canadian officials took a similar approach, first drawing a hard line in the sand and dealing sternly with the offenders, then easing off. In the end, the death sentences of all twenty-five Fenian prisoners in Canada were commuted to twenty years of hard labor in the penitentiary.[75] But the British made one important caveat: they conceded nothing on the bigger issue of citizenship, holding fast to the doctrine of perpetual allegiance.[76] That was good enough for Adams. Almost a year after the habeas corpus crisis, Adams cheerfully told Seward on February 6, 1867, that the Fenian panic "is rapidly passing away." Perhaps now he could go home.[77]

But Adams often underestimated the Fenians. Thomas Larcom, the undersecretary at Dublin Castle and a close observer of the Fenians, was nearer the mark in his letter to Lord Naas, the chief secretary, in March 1867. "We are much as usual—smouldering," wrote Larcom. "We hold [Fenianism] by the throat as you would a burglar—but the moment you relax up it springs as strong as ever." For Irish Americans could not forget, or forgive, their forced exile from Ireland, or Britain's iron-fisted grasp on Ireland and Irish Americans. The "manure" for the Fenian movement, noted Larcom, was "the discontent of a million and a half of people, mourning and brooding over a grievance—expatriation."[78]

TWO

Citizenship on Trial

5

A Floating Rebellion

SINCE 1864, John Warren had urged his compatriots to be on alert for the coming Irish rebellion, when Ireland would be freed through a "baptism of blood." He repeatedly warned: "The day is fast approaching," "The important hour is at hand," "The hour is near."[1] After pledging that 1865 would be the "year of action," James Stephens, the leader of the Irish Fenians, had stalled, promising an Irish rebellion by January 1, 1867. When on December 15, 1866, Stephens tried to delay the rising yet again, warning that the Fenians were woefully short of funds and arms, his military advisors declared him a coward and deposed him. Colonel Thomas J. Kelly took charge of the Fenian cause in Ireland, and finally, on March 5, 1867, the long-awaited Rising erupted. Thousands of Fenians launched attacks on police stations and military installations, reaching from Drogheda in the north to Warren's native Cork in the south, tearing up railways and cutting telegraph lines. Kelly's ultimate goal: to take Dublin and hold it until reinforcements arrived from the United States.[2]

News of the Irish rebellion electrified New Yorkers. Throngs of people crowded the *New York Herald* office, eagerly awaiting the latest news arriving through the new Atlantic cable, which allowed messages to fly across the ocean with lightning speed. Supporters filled the Fenian headquarters, spilling out onto the street, sharing any tidbit of news and speculating wildly on the progress of the long-awaited revolution. Even "lukewarm Irishmen" became ardent nationalists for the moment, sporting the green ties and scarves that popped up throughout the city. New York Irish rejoiced at the news of the establishment of an Irish Provisional Government, which issued a ringing proclamation declaring its determination to "repossess" Ireland or die trying. Fenian circles held emergency meetings, and 10,000 supporters showed up at a boisterous rally

John Warren, co-commander of *Erin's Hope*, 1867. Officials at Kilmainham Gaol took photos of all prisoners suspected of being Fenians and recorded their physical descriptions. Warren was described as being 5′11″ tall, thirty-three years of age, and "very stout" in build, with auburn hair, brown eyes, and a "fresh" complexion.

at Union Square on a bitterly cold and rainy night on March 13 to cheer on the "boys in green." General James Gleeson reportedly ordered 2,000 uniforms of "bright emerald green" to clothe two Fenian regiments as they prepared for the anticipated battle.[3]

Yet anxiety tempered the joy of Irish Americans, especially as the terse dispatches provided meager details, leaving the watchful in "a sort of maddening suspense." News of Fenian defeats alternated with assurances that the Fenian rebellion was not only alive and strong but on the rise, throwing the Irish government into a fevered panic as its military forces dashed about the country trying to squelch the Fenian fire. New York newspapers and Fenian Brotherhood leaders cautioned repeatedly that discouraging news arriving from Ireland by cable was not to be trusted, as England controlled the dispatches. But even the most devout Fenian leaders realized that the rebellion in Ireland stood on shaky ground and tested the mettle not only of the Irish rebels but of Irish Americans as well. Without American support, the insurgency would soon collapse.[4]

Time was of the essence, Fenian leaders urged, as they exhorted Irish Americans to unite and give aid—particularly money—to the rebellion in Ireland. Colonel Kelly, the American commander of the Irish rebels, prodded the pride and conscience of those sitting safely in New York: "If we sink before aid arrives, the wails of our men through prison bars should haunt the bed of every Irishman in America." The Irish rebels would try to hold on until the much-needed money, men, and arms arrived from America, Kelly wrote in his letters of March 15 and 19. But he urged them to "hurry, hurry, hurry!"[5]

The Fenian Brotherhood leaders in the United States tried to hurry, but rapid action proved difficult. They drew thousands of "wonderfully enthusiastic" participants to lively rallies but failed to pry much money from the pockets of Irish Americans, many of whom had little extra to share and had already given to the cause.[6] Nor did the leaders find it easy to agree upon the best means to "help the gallant patriots" in Ireland. Irish American officers from the Civil War gathered at a meeting on March 9 to discuss possible strategies but quickly fell into "spicy debate." Elected secretary of the meeting, John Warren had a front-row seat to what became a free-for-all. Some participants moved to expel Irish American officers who had served in the Confederate Army from the meeting. In a separate motion, Warren proposed that the group appeal to Irish millionaires to contribute liberally to the cause. These and other proposals generated "a row that lasted considerable time. Rebukes and counter-rebukes were now indulged in. The chairman had little control."[7] These were minor differences compared to the long-festering feud between the O'Mahony wing, favoring rebellion in Ireland, and the Roberts wing, focusing on the invasion of Canada. With an actual rebellion under way in Ireland, the Roberts wing faced considerable pressure to fall in line and throw their support and resources behind the cause. Warren, who had supported both factions at various times, sought to unite the opposing forces even before the rebellion started. In an appeal published in the *New York Herald* on

December 1, 1866, Warren warned that soon an "Irish army will be battling on Irish soil" so "in God's name, . . . unite. Rally round them as one man," he urged.[8]

The Fenian leaders in America agreed on one thing: ships were crucial to the success of the Irish rebellion. Fenians in the O'Mahony wing had long threatened that a deadly Fenian fleet of warships and privateers would free Ireland one day and wreak revenge on Britain for its dastardly role in outfitting the Confederates with privateers in the Civil War.[9] Anticipating a rush of Fenian mariners and ships, the Fenian Brotherhood drew up forms to commission privateers, authorizing them to seize British merchant ships and their cargo with the goal of driving British commerce "from the ocean."[10] The Roberts wing thought such plans foolish. Fenian vessels would find it impossible to "leave the United States and sail to Ireland without being apprehended," much less "be able to land men and ammunition."[11] How could they take on the Royal Navy, the largest in the world? But the Rising gave new urgency to the call for a Fenian fleet. What Ireland needed, wrote one New York merchant, was "two or three first class vessels-of-war—a Dunderberg or two," referring to the new massive ironclad warship that had been completed too late to see service in the Civil War.[12] Colonel Kelly, waiting for help in Ireland, agreed. "Where are those ironclads?" he demanded. "A landing in Sligo at the present time would be of infinite service."[13]

QUIETLY, a group of intrepid Fenians plotted just such a mission.[14] Colonel James Kelly, head of the Fenian military council in New York, found a ship, but it was no *Dunderberg*. While *Dunderberg* (Swedish for "thunder mountain"), was 377 feet long, with a beam of 72 feet, *Jacmel Packet* was a small, 138-ton brigantine, measuring 81 feet long with a beam of 20 feet.[15] Built in Medford, Massachusetts, in 1861, the vessel already had an adventurous and illicit past. In 1866, Captain John Dawes, master of *Jacmel*, left Singapore with a cargo of pepper and other spices destined for Melbourne, but absconded with the shipowner's merchandise and vessel and landed in Aspinwall (current-day Colón, Panama), claiming a storm had blown him off course and destroyed the ship's mainsail. Another account suggests even deeper intrigue—that *Jacmel* carried guns to arm the insurgents fighting Maximilian I in Mexico. Whatever he was delivering, the captain quickly sold the cargo and the ship, but the American consul suspected fraud and seized the vessel. *Jacmel* ended up in New York in February 1867, where it remained under the custody of the United States Collector of Customs.[16]

Jacmel was far from a perfect ship. It needed substantial repairs just to get from Panama to New York, and remained "not very well found in sails and appliances for a vessel of her class."[17] But when the ship became available to the Fenian Brotherhood—whether for free or for purchase is unclear—James Kelly jumped at the opportunity. Having finally secured a Fenian "warship," Kelly hired carpenters to build berths and stashed the hold with guns and ammunition. While the ship was being readied for its Atlantic voyage, Kelly turned to the most important task of all: finding the bold Fenian men able and willing to make the audacious voyage.[18]

The men Kelly recruited, about forty-five in all, had much in common. Like most Fenians, they were young men who hailed from the aspiring classes. While John Cade was a "bar boy" and John Rooney a laborer, most of *Jacmel's* rank and file were skilled tradesmen, including a carpenter, tailor, painter, shoemaker, jeweler, glasscutter, boilermaker, bricklayer, and cooper. Others had achieved somewhat higher status, eking out a living in small businesses or clerkships obtained through government patronage. Most of them likely identified as that new breed, "Irish American," born in Ireland but living in New York or New England, many since childhood. Almost all had served in the Union Army or Navy in the Civil War, several in Meagher's Irish Brigade. And all had demonstrated, in some manner, an exceptional dedication to the cause of Irish independence. Some were veterans of the Fenian filibustering expeditions to Canada in the summer of 1866. Others, such as the young actor Augustine E. Costello, served as "head centres" for Fenian circles and gained recognition for their oratory skills.[19]

The commander of the expedition, James E. Kerrigan, certainly had the fighting spirit treasured by Fenians. Kerrigan hailed from Five Points in New York City, "the most notorious neighborhood in nineteenth-century America," renowned for its violence, poverty, and rowdy entertainment. Five Points bred the Bowery B'hoys, William "Bill the Butcher" Poole, Tammany Hall politician William "Boss" Tweed, the bare-knuckle prizefighter Jim Sullivan—and James Kerrigan. Kerrigan proved to be as colorful and brash as the neighborhood that nurtured him. Always ready for adventure, Kerrigan had left Fordham University when only seventeen years old to fight in the Mexican-American War, and in 1856 he joined William Walker's filibustering mission to annex Nicaragua. He returned home in time to defend his position as councilman from the Sixth Ward in a hotly contested political race that erupted into a huge street fight as rival political gangs sought to settle the election with their fists and revolvers. While serving a term in Congress (1861–1862), Kerrigan also held a commission as colonel of the 25th New York Voluntary Regiment, only to be mustered out in less than a year after a court-martial found him guilty of habitual neglect of duty and failure to train his men. But Kerrigan soon secured a higher rank, appointed a brigadier general in the Fenian Army. The daring intrigue of the *Jacmel* expedition undoubtedly held much allure for such an intrepid soul.[20]

Assisting Kerrigan were the Fenian colonels William J. Nagle and John Warren. Warren was undoubtedly delighted to have been chosen for such a prominent position on the expedition, an apt reward for his dedicated service to the Fenian Brotherhood and its military mission. Warren would be third in command, just below Nagle.[21] A native New Yorker, born in 1828, Nagle was the son of an Irish rebel—and not just any Irish rebel, if his father's story can be believed. In a confidential letter to Irish government authorities in 1868, his father, David Nagle, claimed to be the infamous "Captain Rock" of County Cork, the man who led the exceptionally violent agrarian Rockite movement in southern Ireland between 1821 and 1824, resorting to arson, murder, and intimidation to protest high rents, the collection of tithes, and the Protestant Ascendancy. Captain Rock was a mythical figure, but several real-life leaders, or "captains," sprang up in various districts to coordinate the rebellion, David Nagle becoming known as "'the Captain Rock' of the North Liberties" of Cork City. He reportedly cut "a fine figure—dressed in a blue coat with a sash and sword and wearing a military cap with a big white feather," and he caused considerable havoc for the British government in Ireland before his capture in 1823.[22] Whether William's father was indeed the Rockite David Nagle is unknown, but William clearly displayed a similar mix of rebellious discipline and leadership ability. A "War Democrat," the thirty-two-year old William Nagle left his job at the customs office, his wife, Sarah, and their four-year-old daughter to join Meagher's Irish Brigade in 1861, the prominent citizens of South Brooklyn sending him off with "a splendid sword, sash and belts" presented at a "very festive affair." Like Warren, Nagle raised his own company, commanding Company F of the 88th New York Regiment through some of the bloodiest battles fought by the Army of the Potomac before he was mustered out in the summer of 1863. His four brothers served as well, but only two survived. After leaving the Union Army, William Nagle joined the Fenian Army, becoming the military inspector general of the O'Mahony wing.[23]

With the ship secured, the men assembled, and the arsenal of weapons stowed beneath the deck, by April 12 the expedition was ready to go.

William J. Nagle, co-commander of *Erin's Hope*, 1867. Officials described Nagle as 5'10½" tall, of "slender make," with brown hair "turning grey," hazel eyes, and "contraction of sinews" in "right hand, the 4 fingers crippled."

"TELL NONE of our plans to anybody," Colonel Thomas Kelly advised the leaders of the expedition.[24] When Daniel Buckley, a twenty-three-year-old Irish American jeweler, showed up at a house on East Broadway on April 12, as instructed, he claimed to know little about what was about to transpire. He and the other men climbed aboard *Jacmel* at Sandy Hook, New Jersey, entrusting their lives to their Fenian commanders and the skilled mariner, Captain John

Kavanagh, an experienced Civil War navy veteran, who stood at the helm with five sailors as his crew.[25] Late in the day on April 13 the ship slipped away, Kavanagh initially sailing southward, as if to travel the usual "West India track." But after a day he stealthily changed course, shifting northeast toward Ireland.[26]

Despite such deceptive ploys, the ever-watchful British consul in New York thought something was up. On April 13, just as *Jacmel* set sail, acting consul Pierrepont Edwards warned Larcom in Dublin that "an experienced Irish-American officer named Tresilian was preparing to set sail for Ireland along with other fenian agents." Tresilian, a "first class engineer" who had served with General John A. Logan in the Civil War before joining Sweeny's forces in 1866 to invade Canada, was indeed on board, just below Warren in the chain of command. "We must look out for Colonel Tresilian," Larcom wrote to Lord Naas on April 29, but he did little more.[27] Edwards's warning was just one among many vague tips Larcom received about suspected Fenian activities, so perhaps Larcom failed to take it seriously given other tasks at hand.

Jacmel had a charmed voyage the first week out, making good time and arousing no suspicion, flying the British flag to disguise its true identity. So the men were in good spirits on Easter Sunday, April 21, when Captain Kavanagh gathered them together to reveal their mission. On that day, no Union Jack would fly. The crew raised "Erin's war standard," a green flag with the yellow sunburst, a fitting symbol of the promised resurrection of an independent Ireland. They hauled out the three small artillery guns from the hold and saluted the flag with armed fire. Then Kavanagh unsealed the orders he had been given in New York. Captain John Powell, chief of naval affairs, directed the men to land their arms at Sligo, on the northwest coast of Ireland, or elsewhere if landing at Sligo proved impossible. If intercepted, the men were to blow up the vessel and its contents to avoid its capture. Having read the orders to the men, Kavanagh re-christened the ship. *Jacmel* became *Erin's Hope*.[28]

Soon, however, *Erin's Hope* began to run into trouble, making a mockery of its new name. Heavy seas and storms slowed the ship's progress and dampened the men's spirits. Relieved to reach Sligo in late May, after more than a month at sea, the men were anxious to fulfill their mission. Captain Kavanagh hovered off the coast between Sligo and Donegal for days, sending the signals given to him by his commanding officers in New York. But no one responded. And no one was waiting.

The Rising had collapsed long before *Jacmel* arrived. Officials at Dublin Castle knew of the rebellion well before it started, its paid informers providing detailed information about when and where the insurgents would strike.

British forces in Ireland were armed and ready on the appointed day. "Flying squadrons" moved quickly to subdue Fenian fighters wherever they arose, forcing Fenians to take refuge in the mountains during a bitterly cold and snowy spring. Within two weeks the insurrection had been stamped out, its leaders quickly placed on trial and convicted of high treason by early May. Even as *Erin's Hope* hovered off the coast of Sligo, the lord chief justice in Dublin donned his black cap and imposed the "awful sentence of the law" upon convicted rebels: to be "hanged by the neck until each of you be dead; that afterwards your heads be severed from your bodies; and that your bodies be divided into four parts, and that those parts be disposed of as Her Majesty . . . shall think fit." The government's stern reprisals "produced a panic through the country," inducing young men to lie low or flee and dampening the fire of rebellion.[29]

So *Erin's Hope* signaled in vain. Puzzled, the leaders sent Colonels Philip Doherty and Jeremiah O'Shea ashore on May 23 to establish contact, determining that after twenty-four hours the remaining men of *Erin's Hope* would proceed with their own plan of attack.[30] Captain Kavanagh would "run the vessel into Sligo, seize the town, land the arms and stores, muster the friends of the Fenian cause in the vicinity, and entrench himself there to await the general insurrection that he confidently expected would follow [after news spread] that an American force had landed and that the Irish flag floated over Sligo town." As a 1916 account of the expedition suggests, Kavanagh's plan was "highly dangerous"—and, one might add, highly improbable. Sligo had a population of about 10,000, and British Coast Guard stations dotted the shoreline. A force of forty Irish American men would seem to have had little chance of taking Sligo.[31]

As the men made preparations for the possible seizure of Sligo, the expedition began to unravel. *Erin's Hope* had not gone totally unnoticed. On shore, an experienced local pilot, Michael Gallagher, watched the ship for two days and decided he might land a job guiding the vessel. At noon on Friday, May 24, he approached the ship, offering his services as a pilot. What happened next became a matter of dispute in later trials. Gallagher claimed that the "man in charge" said the ship was carrying a cargo of fruit from Spain to Glasgow and offered him two guineas to guide the ship across the bay. But Gallagher soon discovered the ruse. Gallagher later testified that the "man in charge" (likely Kerrigan or Kavanagh) called him into the cabin and, in the presence of Nagle and Warren, asked him if he was a Fenian. When he declared that he was not, the commander put a gun to his head and forced him to swear on the Bible "not to tell anyone on shore that I saw them in the cabin; or if I would take notice of anything in the ship or of them, not to report it on shore," nor "give a description of the ship." Gallagher, "in terror," then turned to his job of piloting the vessel toward Streedagh, an isolated strand of beach to the north of Sligo.[32]

As darkness fell, a fishing boat appeared with a most important passenger: Ricard O'Sullivan Burke. Burke would later be described admiringly by the Irish American press as a master of disguises. Eluding a warrant for arrest for his participation in the March 5 Rising, Burke had roamed the Irish countryside under a variety of assumed identities. Now posing as a wealthy artist on vacation, he was waiting for the Fenian vessel to arrive in Sligo. Burke brought unwelcome news: the rebellion had been "put down" and "it would be foolish to attack the town of Sligo." The ship should try instead to land its cargo on the southern coast of Cork, where there remained active pockets of resistance. Burke then returned to shore along with three of the Fenian colonels.[33]

As the expedition faltered, tempers began to fray and some began to doubt the wisdom of the mission. Daniel J. Buckley, who would be the Irish government's key witness in the later *Erin's Hope* trials, began to lose his nerve after overhearing the commanders' consultations. Sometime on Friday the twenty-fifth, Buckley shot two of the crew, wounding Daniel Coffey (also known as James Nolan) in the ankle and John O'Connor (alias John Smith) in the thigh. Buckley claimed he shot the men accidentally when he was cleaning his gun, but later accounts suggested a fight broke out between the men, resulting in the shooting. Around one in the morning, Captain Kavanagh put the two wounded men ashore along with another *Erin's Hope* man, Patrick Nugent, and the pilot, Gallagher. All four were quickly apprehended by the Coast Guard while *Erin's Hope* sailed south toward Cork.[34]

With their original mission in shambles, the men grew hungry, tired, and mutinous. On May 25, Nagle noted the meager amounts of bread, beans, and coffee remaining on board; the crew existed on rations of one pint of water per day.[35] Buckley, the "Judas of the expedition," continued to be a disruptive force, prodding the men to hold a council about whether to still attempt a landing or, instead, to travel to the Azores to replenish their supplies and then head home to New York. The expedition's leaders, Kerrigan, Warren, and Nagle, refused to attend the meeting but were soon informed of the men's decision: they voted twenty-two to ten to abandon the mission and return home. Captain Kavanagh, however, upstaged Buckley by persuading the men to land if he could find a suitable place.[36] With the fragile agreement in place, Kavanagh patrolled the southern coast, not far from Warren's hometown, Clonakilty, sending out signals that, again, failed to yield a response. Growing desperate, the officers hatched a hasty plan to land most of the men while Warren contacted friends in the area to obtain provisions and arrange to land the arms. Once the arrangements were made, Warren would signal *Erin's Hope* to pick them up.[37]

Kavanagh took advantage of an opportunity to send the men ashore on Saturday, June 1, at Helvick Head, the tip of the Ring peninsula reaching out beyond Dungarvan in Waterford County. A heavy mist lay on the waters, so the men could disembark without being seen. Irish-speaking Patrick Whelan (Paid Mor O'Faolain) and three other fishermen had been out in rough seas since six that morning and their luck had not been good. So when Kavanagh hailed Whelan and offered him two pounds to take two men ashore, he agreed. But instead of two, thirty men jumped into the fishing boat, nearly capsizing it, and Whelan despaired: "We are all lost now." The fishermen bailed out the water as quickly as possible and headed with the men to shore, bypassing the Coast Guard station at Helvick Head and landing the men about three miles away on a sandbar in the water. The men waded to shore in water three and a half feet deep, finally touching land after seven weeks at sea.[38]

Once ashore, the tired men split up. A few men headed straight for Miss Power's public house in Dungarvan to quench their thirst, while others hurried southwest toward Cork, some hoping to find passage out of Ireland. Patrick Kane and Frederick Fitzgibbon tried to blend in, trading their American-style clothes for the flea-ridden "wretched wearables" of the locals—"corduroy trowsers" and tattered heavy woolen jackets—but keeping their hats with the telltale "peculiar American slouch" and their "boots of Yankee cut."[39] John Warren and William Nagle, posing as "John Donovan" and "William Palmer," stayed true to their mission. They paid farmer Andrew Roche five shillings to drive them in his horse and cart to Youghal, making their way to find help for their expedition.[40]

GEORGE JONES, stationed with the Coast Guard at Helvick Head, watched from a distance as "some thirty suspicious looking men" struggled to shore, arriving wet and sandy. The earlier fog had lifted, offering him a clear view of the men as they split into groups of three and four and headed south. Jones rushed to report the landing to resident magistrate Henry E. Redmond, sitting at petty sessions in Dungarvan, who immediately telegraphed authorities at Youghal to be on the lookout and then gathered all of the available forces in town—two justices of the peace and twelve constables—to pursue the men. Within a few hours, all but two had been captured. They were not difficult to find, most traveling on foot and wet and sandy. Patrick Kane and Frederick Fitzgibbon eluded arrest until Tuesday, June 4, when keen-eyed constables detected their Yankee hats and boots.[41]

Nobody quite knew what to make of the mysterious prisoners. Their arrival in the coastal town of Dungarvan "electrified the inhabitants," who viewed the strangers as "veritable wonders."[42] The men carried no identifying papers or weapons and said very little.[43] When the twenty-four men were brought before the magistrates at the Dungarvan courthouse for examination, they ringed the room on three sides, making a "most remarkable" impression. Officials reported they were "intelligent," "fairly well educated," clearly military men "fresh from the drill sergeant," but "very 'dark'" and secretive. They claimed to be immigrating to the "Brazils" but said their ship had sunk, forcing them to take shelter on shore. Beyond that, they appeared remarkably ignorant for "intelligent men," claiming to know nothing about their specific destination or the name of the vessel or its commander. Their reticence only confirmed the suspicion that these men were up to no good. "A more dangerous set to let loose in this country I do not think you could meet," warned Magistrate FitzMaurice Bloomfield in his report to Lord Naas.[44]

The men made the "country gentry" in the south of Ireland "very uneasy," as their arrival renewed the "Fenian craze" among local inhabitants of Dungarvan and Waterford. When the men were transferred to the jail in Waterford, the county seat, they entered the city as heroes. Women serenaded the prisoners with the ballad "Bold Fenian Men," but the crowd of 4,000 greeted the constable and his small force of men with jeers, brickbats, and stones, "some of considerable size," as they tried to make their way to the jail. "They were wicked," declared George Goold, resident magistrate at Waterford. As the crowd rushed the police who came to the constable's aid, the "horse police rode through the crowd right and left, trampling down all before them." By the end, Denis Walsh, a young "salter" from the local bacon-curing establishment, lay dead and a policeman seemed to be at death's door. Over thirty men, many of them policemen, sustained serious wounds. The Waterford protesters accused the police of an unprovoked "wanton attack on the people," while Irish officials, in turn, argued the police had acted in self-defense during the "Waterford riot."[45]

Lord Naas surely was not happy to hear about yet another Fenian threat, just when the Irish government hoped that the turmoil over the Rising was beginning to die down. Officials worried that the Dungarvan prisoners—"a better class of men than we have yet seen"—were the "forerunners" of a new

Fenian offensive.[46] That the Dungarvan prisoners were "all Americans or Irish Americans & will give no satisfactory account of themselves" likely came as no surprise to Lord Naas.[47] "I can get no information as to the Dungarvan suspects," Naas confided to Undersecretary Thomas Larcom, but "I feel certain that they are important. . . . If we could get one or two of them to Peach we might perhaps discern a great deal."[48]

Getting Fenians to "peach"—that is, to inform on others—proved to be surprisingly easy and increasingly central to the British government's fight against Fenianism. The lure of easy money, the desire to escape jail and harsh punishments, resentment at being poorly treated by one's comrades—all led some Fenians to offer their services to the government, at a price.[49] Irish authorities soon found *Jacmel* prisoners who were willing to tell all they knew. Feeling "badly used" by his Fenian comrades, William Millen (or Million) provided "startling information" to George Goold in Waterford on June 14, revealing the mission of the *Erin's Hope* and its cargo and identifying Warren and Nagle as the leaders.[50]

Naas was alarmed but still did not know what to do with the prisoners. The men had not committed any explicit crime in Ireland, though Naas did not underestimate the danger they posed and wanted to deter future troublemakers, already rumored to be at work. Millen warned that "another expedition was to sail . . . six weeks after us with men and arms," and police superintendent Daniel Ryan reported rumors that "10,000 rifles of very superior quality have been landed in Ireland recently" on the west coast.[51] Yet the last thing Naas wanted was to stoke the fires of rebellion by making martyrs out of Fenian prisoners. Over 3,000, "many of them of a respectable class," turned out in Waterford to mourn Salter, the man killed by police.[52] The military commander of Ireland, Lord Strathnairn, warned the British cabinet on June 7 of widespread disaffection among the Irish middle class who "sympathize with the Fenians" and "the movement's hostility to British rule."[53] If the government struck too hard, it would simply fan the flames of discontent and provide grist for Fenian propaganda.

The best thing to do, concluded Naas, was to leave the *Jacmel* men locked up for the time being—an easy task, as England had renewed the suspension of the writ of habeas corpus in Ireland in May 1867, allowing Irish authorities to arrest and detain any "suspicious" persons indefinitely, without lodging official charges against them.[54] Irish officials moved Warren, Nagle, and other members of the *Erin's Hope* expedition from Waterford to Dublin's Kilmainham Gaol, the imposing stone fortress already notorious for holding political prisoners.[55] But neither Naas nor Larcom fooled themselves into thinking they had succeeded in eliminating the Fenian threat.

ERIN'S HOPE, meanwhile, sailed between England and Ireland, returning, as prearranged, to pick up the men on June 7 near Dungarvan. But, of course, no one was there. Not wishing to abandon their comrades, the remaining members of the expedition hovered along the southern coast for several more days before giving up and setting sail for home on June 11. Their cargo remained intact, but the ship was considerably emptier and still desperately short on provisions. Thirty-two of the original forty-five men were in jail. The ship ran out of food by the time it reached the Grand Banks of Newfoundland, but after replenishing their supplies, the men eventually made it back to New York by August 1. In America, Erin's Hope became Jacmel Packet once more, embroiled in bitter lawsuits stemming from Captain Dawes's fraud in Panama and sold to satisfy unpaid seamen's wages.[56]

As the story of the improbable expedition began to leak out, many scratched their heads, wondering just what the men had hoped to accomplish. The Freeman's Journal in Dublin would call "that Jacknell business" the "most pitiful part of the tragi-comedy. A number of men—many of them educated and intelligent—embarked in a wretched craft, ill provisioned, and apparently with no other armament than a few revolvers [the Freeman's Journal was obviously misinformed on that point] and sailed away to Ireland to join an insurrection which had existence only in the heated imaginations of fanatical enthusiasts."[57] The New York correspondent for the Milwaukee Daily Sentinel warned, however, that "if any one supposes these men are all blundering, lathering, brainless Irishmen, he miscalculates." Having spoken with Kerrigan and several others who managed to make it back to New York, the correspondent would find them "keen, far-seeing, determined plotters" who aimed with their expedition "to keep the Fenian question before the world" and to demonstrate "the value of persistency and what Abe Lincoln called 'pegging away.'"[58]

The New York reporter was on to something. The expedition might be over, but its mission was not. The most immediate legacy of the Erin's Hope expedition would be not at sea but in Irish prisons and courtrooms.

6

The Voice from the Dungeon

BY JUNE 14, twenty-eight of the *Jacmel* crew sat behind bars in Dublin's prisons, and three more were imprisoned in Sligo, waiting. But for what? What would become of them was a bit of a mystery, not only to the prisoners but to the officials who had put them there as they gathered evidence and decided what to do with the Irish Americans. The suspension of habeas corpus provided little legal recourse for the prisoners. The government could keep them in jail without charges and no release date for days or months if it chose to. Detention was an end in itself. It kept potential troublemakers locked up and gave them a taste of what lay in store if they continued to rebel against British authority. But, as Charles Adams would suggest in a letter to Seward, "the government would . . . be glad to get rid" of the *Jacmel* prisoners if it could do so safely, for in many ways the Fenians proved to be just as troublesome in jail as out.[1] Though behind bars and subject to the harsh discipline of Victorian-era prisons, the *Jacmel* Fenians found new power in their roles as political prisoners. The longer their stay in jail, the more potent their voices became in Ireland and the United States. What was at stake was not only their freedom, urged the prisoners, but the liberty of all Americans.

WAITING without a clear end in sight could wear on a man, for prison life was not pleasant in Ireland, even for those housed in the new East Wing of Kilmainham Gaol, the destination of many Fenian detainees. Completed in 1861, the East Wing reflected the most modern theories of prison design, with its vast oval interior ringed by three levels of cells, connected by open platforms and stairways that allowed prison guards, called warders, a constant and unobstructed view of all the prisoners. "A spectator might fancy himself in a fort or the hull of a huge man-of-war with ports closed," observed one visitor in admiration, but the new addition to Kilmainham Gaol more closely approximated the model panopticon imagined by philosopher Jeremy Bentham, allowing constant surveillance.[2] No dark dungeon, the East Wing was full of light provided by the glass ceiling. Each cell had a small, high window through which the prisoner could glimpse the sky and, hopefully, salvation for his sinful soul. Even at night, the whitewashed cells remained bright, lit by new gas lamps, to expose prisoners to the warders' watchful gaze. Prisoners complained that the glare off the white walls was so bright that it weakened their eyesight.[3]

On each cell door, the prisoner could read a copy of the prison rules: Obey prison officials. In the exercise yard, walk three to four yards apart and keep eyes straight ahead. Hands must be kept out of pockets at all times. And no talking. The rule of silence, common in the era as necessary for prison discipline and for the reflection required for individual redemption, was probably "the most severe" for the Fenians, joked one journalist, given "their powers of speech."[4] But the limits on contact were no laughing matter for the men. They received visitors only once a week, had no writing materials aside from those given them to write occasional letters, and had no access to newspapers. Prison officials read and censored all correspondence. Those who broke the rules might be denied blankets, put on reduced rations, or be placed in solitary confinement in pitch-black basement cells.[5]

Still, since the Fenians remained uncharged of any specific crime, they enjoyed somewhat greater privileges than convicts. They wore their own clothes rather than the convict uniform, and if they had money or sympathetic friends in Dublin, they often enjoyed a better diet than the usual fare allotted to prisoners: "stirabout" (oatmeal porridge) for breakfast, bread and milk for dinner at midday, and bread and milk for supper at night, with a stew of beef and potatoes provided on two days of the week.[6] The Fenians' Ladies Committee provided food, clothes, and books to prisoners, as well as weekly allowances for their families at home, all the while urging them to stay true to the cause. Those prisoners who could verify their American citizenship could have confidential meetings with the American consul, William West, providing at least one social interaction.[7]

Yet Fenian prisoners experienced worse treatment in some respects than the convicts. Worried, not without cause, about the possibility of escape and the exchange of information among Fenian prisoners, Irish officials tightened prison security. More warders guarded the cells, and cavalry patrols kept watch outside the prison walls. Fenian prisoners remained in their cells for twenty-two hours a day, strictly isolated from one another without even the monotonous prison work of picking oakum (picking apart old ropes for reuse in shipbuilding) to relieve the tedium of the hours.[8] There was little to do in the silence of one's small cell, said John Warren, but "to sit down and meditate": "Just think of your coming home from business and meeting a happy family. Think of your hot flap-jacks, your doughnuts and chops. Oh, don't; 'tis murder!"[9]

For others, the isolation and silence bred less welcome visions, perhaps scenes from the bloody battles of the Civil War. The men bore physical scars of the conflict; "hardly an inch" of the body of Patrick Kane, who had served as a captain in the 99th Regiment, was "unmarked by sword-cuts or bullet-marks," claimed the *Irishman* newspaper.[10] Some also carried emotional and mental scars, as well as recurring illnesses, from the war. William J. Nagle, the veteran of some of the war's deadliest battles at Chancellorsville, Fredericks-burg, and Antietam, was perhaps one of the most experienced soldiers on the *Jacmel* expedition, his "crippled" right hand most likely a remnant of the war. Resolute, respected, determined—Nagle was all these things, but he also seemed in some ways the most fragile of the famed *Jacmel* prisoners. Several *Jacmel* prisoners complained of ill health while in prison, but Nagle's pleas to West, the consul at Dublin, stand out in their poignancy. Since the war, Nagle had suffered from "severe intermittent fever," or malaria, one of the most common diseases among Union soldiers. The debilitating disease returned with force under prison conditions. But, even more, Nagle could not abide the solitary confinement, which "he compared to a 'living death,'" saying "that his own voice became strange to him."[11]

Nerves could snap, especially as weeks and months passed. Robert McDonnell, the prison doctor at Dublin's Mountjoy Prison, repeatedly criticized the "rule of silence" and solitary confinement so popular among prisons in the era, arguing such practices generated a "morbid state of mind" and even "sui-cidal attempts." "A perfectly quiet dog, if kept constantly chained up, becomes savage," the doctor warned.[12] The *Jacmel* men became defiant one bitterly cold day as they walked in the exercise yard. A few tried to warm their numb fin-gers in their pockets, but the warders, adhering to prison rules, ordered them to take their hands out. Chafing at this "piece of petty tyranny," all of the pris-oners put their hands in their pockets. The warders called a halt to the exercise period, ordering the prisoners to their cells. The following day, the same thing occurred, the men keeping their hands in their pockets and the warders ordering them inside. A tense standoff ensued, ending only after Nagle intervened to avoid bloodshed. "I feel mad, and do not care a damn for the whole set," Nagle confessed to Warren. "They will not get me foul, however, through any passion. A cool, determined, independent bearing is the only safety now." The men returned to their cells, to be punished with half rations.[13]

Impatient with their confinement and anxious to use their imprisonment to the most powerful political ends, the *Jacmel* prisoners did not wait quietly. They did what previous prisoners had done: they wrote, often in defiance of the censors. They wrote letters home to family, notifying them of their capture and urging fathers, wives, and friends to mount a protest on their behalf.[14] They penned poems, such as Augustine Costello's "The Patriot," defiantly declaring, "What are your bolts and bars to me? / What care I for the dungeon's gloom?"[15] They slipped furtive notes to each other in prison, Nagle encouraging Warren to "do all in our power to keep the spirit that animates the boys alive."[16] They sent dramatic testimonials about "life in the bastille" to Irish and Irish American newspapers.[17] And they sent demands to the American government for protection. They wrote to county clerks for proof of their citizenship; to diplomatic officials, West and Adams, urging their intercession; to mayors and congressional representatives as their constituents; and to President "Andy" Johnson trying to "rouse his old Hickoryism" to take a more aggressive stance with "John Bull." John Warren urged President "Andy" to send a dispatch saying, "Drop that Irishman, Warren, you have in No. 17 Kilmainham. The keeping of him 24 hours longer won't be conducive to your health." How they were able to be so prolific, given the tight security in Dublin prisons remains puzzling, especially as, with each leak, prison officials clamped down tighter.[18]

Like the best writers, the *Jacmel* prisoners crafted their letters and petitions with care, always keeping in mind their intended audience: the "reading public." Though the letters might be addressed to a loved one, the writers hoped that they would be read widely in newspapers, the most popular media of the day. "It is amusing to notice how universal is the habit of reading a morning paper," observed the editor of the *North American Review* in 1866. Not just businessmen consumed the daily news, but so did "the torrent of workingmen pouring down town, many of them reading as they go."[19] Newspapers had exploded in number and dropped in cost in both the United States and Ireland by the mid-nineteenth century, allowing migrants flung across the globe to stay connected. Workingmen, noses in their papers as they walked to work, might have been reading the major city daily paper, but they also might have been absorbed by the

Boston *Pilot* or the *Irish American*, a weekly from New York—or even John Warren's *Fenian Spirit*.[20] Readers caught up on news in the United States and Ireland, weighed the often fiery editorials, enjoyed folksy anecdotes and jokes, scanned the announcements of local meetings and events, and looked through the "Missing Friends" or "Information Wanted" section to find lost loved ones, separated through migration.[21]

Newspapers could shrink geographic and cultural space, providing a sense of immediacy, but also generating a common bond—"imagined communities"— among their readers who might never meet face-to-face. The rise of nationalism and the expansion of print media in the early nineteenth century went hand in hand, newspapers making it possible to think of oneself as "part and parcel of the whole."[22] When William Nagle described solitary confinement as a "living death," he complained not only of not being able to talk to his fellow prisoners but also of being without even the comfort of a newspaper to "converse" with. (West left him a copy of the *New York Times* to keep him company.)[23]

Both the government and Irish nationalists understood the power of newspapers to draw people together in common sentiment and cause. Believing that "the Fenian Press has been the fountainhead of all sedition and treason in Ireland," one of the Irish government's first organized attempts to subdue Fenianism was its raid in 1865 on the *Irish People*'s office in Dublin. Desperate to silence the papers, the government not only shut down the *Irish People* but also ordered the Irish post office to seize "treasonous" newspapers arriving from the United States. But the press could not be stopped. The *Irishman* picked up the nationalist banner after the suppression of the *Irish People*, using the government's campaign against the press as proof that the famed "British liberties" had little hold in Ireland.[24]

It was no surprise, then, that Nagle told Warren as they waited in prison, "I must do all I can to create a public sentiment here, and in the U.S., through the papers. No doubt my letter home of 2nd August will be published and copied here." It helped that Warren, with his newspaper experience, had ties to the press on both sides of the Atlantic. Nagle asked Warren to "send for your friend Sullivan [most likely Alexander M. Sullivan, editor of the *Nation* and the *Weekly News* in Dublin] and tell him enough that it would be sure to reach the papers" and perhaps even "interest the *Herald* correspondent."[25] Nagle's plan worked. His letter to his father in New York City popped up in the *Freeman's Journal* and the *Irishman* in Dublin and in the *Irish American* in New York, which used such missives to reinforce the central mission of their press: to build Irish nationalist fervor and spread their call to arms against British tyranny. The *Jacmel* prisoners' letters rarely found a home in the *New York Times*, but a letter that appeared in the Boston *Pilot* or the *Irishman* might migrate to the pages of the *New York Herald* or the *New York Tribune* and gain a wider readership. Letters spawned other letters, as indignant readers and organizations wrote to protest the Fenians' treatment and government inaction. Newspaper editors sympathetic to the Fenian cause clustered the letters together with news of the *Jacmel* and other Fenian exploits, using headlines and editorial comments that dramatized the prisoners' plight: "Life in the Bastille," "The Humiliation of the Stars and Stripes," "News from a Fenian Martyr."[26]

The *Jacmel* prisoners honed their message, sticking to the same three themes: They had done nothing wrong. What happened to them could happen to any American. And American honor and national status hung in the balance.

IMAGINE, encouraged John Warren in his vivid letter "A Voice from the Dungeon," printed in both Irish and American newspapers, that "you arrive" in Ireland. "You may have been supplied with a passport, and consider yourself perfectly safe . . . you wear a good coat and a villainous mustache, and you have acquired a habit of standing erect and dashing ahead, swinging your hand, and, your republican barbarism, if you meet a lord, you don't take your hat off; you look him right in the face; you don't get nervous. You wear the murdering square-toe [boots]. . . . All go to prove that your education is dangerous; that you don't worship monarchy; that you're a republican—a freeman." Then "you're pounced on." Putting his American readers in his shoes, Warren tried to raise their indignation as he urged "my case is your case."[27]

Repeatedly the prisoners joined in the same refrain: their only offense was "being an American." "Have I done an[y] wrong? Have I broken any law that I should be kept here surrounded with guns and bayonets?" one of the prisoners reportedly demanded when first arrested in Dungarvan.[28] "I have violated no English law," Warren wrote to President Johnson, but was merely "a member of the press, collecting notes, coupled with the desire to see the old scenes, and to meet the old friends of my boyhood and near and dear relatives."[29] Nagle complained to his father that "no evidence of any kind is shown or charge made, other than 'suspicion,' which is applied as a general rule to all Americans."[30]

At most, the prisoners argued, they were arrested for things they had said or done in the United States, actions that were far beyond the control of the

British government. As the *Jacmel* prisoners awaited their fate, the case of Stephen J. Meany was winding to a close and offered an important preview of how the Irish government would proceed against the Fenian crew. Meany, a newspaper editor from Ohio and veteran of the Young Ireland movement of 1848, enthusiastically embraced the Fenian cause. As a "district centre" in Ohio, Meany made rousing speeches urging Irish Americans to buy "Fenian bonds" to finance Irish rebellion. When Meany traveled to London in December 1866, British authorities promptly arrested him and sent him to Ireland for trial, charging him with conspiracy to "levy war against the Queen." The evidence: Meany's speeches and fund-raising activities in the United States. Even the judge presiding over his trial wondered whether he had jurisdiction to hear the case.[31] Typically, under the common law, only crimes committed within a state's borders could be prosecuted. But the attorney general of Ireland persuaded a majority of judges on the Criminal Court of Appeal in Dublin that "Meany was as liable in America, once he joined the [Fenian] conspiracy, for all the acts done in Dublin, as if he was present when they were committed."[32] That Americans— even Irish-born naturalized Americans—could be punished by the Irish government for things they had said or done in the United States sparked outrage. This "is not a Fenian case, nor yet an Irish case," argued P.A.C. in his letter to the Boston *Pilot*, but "the cause of every American citizen."[33]

Nor were the nation's honor and status secure in the world, noted critics. "The Stars and Stripes are towered over by the Union Jack, and the bedraggled British Lion has placed his paw on the Eagle of the Republic," cried the *Irishman* in an article reprinted prominently in the *Pilot*.[34] Editors repeatedly reminded their readers of the Koszta case of 1853, when the fearless leader Captain Ingraham had taken a "haughtier position" and unhesitatingly stepped in to rescue Koszta, not even a fully naturalized citizen, from the grasp of the Austrian Empire.[35] Now, in 1867, the United States had even greater power in the world and should not stand for being the "door-mat" of England, to be "trampled upon" at its will. "It is quite time for Americans to be respected abroad," P.A.C. declared in the *Pilot*. It is "quite time" for America "to make herself known among the nations of the earth."[36]

And quite time, the Fenians added, for American diplomats to step up to lead the charge on behalf of their countrymen.[37] "You know old Seward is slow and needs to be poked under the short rib occasionally," advised one prisoner.[38] Impatient with diplomats, but reliant upon them as one of their few powerful and accessible allies while in jail, the *Jacmel* prisoners poked and prodded the

State Department's officials into action, demanding they secure them either a trial or their liberation.

"WHAT ARE you doing, *Hon.* Charles Francis Adams?" demanded a writer named Tyrone in the *Irish Republic* of Chicago. Not much, imagined John Warren in "A Voice from the Dungeon," as he painted for his readers an unflattering portrayal of Adams, "as stiff and starch as a lord." "He is sitting at his desk, and in turning a lot of papers yours (you're lucky) fortunately turns up. He reads, turns to a clerk and instructs him to write to the castle in Dublin for a copy of documents and papers connected with your arrest. He receives an answer that they will be furnished at the earliest opportunity. He is satisfied. . . . Diplomacy!" sneered Warren.[39]

What *was* Adams doing in the summer of 1867, while the *Jacmel* men waited in prison? Warren's fantasy of Adams's distant and perfunctory attitude toward his work was not altogether wrong. Adams had run out of patience with the Fenians and his post in London long before. The Fenians "still continue to occupy my time," Adams wrote wearily on June 10, 1867, but they did not seem worth the effort, nor did their cases involve the grand questions of state relations that had marked Adams's early years in London. Adams seemed happiest when he was traveling with his family in Europe or absorbed in writing a history of his mission in London during the war. The routine work at the legation was often an unwelcome chore.[40] "Mr. Adams shuns this den as if we had the plague," complained Benjamin Moran, the assistant secretary of the U.S. legation in London, on August 2, 1867. He "gets more and more indifferent every day."[41] If the *Jacmel* men were going to get action, they would have to lean directly on Secretary of State Seward, long seen as an ally of the Irish and the foreign-born.

Seward worked hard during his political career to woo Irish Americans, cultivating a controversial friendship with the Catholic archbishop John Hughes and even claiming Irish ancestry (though of the Protestant persuasion) through his maternal grandmother. As governor of New York, Seward took a particularly bold and controversial stand on the issue of public education of Irish Catholics in the 1840s, pushing to free schools from the domination of Protestants. And in the 1850s Seward had been one of the most vocal critics of the Know-Nothing movement. Seward lured few New York Irish away from the Democratic Party and alienated many native-born Americans, his pro-immigrant views perhaps even costing him the presidential nomination in

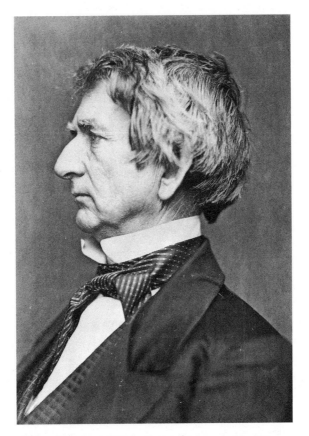

William H. Seward, U.S. Secretary of State, ca. 1860–1865.

1860.[42] Still, Seward earned the respect of many foreign-born. "You have always been the friend of our race and religion," wrote one Fenian prisoner.[43]

William Nagle had deeper ties to Seward. Nagle's father, David, proved to be that rare thing, an Irish American Whig (and, later, Republican), and had cast his lot with Seward in the early 1840s, working to build Seward's political support among "our Naturalized citizens" in exchange for Seward's help in securing jobs on the public payroll. Tutored by his father in the workings of nineteenth-century patronage, William had turned frequently to Seward since 1852, alternating flattery with offers of political service and desperate pleas for help in finding work. "I have been taught since I was a boy 12 years of age to revere you as my Father's friend and benefactor," William wrote in his first letter to Seward, "and years have but added strength to my admiration of your great talents and liberal and just mind." Over the years, Seward had helped William obtain work as a customs inspector, as a ship's purser, and in the U.S. Appraiser's Office, and now Nagle turned to his former benefactor once again.[44]

Seward saw the Fenian crisis as both challenge and opportunity, especially as he sought to secure his legacy as secretary of state. Seward devoted his postwar career to the objective dearest to his heart: empire building. He envisioned the United States, on the verge of becoming a vast commercial empire, achieving global supremacy through its trade and industrial might. But Seward could only accomplish so much on his own as secretary of state. He needed the cooperation of Congress to acquire new territory, ratify treaties and trade agreements, confirm nominations to diplomatic posts, and provide the State Department with the necessary money to run its operations. And by the summer of 1867, the Republican-dominated Congress was not in a cooperative mood, so alienated had it become by Democratic president Johnson's bitter resistance to its Reconstruction program. Republicans had originally viewed Seward, a founding member of the party, as one of their own, but by 1867 many saw him as hopelessly tarnished by his association with Johnson's administration. Seward's State Department became caught in the crossfire between Johnson and Congress, as the Senate refused to confirm several of Seward's nominations for diplomatic posts and the House combed over Seward's State Department budget with a stingy eye.[45]

Power abroad began with power at home, Seward realized, and he saw his foreign and domestic political agendas as deeply connected.[46] Seward worked hard to soothe disgruntled Republicans in Congress while also appealing to American voters, most especially the foreign-born, who had gained in numbers and in political power by the end of the Civil War. Yet Seward could not take the loyalty of Irish Americans and other foreign-born voters for granted, especially in 1867. The Fenian Congress in September 1867 urged that the only way the Fenian Brotherhood "would become a power to be felt and heard in America" was by throwing its support behind whichever political party proved the most responsive to its cause.[47] Republicans had done their best to woo Irish Americans away from the Democrats in hard-fought elections, capitalizing on Irish Americans' frustration with the Johnson administration's handling of the Fenian invasions of Canada.[48] Seward tried hard to mend fences with Irish Americans, arranging for the federal government to dismiss all charges against Fenians arrested for violating American neutrality laws at the Canadian border at Buffalo, New York. For some, Seward's actions were too little too late, the *Irish Republic* of Chicago calling Seward a traitor for his deceptive response to the Canadian invasion.[49]

By late summer of 1867, the *Jacmel* cause was gaining momentum and becoming another test for Irish Americans of Seward's commitment to foreign-born Americans. The *New York Tribune* praised the Fenian movement in June 1867 as a cause worthy of the support of "every true friend of liberty and justice."[50] Fernando Wood, congressional representative and the former Democratic mayor of New York City, who had long competed with Seward for the votes of Irish Americans, wrote a letter to Johnson calling the arrests of Warren and Nagle a "national insult." He joined Fenian congressman William S. Robinson in demanding that the House Committee on Foreign Affairs investigate whether Americans were being tried for "words spoken or deeds done" in the United States.[51] The Constitutional Union Association of New York petitioned President Johnson and Seward for the release of the "gallant soldiers," Colonels Nagle and Warren, and the New York Democratic Party included in its platform a demand that the U.S. government protect naturalized citizens as well as the native-born while abroad.[52] By late August, John Warren and William Nagle had become a topic of discussion at President Johnson's meeting with his cabinet.[53]

Just as the *Jacmel* cases began to grab public attention, the *Alabama* claims controversy resurfaced. In August 1867, newspapers published the just-released diplomatic correspondence on the *Alabama* claims, often sitting side by side with news of the Fenians. The *New York Times* reprinted Seward's lengthy dispatch to Adams, written a year earlier, insisting that settlement of the claims was "urgently necessary to a reestablishment of . . . friendly relations between the United States and Great Britain." Attached to the memo was a very long list of the specific claims filed by individuals and insurance companies, impressive in its length and details, ranging from the loss of sixty-eight barrels of spermaceti oil and the whaling ship the *Elisha Dunbar*, sunk after a forty-month whaling voyage, to the lost wages and clothing of crew members unfortunate enough to be on board ships targeted by raiders. The final tally of damages to Americans: the loss of ninety-five ships and over $10 million in property. Written a year earlier, the memo's publication was a stark reminder that American demands for compensation had yet to be met—and a reminder that the British had grown only bolder in its dealings with the United States, as evidenced by its cavalier treatment of Irish American citizens.[54]

Seward, like the reading public, linked the *Alabama* claims with the Fenian crisis but saw them as part of his broader mission of making the United States a more powerful player in the global arena. Britain, as the world's leading commercial and military power, stood as both a model and a rival in Seward's mind. Disputes had lingered for years between the two nations over contested boundary lines in the Pacific Northwest, access to valuable fisheries in the waters between Canada and the United States, and competing interests in Latin America and the Caribbean, as the leading commercial nations sought appealing harbors and islands that could serve as coaling stations and potential canal routes that would expedite shipping and trade. On top of these disputes came the *Alabama* claims and the Fenian controversy. All of these questions involved specific strategic interests but also broader questions of national sovereignty and jurisdiction as the two nations struggled for control over territory, resources, and people.[55]

So Seward responded when "poked in the short rib" by the *Jacmel* prisoners and their supporters. Most likely Seward did not want the new crisis to land on his desk and did not relish the flow of new letters that demanded immediate action. But Seward doubtlessly realized that the *Jacmel* cause provided a vehicle to restore credibility among foreign-born voters. And it had even more potential as leverage for American foreign policy in the hands of the savvy diplomat, especially as the *Jacmel* case became framed as an American cause, as opposed to merely an Irish one. Poked by the Fenians, Seward prodded Adams into action.

ADAMS AWOKE in the middle of the night of August 23 to a "thundering knock" at the door of his London home. Much to his disgust, it was a telegram from Washington about "Fenian complaints in Ireland," sent over the new engineering marvel, the Atlantic cable, which had been stretched across the ocean floor in 1866 and speeded communication between the continents. A message that could have taken days or weeks to travel across the Atlantic by ship could now be transmitted within minutes. Adams intensely disliked the new technology, which struck him as almost unseemly in its haste and brevity. The revolution in communication allowed Seward to send more frequent directives, often on minor details, and to manage diplomatic negotiations more closely. "His telegrams are a marvel," Adams snidely noted in his diary a few months later, after receiving yet another in a long string of telegrams about the Fenians. Seward's constant harping about the Fenians proved almost as wearing as the Fenians themselves. "I confess they strongly contribute to my desire to get out of the place," Adams said about the telegrams, but he could just as easily have been speaking about the Fenians.[56]

Adams read the letters—and telegrams—from both Seward and the Fenian prisoners with an increasingly cynical eye. Seward was his "dear friend" and a mentor of sorts, but Adams never fully understood or shared Seward's sympathies for Irish patriotism and Fenianism.[57] More troubling to Adams was Seward's aggressive approach to foreign affairs in 1867. Seward's dispatches frequently were "calculated to provoke rather than to conciliate foreign powers" and left "open all unsettled questions." The result, Adams worried, would be not just to further antagonize Great Britain but also "to alienate all other nations most uselessly."[58] But Adams grudgingly went along with Seward, who warned that "special interest is felt in these cases by a large number of highly respectable and influential citizens," over a thousand of whom (including the mayor of Brooklyn and several judges and civil officers) signed a petition addressed to President Johnson. American officials knew little about the *Jacmel* expedition at first and the British government did little to enlighten them, which only encouraged the growing belief that the men were unjustly imprisoned. Seward worried that the cases threatened to spin out of control.[59]

By September 1867, both the prisoners and Seward had become testy, running out of patience with the long detention and no end in sight. Augustine Costello bitterly protested his continued imprisonment. If the Irish government had evidence, why didn't it just go ahead and try him? The answer seemed simple: there was no such evidence. "I was not two hours in the country when arrested and imprisoned—a short time to concoct or plot treason," said Costello. Costello captured the prisoners' common refrain: "My liberty or a trial is what I want and what I demand."[60] Surely the United States had waited long enough for a satisfactory answer from the British, Nagle declared. Seward agreed, firing off a series of terse telegrams to Adams: "Obtain definite answer about Warren and Nagle." "Urge prompt release of Nagle and Warren." "Affair is embarrassing."[61]

Adams had little faith in the prisoners' innocence, warning Seward that Warren and Nagle were setting a "trap" for the American people "to force the two governments into a conflict."[62] Nonetheless, he dutifully wrote to Lord Stanley that "my government has sent very strong instructions to do all in my power" to release the prisoners, making a special plea for "Colonel Nagle," whose treatment even Adams believed to be "unreasonably harsh." When West visited Nagle at his request on September 9, he found Nagle "depressed in spirit and health," no longer able to eat. Adams secured the transfer of Warren and Nagle to Mountjoy Prison, which allowed habeas corpus prisoners more interaction and freedom.[63] Adams hoped the Irish government would take the next step and release the prisoners. Surely the imprisonment and "severe treatment" the men had already experienced was punishment enough, Adams said to Stanley. Whatever their intent, the prisoners "could not have committed any act of hostility" before they were arrested and the Irish government would have no chance of securing a verdict against them at trial.[64]

The British foreign officials threw their support behind Adams and Seward, stressing the potentially explosive political situation in America in their own letters to Lord Mayo (the former Lord Naas, who inherited his father's title as Earl of Mayo in 1867). Sir Frederick Bruce, working in the tumultuous political climate of Washington, D.C., perhaps understood better than any other British official the strain on Seward in the late summer of 1867, and in his telegram of August 23 to Lord Stanley he urged the release of Nagle and Warren. Lord Stanley, in turn, gently pressed the Home Office in England and Lord Mayo to be merciful with the prisoners, writing to the Irish chief secretary three times in the course of ten days in September 1867. "I am not anxious to interfere with your decision," Stanley told Mayo, as "you have Irish opinion to consider as well as American." But "if you can liberate them, so much the better diplomatically."[65]

The Home Office of the British government was not easily swayed, tired of repeatedly giving in to Americans when it came to the Fenians. The British government had just backed down—again—in commuting the death sentences for the Fenians involved in the Rising of March 5.[66] But showing mercy had done nothing to deter future Fenian attacks. Lord Derby, the British prime minister, found little in Warren and Nagle's case that warranted any "special favour" and cared little about the political unrest their detention had provoked in the United States. Derby treated Bruce's urgent but "very meager" telegram skeptically, saying, "Bruce is always inclined to err on the side of overcaution and to attach more importance to American 'bounce' than it is entitled to." To the prisoners' repeated claims that they had done nothing wrong, Derby scoffed that it was only because "they have had no opportunity of doing so" because they were "almost immediately arrested." They were still guilty, he argued, of leading "a piratical attempt at invasion" and should not be regarded lightly. Finally, Derby resurrected the thorny dispute over citizenship, refusing to act until Adams could provide proof that the men were native-born American citizens and thus "entitled to his good offices."[67]

The *Jacmel* prisoners did little to help themselves, complained Adams. Their publicity campaign might "keep up agitation in America" but did nothing to endear them to Irish officials, especially as furor over the cases filled the Dublin newspapers. Nor did the Irish government believe the prisoners when they promised to leave Ireland if released and "never return unless permitted." The same promises had been made by several of the *Jacmel* crew, arrested and released during the raids of 1866, Adams reported, yet here they were in Ireland again. If the Irish American prisoners could have been trusted to keep their word, "I have little doubt that nearly all would have been released before this," said Adams on August 27.[68]

From Adams's point of view, the Irish American prisoners betrayed even those who tried to help them. "I do all I can for them," Adams wrote plaintively, "yet they do their best to abuse me."[69] His successful efforts to transfer the "fretful" Nagle from the stringent confines of Kilmainham to the somewhat more congenial environment of Mountjoy Prison yielded not thanks but rather a bitter public condemnation of the "cold and spiritless action" of "our most *patient* Minister" Adams.[70] West fared little better, as he became besieged by prisoners who alternately pleaded for his sympathy and then issued imperious demands for visits and immediate answers to their letters.[71] And what did he get for his trouble? A scathing denunciation by John Warren as a "proud . . . peacock" who cared more about hobnobbing with Irish officials at Dublin Castle over a game of billiards than he did about American citizens.[72] A scornful letter from William Nugent, one of the *Jacmel* prisoners, said, "I can safely say that you have done nothing for me."[73] No wonder Adams became increasingly antsy to leave England and the Fenians behind. No wonder West became ill in early September, too ill to keep up with the incessant correspondence or to visit the ungrateful prisoners who took up all his time and strength.[74]

But the dramatic and deadly "Manchester rescue" of September 18 became the biggest obstacle to securing the *Jacmel* prisoners' release, in Adams's opinion. Undeterred by the failure of the March Rising in Ireland, the Fenian leader Thomas Kelly had shifted the Fenians' focus to England, busily creating networks of supporters in key Irish centers such as Liverpool and Manchester. News of the Fenians bringing their revolutionary activity to England put the British government on high alert.[75] Manchester police had the good luck to stumble upon Kelly and arrested him, along with Timothy Deasy, on suspicion that they were burglars, only later discovering that they had "caught the leading Fenian of them all."[76] British triumph over their catch led to mortifying despair a week later when Kelly and Deasy escaped. A group of about thirty men attacked the police van carrying Kelly and Deasy from the Manchester court to the local jail, freeing the men but killing a police officer, Sergeant Charles Brett, in the process. The rescue led to scores of arrests of Irish suspected of being involved and fueled what one newspaper called "Fenian mania." Rumors circulated of Fenian plots, from disrupting the Manchester gasworks and plunging the city into darkness to kidnapping Queen Victoria and using her as a hostage in negotiations to release those arrested for the Manchester Rescue.[77]

Not surprisingly, such news did not increase the queen's "desire to yield anything in favor of the Fenians," despite Adams's efforts on their behalf. Indeed, said the British home secretary, "Mr. Adams' . . . interference is a very sore subject with her."[78] The arrival of the "Dungarvan men" off the coast of Ireland around the time of Kelly's renewed activities in England seemed too neat to be coincidental. "The authorities are becoming less and less disposed to grant releases upon any conditions whatever," Adams informed Seward on September 21. "I very much fear the temper of both the government and people will not be much longer restrained from dealing with the offenders with the utmost severity."[79]

The news must have been frustrating for Seward, for now he had yet another potentially explosive Fenian conflict that could arouse public agitation in the United States. The *Jacmel* prisoners and their supporters, no doubt worried about the likely impact of the Manchester case, stepped up their pressure. What did the Manchester rescue have "to do with the incarceration of Col. Nagle, an American citizen?" asked the Boston *Pilot*. "We are angered that Mr. Adams should accept such a ridiculous plea as a reason for his detention."[80] Seward, too, went on the offensive. While expressing regret about the Manchester incident, Seward declared that these "new embarrassments" could not be used to justify the "arbitrary and indefinite imprisonment" of United States citizens "who have neither committed or attempted to commit any offence in Ireland." The time had come, Seward demanded, for Britain to explain its actions to the American people.[81]

Officials in Ireland were not idle. They were biding their time, waiting to see how the evidence was shaping up. Robert Warren, the Irish attorney general, told Lord Mayo on September 27, "I think there is sufficient evidence to convict both the prisoners," though he admitted that informers provided the heart of the case and there was little to corroborate their stories. He played for time, perhaps hoping for more evidence to appear. Arthur Forrester, arrested during the Rising in March, wrote a letter to the *Irishman* explaining how officials gathered evidence, or in the newspaper's words, "how information is manufactured in Fenian cases." A warder named Biggers had approached Forrester in his cell to "terrify me," threatening the certainty of a long prison term, punctuated by regular floggings every six months. Then, "taking pity on my youth," the warder suggested Forrester had been led astray and offered to help him if he told everything he knew about "the affair." Similar tactics were now being used, Forrester warned on October 11, in the Dungarvan case, and "I am sorry to state that it is thought with some success" as "high officials" had tempted a man named Nugent and also Daniel J. Buckley with similar offers. "Should he or Nugent ever appear as approvers, your readers will remember this."[82]

Neither of the two Nugents on the expedition—Patrick and William— appears to have "peached," but on September 12 Daniel Buckley, the leader of the mutinous forces aboard the *Erin's Hope*, did indeed become an "approver," giving a sworn statement at Kilmainham Gaol that provided invaluable details for the prosecution. Buckley would be the government's star witness in the trials of the *Jacmel* crew.[83] James Nolan, one of the men wounded by Buckley and landed in Sligo, also "made a full statement of what he knows of the Jackmel Expedition," and after being discharged from prison on September 30 he left for Liverpool, where he became a valuable secret informant for the head constable on Fenian activities.[84] By October 8, Robert Warren felt ready to proceed. He had his witnesses lined up and "two satisfactory judges" to hear the case. Having finally decided to proceed, the attorney general was anxious to get started, "the sooner the better."[85]

Warren, Nagle, and the *Jacmel* crew would finally have their day in court.

7

All the World's a Stage

"TODAY COMMENCES the irrepressible conflict," Augustine Costello wrote to West on the morning of October 25, 1867. "We go before the Court at 10 o'clock this morning." Costello's choice of words was revealing, drawing on a famous speech of Seward's in 1858. Seward had declared that the United States, sharply divided over slavery, was headed toward an "irrepressible conflict." Costello pitched the *Jacmel* men's trial as the inevitable showdown between Ireland and Britain over Irish enslavement—and between British and American sovereignty. The *Jacmel* prisoners looked forward to their day in court, but not because they believed they would be found innocent. While continually declaring their innocence, they typically saw their trials as tragic farces with predictable outcomes: a verdict of guilty. But they understood the power of trials as dramatic public forums. What was really on trial, the defendants insisted, was America's resolve to defend its sovereignty—and its adopted citizens—against imperious British overreaching.[1]

Costello was not alone in framing the trial in sensational terms and spinning the narrative the public was about to hear. Lord Chief Baron David Pigot promised the Irish grand jurors, gathered to decide whether to indict the *Jacmel* men for treason-felony, that they would hear an astonishing tale, "one of the wildest dreams that could enter the brain of men": the effort of a handful of men to take on England, one of the most powerful nations in the world. "It will be impossible for you to consider a charge of this sort," Pigot sympathized, "without some feeling of amazement that such a design as this . . . should be entertained by reasonable men." Pigot could only conclude that "truth is often more wonderful than fiction." The case had nothing to do with American power or Irish freedom, he argued. What was at stake was the security and stability of British rule in Ireland, put in danger by a handful of half-crazed Irish Americans. British authorities understood as well as the *Jacmel* defendants that the Fenian trials put their governance on stage. They decided to prosecute the *Jacmel* defendants to showcase just how fair and generous British rule was, operating not by naked acts of power but through civilized legal procedures. What better way to highlight the contrast between British regard for the rule of law and the lawless violence of Irish American Fenians?[2]

THE OPENING day of the trial on October 25, 1867, began dramatically enough. The thirty-one *Jacmel* prisoners left the stone fortress of Kilmainham Gaol in two prison vans under heavy guard, surrounded by two troops of the 12th Lancers, revolvers in hand, and a number of mounted policemen. Clearly, Dublin officials were taking no chances that there would be another Manchester-type rescue effort. The caravan threaded through Dublin, crossing the River Liffey to its northern bank and arriving at Green Street Courthouse without incident. As the defendants crossed the threshold into the historic court, they entered an arena rich with political and historic symbolism.[3]

The Green Street Courthouse was no ordinary venue. Built in 1796, on the eve of the 1798 Rebellion, the courthouse had been home to the most notorious political showcase trials in Irish history. Here the Irish rebel Robert Emmet had been condemned to death in 1803 and made his famous defiant speech to his fellow Irish on the eve of his execution. "Let no man write my epitaph," he demanded, until "my country takes her place among the nations of the earth." The Crown tried a succession of Irish nationalist heroes at the Green Street Courthouse—the Young Ireland leaders of 1848, the publishers of the *Irish People* in 1865, and, more recently, the commanders of the March 5 Rising. Small wonder that Augustine Costello would declare the dock where he and the other *Jacmel* defendants stood on trial "a holy place, where stood those whom I revere as much as I do any of our saints."[4]

The judges, wearing their white wigs and ermine-trimmed scarlet robes, sat at center stage.[5] The Irish government strategized over which judges would be most valuable to have on the bench in the treason-felony cases, selecting Chief Baron David Richard Pigot and Judge William Nicholas Keogh to hear the cases of the *Jacmel* prisoners.[6] The most hated of Irish judges, Keogh presided over many treason-felony trials, earning him a popular reputation, some say undeservedly, as a hanging judge afflicted with "Feniophobia" and "an

Fenian prisoners before the Special Commission Court, Green Street Courthouse, Dublin, 1867. Drawn from an earlier Fenian trial after the Rising of March 5, 1867, the print reveals the dramatic courtroom setting of Warren's trial in November 1867.

appetite for 'eating up' Fenians." Keen to have Keogh on the case, the government delayed Warren's trial so that the judge could return from his mother's funeral. Keogh's appointment came as no surprise to Irish nationalists. "Packing the bench" was business as usual for the British-dominated Irish legal system, the *Irishman* newspaper charged, turning "judicial trials into solemn farces, its ermined judges into bad actors."[7]

Nor did Irish nationalists have much faith in the objectivity of the jurors sworn in to hear their cases. "Jury packing" was even more common than packing the bench.[8] Britain celebrated the right to a jury trial as proof of its liberal administration in Ireland and its reverence for the rule of law. Yet Crown prosecutors did not entirely trust Irish jurors, who acquitted defendants at higher rates compared to jurors in England and Scotland. British law gave Irish prosecutors the upper hand in selecting jurors, allowing defendants to exclude without cause only twenty potential jurors, while permitting the government unlimited challenges of jurors for any reason.[9] The trial transcripts reveal little about the men who served as jurors in the *Jacmel* trials but, given the property qualifications for jury duty, few if any of the jurors would have been drawn from the ranks of the young Irish artisans who, as a group, had been the most enthusiastic recruits to the Fenian movement in Dublin. Few Catholics made it onto juries, either, especially in political trials. Finally, the jurymen were Dubliners, who statistically were more willing to convict defendants in criminal and political trials. The Irish government could have brought Warren and the *Jacmel* crew to trial in County Waterford, where they were arrested, but the "Waterford riot" and the sympathy of the residents for the "Dungarvan men" strongly suggested that a Dublin jury would be a safer bet for conviction. In sum, the men who sat in judgment at the Green Street Courthouse were not a jury of the *Jacmel* men's peers, nor were they meant to be.[10]

Yet if the jury was the best the government could hope for, the jurors were not always compliant. When Judge Keogh finally arrived to begin John Warren's trial on October 30, the court encountered yet another delay: several jurors failed to show up. It was not easy to be a juror. Jurors faced the possibility of retaliation from defendants and their allies if they sided with the government and harassment by the government should they evade what increasingly became viewed as an onerous duty. At Warren's trial, Pigot fined the missing jurors £20 and gave them an hour to appear or suffer an additional fine of £50, astounding sums for the time. The fines did the trick in compelling jurors to attend, but they did not appear happy about it.[11]

There was one more no-show at the trial: the public. The Manchester rescue trials, occurring in England at the same time as the *Jacmel* trials in Dublin, seemed destined to grab the spotlight with its prosecution of leading Fenians for the murder of police officer Sergeant Brett. Irish officials attributed the low turnout to the public's growing impatience with Fenian conspiracies, but the attorney for the *Jacmel* men argued the Irish government had kept the public out. Policemen "rudely and insolently" turned people away, leaving little doubt this was to be a "sham trial."[12]

But there was another possible reason for the light attendance. Unlike the sensational tale of the Manchester rescue, many heard the story of the *Jacmel*'s doomed but audacious voyage only after the trial began. Even the American consul William West, who had communicated with the *Jacmel* men frequently, appeared startled by the tale told by the Irish attorney general in his opening remarks to the jury. "If one half of what he said . . . is proved," West wrote to Adams at the end of the first day of trial, "there can be little doubt of the results."[13] The press quickly turned its readers' attention to the "astonishing tale" of the *Erin's Hope*, promising that the *Jacmel* trials "are destined to unfold a tale of more novelty and greater interest" than the better-known Manchester trials.[14] Coverage of the *Jacmel* trials filled local newspapers, with the *Freeman's Journal* providing transcripts of the proceedings that rivaled the official record in its level of detail and eventually became part of the American public record, published in the *Congressional Record*. The public might not be sitting in the gallery, but they could become virtual spectators as they sat in pubs, trains, and homes, reading and listening to the trial unfold. The courtroom actors in Green Street never forgot for whom they were performing.

FINALLY, on October 30, 1867, at high noon, the key players took their places and the trial of John Warren began. And it began, like many legal contests, with a battle over words. Warren's eminent counsel, Denis Caulfield Heron and Richard Dowse, both with long histories of defending Irish nationalists at trial, sparred with the top Irish legal officials, Irish attorney general Robert Warren and Irish solicitor general Michael Harrison, over the form of the indictment and the wording of the defense's opening motions as Warren came forward to plead not guilty.[15] As good lawyers—and they were some of the best in Ireland—they knew that getting the words right mattered. Warren's defense counsel used words to stake claims and delineate boundaries to make their central point: that the Irish court had no legitimate jurisdiction over him.

Warren's counsel made that point forcefully when, at the outset of the trial, Heron and Dowse made an unusual request: as an American citizen, Warren was an alien, and so his case should be heard by a "mixed jury," composed half of "natives" and half of "aliens" born in the United States. Today the mixed jury seems an odd idea, but even in 1867, the mixed jury struck observers as a strange, antiquated practice that had lost much of its original rationale. The mixed jury reached back at least to the twelfth century, long before England became a centralized nation-state, to recognize that diverse communities made up of local residents as well as foreign merchants and artisans had distinctive "courts, customs, dialects and even units of measurement." In an era when jurors exercised much greater power in establishing and interpreting local law, the mixed jury sought to give voice to both local and foreign law to arrive at just verdicts. By the nineteenth century, however, England sat at the center of a vast empire and its centralized and increasingly codified legal system did much less to accommodate non-English customs and practices. Both the subjects of its far-flung kingdom and "strangers" that ventured into its territory had to submit to its law and the standard jury.[16]

Warren's demand for a mixed jury was a brilliant move—as a publicity stunt, for starters. By the 1860s the mixed jury had become a rarity, most recently demanded—but denied—in a notorious murder trial of a British husband and a Swiss-born wife in 1849, so its use by the Fenians was sure to draw attention.[17] But the mixed jury proved more important in underscoring two critical issues. One was the legitimacy of the Irish legal system. The demand for a mixed jury implicitly questioned the ability of a purely Irish jury to provide impartial justice. But, even more important, the mixed jury, afforded only to aliens, allowed defense counsel to raise the crucial point: that a citizen of the United States of America could not also be a subject of the British queen. The demand for the mixed jury forced the court to confront the thorny issue of conflicting membership rules from the outset and allowed the defense to seize the initiative in defining the trial as a much grander international struggle over citizenship and sovereignty.[18]

Warren was not the first Fenian to demand a mixed jury, but he was the first naturalized American to make the request a central feature of his trial. In 1865 Captain John McCafferty, a native of Ohio, had succeeded in obtaining a mixed jury in his treason-felony trial in Cork held before Judge Keogh. It took some time before the court could round up enough aliens to serve, but in the end McCafferty had his half-alien jury, as the sheriff brought in a Swiss watchmaker, a vice consul for Greece, a French hatmaker, and a professor of modern languages at Queen's College, among others. The special commission court readily granted McCafferty's request for the mixed jury, seeing his birth in the United States as establishing his status as an alien. But John Warren, born in Ireland, would run into considerable more difficulty.[19]

The attorney general quickly exposed the key issue: what made Warren an "alien"? To be an alien, Warren would have to show that he had been born in another country, and even then he could still be a subject if his parents were Britons living abroad. Heron and Dowse resisted the attorney general's demand that Warren's request for a mixed jury include his place of birth, until Judge Keogh impatiently intervened and cut to the chase: "You want to raise the question that a British subject can adopt the American allegiance." Dowse replied, "That is not the question, exactly," and pointed out that even Blackstone had suggested that British subjects might pledge their allegiance to another prince. The issue was whether the act of swearing allegiance to another made one an alien in the eyes of the former sovereign. Dowse insisted that Warren's naturalization turned him into an alien in Britain, pointing to the absurdity of sustaining dual allegiances. "A man cannot be the subject of a republic and a monarchy at the same time," Dowse quipped—a suggestion so preposterous that the spectators in the courtroom laughed.[20]

Heron finally agreed to include Warren's birthplace in the motion, amending it to read "John Warren was born in Cork, in Ireland," but the attorney general still objected that the motion did not clarify Warren's nationality, as it said nothing about the status of his parents: "he might have been born of American parents in Cork," thus making him an American. Dowse joked, "Sure no American would come over here to have a child born in Cork"—a prospect again so absurd, given the one-way immigration of Irish to America, that it provoked laughter. The attorney general, backed by the judges, insisted that Warren's counsel add that he was "born in Cork, and of British parents." "Very well, my lord; I will do that," said Heron. "I will add the statement, 'born in Cork, of *Irish* parents,'" prompting another outburst of laughter at the attorney's cheeky resistance to British domination, even if only in wordplay.[21]

But what about allegiance? asked the solicitor general. Allegiance was indeed at the heart of the dispute between the parties, and between the United States and Great Britain. "Add the statement—'born of British parents under the allegiance of Her Majesty,'" commanded Chief Baron Pigot, and then the court would finally rule on the mixed-jury request. Heron resisted again: "I will say under the allegiance of the United Kingdom." "No," the attorney general insisted, "under the allegiance of the Queen." Determined to reject any indication that Warren, or his parents, owed allegiance to Queen Victoria, Heron wrote instead, "Born in Cork of Irish parents in Ireland, then under the allegiance of King William the Fourth."[22]

Perhaps the Crown officials tired of the banter, as they allowed Warren's counsel to have the last word on the phrasing. After all, the chances that the judges would grant the request were slim. But that had not been the point of Warren's attorneys' opening act. Warren's attorneys sought political rather than legal victory, playing to the public rather than to the judges.

The judges, predictably, turned down the request for the mixed jury and rejected Warren's claim to be an alien. Chief Baron Pigot could not resist the opportunity to provide a lecture on the nature of allegiance and subjecthood, aimed primarily at Americans. He had clearly anticipated that the issue of citizenship would arise and had armed himself, turning first to Blackstone and his familiar justification for "perpetual allegiance." A natural-born subject was a subject forever. If the subject swore allegiance to another "prince" and became "entangled" in conflicting obligations, "it is his own act that brings him into these straits and difficulties of owing service to two masters." Pigot then turned—with some glee, one imagines—to the legal treatises by Joseph Story and Chancellor James Kent, quoting liberally from the "two great lights of the laws of America" to show that they, too, embraced Blackstone's theory of perpetual allegiance. Neither British nor American law sheltered naturalized Americans from their just deserts when they came to Ireland bent on rebellion, Pigot warned.[23]

The question of the mixed jury resolved, it seemed the trial would finally get under way. But Warren had another opening gambit. As the Crown's attorney general rose to deliver his opening argument, Warren interrupted, declaring, "My lords, as a citizen of the United States, I protest against being arraigned at this bar, and being tried as a British subject." He then dismissed his attorneys and informed the court that "I place [my case] in the hands of the United States government; which government now becomes the principal of the case."[24]

Declining the aid of counsel was not a novel move in itself. Other Fenians had insisted upon representing themselves, refusing to play along in what they saw as a British charade of brute power masked as "rule of law." Trials without defense counsel also had the potential to make defendants appear more sympathetic, perhaps even heroic. But by firing his attorneys, Warren went further than simply refusing to help legitimize British rule. The real injured party, Warren implied, was not himself but the United States, whose dignity and national power had been attacked by Britain's arrogant disregard of its power to create and protect its citizens. While a representative of the U.S. consul's office observed the trial, Warren proceeded to defend himself—and the United States.[25]

Not that the United States appreciated his efforts. Adams was irked by Warren's courtroom antics. Adams had never thought the United States should hire attorneys for the *Jacmel* leaders in the first place, but Seward had insisted. Then Warren and Nagle had haggled over who would represent them, rejecting the solicitor that West chose.[26] Now Warren rejected the very counsel he had pestered the consulate to hire. Adams knew what Warren was up to by playing the martyr and demanding a mixed jury. "It is evident," he fumed to Seward on November 1, "that he expects to effect the object so long desired" by the Fenians, "of raising a difficulty between the two countries on the question of the right of expatriation."[27]

For the moment, however, the opening act came to a close. The Crown's counsel took center stage to make its case against John Warren.

As the attorney general rose to deliver the crucial opening remarks to the jury—laying out the charges against Warren and telling the story of the *Jacmel* for the first time in public—he was pretty sure he had a good case against Warren. Certainly he did not reveal any doubts to the jury, delivering his speech with force and persuasion. Warren and the other *Jacmel* defendants were part of a wicked transatlantic Fenian conspiracy, the attorney general charged, organized to destroy "the social system of the country" by establishing a republic in Ireland and deposing the queen. Their treasonable designs left little doubt in the attorney general's mind that they were guilty of conspiracy under the Treason-Felony Act of 1848, making it a crime to conspire to deprive the queen of her crown, levy war against the queen, or to "stir up" foreigners to invade the queen's realm.[28]

But a month earlier Attorney General Robert Warren had admitted to Lord Mayo that the case presented some challenges. First and foremost, the *Jacmel* men had not actually *done* anything in Ireland. There was no "smoking gun"—in fact, there were no guns or weapons found on the men at all. There was no ship in the Crown's custody. (Throughout his trial, John Warren repeatedly and scornfully referred to the "imaginary ship.") The only physical evidence collected were scraps of paper found in Nagle's pocket, providing a list of names, ranks, and occupations, as well as a brief description of *Erin's Hope* and a list of provisions, but the attorney general remained uncertain whether the notes could be admitted as evidence in Warren's trial.[29]

Making the charge of conspiracy to commit treason-felony stick might be challenging, but Irish judges had made the attorney general's job much easier with their recent rulings expanding the definition of "conspiracy." The law of conspiracy for treason-felony required proof of "overt acts," but what counted as an overt act?[30] Clearly, those who took up sharpened pikes and guns in the failed Rising of March 5 had committed an overt act under the Treason-Felony Act. But Chief Baron Pigot clarified, based on recent appellate court rulings in Fenian cases, that overt acts also included meeting, organizing, writing, or speaking about freeing Ireland from British rule and establishing a republic—even if those activities occurred *outside* of Ireland. Recall the case of Stephen Meany, decided by a divided appellate court in July 1867 while the *Jacmel* men awaited trial. Meany had been nowhere near Ireland during the recent Fenian activity. Yet when he landed in England in December 1866 he was promptly arrested, whisked away to Dublin for trial for treason-felony, and convicted of being part of the Fenian conspiracy. The only evidence the jury considered was whether Meany had participated in the Fenian organization in the United States.

Meany's conviction raised major, controversial questions about jurisdiction. How could an Irish court punish an individual for something he did in America—in this case, participating in the Fenian Brotherhood? Traditionally, criminal courts had jurisdiction only over crimes committed within their physical territory (within their "venue"). The "crime, having been committed in America, was not triable here," argued Judge O'Hagan of the Irish appellate court.[31] Chief Baron Pigot, interestingly, had denounced the Crown's argument in the Meany case as "preposterous," as "the prisoner never was in Ireland at all up to the period of his arrest."[32] But the Crown persuaded the majority of Irish judges in Meany's appeal, drawing on the common-law rule that a conspirator is liable for the acts of his co-conspirators. To take a modern example, if two men plan to rob a bank and one of them kills a guard during the robbery, the other man is also liable for murder as a co-conspirator, even if he did not pull the trigger.[33] Drawing on such logic, the Crown's counsel declared that "Meany was as liable in America, once he joined the [Fenian] conspiracy, for all the acts done in Dublin as if he were present when they were performed."[34] Even judges who expressed discomfort with the Crown's bold expansion of jurisdiction upheld Meany's conviction, convinced by the government that it needed to be more aggressive to defeat "one of the most gigantic and wide-spread conspiracies the world has ever seen."[35]

Perhaps Britain was reaching too far into what would normally be considered American territory and jurisdiction. But Americans were intruding too far into Irish affairs as well, declared the Crown. America had "a future of greatness—exceeding, perhaps, that of Rome, perhaps that of Britain," Robert Warren conceded to the jury. But Americans should stay at home and devote their energies to building their own nation. "Let them not seek to disturb the peace of other kingdoms . . . let them not come to our country."[36] Armed with the expanded definition of conspiracy, the attorney general charged Warren with being part of the Fenian conspiracy in America, making him a co-conspirator in the March 5 Rising, and with sailing on the *Jacmel* with the intent of landing arms and men "for the purpose of fighting against the Queen and raising an insurrection in Ireland."[37]

The Crown's counsel had the law behind them, but they still needed evidence to convict Warren. Informants proved key to the Crown's case, as they did in most Fenian treason-felony cases. The government had succeeded in getting three of the *Jacmel* men to "peach." William Millen confessed shortly after his arrest in Dungarvan, hoping to remain a "secret informer" and leaving for America well before the trial, but his comrades soon suspected that he had "turned informer." Nagle saw him as a "most accursed traitor" who had to be stopped at all costs. "I know someone who will look after him," said Nagle. A few days after he returned to New York, Millen was shot to death, reportedly by a Fenian assassin.[38] James Nolan, one of the men shot by Daniel Buckley off the coast of Sligo, also confessed and then left for Liverpool to help the government uncover Fenian activity. The attorney general called him to testify at Warren's trial, but Nolan returned very reluctantly and, once on the stand, refused to say a word. The third informer, Daniel J. Buckley, proved more than willing to tell all he knew about the *Jacmel*'s mission and the men who had led it. He became the Crown's star witness and was the first to testify.

Buckley's betrayal probably did not surprise Warren and the other defendants. It had been Buckley, after all, who had led the mutiny attempt after the failed landing at Sligo. Buckley had a certain swagger, at least as displayed in the photograph taken of him in Kilmainham Gaol. In that photo, he sprawls before the camera, with his vest popping open and his hand in his pocket, his hazel eyes staring at the photographer boldly—perhaps even insolently. A handsome young man with fair features and a stylish tuft of chin hair, Buckley appears decidedly unfazed by his predicament.[39] When asked why he had decided to inform on his associates, Buckley flippantly replied "so I wouldn't end up like the prisoner."[40]

Buckley provided a gripping eyewitness account of the *Jacmel*'s voyage from the time the men left New York to the morning seven weeks later when they straggled to shore near Dungarvan in search of food and supplies. Remarkably vague on the specifics of his own life—saying he was twenty-five years old, "as far as I know," and that he thought he had been born in Munster—Buckley provided colorful details about life as a Fenian and baldly stated the purpose of the expedition: "to arm a revolutionary party . . . for the purpose of revolutionizing [Ireland]." Buckley named names, particularly noting that Warren and Nagle had leadership positions, serving as colonels. He described the deadly assortment of weapons stashed in the hold of the ship and told of the arrival of Ricard O'Sullivan Burke, a notorious leader in the March 5 Rising, who warned Warren and others against their landing the arms at Sligo. And, critically, Buckley testified that when the pilot, Michael Gallagher, boarded the ship to offer to guide it through Sligo Bay, Warren and Nagle forced him to

Daniel Buckley, crew member aboard *Erin's Hope* and chief Crown witness against John Warren, for which he would be called the "Judas" of the expedition.

swear an oath not to divulge anything of what he had seen or heard on board before they would allow Gallagher to leave. All the details proved damning for Warren, supporting the Crown's charge that he had sailed to Ireland on the *Jacmel* with the intent of levying war against the queen.[41]

The government moved to the final charges against Warren: that he had joined the Fenian Brotherhood in the United States, making him criminally liable as a co-conspirator for the Rising of March 5. To document Warren's Fenian activities, the attorney general trotted out the government's star "approver" in state trials, John Joseph Corydon. No Fenian treason-felony trial would have been complete without the testimony of the informer Corydon, who was kept on the British government's payroll and prided himself on identifying "a great many" people. No informer was more hated than the "blood selling scamp" Corydon. When officials brought Corydon to Waterford to identify the *Jacmel* prisoners, they barely got him out alive, as his carriage "was almost smashed with stones," his attackers "chiefly girls from sixteen to twenty" who "bared their arms" and urged the police officers to allow them two seconds alone with the "rascal."[42] Corydon felt no shame about being a paid informer, boasting, "I will take all I get."[43] He earned his keep in Warren's trial. Corydon claimed to know Warren well, both as a Fenian and as a soldier, as Corydon had served in Warren's regiment during the war. Warren was a Fenian through and through, said Corydon, and served as "state centre" for Massachusetts.[44]

The testimony of Buckley and Corydon, while valuable, would not suffice. Buckley, after all, had been an accomplice in the conspiracy, and, as even judges admitted, informers had an "odious character," tainted with betrayal and self-serving motives. To protect against loose accusations by unscrupulous men, the Treason-Felony Act of 1848 required at least two "credible witnesses" to establish an overt act of treason. Michael Gallagher, the unfortunate pilot from County Donegal who happened upon *Jacmel* in Sligo Bay, followed Buckley on the stand and was as critical as Buckley to the Crown's case.[45]

Gallagher must have rued the day he rowed out to *Jacmel* with his crew in search of a little work. A pilot for twenty-five years, with a large family—seven children, a wife, and a mother—to support, Gallagher had not been looking for trouble. Not only did he stumble upon a band of Fenians, but Gallagher ended up spending weeks in local jails and eventually Kilmainham Gaol. "I never was in gaol until I got into this case," Gallagher declared. "I got enough of gaols since; it put my family and myself to beggary."[46] And he had never even been paid the promised two guineas from the "man in charge" of *Jacmel* for his pilotage, Gallagher complained bitterly at the trial.[47]

Each time Gallagher told his story, it became longer and more full of vital details. When Gallagher had been questioned by two Streedagh Coast Guard men, he said little: that he had been out fishing, boarded the brigantine to pilot her to Killybegs, and then got off and headed for Streedagh shore. He had seen only eight or nine men on board. It was a Spanish vessel on its way to Glasgow. Beyond that, he swore, he knew nothing.[48] But by the time of the trial, Gallagher had much more to say. After he boarded the ship and made the deal to pilot the ship into Sligo Bay, he took charge of the vessel but was called down to the captain's cabin, where Warren, Nagle, and the "man in charge" waited.

There Nagle asked him if he was a Fenian, to which Gallagher replied no; "I said I didn't think there were any Fenians in the county Donegal." The "man in charge then said, 'Swear him.' I told him for God's sake not to swear me, . . . as I was a man of age and had a large family." But "the man in charge" held a gun to his head, Gallagher insisted, and Nagle handed him "the book," forcing him to swear not to tell anyone what he had seen on the ship. Gallagher sealed the oath by kissing the Bible and returned, "in terror," to his duties of piloting the ship, trying to steer the ship close to one of the many Coast Guard stations that dotted the shore in hopes of attracting the attention of the guardsmen. Gallagher tried to escape, saying, "I am long enough watching the vessel," and jumped into a small boat, only to be dragged out. Finally, at one in the morning, after being on the ship since noon, Gallagher left with the two wounded men and three others and "pulled for the shore." Once he touched shore, he immediately began the fifty-mile trek home, not even stopping to help unload the wounded crew members in his hurry to get away from the Fenians.[49]

Gallagher's testimony at trial was much more incriminating than earlier statements he had given to officials on May 27 and June 15. It was not until October 12, as the Crown law officers prepared the case for trial, that Gallagher told of the secret oath he had been forced to swear—a vital detail allowing prosecutors to charge Warren with a crime committed within British jurisdiction. Interestingly, Daniel Buckley also included the story for the first time in his deposition on October 10, failing to mention it in his first sworn statement of September 12. Warren asked skeptically why the story hadn't come up sooner, and how it was that the witnesses suddenly remembered so many more details. Gallagher replied that he felt bound by his oath: "I was sworn in the vessel, and I could not give fair evidence."[50] Buckley blithely said his memory was "refreshed" after having a chance to sit down and recollect what happened.[51]

Warren had a different explanation for the discrepancies: the witnesses had been coached by the Crown's legal team. Gallagher's testimony was a "tissue of perjury from first to last," made either for pay or to obtain release from jail, about an "imaginary ship."[52] Of course, the ship was not imaginary, as Warren and other Fenians would later not only admit but celebrate. And, as the attorney general suggested, Gallagher's testimony had a ring of truth to it. But Warren's charges that the Irish law officers had "cooked" the evidence are not improbable. When the attorney general wrote to Lord Mayo on September 27, a month before the trial began, he worried that he only had "slight" evidence "to corroborate the informers."[53] Two weeks later, he had a better case, with the sworn statements of Buckley and Gallagher both attesting to a "secret oath" that had not come up previously. Even during the trial, Warren noted, the witnesses heard each other testify, allowing them to adjust their stories accordingly. Chief Baron Pigot apparently had not noticed, or feigned ignorance, saying, "That should not have been. The usual course is to have the witnesses out of court." But by then, of course, it was too late.[54]

The direct evidence of Warren's guilt was hardly overwhelming, tainted by informants and possible prosecutorial misconduct. So the solicitor general leaned heavily on circumstantial evidence in his closing remarks to the jurors, asking: Just why had Warren come to Ireland? Was he simply "a member of the press, collecting notes," and visiting the "old scenes" and "old friends of my boyhood and near and dear relatives," as he claimed?[55] The Crown's attorney reminded the jury that a bunch of well-dressed men, apparently from America, had washed up on shore one day, without a credible story to explain themselves, at a time when Fenianism gripped the countryside. The fishermen from Dungarvan testified that the men had commandeered their small boat, forcing them to land thirty men and to avoid the Coast Guard station.[56] Warren and Nagle had hidden their identities, posing as "William Palmer" and "John Donovan" when they paid farmer Andrew Roche to take them to Youghal. They had told Police-Sergeant James Norris they were from Cork when he stopped them on Youghal Bridge, just a mile from their destination. When Norris took them into custody, he confiscated incriminating "papers with pencilling on them" from Nagle.[57] Giving false names, dodging the Coast Guard, misleading Whelan and his crew—all together, the Crown's counsel argued, the circumstances of Warren's landing and arrest suggested the men were up to no good. "What brought [Warren] to Ireland on the 1st of June?" asked the solicitor general skeptically. "What difficulty could he . . . have in showing how he came to Ireland, and for what purpose—if it was not a wicked one?"[58]

The jury arrived at its answer with little difficulty. The jurors began deliberating at 4:20 P.M. on November 5 and returned by 4:55 with the expected verdict: John Warren was guilty on all counts.[59] Warren was returned to Kilmainham Gaol to await his sentencing and his chance to deliver the all-important speech from the dock.

ON NOVEMBER 17, 1867, the courtroom players gathered for the final act in the *Jacmel* trials. By that point, Irish officials had tried a second *Jacmel* prisoner, the dashing Augustine Costello, but found the jury less compliant. The first jury could not agree on a verdict, and the second convicted him reluctantly. Costello "had many friends on the jury, myself among the number, who were most anxious to acquit him," said John A. Walker.[60] The jury's ambivalence in Costello's case and the allegations of witness tampering in Warren's did little to persuade skeptics that the British legal system afforded true justice. But if justice could not be expected to come from an Irish bench, wrote the Irish *Nation*'s editor, Alexander Martin Sullivan, the prisoner could still redeem the trial by imparting vital moral and political lessons in a speech from the dock. As Warren and Costello arrived to be sentenced, they found the courtroom "densely crowded" with spectators, anxious to witness the climax of the political drama when the defendants gave their final speeches before being sentenced.[61]

The defendants reportedly "entered the dock with a firm step." Warren, with his "squat," "very stout" build and thinning auburn hair, did not look the part of romantic adventurer to curious onlookers. While Warren liked to think of himself as a "military man," to courtroom spectators he could have passed for someone "studying for the clerical profession, or, indeed, any other pursuit than that of war."[62] But Warren's words had always been his most dangerous weapon, and as he rose to give his culminating speech, he knew how critical it could be in shaping how his trial would be understood by transatlantic audiences. Sir Frederick Bruce, the British ambassador to the United States during the Fenian crisis, had pointed out that if Irish nationalists could "appeal to . . . American interests [rather] than to American sympathies, their influence in [the United States] would become far more dangerous."[63] Warren took this advice to heart. He deftly shifted attention away from his Fenian activities and his possible guilt to the real issue in the case: British contempt for American sovereignty and the United States' commitment to its adopted citizens.

"I protest against the entire jurisdiction of this Court," Warren declared, returning to his opening salvo. The British imperiously intruded on American territorial jurisdiction with their expansive definition of conspiracy, but, more important, they insolently refused to acknowledge naturalized Americans as U.S. citizens. Just think about the potential consequences of the British doctrine of perpetual allegiance, he warned his fellow Americans. Under the court's absurd theory, not only were those born in Britain perpetual subjects but so, too, were their children and grandchildren who lived abroad. They could "claim as British subjects Andrew Johnson, our President, Secretary Seward, and Governor Fenton, of New York." Even General Washington, and Benjamin Franklin "lived and died British subjects," Warren cried, and the British "could hang the whole of them if convicted of high treason."[64] Warren ended his impassioned speech with a call to arms in America, demanding that the United States honor its obligation to protect all Americans, naturalized and native-born alike. "If England is allowed to abuse me as she has done, and if America does not resent England's conduct towards me; if the only allegiance I ever acknowledged is not to be vindicated, then thirteen millions of the sons of Ireland who have lived in happiness in the United States up to this will have become the slaves of England."[65]

Warren would have said much more if Chief Baron Pigot had not cut him off repeatedly. Pigot had no intention of allowing Warren to use his court as a political soapbox to arouse the sympathies of Americans or to denounce the governments of either the United States or Britain. "We have nothing to do with the conduct of any government," Pigot said primly. "We are here to dispense justice according to law and whatever the officials of our government or the American government have done cannot have the slightest influence upon our judgment." Pigot was trying as hard as Warren to have the last word on how the trial would be framed. By preserving the fiction that the Irish court had nothing to do with politics but just followed the dictates of the law, Pigot insistently championed the *Jacmel* trials as the model of legitimate British rule.[66] He reminded the defendants that no matter what the men had pledged in America, their native allegiance "binds you by bonds from which you cannot be freed." As British subjects who had conspired to depose their queen, in a most foolish and "astonishing" scheme, Warren and Costello fell firmly within the court's jurisdiction. Pigot then sentenced Warren to fifteen years of prison at hard labor and Costello to twelve.[67]

With the sentences passed, the prisoners left the dock, Warren flinging his final defiant words: "I would not take a lease of this kingdom for thirty-seven and a half cents!"[68] As Warren passed Governor Price, the director of Kilmainham Gaol, they exchanged heated words, tempers flared, and spectators thought Warren might punch Price. But instead, the prisoners returned to Kilmainham Gaol under heavy guard as convicted felons. The show was over.[69]

BUT THIS wasn't really the final act. William Nagle, a native-born citizen, still waited to be tried. Nagle had been at the forefront of the *Jacmel* controversy before the trials began, his name joined with Warren's in newspaper accounts and petitions. But by November, newspapers spoke of "Warren and Costello," Nagle on the sidelines for the moment as the Crown delayed his trial. Nagle desperately wanted to be tried and have his day in court. Anything was better than sitting in prison, enduring "this torture of lingering death." His health deteriorating, Nagle wrote a long, defiant letter to Adams, saying he had been punished long enough and that further detention would most likely "be fatal to my life."[70] At the conclusion of the sentencing hearing for Warren and Costello, Heron asked the court to either try Nagle immediately or release him on bail. Why had the trial of the prisoner been "so often postponed?" Heron demanded.[71]

The attorney general had originally planned to prosecute Nagle after Warren, but he ran into a legal snag. The Dublin court had no jurisdiction over Nagle, he concluded, because Nagle was a native-born American citizen and thus, unlike Warren, an alien. Even enthusiastic supporters of the broadened definition of conspiracy hesitated to extend the principle to foreigners.[72] Unable to charge Nagle with being a co-conspirator in the Rising of March 5, they had to rest their case on the "illegal oath" that he supposedly administered to Michael Gallagher off the coast of Sligo. Nagle and the rest of the *Jacmel* prisoners would have to be tried in Sligo, where the offense had occurred, the attorney general decided, and Nagle would be eligible for a mixed jury.[73]

Here was infuriating proof of the stark difference that American birth could make. Aside from his being born in the United States, Nagle's situation varied little from Warren's. Both men had earned reputations as loyal Civil War leaders. Both had dedicated themselves to the Fenian cause of Irish independence. Both had shared command as colonels on *Jacmel*. Yet British law could hunt down Irish-born naturalized Americans wherever they went, while American-born Irish could claim the protective shield of the American government. Where was the justice in that? demanded Irish Americans. "It is full time the people should know what is the meaning of the phrase '*American citizen*,' or if it has any meaning at all," demanded John Savage, the new president of the Fenian Brotherhood.[74] Were adopted Americans citizens deserving of the same regard and protection as native-born Americans, or were they not?

Warren and Costello's case hit a nerve not just among Irish Americans but among other naturalized Americans as well. On the heels of their convictions came the executions of the "Manchester Martyrs" for the murder of Sergeant Brett, their hanging described in gruesome detail in newspapers throughout the world. The executions, denounced as "judicial murder," often became conflated with the *Jacmel* cases, sparking widespread protests and rallies.[75] Within weeks the Boston *Pilot* reported "immense and enthusiastic" meetings popping up around the nation, revealing that "the feeling throughout the land is very generally awakened," not only among Irish Americans but also among Poles, Germans, Austrians, and others who had made America their home.[76] Angry letters and petitions poured into Congress and rallies spread throughout the United States, demanding protection of the "Rights of American Citizens Abroad."[77]

Nagle's trial, still to come, promised to stoke the burning resentment among naturalized Americans. But for now, the controversy shifted from the courtrooms of Ireland to American streets and the floor of the United States Congress.

THREE

Reconstructing Citizenship

8

Are Naturalized Americans, Americans?

JOHN WARREN had to wonder, he wrote to Congress from his prison cell at Kilmainham Gaol, "what feeling must I have towards my government . . . as I lie to-night in my lonely dungeon, cut away from mother, wife, sisters, children and friends, immured in a living tomb." Now "clothed in a suit of convict gray," facing a fifteen-year sentence in an English prison for the crime of belonging to an Irish national organization in America, convicted on the testimony of vile spies and informers, Warren pondered what exactly his oath of allegiance to the United States had meant. Why had the United States conferred the supposedly priceless possession of citizenship upon him if it had no intention of standing up and protecting its adopted citizens from insolent British bullies? *Do* something, he urged Congress.[1]

One might have imagined that Charles Sumner, U.S. senator from Massachusetts and chair of the Senate Committee on Foreign Relations, would have been an ideal champion for the right of expatriation. Few men spoke so passionately—or so incessantly—about the moral necessity of absolute equality than Sumner. Few prodded the nation's conscience more than he, challenging his fellow Americans to live up to the ideals of the Declaration of Independence, which in Sumner's view was more important than the Constitution in expressing the fundamental principles of the United States. Few embraced the need for a strong nation-state more than Sumner, who saw a bold, empowered federal government as going hand in hand with the expansion of citizens' rights. And for Sumner, the question of citizenship and its rights lay at the heart of the Republican Party's Reconstruction program following the Civil War. Politically, of course, as a senator from Massachusetts, with its large Irish American population, Sumner would have much to gain from leading the charge in the expatriation campaign.[2]

But Sumner showed little interest in expatriation, sharing Adams's view that Fenians had trumped up the cause to launch the United States into war with England. When Sumner and his fellow Radical Republicans spoke of citizenship, equality of rights, and freedom of movement, all protected by a strong nation-state, they had a very specific group in mind: African Americans, who had borne the brunt of the sin of slavery and for whom true liberty would be achieved only by absolute equality of civil and political rights. But Sumner's declaration of "equal rights of all" promised much more during the volatile postwar era. As Warren challenged Congress to step up and protect foreign-born citizens abroad, he joined a boisterous fight during Reconstruction over the parameters of citizenship and government power at home.[3]

"ARE WE A NATION?" Charles Sumner asked the young Republican men gathered at Cooper Union on November 19, 1867, within weeks of Warren's sentencing. For Sumner, the answer was an obvious and resounding yes. But it is telling that Sumner felt a need to pose the question. At the end of the Civil War, the country was still split apart, despite the Union's victory, and many questioned whether and how the nation could be put back together again. After a traumatic war that had spread unprecedented death and destruction, the victors turned to the difficult, contentious task of rebuilding the nation—and reconstructing American citizenship.[4]

Sumner rejoiced at the work ahead. The future had never looked "so grand, & fair, & beautiful," he said to his abolitionist friend Wendell Phillips in May 1865. For the war had brought an end to slavery, a cause Sumner had pursued for years with relentless passion, alienating many in the process. In 1856, Sumner's fiery speech denouncing the hold of "the harlot slavery" on Kansas sparked a violent attack by Congressman Preston Brooks of South Carolina, who beat Sumner senseless with his gold-tipped cane on the Senate floor. When Sumner finally returned to the Senate in 1860, having taken several years to recover from the beating, he was unchastened, more self-righteous, and even more determined never to compromise on the question of "Human Rights."[5] At war's end, prospects seemed bright when Congress passed the Thirteenth Amendment to the Constitution, outlawing slavery.[6]

Sumner's gleeful optimism quickly turned to despair. Andrew Johnson, assuming the presidency after the assassination of Abraham Lincoln, had seemed so promising at first, vowing that "treason shall be punished" in the South and appearing to be the "sincere friend of the negro." But Johnson proved a fickle friend. Johnson's Reconstruction policy was so lenient, in the eyes of Sumner and his Republican allies, that the South—which had been "ready to accept" their defeat—soon became emboldened, restoring former Confederates to public office and using "Black Codes" to keep freedpeople at work on plantations in a system all too reminiscent of slavery. African Americans and white Republicans in the South pleaded with Congress for protection against rapidly escalating violence. On July 30, 1866, when white and black delegates gathered in New Orleans to protest the passage of the Louisiana Black Code, they were met by a white mob organized by the mayor, a former Confederate, spurring a melee that ended with the death of forty-eight people, all but four African American. A riot in Memphis two months earlier had ended with forty-six African American deaths and the burning of hundreds of black homes, churches, and schools.[7] Cries of "states' rights"—the doctrine that had led to "civil war, wasted treasure, wounds and death"—surged once again, calling people to resist "centralism" in the federal government.[8]

African Americans remained especially vulnerable to attacks, argued Republicans, because their citizenship remained in doubt, a legacy of the *Dred Scott* decision in 1857. In that "outrageous" decision, which "horrified" the nation, Justice Roger B. Taney ruled that free African Americans were not citizens of the United States, regardless of their free status or their birth within the United States. African Americans had "no rights which the white man was bound to respect," Taney famously declared.[9] That enslaved blacks had little recourse under the law had not been a surprise. But the idea that a free African American, born in the United States, could not claim American citizenship shocked many, though *Harper's Weekly* quickly pointed out that the critics who "fume, and fret, and bubble, and squeak" at the Court's decision often discriminated against African Americans on a daily basis.[10]

The North stood in as much need of reconstruction as the South when it came to racial inequality. Northern laws barred blacks from juries, from state militias, and as witnesses in legal proceedings; they denied black men the vote; they segregated trains, streetcars, and schools; some hampered that most basic of human rights, the "freedom of locomotion," limiting African Americans' entry and residency in several northern states. Even the parade in New York City to mourn President Lincoln in 1865 turned into a racial battleground, African Americans securing a place in the funeral procession only after strenuous political lobbying and only under heavy guard by federal troops to protect them from angry white spectators.[11] In the nation's capital, the State Department had routinely denied U.S. passports to free African Americans, based on what it viewed as dubious claims to American citizenship and a desire not to inflame the already tense relationship between North and South. Even after the Civil War began, Secretary of State William Seward balked initially when Sumner asked him for a passport for the son of Robert Morris, the pioneering African American lawyer who had led the legal battle against segregated schools in Boston. "This will never do," Seward reportedly protested. "It won't do to acknowledge colored men as citizens."[12]

The *Dred Scott* decision cast a long shadow, as the highest court in the land had thrown the status of African Americans into limbo, legitimizing their unequal treatment under the law. Stateless, both slaves and free blacks existed outside the logic of nineteenth-century citizenship, owing allegiance to the government because they lived within its territorial jurisdiction but unable to claim the protection that allegiance was supposed to require.[13] Even after emancipation and the end of the war, even after 180,000 black soldiers—one-fifth of the eligible adult male black population—had served in the Union Army, African Americans found their citizenship in doubt, their opponents dragging up *Dred Scott* to deny them a place in the polity.[14]

Citizenship mattered, Republicans argued, if African Americans were to be truly free and equal. "From the first," recalled Frederick Douglass, the former slave and great abolitionist, "I saw no chance of bettering the condition of the freedman until he should cease to be a freedman and become a citizen."[15] Henry J. Raymond, congressional representative and editor of the *New York Times,* saw citizenship as the foundation for all other rights: "Make the colored man a citizen of the United States, and he has every right which you or I have . . . He has the right of free passage from one State to another . . . He has a defined *status;* he has a country and a home, a right to defend himself and his wife and children."[16] Some Republicans and Democrats had thought emancipation, as guaranteed by the Thirteenth Amendment, would be enough to secure African Americans' "final freedom." But many soon agreed, especially in the face of bitter resistance in the South, that Congress needed to define American citizenship and its rights more clearly.[17]

"This Republic cannot be lost," Sumner urged. "We must work hard to save it."[18]

REPUBLICANS in Congress mounted what many saw as a revolution in civil rights, defining national citizenship for the first time.[19] The Civil Rights Act of 1866 aimed to vanquish the ghost of *Dred Scott,* declaring clearly—and defiantly—that *all* persons born in the United States were American citizens. And those citizens, "of every race and color," wherever they roamed within the United States, had the same civil rights as those enjoyed by white people: the right to own property, to make contracts, to file lawsuits, to give testimony in courts. Two months later, Congress went further to lodge the principle of equal citizenship more firmly in the Constitution, ensuring that African Americans had rights that white men had to respect. The Fourteenth Amendment reiterated that all persons born or naturalized in the United States "are citizens of the United States and of the states wherein they reside."[20]

"We are making a nation," observed Thaddeus Stevens, Sumner's Radical Republican ally in the House.[21] No longer would Americans be plagued by "so-called double allegiance," a "barbaric" and "political absurdity" that had only caused "great mischief." Justice Taney had declared in *Dred Scott* that Americans had two separate statuses: they were citizens of sovereign states *and* citizens of the United States. Massachusetts might recognize a black man as a citizen, for example, but he would not be a citizen of the United States in Taney's eyes. Now, though, the concept of divided citizenship had to be swept away, joining "state sovereignty" in the historical dustbin. "We cannot faithfully serve two masters," argued the eminent social theorist Francis Lieber, a close friend of Sumner's. Nationalization—the consolidation of power in the federal government and the creation of a unitary national citizenship—would allow the United States to return to its historic mission as the most advanced liberal republic. Americans would be "one people, under one sovereignty," bound to a dedication of "Human Rights."[22]

The Fourteenth Amendment put federal force behind protection of universal rights. In sweeping, broad language that would keep future constitutional scholars busy for generations trying to parse out its meaning, the amendment commanded that no state shall abridge the "privileges and immunities" of an American citizen, nor deny any person life, liberty, or property without due process of law or equal protection of the laws. "Every person, no matter what his birth, condition or color, who can raise the cry, 'I am an American citizen,'" has a right to demand that the nation protect his rights of citizenship against any and all detractors, Sumner thundered. A citizen should be a citizen wherever he goes.[23]

Sumner launched an ambitious national lecture tour in the fall of 1867 with twenty-two stops in six weeks to push the Republicans' Reconstruction plan, with its nationalization of citizenship and civil rights, as the only path to restoring the Union. "State Rights . . . must be trampled out forever," he urged, so that the United States could be "in reality as in name, a Nation." By then Congress had gone even further, imposing martial law upon the South in the spring of 1867 and insisting that before their readmission to the Union, southern states must ratify the Fourteenth Amendment and extend suffrage to black men. The young Republican men in New York City's Cooper Union and other supporters cheered Sumner on, but Sumner's relentless lecturing left others cold. In Milwaukee, bored audience members walked out in the middle of Sumner's two-hour speech, drawing the silent wrath of the self-righteous senator, who paused and fixed a furious glare on them as they left. Clearly not everyone shared Sumner's passion for a centralized nation of equal citizens.[24]

President Johnson spoke for many Democrats who were appalled by the Republicans' Reconstruction program. When the Civil Rights Act of 1866 landed on his desk, Johnson promptly vetoed it. Emancipation was one thing, equality quite another. Like most Union Democrats in both North and South, Johnson had supported the Thirteenth Amendment, seeing the abolition of slavery as a necessary outcome of the war, though even that amendment had been hard fought. But Johnson Democrats—and many conservative Republicans—balked at calls for equal rights and resisted the expansion of federal government power. The sweeping definition of citizenship in the Civil Rights Act astounded Johnson, as it "comprehends the Chinese of the Pacific States, Indians subject to taxation, the people called Gipsies, as well as the entire race designated as black, people of color, negroes, mulattoes, and persons of African blood." He could not abide thrusting 4 million people who "have just emerged from slavery into freedom" into the cherished status of citizens, especially when eleven of the former Confederate states, still unrepresented in Congress after the war, had no say in the matter. States had always had the right to decide rules of citizenship for themselves, Johnson insisted, and the war had done nothing to change that. With the Civil Rights Act, Congress arrogantly intruded into state jurisdiction, not only imposing its definition of citizenship but spelling out citizens' fundamental civil rights, rights that belonged to the states to define. What would Congress do next, Johnson wondered, in its perplexing quest for "perfect equality of the white and colored races"? Allow "revolting" intermarriage between whites and blacks? The act violated the Constitution and good sense, Johnson declared.[25]

Taken aback by Johnson's resistance, Congress quickly overrode his veto in April 1866.[26] But while the Republican Reconstruction program swept the party to victory in the fall elections of 1867, thanks largely to black support, Republicans faced crippling defeats in the North. Democrats in the North—the party that proved most supportive of the Fenians and the right of expatriation—denounced the "Radical Party" for usurping power in the South "by establishing negro supremacy . . . by military force."[27] By the fall of 1867, as the expatriation crisis mounted, the Fourteenth Amendment still lay before the states for ratification. Southern legislatures, unsurprisingly, had defiantly rejected the new amendment as "an insulting outrage," but northern opposition to the amendment grew as well.[28] Three northern states—Ohio, New Jersey, and Oregon—actually rescinded their ratification of the Fourteenth Amendment soon after the elections. Conservative Republicans, too, worried that Congress reached too far, the *New York Times* cautioning against Sumner's "theory of absolute, tyrannical centralization."[29]

Other critics blasted the Republicans for doing too little, stopping short of full equality. "Civil rights," for most Americans, referred to rights to own property, sue in court, move freely about—the types of rights guaranteed by the Civil Rights Act of 1866. African Americans had been lobbying for more before the war ended, gathering in black conventions and forming the National Equal Rights League to press their cause. "WE ARE COMING UP!" Dr. P. B. Randolph trumpeted in Philadelphia, "and going up to *stay.*" The vote and land—those were what African Americans prized above all else. Black veterans of the Union Army exposed the hypocrisy of the government, so willing to embrace them as soldiers but keeping them at arm's length at the ballot box. "Are we good enough to use bullets, and not good enough to use ballots?" they asked. "Are we citizens when the nation is in peril, and aliens when the nation is in safety?"[30] They demanded that Congress extend political rights and guarantee black male suffrage.[31] Yet for many African Americans and a handful of white supporters, even that vision fell short. As legislators debated the meaning of equality in the nation's capitol, Sojourner Truth defiantly climbed aboard a whites-only Washington, D.C., streetcar, only to be physically removed by the conductor. Truth and other African American activists took to the streets, demonstrating with their actions and their words that nothing less than full social equality, including full access to public spaces—trains, schools, militias, streets, and parks—would remove the "badges of slavery" and secure full freedom.[32]

Reconstruction did not belong just to African Americans, other critics argued. Elizabeth Cady Stanton and Susan B. Anthony, leaders of the woman suffrage campaign, furiously denounced the Fourteenth Amendment for establishing an "aristocracy of sex." Not only did the amendment fail to extend suffrage to women, but it explicitly introduced distinctions based on sex to the

Constitution for the first time, reducing the number of congressional representatives in states that denied "male citizens" the right to vote.[33] The women's rights leaders felt betrayed. Men who had once been their political allies, fellow warriors in the fight for emancipation and universal rights, now told them "this hour belongs to the negro."[34]

It was hard to stuff the genie of equality back in the bottle once Radical Republicans had let it loose. Sumner and the Radical Republicans may have had their eyes fastened on the rights of African Americans, but they spoke in broad strokes, using language that encompassed much more. "The people, everywhere . . . roused from lethargy of the ages, are demanding an extension of rights," claimed the Equal Rights Convention in New York. The "constitutional door is open," declared Stanton, and she and many others who felt they had been excluded from the polity wanted to walk through it, determined to take hold of the "golden moment" to reconfigure the boundaries of American citizenship and declare their equal rights.[35] "Now's the Hour.—Not the 'negro's hour' alone, but everybody's hour."[36]

INTO THIS swirling debate on citizenship and rights stepped the Fenian Brotherhood. Determined that their claims would not be forgotten, the American Fenians worked to keep the *Jacmel* men's plight in the public eye. Only weeks after the Dublin trials ended, Warren and Nagle became immortalized among the "great Fenian heroes and martyrs" in a book written by Fenian Brotherhood president John Savage and rushed to press by Patrick Donahoe, editor of the Boston *Pilot*. Advertised as "the most interesting book ever published," Savage's book ended with a passionate plea for immediate government intervention.[37]

In Boston, Warren's home city, Fenians pulled out all the stops in a grand evening rally on December 7, 1867, to protest his conviction. Led by O'Connor's Brass Band, almost 4,000 protestors marched from Boston Commons to Old Faneuil Hall in support of Warren, holding aloft "transparencies"—banners illuminated from behind with gas lamps—that mingled appeals for Irish independence ("Ireland's Rights or England in a Blaze") with calls for the recognition of all Americans' rights ("We demand our rights as citizens"). The "vast crowd" waiting at Faneuil Hall greeted the marchers with "deafening cheers" and noisily endorsed resolutions demanding the release of Warren and other imprisoned American citizens.[38]

Fenians had high hopes they could unite the foreign-born—especially Germans and Irish—to forge a mighty political force. "This is not a Fenian question, nor a mere Irish Question," wrote one supporter, "but one in which all naturalized citizens, in whatsoever country born, are concerned." Only by coming together could the foreign-born be heard over the "din of party wrangling," suggested John Mitchel, the Young Irelander journalist known for his proslavery views and uncompromising dedication to Irish freedom at any cost. He called for an "Adopted Citizens' Association" that could "act coercively on American politics, and *force* results." If the foreign-born united to elect only those who were willing to stand up to foreign bullies, Mitchel argued, the next time a "lawless outrage" was committed "upon an adopted citizen abroad" the American response would be war, not polite petitions.[39]

Uniting the foreign-born would not be easy. They might live in the same cities and belong to the same Democratic Party, but familiarity did not necessarily breed friendship or understanding.[40] Germans and Irish had often been bitter rivals since their arrival in the United States. Language created one divide. "Even the most educated German is like a child in terms of the language and the customs," complained Albert Augustin in 1861. Despite years of studying and learning "all the tricks and traps in America," Germans "still have to take orders from coarse Irishmen and nasty Americans."[41] If Irish seemed to have the upper hand in terms of language—and their mastery of American politics and greater access to patronage—they lagged behind Germans in skills and economic mobility, breeding resentment of the "damned Dutch" (from the German word *Deutsch* for "German") that erupted in innumerable conflicts, from name-calling to fistfights to riots. Harassed daily at his factory job in Connecticut by an Irish coworker who never left him "one day in peace," German-born Michael Bork finally blew up and threw a piece of iron at his tormentor. "If it'd been me," said his friend Martin Weitz, "I would have knocked the [Irish fellow] down, with those people you can't put up with any nonsense."[42]

Worshipping at the same Catholic Church and fighting side by side in the Union Army often did little to heal the cultural divide. In Catholic parishes, Irish and Germans battled over patron saints, liturgical practices, and the management of their congregations. The small, rural parish of Jackson County, Iowa, became so divided that the congregation insisted on having two separate boards of trustees—one German and the other Irish—and partitioning the cemetery into German and Irish sections.[43] The Union Army adopted a similar strategy, creating all German and all Irish units, a tactic which boosted morale within the groups but often widened cultural gaps. German American soldiers, proud of their German units and leaders, resented the slurs cast by Irish

American and "Yankee" soldiers who called them cowards and "panic-stricken Dutchmen," especially in the wake of the Union's devastating defeat at Chancellorsville in 1863, widely blamed on the "disgraceful flight of the flying Dutchmen."[44] Germans unfortunate enough to be stuck in multi-ethnic units often felt isolated. "I have very little contact with the others [in my regiment] who are mostly Irishmen of the most uncultivated class," wrote Gustav Keppler in 1864.[45]

But politics still had the potential to unite the foreign-born. Irish and Germans had managed to reach across the cultural divide in the past to fight "reforms" by native-born Protestant Americans and elect ethnic leaders sympathetic to the interests of the foreign-born. In Massachusetts, the law making naturalized citizens wait two years before they could vote had enraged not only Irish Americans, the law's immediate target, but also Germans throughout the United States. The law "strikes at the very root" of the "fundamental principle of the Republican party that all citizens had equal rights before the law without any distinction of color or birth," declared a group of German-born Republicans in Toledo, Ohio.[46] The expatriation crisis promised to bring the foreign-born together once again.

Before the Civil War, the loudest voices protesting about the "grasps of tyrants" abroad that turned naturalized citizenship into a "sham" had come from German, French, and even Spanish Americans, who challenged the right of their native sovereigns to demand their military service well after they had become American citizens.[47] Warren's case struck home for foreign-born Americans who, after the war, continued to run into trouble abroad—people like Simon Israel, who in the winter of 1866 begged Joseph A. Wright, U.S. minister to Prussia, to secure his release from the Prussian army. Israel had emigrated to America from Prussia in 1853 and, after becoming a naturalized citizen, returned to visit his family in 1863, only to be "seized by the authorities" and placed in the Prussian army in Stettin. The American consul reported that after two years' compulsory service, Israel "has . . . been made a cripple perhaps for the whole of his life" from injuries received during military drills, but the Prussian authorities insisted that Israel complete his full service "as punishment for having gone to America to evade the military service."[48] Or take the case of Frank (François) Pierre, an employee of the New England Glass Company in Boston, who after fifteen years' residence in the United States returned to his native France in 1866 on business and to visit his family. The French police arrested Pierre as he dined with his uncle, confiscated his naturalization papers, and threw him into prison, claiming he remained liable for military service.[49]

Other foreign-born Americans—especially German Americans—feared returning to their native countries yet could not escape the long arm of the state. George Striebg, who emigrated to the United States at age fourteen, considered himself an American by virtue of his military service during the Civil War. Yet the Bavarian government drafted Striebg into the Bavarian army in absentia when he turned twenty-one. The Bavarian government retaliated for Striebg's alleged desertion through his emigration to the United States by confiscating his father's property and closing his business. "The Bavarian government holds me as a citizen, holds my property, and probably would arrest me as a deserter should I ever set my foot in the place of my birth again," Striebg pleaded to Secretary of State William Henry Seward in February 1866. "Honorable sir, can anything be done in my case? . . . I do not know where I belong."[50]

Plaintive pleas for help turned into indignant demands as Warren's case ignited a political awakening among foreign-born Americans. "Are naturalized Americans, Americans?" the *Pilot* bitterly asked. In pressing Congress to clarify their status in law, foreign-born Americans were actually asking for much more. They sought recognition and acceptance from native-born Americans who had often doubted their allegiance, despite their sworn pledges, and treated them as second-class citizens. The rights of "adopted citizens" consisted only of "being able to vote, and help some great creature into office, picking up a crumb here and there themselves," grumbled the *Pilot*.[51] The expatriation crisis became nothing less than a referendum on the cultural and legal status of the naturalized citizen in America, an inquiry into what kind of "nation of immigrants" America would be.

If Germans and Irish fought bitter turf wars in their local communities, they could agree on one central point: they did not receive the respect they deserved from native-born Americans, despite all they had done to make the United States the great and powerful nation it had become by 1867. Who, after all, had built America—its cities, its railroads, its factories, its farms? Who had shed their blood on the "crimson field of battle" in the war to ensure the nation's survival? Immigrants, answered John Warren in his letter from prison. "By your industry, by your manual labor, by your intellect, by your capital, by your devotion, by your blood on the battle-field, you have . . . done more than any other class of citizens to raise your adopted country to the proud position which she holds to-day." It was the naturalized citizen, he argued, who proved most steadfast in support of American republican principles: "You are the faithful sentinels on the outpost, guarding with a jealous, with a vengeful eye the sacred approaches to republicanism and freedom."[52]

And it was the naturalized citizen who best represented the true spirit of American citizenship. Native-born citizens assumed they were "natural" Americans, born in the republic and bred to liberty, but foreign-born advocates of expatriation argued that birthplace had little to do with one's political allegiance.[53] The Irish born under British jurisdiction felt no allegiance to Britain; theirs was a "birthright of suffering." For the man born under oppressive regimes, "the instinct of naturalization is within his soul," and he seeks his natural political home, which may be oceans removed from where he was born.[54]

Having found their "natural political home" in America, the foreign-born and their American-born sons had fought to defend it, baptized as American citizens by the blood of the Civil War battlefields. Warren and "hundreds of other" Irish freedom fighters bore "the battle scars of the Republic on their breasts," wrote William Grace of the *Irish Republic*. German Americans had outpaced all other immigrant groups in their military service, many serving in German units led by German political exiles from 1848 such as Carl Schurz, Franz Sigel, and August Willich.[55] By joining in the war effort, "I wanted to show everyone who believes that you can only be a worthy citizen if you were born here, that we as Germans are also republicans," explained Willich, the beloved and respected commander of the all-German regiment from Indiana.[56]

Foreign-born Americans spoke reverently of their naturalization papers as "baptismal certificates" and their oaths of allegiance as evidence of their conversion from subjects to republican citizens.[57] When Republican canvassers challenged his citizenship—and right to vote—at a New York city polling station, one German American reportedly went home and returned with "a huge walnut-framed picture" containing his naturalization certificate and discharge from the army. An Irish American voter, when questioned, went further: unable to remove his naturalization certificate, which was "pasted fast" to a door, he unhinged the door and carried it to the polling place. He successfully cast his ballot, to the cheers of bystanders.[58] In such public displays, the naturalization certificate had almost magical properties, used to fend off those who insisted on referring to naturalized citizens as "foreigners"—proving, said the *Pilot*, that "we . . . act as part and parcel of the people of this republic . . . whose rights, duties, interests, and obligations are American," not "alien or foreign."[59]

The oath of allegiance loomed large in the foreign-born's narratives of naturalization—not surprising, perhaps, given the pervasive use of loyalty oaths during and after the Civil War to bind citizens to the nation. President Lincoln had offered amnesty and restoration of American citizenship to former Confederates if they declared their future loyalty to the Union. Federal "oath commissioners" had spread across the South to administer oaths of allegiances to former Confederates. White southerners might pledge their allegiance reluctantly, and perhaps cynically, but the oath nonetheless became the critical mechanism to restore them as citizens.[60] It was not unexpected, then, that naturalized Americans repeatedly focused on their oaths of allegiance as determinative of their status and evidence of their loyalty.[61]

"We are citizens twice over, by the law and by the sword, by adoption and by service, but our claims are now ignored," sang Private Miles O'Reilly, the fictional persona of General Charles G. Halpine, at a meeting of angry Irish American veterans on November 23, 1867, the lecture hall "packed as close as a sardine box." Singing underneath a large banner declaring "American Citizenship, the Panoply of Freedom—it must protect our People the world over," Halpine brought down the house with his new ballad, sung to the tune of the Irish nationalist standard "The Wearing of the Green." By January 1868, other foreign-born Americans had joined the refrain: "Protection in your Starry Flag / No longer can be found." It was time for Uncle Sam to step up and protect his adopted sons.[62]

Boisterous rallies erupted throughout the nation in the winter of 1868 as the Fenian battle cry ignited protests among a large swath of the foreign-born— German, French, Austrian, and Polish Americans, as well as Irish Americans. In an onslaught of resolutions and petitions, naturalized Americans demanded nothing less than a reconstruction program for the foreign-born, borrowing the potent language and logic of Radical Republicans.[63] They, too, were enslaved to their former "masters," the sovereigns of their native lands. They, too, demanded emancipation from their homelands, through the explicit legal guarantee of the right of expatriation. They, too, deserved "equal protection of the laws," to be treated the same as native-born citizens. Radical Republicans may not have claimed the cause of expatriation as their own, but they helped make it possible, providing the vocabulary and a political climate that placed citizenship and its rights at the forefront of the nation's agenda. "The same laws, the same duties—the same rights *for all!*" demanded Charles Munde, a German American doctor and journalist.[64] Sumner could not have said it any better.

9

This Is a White Man's Government!

FOREIGN-BORN activists spoke in broad strokes about equality and natural rights, typical of the Reconstruction Era, as they demanded "the same rights for all!" But the well-known political cartoonist Thomas Nast drew their dedication to equal rights into question in his bitter and devastating cartoon of 1868, "This Is a White Man's Government." Nast depicted an Irish American ape-man, wielding his shillelagh (his power to vote), and clasping hands with Nathan Bedford Forrest, representative of the unreconstructed and violent South, and August Belmont, international banker and the German American chair of the Democratic National Committee. All three keep a fallen African American soldier pinned to the ground beneath their feet as he reaches for the ballot box and the Colored Orphan Asylum burns in the background, a reminder of Irish Americans' role in the deadly draft riots of 1863.[1] Nast's cartoon captured Republicans' fury with foreign-born Democrats' alliance with the forces of illiberal politics but also exposes a perplexing juxtaposition. How do we reconcile the lofty speeches at the scores of expatriation rallies, pitching the naturalized citizen as the very model of American citizenship—as the "sentinels" guarding "republicanism and freedom"—with Nast's savage portrayal?[2]

The domestic debates on expatriation tested not just the nation's commitment to equality but that of foreign-born Americans as well. The right of expatriation—read broadly to encompass the right to choose one's physical and political home—had enormous potential appeal, reaching well beyond European men seeking to escape the grasp of their former sovereigns. Irish American women also flocked to the rallies demanding "rights of our citizens abroad," a visible reminder that women, too, were immigrants. Some had left

"This Is a White Man's Government" (1868). The caption of the cartoon by Thomas Nast continues: "'We regard the Reconstruction Acts (so called) of Congress as usurpations, and unconstitutional, revolutionary, and void'— Democratic Party Platform." Nast depicts Nathan Bedford Forrest (*center*), the infamous Confederate commander during the Fort Pillow massacre of black Union Army prisoners, clasping hands with August Belmont (*right*), German American banker and head of the Democratic National Committee, and an Irish American voter (*left*). Nast denounces the unholy alliance between the foreign-born and the violent, unreconstructed South that keeps African Americans pinned down.

their native lands involuntarily, dragged by their husbands or fathers to new, unfamiliar homes in the United States, while others paved the way for their families, embracing emigration as an opportunity to expand their options and secure the economic stability of their families. Rallies on the Pacific Coast probably included few, if any, Chinese immigrants, but young Chinese men were arriving by the thousands in the American West, defying their emperor's ban on emigration to find work that promised brighter economic futures.[3]

Native-born Americans, especially those who experienced precious little choice over where they lived or their political allegiance, could find the ideals of voluntary expatriation just as intoxicating. "Are we aliens, because we are women?" Angelina Grimké had asked in 1838. "Are we bereft of citizenship, because we are mothers, wives, and daughters of a mighty people? Have women *no* country?" These questions lay unanswered in 1868, Susan B. Anthony and Elizabeth Cady Stanton reminded their country, as women still lay under the legal cloak of "coverture," their domicile and political allegiance determined by their husbands and fathers.[4] Native Americans did not have to read Emer de Vattel's treatises on international law or Fenian tracts to appreciate the importance of "volitional allegiance" and freedom of movement, their repeated involuntary removal from their homes to reservations having brought those lessons home. As the U.S. government sought once again to clear Indians from their land to make way for a new onslaught of white Western expansion after the Civil War, the Ho-Chunk leader Dandy appealed to American citizenship and the "inalienable rights of men" to resist his band's removal in Wisconsin and to secure the freedom to live where they wanted.[5]

African Americans also embraced the spirit underlying voluntary expatriation, especially in light of their limited mobility and "self-ownership" before the Civil War, even for free blacks. Freedom had often come at the price of involuntary expulsion of African Americans from their homes, several states—both southern and northern—banishing freed slaves from their borders and the American Colonization Society pressuring freed slaves to "return" to Africa. In light of that history, the "right of locomotion"—the freedom to go where one wanted and to be recognized as American citizens—was no small matter. No group, perhaps, appreciated the right to leave more than emancipated slaves after the Civil War. Leaving the plantation and their former owners was often the first declaration of independence for freed blacks, who took off to find lost loved ones and friends separated by slavery, to seek new jobs in nearby towns, or even just to experience the joy of going wherever they wanted. Some joined the black exodus to the West, settling in Kansas. A few moved even farther to shake slavery off their feet: Elias Hill and 167 other freedpeople exercised their right of expatriation and left South Carolina for Liberia in 1871.[6]

None of these groups—women, Chinese immigrants, Native Americans, African Americans—came to mind for the advocates of the "right of expatriation," but as they moved from town to town, across the Atlantic, or across the Pacific they repeatedly asserted, with their feet if not their words, their right to leave and join others seeking economic, social, and political freedom. Whether the right to choose one's home and political allegiance would be truly universal, escaping the boundaries of race and gender, remained to be seen. The Reconstruction era raised expectations and hopes for the dawning of a "new birth of freedom" but all too often, commitments to full equality fell far short of the high-sounding ideals.[7] Foreign-born Americans would prove no more consistent than many other Americans who demanded equality, only to deny it to others. No one, perhaps, illustrated both the promises and limits of the foreign-born Americans' campaign for equal rights more than the Fenians' favorite speaker: the flamboyant and rabidly racist George Francis Train.

WHEN PATRICK Donahoe, editor of the Boston *Pilot,* took charge of organizing a fund-raiser in Boston for John Warren's family, he naturally turned to George Francis Train, "one of the best known men in the world" and one of the Fenians' most popular supporters. "It is by no means an easy matter to describe either the man or his manner," the Colorado *Tribune* said of Train in November 1867. Whether an "eccentric genius" or a "crack-brained harlequin and semi-lunatic," Train was a larger-than-life character whose "superabundant vitality" bordered on the manic. Train gained prominence first as an entrepreneur who, according to his own extraordinary memoir, pulled himself up by his bootstraps, having "supported [my]self since babyhood." By the age of twenty, Train had become the business partner of his older cousin Enoch Train, founder of the White Diamond shipping line, which carried goods and immigrants—mostly Irish—between Liverpool and Boston on his packet ships. The shipping business failed to satisfy George Train's entrepreneurial energy, and he spent the 1850s dashing through the American West, Australia, Asia, and England, organizing various speculative ventures, including the notorious Credit Mobilier, created to finance the Union Pacific's transcontinental railroad. By 1867, at the age of thirty-eight, Train had earned a fortune from his ventures but he professed to have "never given a thought to the mere details of money," reveling instead in promoting big ideas and big ventures, the more grandiose the better.[8]

Train's "principal amusement is delivering orations," said the Boston *Daily Advertiser.*[9] Train loved audiences and audiences loved him, partly because he said the most outlandish things. Dressed in an eye-catching, form-fitting blue coat with brass buttons, black pants, black patent-leather shoes, and lavender kid gloves, Train gave a dazzling performance. "He came! He saw! He conquered!" crowed the Lawrence *State Journal,* reporting on one of Train's many speeches in 1867. Even his critics—and he had many, who deplored his "total absence of both decency and common sense" and claimed he was "afflicted with diarrhea of words"—acknowledged that Train had "great influence" over his listeners. His ability to draw crowds and the press made Train a popular figure on the lecture circuit for causes seeking a spotlight. In 1867 Train devoted his powerful oratorical skills to two movements—the woman suffrage movement and the Fenian Brotherhood. Susan B. Anthony and Elizabeth Cady Stanton, feeling abandoned by their former political allies, the abolitionists and Republicans who shelved the cause of woman suffrage until black men secured the vote, accepted Train's offer to speak on their behalf. They hoped the flashy Train would bring much-needed attention to their cause and attract new supporters, especially Irish Democrats.[10]

When Donahoe asked Train to speak at Warren's rally, Train was still stumping for woman suffrage, but enthusiastically agreed to come to Boston. "Turn out by thousands for the benefit of the family of brave John Warren," Train exhorted Boston's Irish Americans in a letter advertising his upcoming lecture in the *Pilot.* "That night I will make a political speech that will shake New England to its centre, and make *old* England read the letters of the 'Handwriting on the Wall.'"[11] Turn out by the thousands they did. Boston's Irish "filled Tremont Temple from hall to dome," on December 18, 1867, paying twenty-five cents to hear their "long-lifed friend" and show their sympathy for Warren. Train did not disappoint, entertaining the cheering crowd for two and a half hours with his free-flowing diatribes against England, Adams, Seward, and the Republicans. "The time for talk [is] past," Train declared. "Seward is lost in a swamp of diplomacy! . . . Charles Francis Adams dines and wines with the British minister while American citizens are hung in Manchester, and are dying in Irish jails!"[12] Settling "the Fenian question" did not have to be so difficult. "Here is a new idea," proclaimed Train. "Let us offer to buy Ireland for the Alabama claims (loud cheers). All in favor say Aye." The resolution passed as the audience shouted aye. Having resolved the question of Irish independence and the *Alabama* claims, Train turned to his favorite pastime: bashing Republicans and their Reconstruction program.

"Where is Charles Sumner" while "poor Captain Warren is wearing his life out in an Irish jail?" asked Train. "Where are your members of Congress?" In reply, Train used a prop, "one of the new Christmas toys, representing a negro dancing." As he asked each question, Train touched the board of the toy "and Sambo would jump while the audience would roar with laughter." Train continued to lay a host of Boston's ills at the feet of African Americans:

> Why are your wharves deserted—no ships, no steamers . . . ? (Sambo becomes wild with jumping and the audience as wild with laughter.) Why is the consolidation of your roads no use to you in getting back the Western trade? (Mr. Train makes the nig dance a new jig, and the audience were convulsed with laughter.) . . . Why are the negroes pouring into a climate not adapted to them, crowding you out of the field? (More dancing.) . . . Why are there no emigrant ships coming here? (Sambo jumps with delight.)[13]

Lawmakers, "as usual, moaning and groaning over the Blacks," left the "white men" to fend for themselves. Turning Justice Taney's infamous line from the *Dred Scott* decision on its head, Train declared: "White men are not citizens! Irishmen have no rights your Congressional delegation are bound to respect!"[14] Train only stopped the "dancing Sambo" tirade when a voice from the audience asked, "What about woman in Kansas?," prompting Train to shift his attention to woman suffrage ("Let a million Irish girls vote!").

Train went on to a host of issues, including currency ("Down with gold and up with greenbacks!") and the possible candidacy of General Ulysses S. Grant for president ("Training for the White House . . . since Shiloh"), while a news reporter struggled to keep up. Train "talks about seven columns an hour," said the reporter, apologizing for how "meagre must be our report," given the limited space of the paper. As Train finally drew to a close, the audience rose with loud cheers and applause, hundreds reaching out to shake his hand as he left the hall. "It was a grand demonstration," the *Pilot* concluded, "and will be long remembered in Boston."

IT'S WORTH pausing to ponder what the audience took away from Train's talk, what exactly they would remember, and what his speeches tell us about the political climate in which the debates over expatriation would unfold. Train dazzled his audiences, but even he worried "the moment they got out of my reach, they got away from me."[15] He hoped, no doubt, that they would leave persuaded by his pitch for woman suffrage—and few would forget his repeated, scathing indictments of the administration and Republican legislators. But, if they recalled anything, his listeners were bound to remember "the dancing of the Negro," the Boston *Advertiser* reporting disapprovingly that "the principal portion of the lecture was devoted to . . . denunciations of the 'nigger' mania of Sumner, Wilson, Banks, and other public men," all of which "created immense applause."[16]

Train's provocative speech aptly illustrated abolitionist William Lloyd Garrison's charge that "the colored people and their advocates have not a more abusive assailant" than Train, who, especially "when he has an Irish audience before him, . . . delights to ring the changes upon the 'nigger,' 'nigger,' 'nigger,' *ad nauseum*."[17] Yet, Train was hardly alone in his race-baiting. The Democratic Party racked up gains in several northern states in the fall of 1867 on the promise to protect "white supremacy" against the "insults" of "black equality," and Democratic leaders hoped to win the presidency in 1868 using the same tactics. "Our position must be condemnation and reversal of negro supremacy," wrote the prominent New York Democrat Samuel J. Tilden. The "race question" would be the winning issue, he predicted, appealing not only "to all the workingmen" and "the young men just becoming voters" but also "to the adopted citizens—whether Irish or Germans."[18]

Train and the Democratic Party leadership harped on race, in part because they thought it would sell, especially to naturalized citizens. But were they right? And if so, why? After all, Fenians often pitched the Irish nationalist cause as part of a broader global struggle for human freedom and dignity. In their numerous letters and speeches, the *Jacmel* prisoners may have called themselves the "slaves" of England, bound by the "slavish" doctrine of perpetual allegiance, but they did not descend to racist arguments or anchor their claims for United States citizenship in their status as white men.[19] In fact, Warren and Nagle were among those rare Irish Americans who joined the Republican rather than the Democratic Party.[20] In a letter to Seward in 1856, Nagle had railed against his fellow Irish Americans for supporting a "party pledged to the extension of Slavery." He praised the election of Lincoln in November 1860 as setting forth the "true issue before this nation; whether this government was instituted for the propagation of Slavery or the spread of Liberty; for the benefit of the whole human family or the building up and sustaining of a tyrannical and usurping aristocracy."[21] Even more German Americans threw their support behind the Republican Party and the cause of emancipation. Embracing the Civil War as "a war of sacred principles," German-born Republicans were among the strongest supporters of Radical Reconstruction policies at war's end.[22] Still, Train's racialized appeals at Warren's rally drew "tremendous applause," suggesting that few in that Irish American audience would be likely recruits for interracial or Republican alliances.

Republicans made an effort to woo the immigrant vote from the Democratic Party, especially in the heated elections during Reconstruction, but they remained profoundly ambivalent about the foreign-born. The Republican Party welcomed immigrants wholeheartedly—at least, as laborers to expand the nation's economic might. After the Civil War, commercial interests gleefully counted dollar signs as well over half a million immigrants arrived at American ports in 1866 and 1867, numbers not seen since the high tide of immigration in 1854. Friedrich Kapp, a German-born member of the New York Board of the Commissioners of Emigration, went to some lengths to estimate the "capital value" of immigrants. Kapp estimated that it cost the United States $1,500— for food, clothing, shelter, and education—to raise an American boy for eventual occupation as a farmer or unskilled laborer. The American girl cost less to produce, approximately $750, because "she becomes useful to the household at an earlier age." Most immigrants, however, arrived as young adults, at the peak of their productive capacity, their home countries having borne all of the expense of "producing" future workers for the United States. Immigration, in Kapp's formula, added up financially: the United States gained more than $400 million a year, and more than $1 million a day, based on the post–Civil War levels of immigration of over 300,000 arrivals a year. No wonder the pro-business Republican editor of the *New York Times* declared, "Let them all come. We have plenty of room for them and for many millions more."[23]

If only the foreign-born would behave and vote the right way, the Republicans raising as their model men like Carl Schurz, the Prussian political exile and antislavery advocate who would become the first German American to be elected to the U.S. Senate in 1868 (as a Republican, of course).[24] But the Democratic Party continued to pull many immigrants to its ranks, fueling Republican anxiety and distrust of the foreign-born, and of the naturalization process. The "conversion of an alien into a citizen" was a "hasty, trifling, fraudulent, and farcical" process, argued Charles A. Page, the United States consul in Zurich, not the "well-considered, well-guarded, weighty and solemn thing it ought to be."[25] When Republicans fared poorly in the 1867 elections in

New York City, they blamed "gigantic and frightful frauds" perpetuated by corrupt naturalization judges and Democratic political machines. The *New York Tribune* estimated that 20,000 voters, relying on false naturalization papers, had registered to vote illegally, bolstering the Democratic Party and threatening to derail the Republican Reconstruction agenda.[26] Republican leaders eyed the coming election of 1868 warily, and with good reason. Tammany Hall, the Democratic Party machine in New York, busily printed thousands of naturalization applications and certificates, paid court fees, and provided witnesses for immigrants—churning out 41,112 newly naturalized voters in New York City by the end of the year.[27]

If swearing an oath transformed immigrants legally into American citizens, critics worried that the naturalization process left them personally unchanged. The foreign-born swore false allegiance, complained the *Brooklyn Union* in the summer of 1867, pledging to become Americans but remaining German, French, or Irish in their hearts. Contrary to the hopes that the Union Army would be a "wonderful school for instilling American ideas [and] sentiments" in foreign-born Americans, the *Brooklyn Union* claimed a new "German spirit" had arisen instead after the war. German immigrants created vibrant communities tied together by their common language, countless German associations, a flourishing German-language press, German-language churches, and German-language parochial schools. German Americans often reconciled their love for Germany and America with the well-known saying "I love Germany as my mother, America is my bride." But to outsiders, distinctive German communities often seemed clannish and "un-American."[28] The Irishman was worse. He "owes an allegiance which is not mentioned in his oath, which he never renounces"—his allegiance to Ireland. "Irish Americans should make up their minds to turn Americans *bona fide*, . . . become useful citizens of the United States, and let the green island drift," lectured Charles Francis Adams.[29]

The Know-Nothingism of the 1850s had died down, but its prejudices lingered on, popping up in cartoon portrayals of Irish as apes and snide comments about the "Irish character." "The Irish does little to elevate himself," wrote a "Veteran Observer" in the *New York Times*. "He reads little and studies less. Generally he is a digger of ditches and maker of railroads." Anti-Catholic sentiments lost some of their prewar punch but constantly resurfaced, especially as Republicans sought to explain Irish Americans' resistance to their Reconstruction programs or to justify black suffrage. The Reverend Mr. King in his 1867 Thanksgiving Day sermon to his Methodist congregation in Fall River, Massachusetts, preached that the Irish "are morally and intellectually less qualified to exercise the elective franchise than the negro," or, as his Irish critics read it, "a nigger was better than an Irishman." Trotting out well-worn arguments, King cast doubt on Irish Catholic men's independence of thought, calling them a "class of men who have no *comprehension* of republican principles, who possess no single element of self-government," as the Pope in Rome controlled what they thought and did.[30] George Marsh, U.S. minister in Italy, went further, blaming "Irish and German-Catholic influence" for the perpetuation of slavery and, indeed, the Civil War itself. If not for foreign-born Catholics, "slavery would long since have died a natural death, and we should have been spared the crimes and the curses of the late rebellion."[31]

Stupid, bigoted, lazy, violent, animalistic, uneducated, puppets of Rome— such stereotypes of the Irish abounded, especially among Protestant, middle-class, native-born Americans. "They never speak of you, except insultingly," Train said. "No more sneers against the Irish," he declared, a sentiment that must have struck a chord with many Irish Americans who deeply resented Nast's "mean caricature" of Irish as apes and any suggestion that Irish Americans were anything less than fully American. Most especially, the Republicans' insinuations that Irish Americans had been disloyal and unpatriotic, ignoring their valiant service in the Civil War, sparked bitter resentment.[32] If the Irish had largely rejected the Republican Party, said the *Pilot*, "they have never given their votes against republicanism." "There is no Irishman stupid enough" to believe that "republicanism and the Republican Party are identical."[33]

Yet, there was little doubt that many Irish Americans, with some significant exceptions, embraced the "white supremacy" platform of the Democratic Party.[34] Perhaps nothing rankled more than the Republicans' claim that blacks were not only the equals of but better than Irish Americans. The Radicals "hold up the negro as our superior," scoffed the *Pilot*, a proposition Irish Americans viewed with alarm and disgust as eroding the color line.[35] The Irish may have been the diggers of ditches, the makers of railroads and canals, the nursemaids and servants of wealthy Americans. They may have occupied the bottom rung of the economic ladder—often taking jobs once held by African Americans. But at least they were white in a world where race mattered. Whiteness conferred a "psychological wage," wrote the black historian W. E. B. Du Bois, offering even the despised Irish the benefits of higher social status and access to public spaces. Economically, the bonus of being white translated into higher wages and access to a greater range of jobs, even though employers discriminated routinely among ethnic groups and by sex.[36]

Perhaps most important, whiteness critically shaped what it meant to be a citizen in the United States. Only "free white persons" could become naturalized citizens under American law. With citizenship came a host of rights—to vote, serve on juries, hold political office, own property—often limited by law or by practice to white men. And with voting came patronage, landing Irish American companies construction contracts and individual men jobs on the public payroll, ranging from maintenance workers to police officers to inspectors in the Customs House. If race distinctions fell, what would become of Irish Americans and their tenuous status—gained largely through their color—in the United States?[37] Train voiced that anxiety in one of his rhymes: "In freeing the Blacks, have we enslaved the Whites, / and lost forever our manhood's rights?"[38]

German Americans worried less about declaring their whiteness to other Americans. Yet they, too, resented the attention they thought Republicans gave to African Americans at the expense of the foreign-born.[39] "Is it right," asked German American doctor and journalist Charles R. Munde, "that the educated German, who shed his blood for the union and for the abolition of slavery, should stand beneath the ignorant negro, whom he helped to liberate from bondage?"[40] While German American Republicans spoke passionately about equal rights, they often supported black equality more in the abstract than in practice, voting down state referenda on black suffrage even as they cheered speeches condemning racial discrimination. In Missouri, the new state constitution of 1865 denied black men the vote but extended suffrage to "declarant" aliens—those who had declared their intention to become American citizens. Germans arrived in the United States "ready to be full citizens," argued the German American press. But African Americans, emerging from slavery, required training and preparation before they could be full citizens with voting privileges.[41]

Democratic politicians hammered the point home: African Americans were more "alien" than European immigrants and should be incorporated into the polity more slowly, if at all. As the expatriation crisis heated up early in 1868, the Democratic Party warned that as the Republicans stood ready to grant black men suffrage, they might also strip foreign-born Americans of their right to vote and all the perks and status that came with it. Samuel J. Tilden, who would go on to be the Democratic presidential candidate in the fateful election of 1876, courted the European-born in March 1868, appealing unabashedly to racist fears of miscegenation. The test for admission into the polity should be the same as for admission into the family, argued Tilden: American whites should exclude from citizenship all races—the Chinese, Native Americans, African Americans—that they would refuse to accept into their family by marriage. White European immigrants "enter the American family without the slightest repugnance on either side," arriving on America's shores practically "a native here almost immediately." But the freedmen, even if their roots in America reached back for generations, might still be "aliens."[42]

President Johnson had drawn on a similar rationale in vetoing the Civil Rights Act of 1866. Far from achieving "perfect equality," Johnson protested, Congress perpetuated racial discrimination—against whites. The act provided freedmen a fast track to citizenship, Johnson argued, allowing them to leapfrog over European immigrants, whom he saw as clearly more qualified for citizenship. The government had always required "persons who are strangers . . . and unfamiliar with our institutions and laws" to "pass through a certain probation," Johnson observed. African Americans may have been born in the United States, but they remained "strangers" in Johnson's eyes, more foreign than "large numbers of intelligent, worthy and patriotic" immigrants who arrived from Europe to "make our land their home." At the very least, Johnson implied, blacks should have to go through the same probationary process as foreigners, proving their fitness for citizenship.[43]

Race remained threaded throughout the claims for the rights of the foreign-born, even if Warren and his colleagues did not frame their demands as white men. Race had been so critical to how citizenship was structured and deployed, and so central to the Reconstruction-era debates on citizenship, that it was impossible to think about questions of allegiance and the "natural and inherent right of all people" to the right of expatriation without seeing race. Foreign-born Americans reached for slavery analogies in describing their own bondage to their native countries because African slaves, and the ambiguous status of free blacks, provided the antithesis of liberal citizenship. Slaves and free African Americans before the war lacked the legal selfhood, the volition to choose, the ability to declare one's allegiance, the power to demand government protection—all of which defined citizenship. Train was not the only commentator to turn to *Dred Scott* to describe the ambiguous status of foreign-born Americans, comparing them to fugitive slaves. If America did not challenge Warren's conviction and bowed to the British rule of perpetual allegiance, claimed the *Irishman* in Dublin, "she puts a halter round the neck of all her adopted citizens, German, French, Italian, British or Irish. . . . The adopted citizen, like [the captured negro runaway], will have no right which his master is bound to respect."[44] Advocates of the right of expatriation, though they used broad universal language, took the white European as their model claimant.[45]

OR, MORE PRECISELY, they took white European *men* as their standard. Gender, too, structured American citizenship, as Susan B. Anthony and Elizabeth Cady Stanton tirelessly argued. Women became citizens of the United States in the nineteenth century, but rarely by choice. Where they were born or whom they married most often determined their political status.[46]

Consider the women in John Warren's family. Joanna Madigan married John probably around 1855, when she was about nineteen years old.[47] When John became a naturalized citizen in 1866, Joanna became a citizen, too, without doing a thing. Joanna signed no papers, swore no oaths of allegiance, appeared before no judge or official to declare her intent to become a citizen. The only oath that Joanna swore was her wedding vow when she married John. That was enough, under the Naturalization Act of 1855, to carry her over the threshold into citizenship. As long as they met the essential requirement for naturalization—being a "free white person"—all foreign-born women became citizens when they married naturalized or native-born American men or when their husbands became naturalized. But Joanna, as a married woman, could not have decided to naturalize on her own, at least not after the 1855 act became law. Only John could determine the family's nationality.[48]

Perhaps John consulted with Joanna before he naturalized and, with a stroke of a pen, changed her nationality as well as his. But it probably did not occur to him to ask, nor did he need her consent. If she had protested, it would probably have done no good. Jane Brand, also from Ireland, married an American citizen in New Orleans; widowed in 1849, before the 1855 law was passed, Brand declared "she never in any manner adopted his nationality," insisting she remained a British subject. Elise Lebret married Pierre, both French at the time, in New Orleans but protested she never agreed to give up her French citizenship when Pierre naturalized in 1840, and she appeared before the French consul twice to declare her desire to remain French. What Brand and Lebret wanted proved irrelevant to legal officials, who found their husbands' decision to naturalize bound their foreign-born wives to American citizenship.[49] "The husband, as the head of the family, is to be considered its political representative," a federal judge later intoned, and "the wife and minor children owe their allegiance to the same sovereign power."

Here lay a paradox: American naturalization and the celebrated doctrine of expatriation rested on volitional allegiance, a concept that touted the natural right of all persons to choose their political homes, yet American law tied married foreign-born women to their husbands' political choices. Policymakers saw nothing compulsory or contradictory in the Act of 1855, seeing the law as a humane measure to protect women from statelessness and ensure the unity of American families. Legislators simply brought American law in line with that of European nations, following a rule that, in their opinion, made good sense for both the governments and women citizens.[50]

The law was not surprising given married women's status under the common-law concept of "coverture," which similarly treated the family as a unit under the husband's control. A single woman (*feme sole*) could make contracts, own property, sue in court, and naturalize, but upon marriage, she (now a *feme covert*) yielded those rights—and more—to her husband, who exercised them on her behalf. The woman experienced "civil death," "covered" by her husband's protective arm and no longer an independent legal agent in her own right. Early feminists, including Stanton, targeted coverture as critical to man's ability to wield "absolute tyranny" over women in the Declaration of Sentiments issued at Seneca Falls, New York, in 1848.[51] By 1855, when the marital naturalization act was passed, coverture had begun to crumble, but the marital naturalization act shored it up under the guise of protecting foreign-born women.[52]

Not all women were married and thereby bound by their husband's choices. John's daughter, Eliza, born in Massachusetts in 1861, automatically became an American citizen by virtue of her birth in the jurisdiction, a privilege that the Fourteenth Amendment secured for African American women as well by 1868. Most courts held that native-born women who married foreigners did not lose their American citizenship. John's sister Anastatia who never married, and his widowed mother, Mary Canty Warren, both immigrated to Massachusetts and had the option to become naturalized citizens in their own right.[53] How many immigrant women availed themselves of this right is very difficult to pin down without more in-depth studies of local court records. But this much is certain: neither the local political party organizations that created the "naturalization mills" to recruit foreign-born men as voters nor the federal government courted women as citizens. In 1870, when census takers dutifully recorded the citizenship status of the nation's inhabitants, they were told to count only male citizens over the age of twenty-one. Women did not "count" as citizens because they did not have the right to vote, the main distinguishing factor, aside from military service, that made one an asset in the polity.[54]

Foreign-born women might still engage in nationalist politics, the Fenian Sisterhood often outstripping men in generous donations of their hard-earned money to the Fenian cause and insisting on having a voice on how it was spent. "We are not raising money for a church, or a school house," but "to sustain a revolution that will free our country," declared Ellen A. Mahony, leader of the Sisterhood. But, while Irish American men welcomed their "sisters'" dollars and fund-raising bazaars, they resisted Train's plea to extend equal rights to women. The *Irishman* in Dublin reported disapprovingly on the emerging woman suffrage campaign in Dublin and London, saying the women's time would be better spent working for "something . . . higher," such as the relief of Irish political prisoners.[55] In German American circles, German American feminist and "Forty-Eighter" Mathilde Franziska Anneke did her best to persuade her radical countrymen to extend their grand "freedom-loving" principles to women. But to no avail. Even the most radical of German American Republicans opposed women's rights, viewing woman suffrage as a direct challenge to German culture.[56]

When the U.S. minister at Berlin, Joseph Wright, spoke in 1866 of the "principle of naturalization as a natural and inherent right of manhood," he likely thought he was speaking in generic terms. The Declaration of Independence, after all, took as its starting point that "all *men* are created equal," "men" serving as the common reference point for human beings. But, as Stanton and Anthony argued, gendered language mattered, revealing assumptions about who constituted the polity and who bore rights that all needed to respect. Recall that when Henry Raymond, congressional representative and editor of the *New York Times,* defended the birthright citizenship provision in the Civil Rights Act of 1866, he said: "Make the colored man a citizen . . . and he has a defined *status;* he has a country and a home, a right to defend himself and his wife and children." African American women, too, became citizens by virtue of the Civil Rights Act and the Fourteenth Amendment, but few noticed the transformative effect of their new status. Citizenship remained the domain of men, whether native-born or foreign-born, even if masked by the slogan "equal rights for all."

Foreign-born men, when they demanded equal rights, invoked masculine narratives of allegiance and mutual obligation. They recalled their sacred oaths of allegiance, their service in the military, their pride in joining the polity. They spoke of their emasculation—the loss of "manhood rights"—when the doctrine of perpetual allegiance hampered their ability to move freely in the world, to seek better homes and jobs to support their families. And they demanded that the United States "be a man" and defend the country's honor and those under its protection, which in turn would allow male citizens to take their rightful places in the household.[57]

IN THE END, it is difficult to conclude what Train's audience took away from his speech, but one theme clearly struck home for thousands of foreign-born American men: they had been left out of the era's reconstruction of citizenship. Foreign-born men deserved at least as much attention as Congress was now giving to reconstructing the South, argued William H. Grace of the *Irish Republic*, a pro-Republican newspaper. "We want a bold and decisive measure that will let the monarchs of Europe know without a doubt" that the United States would protect the "rights of all . . . who have been baptised in the temple of the Republic," he wrote. England's doctrine "'once a subject always a subject' *must be squelched by the pen if she will, but the Cannon if we must.*" It was time for Congress to act. It was time for the nation to answer yes, boldly and force-fully, to the question: Were naturalized Americans citizens, or were they not?[58]

10

The Politics of Expatriation

"WHAT IS to be done with Nagle and the other Jackmels?" asked the annoyed
Irish attorney general, Robert Warren, in March 1868. He longed to be rid of
them. As Warren and Costello began their long prison sentences and Americans
debated the parameters of citizenship, the rest of the *Jacmel* crew still waited in
Dublin jails. The attorney general had decided to prosecute eight men, including
Nagle, in Sligo at the end of February, but moving them to Sligo too soon seemed
risky. England and Ireland remained on edge in the wake of the uproar over
the Manchester executions and, more recently, the Clerkenwell explosion, in
which Fenians detonated a barrel of gunpowder at Clerkenwell Prison in
England to free one of their imprisoned leaders. The "terrific explosion" blew
out windows, toppled buildings, and killed seven local residents, including eight-
year-old Minnie Julia Abbott.[1]

Adams reported widespread panic and growing government surveillance
in England in late December 1867. British ships patrolled harbors, on the lookout
for Fenian war boats and saboteurs. Americans arriving at Queenstown un-
derwent rigorous searches. British inspectors, dressed like "flushers," de-
scended into the stinking sewers near Buckingham Palace, wading through
two feet of sewage to look for possible explosive devices.[2] And British authorities
struck at the Irish nationalist press, convicting A. M. Sullivan, editor of the
Nation and the *Weekly News* (as well as *Speeches from the Dock*), and Richard
Pigott, editor of the *Irishman,* of seditious libel for their coverage of the Fenian
movement and trials, widely reprinted in the United States.[3] Worrying about a
possible rescue effort to free the *Jacmel* men, Edward Cooper, one of the largest
landlords in Sligo and a member of Parliament, cautioned against bringing the
Jacmel prisoners to Sligo "any sooner than is absolutely necessary."[4]

Yet even with the crackdown, British officials remained keenly aware that Americans watched from afar, ever ready to find fault. Seward sent a dispatch to Adams on January 13, 1868, that crackled with impatience. "The trial of John Warren . . . has awakened a general feeling of resentment and deeply wounded our pride of sovereignty," he cautioned. "The people are appealing to this government throughout the whole country, Portland to San Francisco and from St. Paul to Pensacola." Seward had repeatedly warned the British of the importance of "eliminating . . . Fenian excitement" if the United States and England were ever to mend their troubled relations. But the British insisted on stirring the pot of "irritation and jealousy" with their contempt for American citizens. Now the matter of expatriation lay before Congress, beyond Seward's control. Perhaps, said Seward in a barely disguised threat, after "this popular protest" has worked its way through Congress, the British would be more willing to come to terms and restore "cordial and friendly relations."[5]

In England as well as the United States, expatriation and allegiance had become the "problems of the hour" by the winter of 1868.[6]

UNDER THREAT of impeachment and anticipating a showdown with Congress, President Andrew Johnson in December 1867 took a momentary break from denouncing Republicans for their legislative excesses and punitive policies in the South to request that Congress resolve the "embarrassing conflict of laws" that had arisen in the Fenian trials. Johnson encouraged Congress to remove any ambiguity and expressly declare expatriation to be national law.[7] By the end of 1867, even the mainstream press had been swept up in the campaign for more explicit protections of expatriation, though it took care to distance itself from the "Fenian folly." The "monstrous monarchical assumption" of "once a subject, always a subject" was outdated and a threat to American interests, argued the editor of *Frank Leslie's Illustrated Newspaper*. As "the centre of immigration" in the world, with a significant proportion of its population "made up of adopted citizens" and mass migration showing only signs of increasing, "it has become indispensable for us, as a great nation, to have this right recognized."[8] Failure of the government to act, warned the foreign-born, would be not only unjust but also "highly impolitic." The *Pilot* threatened that "politicians who are shaky on the subject, if they value their places and popularity, had better act promptly."[9]

Congress got the message. Keenly aware of the upcoming presidential election in the fall, representatives and senators scrambled to introduce resolutions,

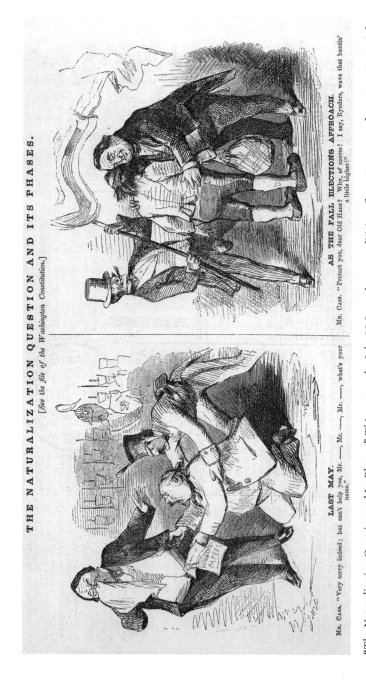

THE NATURALIZATION QUESTION AND ITS PHASES.

[See the file of the *Washington Constitution*.]

LAST MAY.

Mr. Cass. "Very sorry indeed; but can't help you, Mr. ——, Mr. ——, Mr. ——, what's your name."

AS THE FALL ELECTIONS APPROACH.

Mr. Cass. "Protect you, dear Old Hans? Why, of course! I say, Rynders, wave that buntin' a little higher!"

"The Naturalization Question and Its Phases." This cartoon by John McLean skewers politicians (here, Secretary of State Lewis Cass) for their fickle positions on expatriation. As elections drew closer, politicians such as Cass became more enthusiastic about protecting the foreign-born from their former governments.

each wanting to show he had done his part to protect naturalized Americans abroad. So many resolutions, all more or less the same, rained down on Congress that when yet another representative rose to introduce his, Representative Henry L. Dawes protested, "I object. We have had enough of the Fenians." But his objection could barely be heard above the clamor of the political parties competing for foreign-born support.[10]

No one, perhaps, held his finger to the political winds more than Nathaniel P. Banks, author of the bill that eventually became the Expatriation Act of 1868. A Republican congressional representative from Massachusetts and chair of the House Committee on Foreign Affairs, Banks seemed to have much in common with his counterpart in the Senate, Charles Sumner. Both hailed from Warren's home state, both were Republicans, and both held leadership positions in their respective chambers as the head of Committees on Foreign Relations. But there the resemblance ended. Sumner disdained politicking, even if he engaged in it when necessary; Banks embraced politics as a career, viewing it as a way to move up the social ladder. Sumner was unyielding in matters of principle, even if it meant making enemies; Banks compromised a great deal. His biographer calls him a "pragmatic politician" with a "talent for accommodation," but Banks's contemporaries, especially those in Sumner's circles, were less kind, denouncing him as a "charlatan," "demagogue," and "political quack."[11]

Banks had not always been held in such contempt. Elected first to the Massachusetts legislature in 1848, he landed in the House of Representatives in 1854, became Speaker of the House in 1855, and was elected governor of Massachusetts in 1858. By 1860, his name even circulated as a possible candidate for the presidency, and he had become one of Lincoln's "political generals" in the Civil War—not bad for "the bobbin boy" of Waltham who had left school at the age of fourteen to work with his father, a skilled laborer, at the Boston Manufacturing Company's textile mill. Perhaps most important to his future political career, Nat could deliver a speech at the drop of a hat. Even as a boy, Nat always had a speech "at his tongue's end, which would roll off, at his bidding, as easily as thread unwinds from a spool," and fill his audience "with surprise and wonder."[12]

But some critics thought Banks's words flowed far too easily and shifted with the political moment. Banks trimmed his political sails as he navigated the turbulent party politics of the 1850s, seeking the course that would keep him in office. He changed political allegiances frequently, beginning as a Jacksonian Democrat before joining, in succession, the Free Soil Party, the American

Party, and the Republican Party. While he never completely abandoned certain core principles—antislavery, for example—he proved more than ready to compromise on them, searching for a middle ground and his own political survival.[13]

Critics saw Banks's enthusiastic embrace of the Fenian cause as proof of his flexible principles. Though drawn to the American Party primarily for its antislavery sentiments, Banks rang the nativist alarm about the "swelling tide of emigration" and the divided allegiances of Catholic Americans when elected to Congress as a Know-Nothing in 1854. As governor of Massachusetts, he supported more restrictive naturalization laws to stop the "irresponsible creation of voters on the eve of election."[14] Yet by the end of the Civil War, Banks had repositioned himself as the champion of immigrants and the Irish cause, trying to woo them into the Republican Party. When the federal government arrested Fenians for violating American neutrality after their failed invasion of Canada, Banks pushed a new law through the House of Representatives to relax the definition of neutrality and reduce penalties for its violation. "He undoubtedly was striving for Fenian votes," sniped a critic, and Sumner quickly put an end to "that bad Banks bill" by putting it "to sleep" in the Senate Foreign Relations Committee.[15] But Irish Americans praised Banks for his "splendid efforts" in taking the side of "freedom and right," and rumors circulated once again about Banks as a possible presidential candidate. As the question of American citizens abroad heated up, becoming "the most popular political issue" of the day, Banks once again took the lead, introducing his long-awaited bill on January 29, 1868.[16]

"It is a difficult subject to treat," Banks cautiously admitted. Everyone wanted immediate action, yet few had concrete answers about what Congress could actually do, especially given the international dimensions of the issue. Congress had jurisdiction over domestic matters, but how far could it reach in shaping the actions of foreign Governments? If diplomats had struggled with defining the boundaries of national sovereignty and the obligations of states to their citizens, so, too, did legislators. Banks strived, as usual, to find a politically popular solution that would accommodate a range of views.[17]

His bill declared that all naturalized Americans were entitled to the same protection as native-born citizens while abroad, but with certain exceptions. Naturalized citizens could not claim protection from the American government if they had committed a crime in a foreign state or treason in the United States, deserted from "actual service" in a foreign military, acquired naturalization through fraud, enlisted in a foreign army, or lived outside the United

States for more than five years and failed to pay taxes while residing abroad. If a foreign state arrested and detained American citizens without cause or held naturalized Americans as their subjects, the bill's "hostage" clause empowered the president to retaliate by detaining any subject of a foreign state then in the United States.[18]

Banks's bill quickly became controversial for doing both too little and too much. Perhaps the strangest thing about the Banks bill was that it said nothing about the right of expatriation. If protest rallies and petitions offered few concrete solutions to the expatriation crisis, the foreign-born appeared unanimous on one demand: Congress needed to state unequivocally that individuals had the right of expatriation.[19] Banks's committee tried to explain its silence on the issue. Expatriation was an inherent, natural right and thus the law, whatever Congress or the courts said. An explicit guarantee now would imply that expatriation was a new right, a law only because Congress said so rather than a natural right mandated by God. Even worse, perhaps, "the Governments of Europe [would] taunt us saying, 'it was not until 1868 that you placed the declaration on your statute-book,' ignoring all past history on the subject." The United States' long insistence on its "American doctrine" of expatriation would be contemptuously swept aside. Many legislators remained unpersuaded, however, insisting on an explicit declaration to remove any doubts, at home or abroad.[20]

Foreign-born advocates skewered the bill for the exceptions it made, one representative warning "the whole German press is in a rage" over the limited protections it offered to the foreign-born. "Why does [Banks] make distinctions between native and adopted citizens?" demanded one prominent German American. Congress would never dare yank citizenship from native-born Americans who resided abroad, as it now threatened to do for naturalized citizens.[21] German Americans objected even more to the exemption of those in "actual" military service from American government protection. German states used a broad definition of "service" and "desertion," insisted Norman Judd, the former U.S. minister to Berlin during the Civil War. In Prussia every male "is a conscript from his birth," remaining liable for service for years, and the Banks bill would leave the vast majority of German American men vulnerable to arrest for military desertion. Far better to "kill" the bill "if you can get no better one," concluded one critic.[22]

If some saw the bill as too weak, others condemned it as far too aggressive, especially in its so-called hostage or reprisals provision. The "hostages" approach had worked before, Banks reminded the House, pointing to American use of reprisals in the War of 1812. If the bill was going to be more than a "naked declaration of principle," the reprisals clause was necessary to give the bill some teeth, argued Indiana Republican congressman Godlove Orth. But most legislators denounced reprisals as "barbarous," "inhuman," and "unwise." Retaliation would turn foreign relations into a "farce," perhaps even provoking a war while punishing innocent victims for the crimes of their sovereigns.[23] Perhaps it would be better, some suggested, to suspend commercial or diplomatic relations with offending European countries, a solution others opposed as harming America's self-interest. They did not want to "shock industry" or "cause a general outcry" among commercial interests, warned Banks and others.[24]

Two weeks after its introduction, Banks's bill had not made much progress. As representatives began proposing amendment after amendment, Banks took his bill back to the Committee on Foreign Relations. They would try again.[25]

As politicians wrangled over the expatriation bill, George Francis Train once again thrust himself into the spotlight. He left for Ireland with Thomas Clark Durant, his savvy (many might say corrupt) business partner and family friend. Ostensibly Train was traveling to Ireland on business, but in his parting words, Train declared that he would settle, singlehandedly, "the rights of American citizens abroad, the Alabama claims, Ireland for the Irish, and the rights of women." "Stephen J. Meany and Capt. Warren I will see," Train announced. "One native-born American citizen, at least as long as I live, will be as true to American Liberty as our Irish American citizens . . . no Adams toadying away of our American birthright of 'liberty and equality for all men and all women, where our flag floats.'" Train promised that within "forty-eight hours after I land on British soil, all Europe and America will ring with America's rights and George Francis Train."[26]

Train often made grand claims about his influence, but this time he was right. The minute Train landed in Queenstown, Irish police arrested him "on charges of Fenianism," based on newspaper clippings in his luggage reporting his inflammatory speeches in Boston and elsewhere. Train relished the chance to play the part of the unjustly imprisoned American. He immediately publicized his arrest, firing off telegrams to Charles Francis Adams and newspaper editors, declaring, "I am under arrest for words spoken in America and on the high

"All Aboard for Ireland." A favorite speaker on the Fenian circuit, George Francis Train left for Ireland in January 1868, promising to free John Warren and defend American citizens' rights abroad. Thomas Nast's cartoon captures Train's manic, flamboyant style.

seas."[27] Referring to himself as the "Independent Ambassador" of America, Train lodged a loud protest with the British government, claiming to act "in the name of the American people—as the American Government are power-less to protect their citizens."[28]

American newspapers had a "jolly chuckle" over British efforts to contain the irrepressible Train, but also expressed astonishment that Train had been arrested for things he had said and done in the United States. If Warren and Costello's convictions had raised the ire of the foreign born, Train's arrest struck closer to home for many more Americans, reinforcing a growing national concern about British overreach. "It was hard work to stir up public sympathy with intriguing or murdering Irishmen," observed one New York newspaper, "but when a thoroughbred Yankee falls into British hands, and is thence transferred to a British dungeon, the case is different."[29] Newspaper editors burst with furious indignation: "It is not to be tolerated that a citizen of the United States shall be snapped up and imprisoned on his way to a foreign country for no better reason than because he indulges in eccentricities at home," thundered the *New York World*. "It is an outrage to which this country ought not, and will not, submit," echoed the *New York Times*.[30]

Dublin Castle officials and the British foreign minister, Lord Stanley, were as surprised as Americans to learn of Train's arrest. Neither American nor British diplomats wanted to inflame already tense relations. Charles Francis Adams had little sympathy for Train but warned Lord Stanley that it would be "extreme folly to raise him into a martyr."[31] Lord Stanley readily agreed, asking Lord Mayo, lord lieutenant of Ireland, to release Train. "He is . . . more than half cracked, and . . . will give you no end of trouble," Stanley predicted. By the next day, Train had been released from jail, though only after promising he would not promote Fenianism while in Ireland.[32]

But the minute he was free, Train entertained newspaper reporters with stories of his capture and met with the Fenian head center in Cork. Then he set out to "stump the country," delighting Irish audiences with his "vigour," "originality," and "wildly extravagant" ideas.[33] Officials watched nervously as Train gathered steam in Ireland, worrying that his "wildly enthusiastic" reception fanned the Fenian fires. They could hardly arrest Train again without creating another international ruckus, so they kept a wary eye on him, hoping his novelty would soon wear off.[34]

But Train was never one to let things die down. In late February he abruptly left southern Ireland—not, as Adams might have hoped, to return to the United States. He headed for Sligo on the west coast of Ireland. His mission? To save William Nagle, the *Jacmel* leader.

ON SATURDAY, February 29, Nagle finally entered the dock in the heavily guarded Sligo County Courthouse to begin his long-awaited trial. The "eyes of the whole Country," and likely those of America, were on the case, Lord Mayo warned the Irish attorney general. Much had changed since Warren's trial only a few months earlier. Not only had the "state of feeling in America" reached a boiling point, "raised higher" by Train's arrest, but public opinion in England had also begun to shift. Sir William Vernon Harcourt, one of England's foremost authorities on international law, had launched a series of articles in the London *Times*, slowly but surely making the case that England should abandon its "ancient" doctrine of perpetual allegiance. On the morning of Nagle's trial, the *Times* questioned whether the prosecution should be carried out at all. "Is the conviction of these men a matter of so much importance that it is worth while . . . to run the risk of interfering with the friendly settlement of a troublesome question?" The government had Warren and Costello behind bars already. It would be wiser to "relax our stringency in the less important and less certain cases," the *Times* advised. Disgruntled by the *Times*'s betrayal and the unwelcome attention to the case, Lord Mayo was anxious to have the trial over and done with: "If Nagle was either convicted or acquitted, a great difficulty would be removed."[35]

Unfortunately for Mayo, Nagle's trial quickly ground to a halt as the Crown's prosecutors struggled to round up enough jurors. British officials, anxious to show they gave American citizens—if native-born—every benefit under the law, had readily granted Nagle's request for a mixed jury of half aliens and half British subjects. The court quickly called sixty-six British subjects as potential jurors, but the sheriff could find precious few aliens in Sligo. He finally scrounged up some Prussian sailors, who neither spoke nor understood English, on a ship anchored in Sligo harbor. But by the day of the trial, the Prussians had sailed away. There remained one alien in the courtroom who was happy to sit on the mixed jury: "Train is here and has applied to the sheriff to be put on the jury which the sheriff has properly declined to do," the Irish solicitor general reported.[36]

The sheriff tried again. This time six aliens showed up, but three were soldiers in the Sligo militia, dressed in British uniforms and in the queen's service. Even the Crown prosecutor agreed they were not acceptable as jurors.

Nagle's attorney demanded the trial be postponed and moved to a venue, Dublin in all likelihood, "where aliens can be had." Legally, Judge John FitzGerald did not have to provide Nagle a mixed jury, since it was a privilege, not an absolute right. But FitzGerald and the attorney general agreed that to deny Nagle the mixed jury at this point would be very impolitic. "It could be said we had sent N. [Nagle] to Sligo for the purpose of depriving him of a privilege that he is entitled to as an American citizen," cautioned the attorney general. "Of course," he added, "I would rather have done with the Jackmel and her crew for ever." Faced with limited options, Judge FitzGerald officially postponed Nagle's trial and ordered it removed to the Queen's Bench in a venue where a mixed jury could be formed more easily.[37]

The collapse of Nagle's case was a major setback for the Crown prosecutors, but they tried to regroup as they pressed forward with the trials of the other *Jacmel* prisoners, all of whom were Irish-born. As British subjects, they could not claim mixed juries. Yet the first trial lasted only half a day before it, too, fell apart. The trial of Patrick Nugent began promisingly enough. Nugent had been one of the crew left behind on Streedagh Strand, north of Sligo, along with the two wounded *Jacmel* men. On the first day of Nugent's trial, Buckley, Corydon, and Gallagher all testified, much as they had in Warren's case. Then the jury retired for the night, sequestered under the care of the sheriff. The next morning, one of the jurors was so ill he could not continue. The doctor diagnosed him as having "English cholera," a general term used to describe attacks of diarrhea and vomiting. The *Times* implied that the juror suffered from too much drinking, and suspicion fell on the sheriff for plying the jurors with so much liquor that they would be unfit to serve.[38]

Whatever the cause, the government gave up. "This was too much for the Crown to bear after the shock of the Nagle mishap," speculated the *Times*. Nugent's trial came to a halt, and the Crown prosecutors decided to send all the prisoners back to Dublin, leading to speculation that they might be released. Opinion remained divided about whether the government should try again or simply "abandon the case against the Americans altogether." The *Freeman's Journal* likely spoke for many in its weary disgust with the "crazy Jacknell business." "It would be well to bring to a close the Fenian trials," it said. "We have had enough of them."[39]

"OUR TRANSATLANTIC cousin, John Bull, is becoming practical," observed the *Philadelphia Inquirer* on St. Patrick's Day, 1868. Soon, the paper predicted,

Fenians would be preparing a grand reception for Nagle and the *Jacmel* crew.[40] Indeed, British officials were more than willing to get rid of the untried *Jacmel* prisoners, Adams reported to Seward, and even more anxious to resolve the larger, vexed question of expatriation.[41] Even before Nagle's trial, British officials had approached Adams about the possibility of negotiating an agreement on naturalization and removing at least one prickly issue from Anglo-American relations. But Seward had brushed aside their tentative overtures, arguing the British offer was too little too late and the issue now lay with Congress.[42] While pretending to be powerless, Seward likely used the threat of congressional action to bring Britain to the negotiating table to settle all the outstanding issues between the two countries—especially the *Alabama* claims—on American terms. Seward knew that the British government much preferred to keep such matters out of the hands of Congress, with its "loud and blustering" anti-British tendencies, made all the worse in the presidential election year.[43]

Suddenly, soon after the Sligo trials fell apart, a resolution of the expatriation crisis seemed possible. Congress, indeed, the entire nation, became absorbed by the "great impeachment question" as President Johnson's trial began in the Senate on March 13.[44] In the lull, Seward abruptly reversed his priorities. He had previously refused to discuss the naturalization question until the *Alabama* claims had been settled, but, on March 7, Seward declared that the naturalization question now took precedence. Puzzled by the rapid turnabout, Adams speculated that Seward, facing the possibility of being turned out of office if Johnson was convicted, wanted to secure his legacy by settling the expatriation question that had so long dogged Anglo-American relations. Whatever the cause, Seward wanted a treaty on naturalization as soon as possible, along with the release of Warren and Costello, the convicted Fenians in Canada, and the untried *Jacmel* prisoners. Only then would the United States consider the *Alabama* matter and other issues dividing the two countries.[45]

The British government had no intention of letting Warren and Costello go but was willing to settle the contentious issue of expatriation in a "business-like and rational" way. In the meantime, it was "glad to relieve itself of the burden" of Nagle and the other untried *Jacmel* prisoners—once they had signed a written confession and promised to leave Ireland immediately. Most readily complied with the conditions, and by May only seven untried *Jacmel* prisoners, including Nagle, remained in Dublin jails. But they proved a stubborn lot. The prisoners refused to go, at least not on the terms offered by Irish authorities.[46]

Give us a trial or an unconditional discharge, Nagle and the remaining prisoners demanded. They desperately wanted to leave prison. Nagle protested to Adams, "I have been over ten months in close confinement deprived of every right belonging to a free man, suffering in body and mind—my health broken, my family injured, my social and business connections destroyed."[47] But they would be signing no confessions, as that would play into the hands of British authorities. The prisoners understood the British officials' dilemma. Without trying the *Jacmel* prisoners, confessions provided the only way to demonstrate their guilt and vindicate their lengthy detention. Increasingly, Dublin Castle officials saw Nagle as the solution to the impasse. If they could persuade him to confess, the others would follow. But Nagle "stoutly refused" a conditional discharge.[48]

Or he did until May 5, when Nagle and Patrick Nugent signed a document acknowledging that "we came to Ireland in May last (1867) in the Brigantine Jacknell along with others, believing that the people of Ireland were but awaiting the assistance of men and arms to raise an insurrection against the government. We hereby express our regret at having done so & undertake if now discharged to leave Ireland and not again visit Ireland." Only two weeks earlier, Nagle had written to West again demanding his release. Why did Nagle change his mind so suddenly? Perhaps Nagle's declining health or personal affairs at home finally pushed him into confessing.[49] An account left by Samuel Anderson, the crown solicitor of Ireland, suggests an alternative explanation: that the British government may have blackmailed Nagle.

Anderson admitted that Nagle's confession had been attained "with some difficulty" and "the exercise of not a little ingenuity." Immediately before Nagle's release, authorities received a letter from Nagle's father, David, "offering to give every assistance in his power to the government in the discovery of the Fenian plans, if his son were given his liberty and permitted to return home." David Nagle also claimed to be "no other than the famous 'Captain Rock,'" the same David Nagle who had led the violent Rockite movement in Cork city in 1821–1823 and who, after his capture, escaped execution by informing on his comrades. David Nagle now offered to do much the same, sell out the Fenian Brotherhood in exchange for his son's freedom.[50] Imagine William Nagle's reaction if Irish authorities had shown him this letter. It would have been a crushing blow, the knowledge that his own father was a vile informer, no better than William Millen and Daniel Buckley, the *Jacmel* Judases. Had Irish authorities threatened to publicize the letter and expose David Nagle—and, by extension, William—as informants? Whatever the reason, Nagle signed the confession, and the other prisoners "soon followed the example of their leader." When the last of the *Jacmel* crew finally left prison on

May 21, the American consul William West exulted quietly, writing at the bottom of his ledger: "(Finis!)"[51]

Charles Francis Adams also indulged in a private celebration, declaring in his diary, "Io triumphe!"—the acclamation shouted in triumphal processions in ancient Rome. Adams was only days away from finally leaving his post in England after seven long and dreary years. The Fenians had been a thorn in his side in the last two years, seriously tarnishing his reputation at home and seeming to erase from public memory all he had done during the Civil War to keep England at bay. Threatened with assassination and impeachment, Adams had submitted his resignation to Seward, effective April 1, 1868, saying, "I find myself doing nothing but reclaiming Irishmen from punishment which most of them seem to me richly to deserve."[52] Adams noted the irony that on the eve of his departure he was more popular in England than in America. The British press lavished its highest praise on Adams, saying he "belongs to the true aristocracy of America" and expressing the hope that Adams, a judicious and well-bred man, might become the next American president.[53] Adams dreaded the possibility, now being floated about in Democratic Party circles, of being a presidential candidate, nor did he think it likely given the "hostility of the Irish to me." He just wanted to finish his job in London and go home. Nagle's release brought a welcome sense of closure. "This is the last of the annoyances in my public position," he reflected."[54]

On May 13, Adams finished his accounts at the legation, gave his regards to the foreign secretary, Lord Stanley, and then went to Buckingham Palace for a private audience with Queen Victoria to tender formal notice of his departure. It was a powerful moment, and Adams became uncharacteristically nervous, forgetting for the moment "what I was to call her." Adams reflected with the queen on the "difficulties and trials" of the past seven years that the two countries had survived, ultimately, with a "friendly spirit." At 8:30 P.M. Adams left London, recording in his diary with relief: "I was once more a free man."[55]

In a fitting coincidence of historical timing, Nagle departed Ireland on the same day. If Adams slipped away quietly, Nagle left amidst cheers shouted from crowds who gathered to send him off at the port of Queenstown. George Francis Train turned up to take credit for liberating the prisoners, credit they were happy to give him. "We feel that you are our liberator," wrote one of the last prisoners to leave, "whatever the authorities may say." As the men made their way to SS *Tripoli*, bound for Boston, the crowd raised "hundreds of green boughs" in the air, while Nagle stood on deck, "kissing farewell to Ireland and the assembled throng." Train "shouted wildly" for "three last cheers for Colonel Nagle and the men of the Jacknell, which rose in one fierce hurrah from every mouth on the wharf." Nagle, after almost a year in Irish prisons, finally left for home. Train blasted a victorious telegram: "Saw Nagle off. Shall release Warren and Costelloe at once. Hurrah!"[56]

"HE IS SET FREE!!!" yelled the *Irishman*, in astonishment rather than delight. "What! Is it possible? Are these the impartial laws—is this the equal and indifferent justice of which we hear so much?" Nagle's release did little to placate Fenians or the foreign-born advocates of expatriation, his liberation pointing yet again to the unjust distinctions made between native-born and naturalized citizens. The native-born Nagle "is 'guiltier' than any," argued the *Irishman*, but he was set free while Warren and Costello, because they were naturalized citizens, rotted in English prisons.[57]

Nagle's return helped to revive the expatriation issue, temporarily sidetracked by Johnson's impeachment trial. Just days before Nagle arrived in Boston, the trial ended with Johnson's narrow acquittal. Seeking to recapture the spotlight, the Fenian Brotherhood threw a grand reception for Nagle at Cooper Union in New York City on June 10, with over 3,000 greeting the hero "with a perfect tornado of applause." Decked out with the "glorious old green banner of Ireland" and "America's beautiful flag," the platform was surrounded by banners blaring "The priceless boon, 'I am an American citizen,' must be respected the world over," and "A sacred compact—the citizen bound to defend and the nation bound to respect." A welcoming committee of dignitaries, all eager for the Irish and foreign-born vote, sat on the platform: Democratic mayor John Hoffman, running for governor of New York; William "Boss" Tweed of Tammany Hall, at the peak of his political control over city and state politics; and Susan B. Anthony and Elizabeth Cady Stanton, still hoping to court Irish male support for woman suffrage.[58] Not to be outdone, the Republican Party at its Chicago convention on May 20, 1868, made a strong pitch for the foreign-born vote in its platform, declaring that the right of expatriation must be established "at every hazard." The Democratic Party soon followed suit in its platform.[59] With both political parties committed, one would have expected Banks's expatriation bill to sail through Congress. But it soon stalled out in the Senate.

ON FEBRUARY 20, Banks introduced a revised bill for the House's consideration, showing he had heard his critics loud and clear. The new bill began with a ringing declaration: "The right of expatriation is a natural and inherent right of all people, indispensable to the enjoyment of the rights of life, liberty and the pursuit of happiness." It spoke in sweeping terms of the obligation of the American government to protect all citizens, naturalized and native-born, without any exceptions, when they traveled abroad. But on one point Banks refused to compromise: his new bill kept the reprisals (hostages) clause, and also authorized the president to suspend commercial relations with countries that unlawfully detained American citizens. The bill passed the House with a huge margin: 104 in favor, only 4 against.[60] Critics on both sides of the Atlantic condemned the bill, especially the reprisals clause, the *New York Times* calling it "a stroke of savagery."[61] Opponents hoped, with good reason, that the Senate would put the brakes on the popular will of the House.

Senator Charles Sumner despised the bill, its sponsor, and the Fenians. He had no quarrel with the right of expatriation, calling the British doctrine of perpetual allegiance "absurd" in light of the "gigantic scale" of immigration from Great Britain, which the country had allowed and even fostered.[62] But Sumner denounced the Banks bill as "utterly unworthy of a generous Republic." Though known more for his domestic policies, Sumner also fancied himself an expert on foreign affairs and, as chair of the Senate Foreign Relations Committee, had often fought with Seward for control over foreign policy. He had no intention of disrupting international relations for the sake of self-centered Fenians and was determined not to let the Fenians hijack Republican rhetoric and principles to provoke a war between the United States and Britain.[63]

Sumner did his best to bury the bill in committee. Far better to give diplomacy a chance to work, he thought. And progress suddenly loomed on the horizon. As the expatriation act made its way through Congress, the State Department negotiated a new naturalization treaty with the North German Confederation that promised to settle the question of expatriation and provide a model for agreements with other countries, including England.[64] If he could keep the bill off the Senate floor until after the fall elections, perhaps by then the United States would have a treaty with England and the expatriation bill could die a quiet death, no longer hostage to American politics.[65]

But proponents of the bill were just as determined to get the bill to the Senate floor. The House of Representatives sent a unanimous resolution on June 15 to President Johnson demanding the immediate release of Warren and Costello. Seward, in turn, fired off letters to both the Senate and the acting U.S. minister in London, Benjamin Moran, urging rapid action on both the expatriation bill and an Anglo-American treaty. "Delay hazardous!" he had wired Adams in late March, but by June the English still dawdled, having referred the expatriation issue to a royal commission for further study. Seward wanted to light a fire under the English, in part by using the expatriation bill as leverage.[66] Senator John Conness of California finally forced the bill out of Sumner's committee and onto the floor for debate.[67]

Once the expatriation bill was before the Senate, debate lurched forward in fits and starts, constantly interrupted by other business. Senators often seemed irritable, sweltering in a blistering heat wave, the worst in twenty-five years, that swept the entire Atlantic seaboard in July 1868. Horses pulling streetcars dropped dead from sunstroke and child mortality shot up, the deaths blamed on the "extraordinarily hot weather." Perhaps the senators took the advice of the National Republican and took a small dose of "syrup of rhubarb" or placed grape leaves moistened with water underneath their straw hats to avoid sunstroke.[68] Francis Lieber joked in a letter to Sumner that maybe "the heat of the weather will sweat this Bill out of Congress."[69]

But the bill remained, as did the deadly heat, when the Senate finally began serious debate on July 18. Sumner did what he could to delay the bill further and weaken it by "taking out its worst features." There was no need to rush, Sumner urged. Treaties with the German states to resolve the expatriation crisis were under way and Lord Stanley, the British secretary of foreign affairs, had said only the day before in the House of Commons that the British were prepared to give up their doctrine of perpetual allegiance. If the Senate acted too rashly and passed the "monstrous" Banks bill, it might derail these landmark agreements. At the very least, Sumner was determined to strike out the "barbarous" reprisals section of the Banks bill. "Who shall we seize? What innocent foreigner?" he challenged.[70]

Most senators agreed that hostage taking went too far. But what countermeasures should the government take to defend citizens abroad? And which branch—Congress or the president—should be entrusted with the authority to take action? Embittered by the struggle between Johnson and the Republican legislature, Sumner refused to give the president any more power, proposing that the bill leave it to Congress to take "prompt action" when citizens were detained abroad.[71] Such vague proposals hardly satisfied proponents of the bill, who continued to push for reprisals. "Our citizens wail and lament in prison," and Sumner offered only "lame and impotent" solutions, railed Senator Conness. Only decisive action by a strong executive, who, after all, had power under the Constitution to negotiate with foreign powers, could "satisfy our wounded honor" and bring arrogant countries to heel.[72]

As temperatures rose, so did tempers, the politics of race and rights bubbling close beneath the surface. Sumner would be "very quick to demand the interference of all the powers of this Government in behalf of an arrested American citizen if he were black," accused Senator Conness. "I think it ought to be conceded at this hour of the day that a white man is pretty nearly as good as a black man." Clearly, Sumner's dedication to "equal rights" did not extend to the foreign-born, Conness sniped. Conness could hardly take the high ground on the question of equal rights, charged Sumner and others, pointing to the hostile and discriminatory treatment of Chinese immigrants in his home state of California, much in the news. How could Senators Conness and William Stewart of Nevada, who spoke so passionately of the rights of the foreign-born, deny equal rights to Chinese immigrants, "taxing them as they tax no others, keeping them down . . . as southern rebels would keep the negro down, denying that they are human beings, . . . killing them as soon, as cooly, and with as much impunity as a Texan kills a negro?"[73]

It seemed the debate would go on forever. The heat wave finally broke, but still the bill "drags its slow length along in the Senate, much to the disgust of many Senators" who yearned to be done and adjourn for the rest of the summer. Even Senator Conness, the bill's primary champion in the Senate, lost enthusiasm after his colleagues struck out the reprisals and commercial retaliation clauses, stripping the bill of any real force, in his opinion. Finally, the Senate approved a compromise. It empowered the president to use any "necessary and proper means," but "not amounting to acts of war," to secure the release of American citizens detained unjustly by foreign powers. On July 25, 1868, the Senate approved the Expatriation Act by a vote of 39 to 5. Senator Sumner and other opponents of the bill, recorded as "absent," sat in the Senate chamber but stubbornly refused to participate in the vote. The Senate wrapped up its business and adjourned two days later.[74]

FINALLY, for the first time in its history, the United States declared in law what it had long affirmed in practice: every man had the right to determine "where his citizenship shall be, what country he shall give his allegiance to."[75] Yet, curiously, there was little celebration of the landmark act in the press, with the exception of the Dublin *Irishman*, which trumpeted the law as "Our Victory!" It insisted the law was a "mighty . . . act of justice" with even "mightier" consequences, placing "Irish citizens on a footing of equality with the native-born."

But most observers viewed the final act as weak, a mere shadow of the forceful bill Banks had proposed. The Irish nationalist press and Democratic politicians in the United States decried the Expatriation Act as an ineffectual sham engineered by the English-loving Sumner. For once, the *New York Times* agreed with the Irish nationalist press, saying Congress "could hardly pass a more harmless bill."[76]

Two issues loomed, undercutting the act's potential reach. One was whether the 1868 law allowed Americans to expatriate. Despite the general declaration of a right of expatriation, the act focused only on the right of foreigners to abandon their homelands to become Americans. Perhaps it seemed unfathomable that Americans might want to leave their blessed land, but some had moved and taken up lives elsewhere, even swearing allegiance to other sovereigns, leaving their status uncertain and the United States open to charges of hypocrisy. Americans "have a good deal to do at home" before it could "urge any demands" against foreign governments, argued the British international lawyer Harcourt. "Physician, heal thyself," he scoffed.[77] Harcourt's critique raised the second major question: Could Congress bind other countries with its act? Most legislators blustered past the issue, but some cautioned that Congress had ventured far beyond its zone of power, legislating on matters of international law that could be addressed only "by the treaty-making power."[78] What the act would mean in practice remained uncertain. Most expected, at the very least, that England would release Warren and Costello but Lord Mayo in Ireland remained steadfast. "The time was hardly yet come" to release men who had "cruised along the [Irish] coast" seeking to "raise insurrection against the Queen," he said. Warren and Costello were going nowhere for the present, whatever Congress said in its Expatriation Act.[79]

What, then, had the Expatriation Act accomplished? Later commentators would dismiss it contemptuously as "flamboyant," a "piece of legislative rhetoric," "mere buncombe."[80] The act, undeniably, invited much political grandstanding, but it cannot be swept aside so easily. The expatriation protests, fanned by the Fenian trials abroad, had forced the American government's hand, pushing it to declare its dedication to the principle of expatriation and—at least on paper—to protect naturalized and native-born citizens no matter where they roamed. Even the anti-Fenian *New York Times* had urged "prompt and vigorous action" on the question of expatriation as the nation's "self-respect" lay on the line. The Fenians and their supporters had successfully transformed the rights and status of immigrants into a national and international issue. By mid-July, as the bill limped through the Senate, the sense of urgency had ebbed for many.

But the protests and congressional debates had brought European monarchies to the bargaining table to solve the issue through treaties.[81] Perhaps that had been Seward's hope all along: to use domestic politics as a lever to force international negotiations.

Foreign-born activists had insisted that the "dearest rights of American citizens" could not be left to the "delusive devices of diplomats" with their "paper pellets," but others came away from the explosive domestic expatriation debates convinced that politics certainly did not provide the answer. International issues were too important to be left to the "fleeting passions of party" or to the machinations of individuals and groups that put their own interests before those of the nation. Much better to let the experts handle the problem of expatriation, calmly and rationally. At least so thought the experts— diplomats and international law specialists who quietly and busily sought their own revolution: the fashioning of a new law of nations for a modern age.[82]

II

Private Diplomatizing

"WHAT TIMES we live in," remarked Francis Lieber, the renowned political theorist, to Charles Sumner in September 1867. Everywhere he looked, Lieber saw massive changes afoot in the United States and the world. As Americans struggled to reconstruct their nation, campaigns to unify Germany and Italy erupted in Europe. Hungarian nationalists battled the Austrian Empire for greater autonomy, while Mexico ousted French invaders and established a new republic under President Benito Juárez. Russia brutally crushed the Polish independence movement yet emancipated the serfs in 1861, an act hailed as another blow against slavery. Even England embraced dramatic change. The Reform Act of 1867 extended male suffrage, doubling the number of eligible voters. And the Fenian insurrection prompted Parliament to consider new measures to pacify Ireland, beginning with the disestablishment of the Irish Anglican Church. No longer, the bill promised, would Irish Catholics have to pay to support the Protestant Church.[1]

It was "possible to discover a law out of all this . . . chaotic whirl and bustle, this tangled skein of human affairs," said John Lathrop Motley, an eminent historian and diplomat, in 1868. "That law is progress—slow, confused, contradictory, but ceaseless development, intellectual and moral, of the human race." The trick was to move *with* history, not against it—to facilitate progress, not frustrate it. That was the message Lieber and his fellow international law experts (referred to as "publicists" in the nineteenth century) hoped to drive home as they engaged in what the American international lawyer George Bemis called "private diplomatizing." Patiently prodding the public and policymakers, the publicists added their voices to the expatriation debates. They cared little about the Fenians' woes, despite their shared interest in expatriation. What was at stake in this fluid world of shifting boundary lines, border crossers, and freedom fighters? Nothing less than the future of civilization. And a new international law that embraced the right of expatriation would "draw the chariot of civilization abreast."[2]

LIEBER saw his own life as a struggle to move toward liberty, whatever the costs. Born in 1798 in Prussia as the Napoleonic Wars raged, Lieber had been shot through the neck and the chest at the famous Battle of Waterloo in 1815 while fighting as a seventeen-year-old soldier against Napoleon's forces. His injuries did nothing to dampen his nationalist passions or liberal ideals. Lieber dashed to Greece to aid its revolt against Turkey in 1821, returned home only to be imprisoned twice on suspicion of radicalism, and then fled his homeland for the United States, via London, in 1827. Lieber wrote a letter of farewell to his family, expressing "the greatest anguish of mind" at the thought of leaving "all my dear ones" behind in his beloved Prussia. Yet, as was his way, Lieber cast his own departure as part of a broader law at work in the universe: "It is the destiny of every family to be established, to multiply, and to be scattered, so that new ones are founded, just as it is the destiny of empires." Lieber had been thrilled to exchange "petrified and ossified" Europe for a new home in a "young republic" and "a land of progress" where an ambitious young man could make his way.[3]

But Lieber soon found himself stuck in South Carolina as a professor of history and political economy—an unhappy position, as he disliked both teaching and slavery. "I do so long [to be] away from a land where the sky is so bright and the negroes so black. . . . I was not born for niggery," Lieber complained to his friends in the North.[4] Yet Lieber could not escape slavery easily. He might declare slavery "wrong" and an "absurd" institution, but a few years after he became a naturalized citizen in 1832, Lieber purchased his first slaves, struggling in his diary to rationalize his decision to become a slave owner. Only after twenty-one years did he finally free himself from South Carolina and from slavery, moving to the North and deciding to vote for Lincoln, even though it meant civil war.[5]

Lieber did not shrink from war or from the massive changes it brought. Only by wiping out the "black blot" of slavery could the nation redeem its soul and fulfill its promise as the republic of liberty. The war had been brutal. Lieber's son Hamilton lost an arm but his eldest, Oscar, lost his life, dying at the Battle of Williamsburg in Wade Hampton's Confederate legion and, in his last moments, reportedly "raving against his father and the North." Only his son Norman, fighting against his brother on the Union side at the Battle of Williamsburg, emerged physically unscathed. Such personal tragedy only made Lieber more determined that "we must conquer the South" and wipe out slavery. While his sons took to the battlefield, Lieber fired with his pen, steeling the North in his pamphlets for the Loyal Publication Society to see the war to its righteous end. The Lincoln administration relied heavily on Lieber for its intellectual ammunition, asking him in 1863 to take on a most daunting task: to write a "law of war" to govern the conduct of the Union Army, and to justify Lincoln's departure from traditional "usages of war."[6]

It was the sort of challenge Lieber loved—creating order out of seeming chaos, submitting even war to the rule of law. Years earlier he had reflected that "our Times often appear to me like the Mississippi [River]—mighty and muddy." Lieber had always seen his job as a publicist to involve identifying and clarifying the patterns that lay hidden beneath "muddy" times. Like the pathbreaking scientists of the nineteenth century who promised to unlock the mysteries of the natural world by classifying, organizing, and explaining the evolution of animate and inanimate beings, Lieber helped to pioneer the new "social sciences," submitting the development of peoples and societies to rigorous critical inquiry.[7]

To create his new code of war, Lieber turned, as always, to the past and the great thinkers, identifying universal principles in the "common law of war." But Lieber's code did not just restate old rules; he reformulated them to suit the needs of modern warfare and to speed the victory of the Union. Lieber had little patience for namby-pamby pacifists or humanitarian claptrap; his code allowed unrelenting warfare, endorsing all methods necessary to victory, with only a few exceptions. "Sharp wars" might be brutal, but they would be shorter and thus ultimately less harmful in the long run. Lieber's pragmatic code, finished in 1863 and rushed into print in a handy pamphlet format so officers could carry it into battle, quickly became hailed as a major contribution to international law, soon adopted in Europe as well as America.[8]

If law could discipline war, what else could it accomplish in the hands of enlightened statesmen at home and abroad? As the end of the Civil War neared, Lieber again urged Americans to rewrite their most fundamental law—their treasured Constitution—to ensure that the victories won on the battlefield would be secured in peace. "All laws must change in course of time," Lieber lectured Americans who hesitated to touch the "sacred" Constitution, unamended for fifty years. "Laws are authoritative rules of action . . . for living men," Lieber

Francis Lieber, ca. 1855–1865. The Prussian American political theorist was author of the Lieber Code of War, adopted during the American Civil War, and also pushed for the modernization of international law and recognition of the right of expatriation.

reminded them. Societies that failed to change their laws to meet new realities would lose vigor and die out.[9]

Lieber advocated legal change, but hardly revolution. National and international law remained yoked to fundamental principles that endured across time. "From early youth I have had a peculiar love for . . . formulations of great truths," he later recalled. As a child, he had decorated the walls of his room in Berlin with pithy passages from the Bible and Tacitus, the early historian of the Roman Empire, "beautifully written by my brother and nicely framed." As he pushed for legal reform at home and abroad, Lieber always kept the "great truths" in sight. "Develop, modify, change, trim, improve," he instructed, "but keep to the back bone."[10]

WHEN LIEBER looked at the unrest abroad, watching states shrink and expand and nationalist movements struggle for independence, he saw great universal principles at work—the same forces that had plunged a divided United States into war and resurrected it into a powerful unified nation. For Lieber, the Civil War laid bare "the roots of evil in our polity." Slavery, that "malignant virus," had thrown the United States off course and weakened the republic's foundation of liberty. But so, too, had the destructive states' rights doctrine, with its confusing fragmentation of power and its insistence that Americans were, in essence, dual citizens—of the states and of the federal government. The victory of the Union swept aside the notions of state sovereignty and divided citizenship. Nationalization—the consolidation of power in the federal government and the creation of a unitary national citizenship—returned America to its destiny and allowed it to become a modern nation-state.[11]

Lieber saw the nationalization of the United States as one example of broader political forces taking hold in Europe as well—forces that created not only new nation-states but also the promise of a new "internationalism." Everywhere the nation-state became the norm, and so, too, did the move to define and protect civil liberties. Past forms of government, whether weak confederations of small states or large "universal monarchies," had become "obsolete," giving way to the "demands of advanced civilization." Such changes seemed natural—perhaps even inevitable—to Lieber, given God's design of human nature and the spread of liberalism around the globe. Humans were at once intensely individualistic, seeking to maximize their own interests and fulfill their unique potential, but also social, yearning to coexist with others. States that placed artificial barriers on people's inherent desires for individual liberty and social interaction—by, for example, restricting trade, access to occupations, or migration—frustrated progress and could not last long. Nation-states that unified disparate people and removed obstacles to their freedom of interaction worked with people's inclinations and proved more resilient.[12]

It was a theory that brilliantly celebrated not only the modern nation-state but also two major developments of the nineteenth century: global capitalism and global migration. The "national period," as Lieber called it, was but the latest and most glorious phase in the history of humanity, a history that could be boiled down to one basic narrative: the story of civilization spreading from its birthplace in ancient Asia and Africa and blossoming to its fullest potential in modern Europe and North America. What drove civilization forward, spreading and broadening its influence? Exchange and emigration, Lieber answered, both part of God's plan. "All human beings have nearly the same desires, appetites and wants," Lieber observed. "All eyes love Blue; all men appreciate wool; all men want iron; all love wine, oil, salt, spice, gold; all desire silk." Yet, since only "limited regions" produce desired goods, "men must exchange" to satisfy their desires. Emigration, another type of exchange, was also driven by human nature. "Through emigration the Almighty has directed mankind to spread over the earth," Lieber argued, and throughout history "men have looked for a better country, when the country of their birth became too crowded or too barren," fulfilling their own desires but also God's will. Exchange of people and goods "is the way the Creator enforces interdependence," Lieber concluded, creating societies that became more uniform in their thoughts, values, and practices.[13]

By the 1860s, Lieber argued, the leading nations had become little more than "different members of the same household," linked together by the exchange of goods, ideas, and people. Western nations shared the same alphabet, "mathematical language," "barometer," "dress and fashion," "manners,"—even "the same toys for our children." Natural barriers—"mountains, rivers, coasts"— no longer posed the same obstacles, overcome by telegraphs and steamships. Before long, Lieber dreamed, a new international "commonwealth of nations" would emerge, the most advanced stage of civilization yet seen in human history—but only if nations could find ways to contain conflict and establish an international rule of law. Increased contact and traffic among peoples generated new tensions, as the expatriation crisis illustrated so well, that could easily result in commercial or military warfare. A modern law of nations, "the glory of our race in modern history," would be the savior of the emerging international commonwealth, Lieber predicted.[14]

A new international law could advance the natural progression of internationalism by smoothing and broadening the paths of commerce. It could finally resolve the question of the freedom to emigrate and expatriate, something that should have been "settled long ago."[15]

LIEBER, in the last years of his life, would prove tireless in his efforts to reform international law, becoming the best-known international law expert in the

United States, but he would not act alone. Lieber served as a linchpin between intellectuals and policymakers in the United States and Europe as he developed a vibrant network of cosmopolitan correspondents. Johann Caspar Bluntschli, professor of law at the University of Heidelberg, never met Lieber but felt an "intimate, personal connection" with him, due to their three-way correspondence with Edouard de Laboulaye, a comparative law professor and passionate antislavery advocate in Paris, known later as the "Father of the Statue of Liberty." Laboulaye proposed the idea for a statue, "Liberty Enlightening the World," in 1865 as a testament to America's monumental act of emancipation during the war and its survival as a democracy, so important as a beacon for freedom the world over. But Laboulaye's gesture also revealed the growing allure of internationalist thinking, seen at work in his correspondence with Bluntschli and Lieber. The three men—a "scientific cloverleaf," "belonging to three different nationalities, to three states, and to three peoples"—illustrated the promise of the new international network of like-minded activists in creating a "community of thought, science, and endeavor."[16] Around the world, a new international spirit arose by the late 1860s, bursting forth in new international organizations and journals and infusing enthusiastic advocates of a modern international law. Even in China, Lieber noted, "our Wheaton's Law of Nations has been translated" and had become required reading "among its high officials."[17]

Yet international law experts in the mid-nineteenth century loved to complain about how little people knew or cared about the "law of nations." Few people in England or America took the time "to study great questions of international law," Charles Francis Adams lamented. Even Seward liked to quip that he had never consulted a book on international law since becoming secretary of state. Lieber scoffed when asked in 1868 whether he might translate Johann Kaspar Bluntschli's most recent work on the law of nations from German into English for publication in the United States. No one would print it, he responded, much less read it—unless, he joked, he inserted drawings of nude women alongside the Code of the Modern Law of Nations.[18]

The average American may not have dived into Wheaton's *Elements of International Law* with relish, but that did not mean Americans had no interest in international law. Americans spoke often and passionately about the conduct of nations, condemning them for violating principles of justice and fair play that transcended national borders. The expatriation crisis, the trials of American citizens abroad, the *Alabama* claims—all involved Americans, as well as Europeans, in vigorous debates about the proper boundaries of sovereign power and the meaning of neutrality in wartime. Congressmen debating the expatriation act in 1868 turned frequently to the great theorists of the law of nations—Grotius, Vattel, Pufendorf—to shore up their arguments, whether for or against. But experts found the popular debates invoking international law even more appalling than outright disinterest. Laypeople made claims and assumptions that were wrong or politically motivated, goaded by Fenians and vote-seeking politicians.

What the world needed, if the right of expatriation was ever going to have a secure foundation, was "thoughtful minds going carefully into the whole subject; collecting facts, stating arguments, and in forcible language, *demonstrating* the truth."[19] It was a job that could be done, Francis Lieber half joked, only by the "sacred ring" of the "brotherhood" devoted to the "law of nations." The publicists could become the *"power* behind the *law-maker,"* predicted one of their admirers.[20]

Publicists, powerful? At first glance the notion seemed laughable. Many, after all, were men like Lieber: professors or lawyers, self-taught specialists in the field of international law, only just beginning to identify professionally as "international lawyers." Some held official positions, serving as diplomats or as legislators, though even they often seemed more absorbed by their intellectual interests. During one week in January 1868, George Bancroft, the U.S. minister to Berlin, went from one gathering to the next: Monday, a party at the home of Herman Grimm, an art historian and the son and nephew of the famed Grimm Brothers; Tuesday, dinner with Professor Magnus, "a great chemist"; Wednesday, the midweek "evening society" for *wissenshaftliche unterhaltungen* (scientific discussion); Thursday, dinner with Karl Lepsius, the Egyptologist who pioneered modern archaeology; Friday, a dinner for Americans living in Berlin—students, professors, and ministers; Saturday, a reception held by historian Dr. Georg Heinrich Pertz, the head of Berlin's Royal Library; Sunday, a visit to Bekker, the "editor of Plato and Aristotle." When he wasn't out socializing, Bancroft, ever the historian, buried himself in the archives or wrote letters—lots of letters—to friends and family but also to leading intellectuals and statesmen who shared an interest in international affairs. Combing through his massive correspondence, one wonders when he actually got any work done. As if anticipating the question, Bancroft assured one of his letter recipients, after describing in glowing detail a ball he attended at the royal palace, "Do not think I wasted my evening; I pushed my treaty forward a great bit."[21]

Bancroft had been working the whole time, it appears. The publicists were "men of letters," as they were called at the time, who cultivated a network of like-minded cosmopolitan thinkers that reached beyond national borders. They spent their time reading, talking, attending meetings, and "scribbling," as George Bemis, the acclaimed international law specialist, put it, writing letters, articles, and books. And it was through their "scribbling" that they hoped to advance the cause of creating a modern international law through "private diplomatizing."[22] Bancroft and other diplomats in the foreign service, as public officials, handled international matters through formal channels; yet, as Bancroft's letters suggest, they might pursue public negotiations in private settings, pushing treaties along as they dined, danced, and discussed the topics of the day.

Just as important, private individuals could shape public diplomacy, even though they held no formal position. In England, Sir William Vernon Harcourt, a lawyer and journalist who was the first Whewell Professor of International Law at Cambridge University, held no official position but became "the spokesman of English policy to the unofficial world." He worked so closely with Lord John Russell in the Foreign Ministry that "it was assumed in the United States that he was the semi-official voice of the Ministry." His articles in the London *Times* were reprinted in the published official correspondence of the U.S. Department of State in its annual report to Congress.[23] In the United States, Lieber had the ear of Charles Sumner, his longtime friend, and Secretary of State Hamilton Fish (who replaced Seward in 1869), and he frequently peppered them with suggestions for new diplomatic initiatives. The American lawyer George Bemis, acclaimed for his analysis of the *Alabama* dispute, also sent Sumner long missives, lecturing him about the fine points of international law.[24]

While patriotic and dedicated to their respective countries' interests, the international law publicists sought to establish themselves as independent thinkers and commentators, Lieber describing himself as an "internationalist." Francis Lieber argued that scholars and lawyers could have greater effect if they remained free of nationalism and on the margins of the political world. Hugo Grotius, one of the founders of international law, "was quoted as authority . . . *because* he was an unofficial man, absent from the strife." Publicists gained legitimacy by standing apart from the fray and shaping public opinion through their writings and letters.[25]

But it was not always easy to remain impartial or objective. Publicists might be men of the world, but they traveled in relatively small circles, tending to be much alike in their social backgrounds and orientations. A striking number of both public and private diplomats in the United States hailed from Massachusetts and New York; they knew the same people and went to the same clubs.[26]

They were much like Lieber: highly educated, at a time when very few went to college, much less high school; enthusiastic liberals who endorsed free markets and global capitalism, despite their often disruptive forces; and passionate reformers who, while insisting on their objectivity, took very decided views on domestic issues and lobbied hard for them. Lieber protested mightily about Congress's "meddling" with the domestic labor market when it legislated an eight-hour working day for federal employees. Harcourt, like Lieber, proved a devout free trader and an opponent of undue government intervention in people's personal and economic lives. "I don't admire a grand-maternal Government," he quipped, "which ties nightcaps on a grown up nation by Act of Parliament."[27]

Finally, publicists had to navigate their own overlapping allegiances and identities. Allegiance "is not a single thread," Lieber noted. Writing to Secretary of State Hamilton Fish, Lieber declared he identified simultaneously "as jurist, as internationalist (if you permit this new word), as naturalized citizen, as a thorough *Civis Americanus*." Even as he insisted on the absolute necessity of having one political allegiance, Lieber confessed to Charles Sumner that his bond to his native land "is deep and cannot be wholly eradicated."[28] Could publicists be both citizens of nations and "citizens of the world"? And where would they draw the "borders of belonging" for the countries of the world? Did all belong to the "family of nations," or just countries like theirs—those populated by the "Europides," as Lieber called Europeans and their descendants in North America, who "seem . . . destined to cover the earth"? Publicists strained to break free of parochial limits, condemning the "virulent nationalism that cultivates the hatred of other nations." But they remained tethered to their own world views and their own places and time. Being cosmopolitan would be more difficult than it seemed.[29]

HARCOURT took up his pen on December 10, 1867, as expatriation protests and rumors of war with England erupted across the United States, and wrote the first of several essays published as letters to the editor of the London *Times*. "Who is a British subject?" he asked, as he prepared England to give up its "ancient" theory of perpetual allegiance. A month later, John Westlake, another well-known British publicist, called for the "immediate examination" of the right of expatriation in his speech before the National Association for the Promotion of Social Science. "Can you not write something important on this subject?" Lieber asked his pen pal Bluntschli in Germany. Bluntschli's subsequent article, published in both German and French, appeared in the first international law journal, *Revue de droit international et de législation comparée.* "It is unworthy of the State to keep members against their will and by force, as serfs or as slaves," Bluntschli declared.[30] As the United States Congress began debates on expatriation, so, too, did Europe, pushed by the publicists who drove home a consistent message: it was time to change the law of allegiance.

Europeans are "rushing to America and Australia," observed John Westlake, and governments could—and should—do little to stop them. "To be absent from home during a considerable part of his life is the normal state of civilized man," whether drawn by business, the search for a more "genial climate," or the thirst for new sights and adventure. "The skilled workman and the unskilled labourer" traveled just as frequently, "attracted by foreign mines, railways, and other sources of employment."[31] The flow of people across oceans and national borders revealed more than just an uptick in immigration. Global migration in the capitalist age announced the arrival of a new, higher stage of social development, one that Sir Henry Maine captured in his soon-to-be classic work, *Ancient Law,* published in 1861. Surveying a thousand years of Roman history, Maine concluded that "the movement of the progressive societies has . . . been a movement *from Status to Contract.*" Once upon a time, Maine said, people were defined by their place—or status—in the social order at birth, but "a new phase of social order" had evolved "in which all . . . relations arise from the free agreement of individuals."[32]

Maine's "status to contract" concept drew people's attention, in part because it captured so neatly and simply the vast changes all around them, reaching from the Enlightenment and the age of revolutions to the rise of free market capitalism. What was the collapse of slavery and the emancipation of the serfs but a stark example of the progress from status to contract? Harcourt, with Maine's lessons in mind and writing under the pen name Historicus, blasted Blackstone's description of perpetual allegiance as a *"principle of universal law,"* seeing it instead as driven by historical circumstances. "The truth is this doctrine has its origin in a system which is obsolete," Harcourt argued. It had arisen in feudal relations, where the subject remained obligated to the lord liege, who provided the subject with land and protection. The law of perpetual allegiance worked when "few people left or moved about," but now the "never-ceasing tide of emigration" created new pressures that "feudal law" and "our forefathers" could never have anticipated. Feudal tenure had disappeared long ago, but the law of feudal allegiance remained, at striking odds with modern conditions. The American Civil War had swept out the remnants of feudalism from the United

States, declared George Yeaman, U.S. minister to Denmark, and freedom of contract now reigned. In Europe, too, individuals had gradually won their liberty from absolute monarchs, rulers who had viewed people as their property and subordinated "everything . . . to their own right and interests." In "modern" nineteenth-century Europe, Johann Bluntschli observed, monarchs ruled through constitutions and legislatures, restrained by the "recognition of natural human rights."[33]

People owned themselves and could choose their own fates, Yeaman trumpeted in his defense of the right of migration and expatriation. In pursuing their interests, they advanced the prosperity and welfare of all. As workers migrated to better their lives and opportunities, they followed "higher" scientific laws of population, production, and exchange, moving where their labor was most needed and would fetch a higher price. "Sending" countries ultimately benefitted from the wondrous laws of supply and demand. As they rid themselves of surplus workers, wages and resources opened up for those who remained at home, and with greater prosperity came greater happiness and less political upheaval.[34]

Holding on to outdated political theories of membership that threatened to strangle commerce and create conflict made little sense, publicists argued, especially when emigrant countries already recognized the right of expatriation in practice if not in law. By allowing their citizens to leave, sometimes even encouraging their departure in times of economic distress and political tension, governments had given their tacit consent to emigration. It seemed "highly unjust," argued Lord Cockburn, to refuse the millions of people who had emigrated to the United States since 1816 the "right of complete expatriation" when they had so clearly severed their ties with their native lands and thrown their fates in with a new land.[35]

What would emigrant countries achieve with their stranglehold on their native subjects? Only embittered subjects, Westlake warned, who yearned to break free of the "halter" round their necks and dragged their native countries into conflicts with their new adopted homelands—precisely what was happening in "the present Fenian conspiracy." Was it really worth risking war for the sake of Fenians or other "useless and unprofitable subjects"? Just as a husband would be foolish to "reclaim" a "run away" wife if "she was determined to go away," so, too, nations would be "extremely unwise" to "want to keep people who wished to go away."[36]

Expatriation was not simply an American problem, even if the United States had the most to gain from a "free trade in men." The problem of multiple allegiances, arising from different national rules of membership, plagued international relations. Britain worried about France's new law compelling foreign nationals' children born in French territory to serve in its armed forces, even though under France's rule of descent the children inherited the nationality of their fathers. Some Latin American countries, frustrated by the failure of foreign residents to contribute their fair share in taxes and manpower to their homes, had resorted to "involuntary naturalization" laws. They declared men who bought land or married native women to be their citizens after living in the country for a specified time, whether they wanted citizenship or not.[37] What if a war broke out between two countries—say, France and Prussia—and both sides claimed an individual as their national, compelling him to fight? No matter which side he fought for, he remained a traitor in the eyes of the other country. Conflicting rules put both states and individuals in impossible situations, placing the "conscientious citizen" on a "fearful seesaw" and setting nation-states on a collision course.[38]

"We cannot faithfully serve two masters," Lieber concluded. "We must single out one country, from among all countries of the globe, to call ours."[39] Publicists roundly denounced the "so-called double allegiance" as "barbaric," "a political absurdity," "an impossibility," which only caused "great mischief" to countries and endangered world peace. One allegiance, one nationality—that was the best policy to strengthen the sovereignty of nation-states and avoid being drawn into needless conflict.[40]

As publicists and diplomats wrested control over expatriation out of the hands of legislators, they had shifted the focus of the debate. If Fenians spoke to and for naturalized Americans, emphasizing the government's duty to protect all citizens, the publicists spoke mainly to state builders and policymakers, highlighting the problem of state sovereignty. Conflicting rules of political membership ensnared both individuals and nation-states in murky and potentially explosive jurisdictional battles and left the nation-state powerless to articulate its territorial or political boundaries, they argued. Let your people go, they urged the states, and you will be stronger, not weaker.

12

Treating Expatriation

"THE PILOT is at the helm, the ship swings from her moorings," historian George Bancroft wrote cheerfully to Secretary of State William Seward as he headed to Europe to take up his post as the United States minister in Berlin. He could not have been happier with his new position. Already the nation's best-known historian, Bancroft looked forward to making history, not just writing about it. Seward had charged him with an important and delicate mission: to settle the "never-ending dispute" between the United States and Europe over that most "troublesome" and "long-vexed" question of expatriation.[1] Bancroft approached his task with supreme confidence, bolstered by the belief that history was on his side. If he did succeed, Bancroft boldly claimed, "it will be the greatest diplomatic success gained for a long time." Once Prussia agreed to a treaty guaranteeing expatriation, Seward and Bancroft expected other countries would soon follow.[2]

Bancroft and other publicists were positively gleeful about the dawning of a new international order, as the United States took "the lead in changing the law of nations." Treaty-making exploded in the nineteenth century, the number of treaties doubling between the late 1830s and 1870 and increasing sevenfold over the course of the century. Seward, alone, claimed to have negotiated fifty-six treaties. If the Expatriation Act of 1868 could not force countries to accept the "American doctrine" of expatriation, treaties offered a way for "civilised States" to bind themselves. Publicists praised treaties as the building blocks of a new international law, the "gentle civilizer" of nations.[3]

But even as they gave unprecedented protection to the right of expatriation, the naturalization treaties exposed fundamental tensions about how far that right reached, as revealed in the treaties the United States made with the

North German Confederation, China, and Great Britain. Policymakers worried about the allegiance of their subjects and citizens. Fenians may have succeeded in creating the explosive expatriation crisis, but they also raised alarms about the ability of foreign-born Americans to harness the state to its own interests. "A great many" Fenians had gone over to Ireland "undoubtedly to stir up trouble," argued Senator William P. Fessenden, and had drawn the American people into a cause that was not in their national interest.[4] Sending states also remained deeply skeptical of subjects who abandoned their native land for America. Even those who professed to be the most ardent supporters of expatriation, such as Nathaniel Banks, had worried about the implications of an unqualified and unconditional right of expatriation. Should individuals really be able to come and go as they liked, to naturalize here and there on their own accord? Was *anyone*—women, Chinese—free to change allegiance?

BANCROFT quickly got to work on the naturalization question once he arrived in Germany in August 1867, encouraged by a warm welcome from the new North German Confederation government. When Bancroft arrived in Berlin, German chancellor Otto von Bismarck took him to King William's country residence, where he received the royal treatment. He met with the foreign minister, who received Bancroft's opening remarks about the prospect of a naturalization treaty "in the most friendly spirit." Things were going splendidly, Bancroft reported to Seward. He hoped to soon "report to you favorable progress."[5]

Bismarck, the "Iron Chancellor," cared little about the right of expatriation, or any "natural rights," despising "liberal ideas" and the "boring humanity blatherers" who embraced them. Yet Bismarck was a pragmatist. "One cannot make a wave, only ride it," he often quipped, eyeing the political landscape.[6] Modern emigration could not be stopped, especially as the demand for labor and industry grew. The North German Confederation embraced freedom of migration in 1867, at least internally, overcoming traditional barriers that had tied individuals to particular towns and guaranteeing to its citizens the freedom to travel, work, and live anywhere within the union. Better to acknowledge new social realities and seek strategic advantage with potential allies, thought Bismarck, than to dig in one's heels against inevitable social forces.[7]

Personal relationships and Prussia's long-term interests greased the diplomatic wheels. It helped that Bancroft, having studied in Germany as a youth, spoke German fluently and lavished praise upon Bismarck as a hero of the modern age. But Bismarck also hoped to cultivate the United States as an ally as he sought to unify the thirty-nine separate German states under Prussia's leadership. He was startlingly successful, quickly winning the Austrian-Prussian War of 1866, which brought two-thirds of Germany under Prussian control in the new North German Confederation. Bismarck busily plotted his next move, including a possible war against France. He saw the United States as a potential ally, despite its relative isolation from the European affairs that engaged him most. Prussia had supported the Union cause, and with the war over, Bismarck hoped that the United States, in turn, would sympathize with his project of German unification.[8]

Still, Bancroft had become more cautious about the treaty's progress after a month in Berlin. "The subject is not without its difficulties," he admitted to Seward, as "strong objections and resistance are made."[9] Military service, as always, was the main sticking point. "From the king down to the most humble official, you hear nothing talked of but the *Army*, the *Prussian Army*," wrote Joseph Wright, Bancroft's predecessor in Berlin, in March 1867. The "great questions of the day" would be decided not by "speeches and majorities" but by "iron and blood," Bismarck declared in 1862 as he laid plans to expand the army. New laws enlarged the military by 50 percent and required young men to serve three years on active duty in the army instead of two.[10] As war with France hovered on the horizon, the War Ministry could little afford to relinquish any potential recruits, complicating Bancroft's task. If Prussia recognized the right of expatriation, what was to stop an endless flood of its most valued resource—young men—from leaving?[11]

It did not help that naturalized German Americans sometimes returned to their homeland to live or do business, using their American citizenship as a shield against the demands of German officials. Hugo Rempel, the son of a prominent merchant, was a case in point. Leaving Prussia for the United States in 1859 at the age of sixteen, "only to avoid military service," in the opinion of the Prussian foreign minister, Rempel made himself a perfect nuisance when he returned in 1865. "He has shown a very determined opposition to the royal government," complained local officials, going out of his way to ridicule soldiers and patriotic public demonstrations celebrating Prussia's victory over Austria in 1866. Fed up after he insulted an army officer on a public street, the Prussian government ordered Rempel back to the United States.[12]

Rempel not only flouted his exemption from military service but also raised the thorny question about whether naturalized German Americans should be allowed to return to their homeland to take up permanent residence. It was one thing to let subjects go if they intended to make their lives in America, but quite another if they returned to live and do business in their native land. Bavarian authorities complained they "had no end of troubles with such hermaphrodite 'citizens' who put forth their American citizenship whenever claims were made upon them by Bavaria and directly changed into Bavarians whenever—for business purposes—they could claim any rights or privileges on that ground." American diplomats and legislators had little sympathy for such fly-by-night citizens but wanted to protect legitimate businessmen and entrepreneurs who took advantage of increasing commercial opportunities around the globe.[13]

Nor could the two governments agree upon when German emigrants crossed the threshold from being "German" to "American," especially when it came to the German government's claim to their military service. German emigrants could naturalize after five years' residence in the United States, but Prussia insisted they remained liable for military service for at least ten years after their departure. William Bardroff, born in Bavaria in 1842, immigrated to the United States as a minor and became a citizen in 1865. When he turned twenty-one, in 1863, the Bavarian government declared him a deserter and sentenced him in absentia, punishing him when he returned as a naturalized American. The United States insisted that German states could only punish nationals who had actually deserted, emigrating while they were in active military service.[14]

Over the next two months, Bancroft and the foreign minister, Bernhard König, worked to find a compromise, hammering out the details of the agreement that would become the model for subsequent naturalization treaties. Bismarck persuaded his government to "accept the American rule" as to the time of residence required for a change of nationality. But Bancroft also made concessions—too many, in the opinion of later critics. The two countries agreed on the following terms: five years' residence and naturalization in the other country would be sufficient to change one's nationality, turning a German into an American (or vice versa) and releasing the emigrant from obligations in the native land. This was the North German Confederation's major compromise, as it relented on its ten-year rule. But the German government insisted, despite Bancroft's efforts, that naturalized German Americans could be tried for crimes committed before they emigrated. Finally, and most provocative, any naturalized German American who "renewed his residence in North Germany, without the intent to return to America . . . shall be held to have renounced his American citizenship," resuming his German nationality. The tricky question was how to know if the individual "intended" to remain in North Germany. The treaty's answer: two years' residence in northern Germany would create the presumption that an individual intended to remain.[15]

Bancroft declared the treaty, signed on February 22, 1868, a great victory. "All is granted that our government ever asked for," he declared triumphantly.[16] Bancroft's supporters showered him with praise for his "brilliant success" in securing the "remarkable treaty," which marked a "complete rupture" in previous European policies on allegiance. Finally, the German government had recognized "the great Republican principle, that the People do not exist for the sake of the government, but the Govt for the people," declared Charles Detmold, a German American engineer and businessman. Soon other countries would follow the North German Confederation's lead, many predicted, and "a great bone of contention" would be removed from American diplomatic relations.[17]

Not all sang Bancroft's praises. "Bismarck got altogether the better of George," wrote the German American lawyer Bernard Roelker. "We shall be worse off than before."[18] Panicked German Americans dashed off letters to Bancroft and their political representatives. They worried especially about Articles II and IV. In specifying that emigrants remained liable for "actions" committed before they left, Article II suggested that German Americans could still be punished for emigrating without permission or without fulfilling their military service.[19] Bismarck assured skeptics that the whole purpose of the treaty was to rid the two countries of the pesky military service question: "Whosoever emigrates *bona fide* with the purpose of residing permanently in America, shall meet with no obstacle on our part." But if that's what the article meant, the editor of *Harper's Weekly* asked, "why does it not say so?" Nor did Bismarck's clarification reassure those who worried about the reach of Article IV. Would German Americans who returned to Germany to live or do business automatically lose their American citizenship after two years' residence? If so, the right of expatriation seemed empty.[20]

The worried letters of German Americans revealed bigger problems in coming to an international solution on the right of expatriation. Mass migration had become a fact of life in the nineteenth century. But as individuals became unmoored, states grappled for ways to secure them more firmly in place. For states, the point was to clear up competing claims to the same individuals, draw territorial and political boundaries more sharply, and pin individuals down to one nationality. And, ideally, nationality would align with residence. The purpose of naturalization, Charles Sumner argued, was to incorporate foreigners "who intend to reside here permanently, to cast their lot with us." But naturalized Americans' lives did not always fit neatly within a single nation's territorial borders, their personal and commercial ties stretching across oceans and political jurisdictions.[21]

Consider the case of Dr. Charles E. Munde, a "hydropathic physician." Munde emigrated to the United States from his native Saxony with his wife, Bertha, and their four children in 1849. By 1854, Munde had acquired American citizenship and established Dr. Munde's Water Cure Establishment near Northampton, Massachusetts. He made a prosperous living until the Civil War intervened and his business burned to the ground in 1865. Munde decided to retire in Germany in 1866, settling in Würzburg. Bertha, his son Paul, twenty-one, and his American-born daughter Elisabeth, fifteen, accompanied Charles, but they left behind three adult children, all naturalized Americans by virtue of Charles's naturalization in 1854. Paul, a doctor and veteran of the Union Army, served as a surgeon during the Austrian-Prussian War of 1866 and again in the Franco-Prussian War of 1870–1871. He then returned to the United States, medical degree in hand from the University of Vienna, and established a thriving medical practice in New York, serving in the New York National Guard and becoming a naturalized citizen in 1875. His father, Charles, spent his remaining years in Germany in "comfort and independence," but "always gloried in his American citizenship."[22]

Here was a family, like many others, who moved back and forth between countries, participating in the civic life of both. Some naturalized citizens doubtless sought to escape onerous obligations of citizenship, whether military service or taxes, but others moved to reconnect with family, pursue education, build businesses, repair their health, or retire in comfort. Native-born Americans, too, spent years abroad, finding after the Civil War that their money went further in Europe.[23] It is likely that only a few left with the intention of yielding their American citizenship.

Charles Munde certainly didn't, as he made clear in the "Würzburg Protest" he circulated to American and German officials. "We *are* citizens for life, unless we renounce our rights voluntarily," he insisted. Native-born citizens who lived abroad could do so without fear of losing their American nationality. Naturalized Americans deserved to be treated the same, under the Constitution. "No plenipotentiary, or government, or Senate, or Congress, have the right to *treat away*" the citizenship of naturalized Americans. "Form clubs," Munde urged German Americans living in Germany, and pressure Seward to be as vigilant in protecting their rights as he was for "our Irish brethren."[24]

Bancroft, irked that all of his hard work might go to waste, undoubtedly breathed a sigh of relief when the Senate and president approved the treaty in May 1868. Bancroft eagerly anticipated future European treaties, declaring optimistically "the right of the individual to choose his home & with it the right to change his country . . . is now universally acknowledged on the continent." Yet Bancroft conceded in a private letter to international law expert W. B. Lawrence in the winter of 1869 that "unsettled questions" and "puzzling cases come up," including when a naturalized citizen loses his adopted citizenship—the very question that alarmed German Americans in Germany.[25]

Even as Bancroft slowly overcame resistance in Europe to the idea of expatriation, he remained stymied at home by those who continued to worry that the treaties curbed rather than furthered the right of expatriation. In the spring of 1869, the treaties he had signed with several southern German states in the summer of 1868 still lay unratified by the Senate. Bancroft pleaded with Sumner to use his position as chair of the Senate Foreign Relations Committee to get the treaties approved. The treaties "concede to us everything," Bancroft insisted, "& we give nothing in return."[26] Charles Munde observed that "the more treaties Mr. Bancroft makes," the better they became, but he still pushed for more. The Burlingame Treaty with China, just signed by Seward on July 4, 1868, spoke grandly and "without any restrictions," recognizing "the inherent and inalienable right of man to change his home and allegiance."[27] The rights of individuals, not the greedy interests of states, should ring out loud and clear, Munde urged. But if the Burlingame Treaty spoke in broad, bold strokes about the right of expatriation, it, too, revealed the limits as well as the possibilities of liberal internationalism.

ZHANG DEYI was relieved to see the golden hills of San Francisco, covered with "yellow flowers," as he sailed on SS *China* into the busy harbor on March 31, 1868. The voyage from his native China had not been an easy one. For days, hurricane-force winds whipped up huge mountains of waves, tossing the ship violently about. "Everything aboard clatters, crashes and booms," Zhang recorded in his diary. The "'Pacific' is scarcely an apt name for this viciously tempestuous Great Eastern Ocean," Zhang observed. It "ought rather to be called 'Perilous' or 'Hurricanic.'"[28] When the passengers finally neared the end of their tumultuous journey, the Westerners on board celebrated, changing "into white for the evening and donning tall, built-up paper hats of various shapes." They "formed circles and ran round and round singing," Zhang noted, with an anthropologist's eye.[29]

The Westerners, for all the ruckus they made, were a distinct minority on the ship, numbering perhaps 40 of the 803 passengers. Zhang was one of more than 700 Chinese passengers who arrived at "Gold Mountain," as Chinese called California. It was a banner year for Chinese immigration, though nowhere near the peak in 1852 when 30,000 Chinese hurried to California to join the gold rush. In 1868, 11,081 Chinese arrived in San Francisco—almost 8,000 more than the previous year. Chinese immigrants came to complete the transcontinental railroad, work on California's farms, transform the waterlogged Sacramento Delta into fertile farmland, or seek their fortunes in the silver-rich Comstock Lode in Nevada or in San Francisco Chinatown's burgeoning industries.[30]

Zhang Deyi, however, had a far different task ahead as he walked off SS *China* onto San Francisco's busy streets. Only twenty-one, Zhang served as an interpreter for the Burlingame Mission, an official Chinese delegation led by Anson Burlingame, a Yankee from Boston and the former U.S. minister to China, and two Chinese envoys, Zhi Gang and Sun Jiagu. Zhang, educated in English and French at the new foreign language school in Beijing created in 1862, was part of a bold experiment by a group of Chinese reformers to increase engagement with the West. Over the next three years, the delegation would travel 42,000 miles to visit all the major powers—England, France, Russia, Italy, Belgium, and the North German Confederation—but the first stop on its well-publicized tour was the United States, a great coup for Secretary of State Seward, who had long seen Asia as key to America's commercial empire. He viewed the Burlingame Treaty, signed during the Chinese embassy's stay in Washington, D.C., as one of the major achievements of his tenure as secretary of state.[31]

The Burlingame Treaty is not usually included among the landmark naturalization treaties the United States signed between 1868 and 1872, in part because the agreement cast a much wider net, covering trade, religious freedom, access to education, and Chinese control over its ports. But, as Munde had noticed, the treaty endorsed the right of expatriation and the freedom of migration much more broadly than did Bancroft's treaties. The treaty with China arose in the thick of the expatriation debates, the Senate ratifying the Burlingame Treaty just one day after it passed the Expatriation Act. The China treaty, like Bancroft's agreements, sought to address a similar problem: exit rules that hampered emigration. The Chinese government's ban on emigration, punishable by death, had been rarely, if ever, enforced, but China had other reasons for finally relaxing its official opposition to emigration and legalizing the well-established Chinese immigration to America.[32] By recognizing the right of migration and expatriation, China sought to persuade Western states that it was one of the "family of nations," a sovereign state with power to govern itself—no different from England, France, Russia, or the United States. For by the 1860s, Chinese sovereignty seemed in danger of disappearing altogether, after more than twenty years of relentless assault by Europe and America.

China had fallen far from its historical position as one of the world's largest and most powerful empires, widely respected as the birthplace of ancient civilization. Western powers, craving China's trade and, increasingly, its workers, poured tremendous energy and military might into "opening" China.[33] After the British introduced opium to China, wreaking havoc as opium addiction and illegal drug dealing spread, the Qing government banned the noxious drug and took steps to shut down the trade. "Every state has . . . a right to prohibit the entrance of foreign merchandises," Commissioner Lin Zexu told Queen Victoria, quoting from the West's own eminent authority on the law of nations, Emer de Vattel. Surely, if England had the power to compel outsiders to obey British laws when on English turf, China had the same right to expect foreigners to comply with Chinese laws while on its territory.[34]

The British responded not with respect for China's sovereign power but with self-righteous indignation and gunboats in the Opium Wars of 1839–1842 and 1858–1860, determined to keep the free trade in opium—its most profitable export—alive. The West brushed aside Lin's efforts to couch China's demands within the West's own cherished principles of the law of nations. Vattel insisted in 1758 that "a perfect equality of rights" existed among nations, but some nations were evidently more equal than others.[35] International law applied only to the "family of nations," explained John Quincy Adams in 1841, that is, "civilized" Christian states that embraced the rule of law and universal human rights, including the right of free trade and migration. China had no sovereignty that Western powers were bound to respect under international law, at least not until it began to behave like a civilized Western state and allow free trade and migration.[36]

The West, the United States included, celebrated the "opening" of China after the British victory in the Opium Wars, but China mourned the beginning of its "century of humiliation" and the era of "unequal treaties." China's ports and interior, once off-limits, became open to foreign merchants, missionaries, and the spread of the opium trade.[37] The West also forced China to relax its official ban on migration, especially after the abolition of African slavery in the British Empire in the 1830s. European powers aggressively recruited Chinese laborers by the late 1840s, binding them to lengthy contracts and shipping them off (often on American vessels) to colonies in Peru, Cuba, Trinidad, and British Guiana, under conditions all too reminiscent of slavery. The infamous coolie labor system had been born, though the vast majority of Chinese continued to migrate not as indentured workers but through their own social networks, as they had in the past.[38]

China's rapid decline in the face of the Western onslaught prompted much soul-searching among Qing government officials. The only way to fight the Western enemy, concluded the reform wing of the government, was by adopting its weapons and learning its ways. The Chinese government again turned to Western international law, hoping that China could gain entry into the "family of nations" and secure recognition by Western powers as an equal, sovereign state.[39] China sent an official goodwill delegation to the West in 1868 to publicize its reforms and to soften Western feelings toward China, choosing as the face of the Chinese mission the congenial American Anson Burlingame, who had just resigned his position as U.S. minister to China. It seemed a surprising choice, an American to head a Chinese delegation, but who better to represent China to the West than a Westerner who knew its customs, values, and languages? And Burlingame seemed particularly sympathetic to China's plight, advocating a new "cooperative policy" of patient diplomacy and respect rather than brute force and harsh treaties. On February 25, 1868, the Burlingame Mission embarked from Shanghai on its global voyage, described at the time as "one of the most remarkable events in history."[40]

The Burlingame Mission was a big hit in the United States.[41] Throngs of people came to gawk at the delegation as it toured first San Francisco and then the East. Society ladies, dressed in their finest, filled the corridors of the White House in the hope of seeing the Chinese embassy when they came to meet the president. Crowds packed the House of Representatives to glimpse the unusual reception of the delegation by Congress. In Boston, Burlingame's hometown, the Chinese embassy was nearly "suffocated with hospitality" by the "rush and the crush and the tear of the multitude" that showered the distinguished visitors with serenades.[42]

Burlingame worked hard to overcome American preconceptions, fostering an image of China as enlightened and modern. China and the United States were not so very different, he repeated. Take the "great doctrine of Confucius . . .

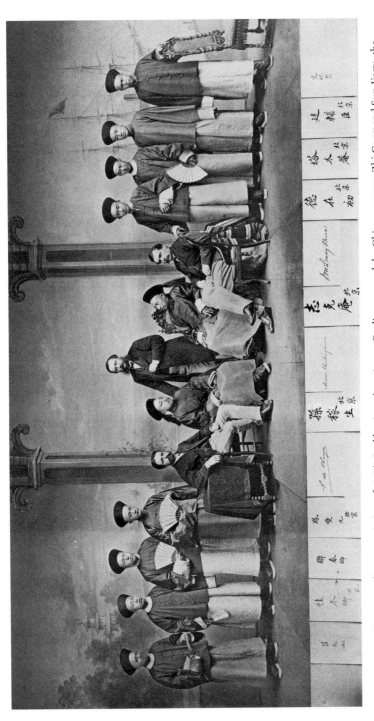

The Chinese Embassy (Burlingame Mission of 1868). Led by American Anson Burlingame and the Chinese envoys Zhi Gang and Sun Jiagu, the Burlingame Mission sought to gain international recognition of China as an equal, sovereign state. Its first stop was in the United States.

'Do not unto others what you would not have others do unto you.'" How strikingly similar it was to the Christian Golden Rule. A Republican ally of both Sumner and Banks, Burlingame also tapped into the Reconstruction-era rhetoric of emancipation and equality to argue for the freedom of China from Western domination. China knew that "she must come into relations" with the West. All China wanted was "fair play," the same independence and equality extended to Western states, Burlingame pleaded. In turn, trade and exchange of people and goods would flourish, bringing together two great civilizations and making "the whole world kin." It was "a mighty revolution" in the making.[43]

The "revolution" culminated with the signing of a new treaty between the United States and China on July 4, 1868—a declaration of independence for China, in Burlingame's eyes, and a model for its new relationship with the West. The treaty seems to have been the brainchild of Seward and Burlingame, not the Chinese imperial government. For Seward, much was at stake: millions of dollars in trade, American national prestige and power, and the immigration of thousands of Chinese workers. Seward had long believed that America's future lay in Asia and the Pacific Ocean and hoped, with the treaty, to capture the Asian trade and edge out England, America's strongest competitor. Seward courted the Chinese envoys shamelessly, even showing his visitors the bedroom where he had almost been killed on the night of Lincoln's assassination.[44] Burlingame happily worked with Seward on the treaty, seeing American and Chinese interests as complementary. "There is no reason why the policy which protects China should not enrich America," observed the *New York Times*.[45]

Hailed as China's first "equal treaty," the Burlingame Treaty was striking in its reciprocity and recognition of Chinese sovereignty, and in its endorsement of expatriation. It recognized the "inherent and inalienable right of man to change his home and allegiance, and also the mutual advantage of the free migration and emigration of their citizens and subjects"—a clear triumph for the American doctrine of expatriation. The treaty also provided one of the few legal shields for Chinese immigrants in the United States against discriminatory laws, entitling them to the same "privileges, immunities and exemptions" extended to other foreign nationals.[46] And China, finally, let go of its emigrants in recognizing the natural right of migration. With his treaty, Seward boasted, he had "emancipated 400,000,000 Chinamen from . . . bondage," freeing them to work in America.[47]

Even American citizenship seemed within Chinese reach. The Naturalization Act of 1790 specified that only "free white persons" could become citizens, making Chinese immigrants perpetual aliens under the law. But the Burlingame Treaty, by extending Chinese the same privileges given other foreign nationals, suggested that citizenship, too, would have to be made available to Chinese immigrants. But that possibility soon disappeared. When the treaty came before the Senate for ratification, Senator John Conness of California—the passionate advocate of the Expatriation Act—introduced a critical amendment, passed by the Senate, declaring that the treaty did *not* confer the right of naturalization upon Chinese in the United States. If Chinese had the right to expatriate from China, they did not necessarily have the right to naturalize in America.[48]

Clearly, not everyone welcomed Chinese immigrants to America as warmly as Seward. Workingmen's organizations and the Democratic Party in California greeted the Burlingame Mission with protests and anti-Chinese riots, denouncing the treaty as an "outrage" that would unleash thousands of Chinese workers to compete against white workingmen, just to satisfy "a few Eastern humanitarians." They fit Chinese into the racialized politics of the era, arguing that Chinese, no less than African Americans, threatened "white supremacy." In vetoing the Civil Rights Act of 1866, President Johnson dangled the unthinkable possibility that it would recognize even "the Chinese of the Pacific States" as birthright citizens.[49] Irish workers, though immigrants themselves, often protested the loudest against the Chinese threat. Chinese and Irish workers had much in common; they were both the "diggers of ditches and the makers of railroads"—and the victims of British imperialism.[50] But few Irish made common cause with Chinese in the United States, especially in light of suggestions that Irish were no better than the "odd" Chinese. In a *Harper's Weekly* cartoon from 1869, Uncle Sam "introduces Eastern Barbarism to Western Civilization," depicting a ragged, simian-featured Irish immigrant, freshly arrived at Castle Garden, bowing to "John Chinaman" with his sharp features and long queue, at the Golden Gate in San Francisco. The Irish immigrant, though from the West, appeared just as uncivilized as the Chinese barbarian from the East. Citizenship provided one crucial distinction between the two groups and one that many Irish workers held on to, arguing that Chinese were not fit to be citizens.[51]

Some elite Americans agreed, even as they cast doubt on the Irish as good citizens. They struggled to reconcile the dignified "Chinese noblemen" on the Burlingame Mission with popular images of Chinese as exotic curiosities at best and dangerous interlopers at worst. "This question of races is a puzzling one," Lucretia Bancroft Farnum confessed to her brother, George Bancroft, writing

"The Only One Barred Out." The caption continues: "Enlightened American Statesman.—'We must draw the line *somewhere*, you know.'" Published in 1882, as Congress was debating the Chinese Exclusion Act, the cartoon highlights the injustice of industrious Chinese immigrants being excluded from the United States while the "Fenian & Hoodlum" are admitted.

from her San Francisco home in 1865. She embraced emancipation and even contemplated black suffrage as a possibility, but derided the Irish. "I never did believe in granting Irishmen [the vote] under less years that a native enjoys it—It takes more than twenty one years to raise an Irishman into a reasoning & reasonable being." But then "there are the Chinese—every fresh arrival landing hundreds of them. . . . [W]ith all my philanthropic interest in the fate of the negro, I cannot control my disgust at these greasy, oblique-eyed people, & I cross the street to avoid meeting them—They are thrifty & industrious—but bah!" Lucretia voiced an all too common view: Chinese might be productive, but with their "unknown tongue" and "strange manners and customs," they would never assimilate into American life.[52]

The Burlingame Treaty, then, embraced Chinese immigrant workers with one hand but barred potential Chinese American citizens with the other. Just as China's status in the family of nations remained ambiguous, so, too, did Chinese immigrants' place in the American polity, circumscribed by debates over where China and Chinese stood as "civilized" people. The Burlingame Treaty revealed a critical limit to the right of expatriation: the right to leave did not guarantee the right to enter. Everyone might have the right to "denationalize himself," but a person could become a citizen elsewhere only if "that country consents to receive him," observed commentator John T. Morse. "No country is prepared to have citizens poured into it like water into a bucket, but prefers rather that they should come through some sort of filter."[53] Race continued to be one "filter" for citizenship. So, too, would gender, as the Anglo-American Naturalization treaty soon revealed.

RIDING high from his success with China and Prussia, Seward turned to Great Britain with renewed determination in July 1868. Seward was tired of British foot-dragging on the issue of expatriation. Time was short. The presidential election loomed in November, and Seward, along with President Johnson, would be out of office by the following March. Settling the long-simmering disputes between the United States and Britain would be a great parting gift for the nation—and for Seward and his legacy. Speak frankly with the British government, Seward instructed Reverdy Johnson, the new U.S. minister to Great Britain. If the North German Union and a growing number of European nations agreed to the principle of expatriation, why couldn't Great Britain? Its delay only increased Americans' "irritation" and "national distrust" of Great Britain, and the United States would not negotiate with Britain on any other issue until the "naturalization question" was settled.[54]

Few British relished the thought of giving in to America's blustering demands, but Sir Vernon Harcourt, with his London *Times* essays under the pen name Historicus, helped persuade policymakers to let go of the outdated doctrine of perpetual allegiance. "We are beginning to see that to claim a dominion over persons is, after all, not such a very fine thing," Harcourt concluded.[55] But the British refused to be hurried into a treaty. Changing nationality rules raised a host of thorny legal issues that would have to be sorted out in British domestic law before Britain could come to any agreement with the United States. British laws on property and inheritance, notoriously complex, posed the biggest challenge, especially since not only wealth but also British political and social power sprang from property ownership. Aliens could not own or inherit property, nor could they hold political office. What would happen if a new treaty suddenly converted naturalized British Americans, previously acknowledged as British subjects, into aliens? Would they lose their property and legal status as heirs? And what about the status of wives and children, also critical to establishing bloodlines and succession? The British government could not act until the Royal Commission on Naturalization, staffed by the leading lights on international law, made its recommendations.[56]

Still, the British government could not resist the opportunity offered when Reverdy Johnson arrived in London, brimming with confidence and eager to resolve all the outstanding disputes between the two countries. Couldn't Lord Stanley agree on a "simple Treaty" that acknowledged "the great principles of expatriation and naturalization," leaving the details to be sorted out after the

"Unconquered Still! The released Political Prisoners, on regaining their liberty, proclaim their fidelity to Ireland and her cause, to the infinite dismay of their jailer, Mr. Bull." The Dublin *Weekly News* depicted Warren and Nagle released from jail but still defiant. (In fact, Augustine E. Costello was released with Warren, not Nagle, who had been freed almost a year earlier.)

commission had done its work?[57] Then, Johnson promised, the two countries could clean up the bothersome *Alabama* claims and settle the long-festering boundary disputes in the Pacific Northwest. The temptation to break the deadlock in Anglo-American relations was appealing, especially as both the United States and Britain faced major elections with the likely prospect of new administrations coming into power. On October 9, 1868, Johnson wrote to Seward triumphantly that "man's clearest right—the search for happiness wherever he may think he can find it"—had finally been secured: he had signed a protocol with Lord Stanley on the naturalization question.[58]

The protocol was not a treaty; instead, it provided a blueprint for what the final treaty might guarantee. It set out the general principles agreed upon by the two countries, recognizing especially the right of expatriation for both U.S. citizens and British subjects. But the protocol would not take effect until Parliament passed domestic laws to change the "perpetual allegiance" doctrine and sort out all the messy details that would entail. Despite Reverdy Johnson's boundless optimism, both he and Seward would be long gone by the time Parliament passed the Naturalization Act on May 12, 1870, followed the next day by the conclusion of the Naturalization Treaty between the two countries. But at least Seward would have the satisfaction of seeing to completion another hard-fought battle: the release of John Warren and Augustine Costello.[59]

IT WAS QUITE a homecoming. Released from Millbank Prison on March 4, 1869, Warren headed for Cork, and then his beloved Clonakilty. "A hundred thousand welcomes greeted the whilom exile and convict on his return to his native town," noted the *Irish Times*. An "immense throng" greeted him at the train station at nearby Bandon, cheering him, the American flag, and the *Jacmel* with "wildest enthusiasm." A band serenaded Warren with national tunes as he and the crowd traveled toward Clonakilty, the road lit by blazing barrels of tar. Arriving in Clonakilty, he found the town "brilliantly illuminated" and its residents turned out to "do honor to the gallant patriot." Until he and Costello, also released, sailed for the United States on April 29, they were toasted, cheered, and celebrated at one reception after another.[60]

Reverdy Johnson rushed to take credit for the prisoners' release, saying he was gratified "to think that the course which I have pursued since my arrival here has in some measure assisted in bringing about this result."[61] But the Fenians were more responsible, although indirectly, for freeing the *Jacmel* leaders. The new British administration, led by William Gladstone, promised to deal a "death blow" to Fenianism by enacting liberal reforms to pacify Ireland. In February 1869, Irish officials, taking the pulse of the country, reported that while there was little immediate danger of an outbreak, "the Fenian spirit" was alive and well, "alarming" in its "extent and intensity."[62] Gladstone promised amnesty for Fenian prisoners, along with land reform and the disestablishment of the Anglican Church, in hopes of sapping the Fenians' appeal. His government ordered the release of forty-nine Fenians in England and Australia on February 22, 1869, including Warren and Costello as a goodwill gesture to the United States. But if Gladstone hoped Ireland would be mollified and grateful, he would be disappointed.[63]

"UNCONQUERED STILL!" blazed the headline in the Dublin *Weekly News.* Warren and Costello showed no repentance as they lashed out at Britain in their victory lap around Ireland. "The sword is the most efficacious weapon to uplift a downtrodden nation," Warren proclaimed before a boisterous Cork crowd. The sword had freed America and "revolutionised the planet"; it could still free Ireland.[64] These did not seem idle words, given the tempestuous crowds and the scandalous speech given by the mayor of Cork at Warren's reception, in which he praised the attempted assassination of Prince Alfred in Australia. "Rank treason!" cried British critics in Parliament. Was this the thanks Britain received for its mercy? Warren and Costello left for the United States, defiantly proclaiming their American citizenship and their love for Ireland, having stirred the pot once more. There would be no further amnesty for Fenian prisoners, announced embittered government officials, given the "poor return" from ungrateful wretches.[65]

WARREN and Costello did little to help along the British Naturalization Act and the treaty. Tensions between the United States and Great Britain flared up once more, as rumors of new Fenian invasions of Canada circulated and the *Alabama* claims, a subject Reverdy Johnson had proclaimed settled with a convention he negotiated with Britain, reignited passions. Unexpectedly, Charles Sumner—usually perceived as Britain's ally in American foreign affairs— delivered a blistering speech against Johnson's *Alabama* treaty in the Senate in April 1869, blasting it for omitting an official apology from Britain or recognition of indirect injuries caused to the nation, which were "mountain-high," perhaps reaching $110 million. The Senate soundly rejected the treaty and Sumner became an overnight hero. But the British were furious over Sumner's "monstrous" betrayal, the foreign secretary concluding that Sumner and recently inaugurated President Ulysses S. Grant wanted war. No matter how much Britain conceded to the United States, Americans never seemed satisfied. The British government dug in its heels, refusing to yield any further. The new secretary of state, Hamilton Fish, counseled that it was time to "take breath" and "allow excitement and irritation to subside" on both sides before any attempt could be made to repair Anglo-American relations.[66]

Quarrelsome Americans aside, British policymakers found it difficult to agree on how to change British nationality rules. The Royal Commission took nine months to study the problem, finally delivering a divided report on February 20, 1869. It took another year before Parliament, on February 25, 1870, took up the naturalization bill. The Royal Commission had been unanimous in one conclusion: "It was high time" to "settle accurately the question 'who is who,'" even if it meant revolutionary changes in British law. The doctrine of perpetual allegiance "is neither reasonable nor convenient," especially in a nation that recognized the "absolute freedom of emigration."[67]

Still, the bill raised the hackles of parliamentary members as it proposed a "very considerable change" in British law, changing a doctrine "interwoven with the whole history of this country." Critics raised a host of questions: Should an individual be able to expatriate himself, without his government's permission? Such a prospect seemed like "robbery," one nation stealing the subjects of another. Should Britain simply give in to the United States on the issue? Wasn't the government moving too quickly, "higgledy-piggledly," in enacting such "a very important change"? An impressive lineup of British officials largely disarmed the opposition, insisting that perpetual allegiance was "indefensible in theory," "unworkable in practice," and far too damaging to British foreign relations to linger any longer.[68]

But one issue could not be easily dismissed: "What is to be done with the wife or child?" wondered the Lord Chancellor. The nationality of wives and especially children proved the most controversial issue during parliamentary debates, as lawmakers struggled to eliminate both dual nationality and statelessness. Ideally, agreed international law experts, all family members should share the same nationality to shield them from hardships during international conflicts and ensure protection for vulnerable wives and children. Harcourt and a minority on the Royal Commission argued that Britain should adopt the European rule of descent, making children's nationality hinge on that of their father's, regardless of where the children were born. But that went too far for the majority in Parliament, the principle of birthright nationality too deeply embedded in British law to uproot. Under the new law, children born in Britain to foreign fathers would remain British, as had always been the law.[69]

But Parliament proved much more willing to innovate when it came to married women. British-born women who married foreigners would now take the nationality of their husbands, a sharp reversal of the traditional common-law rule. Britain joined what was becoming a worldwide trend of "marital dena-tionalization," stripping women who married foreigners of their nationality in order to achieve uniform international rules. A few lone voices protested the radical change, pointing to the irony that Parliament was on the verge of extending greater rights to married women by giving them more control over their personal property while at the same time making the British woman "a foreign subject against her will." But the British attorney general apparently spoke for most in Parliament, insisting that "the question was what rule, on the whole, was most expedient."[70]

Britain's new naturalization act, paving the way for its treaty with the United States, did, indeed, shake British nationality loose from its feudal origins. Seeking to "throw the door open wide to foreigners," Britain liberalized its stingy naturalization process, making it easier and more attractive to become a British subject. The law broadened the rights of aliens, allowing them to own real property in Britain and thus sidestepping the potential problem of natural-ized British Americans losing property or inheritances. It abolished the mixed jury, the rarely used institution that had caused a "considerable fuss" when "traders in politics" such as John Warren used it to inflame Anglo-American relations. And finally, it buried the doctrine of perpetual allegiance as Britain embraced the right of expatriation—except, of course, for married women. The act specified that no "infant, lunatic, idiot, or married woman"—none of whom had the legal capacity to exercise political judgment—could apply for naturalization.[71] It was a thoroughly modern law.

ON APRIL 4, 1870, John Warren once again petitioned Congress. He had been a free man for more than a year, but he could not relinquish the fight. Warren wanted "redress" for his unlawful arrest "while riding peaceably and quietly in a cart" on the road to Youghal and for his imprisonment in a "vile and filthy prison without light or air" for eighteen months. Freed from prison, Warren remained shackled to Britain as its subject, his naturalization certificate not worth the paper it was printed on. "The plain simple issue is, am I a British subject or an American citizen?" Warren asked.[72]

Warren was still an "able writer," but his appeal fell flat, the Anglo-American Naturalization Treaty of May 13, 1870, finally answering the questions he had repeatedly and urgently posed.[73] The treaty fully recognized the right of expatriation, including none of the conditions that had plagued the North German agreement. Anyone who could naturalize under the laws of each country would be allowed to change allegiance. So yes, John Warren was an American citizen. How did Warren react to the news? Not with relief or a victory yell, but with condemnation, calling it "simply a bargain between the United States and England."[74]

Why Warren opposed the treaty remains unelaborated, but he probably realized what Britain and the United States had already concluded: settling the explosive issue of expatriation would give the Fenians one less weapon in their battle to inflame Anglo-American relations. Now the United States government had the unquestioned responsibility for keeping American Fenians within bounds. But Warren may have detected a more significant limitation in the naturalization treaties the United States negotiated with a dozen countries between 1868 and 1872.[75] Deciding "who was who" in international law might free migrants as they left one country to join another, but the treaties— "bargains" between countries—ultimately served states' interests in drawing territorial and political boundaries more sharply. The treaties constrained as much as they liberated, revealing significant anxiety about how states would manage mobile populations in a new era.

The key question, urged Albert Erbe, superintendent of labor exchange at Castle Garden, was this: "Must Expatriation be considered as a *Right* of the citizen, or merely a *License* granted to him by his Government?" The natural right to migrate and expatriate, so celebrated by the leading authorities on the law of nations, butted up repeatedly against another fundamental principle: every nation, being free and independent, was the "mistress of her own actions," having the sovereign power to guard its territorial borders and decide its own laws on membership.[76] The treaties sought to balance the rights of individuals and states, proclaiming the right of expatriation even as they set limits on it.

The Prussian treaty might look liberal, insisted Erbe, but it still rested on the idea that "the consent of Government is an *indispensable requirement* of expatriation," the Prussian government "graciously" extending its consent as long as its conditions—domicile abroad and liability for crimes committed before emigration—were met.[77] The Burlingame Treaty passionately declared the natural right to migrate and expatriate but then hedged, saying the treaty did not confer the right of naturalization on Chinese. Congress in 1870 would speak more plainly. When Sumner moved to strike the "white" requirement from the nation's naturalization law, as befitting a nation that had committed itself to racial equality, he met the angry opposition of Western representatives, who defeated the proposal, worried it would extend citizenship to Chinese. If Chinese did not have the right to become citizens, what good was the right of expatriation? Finally, the Anglo-American treaty appeared a striking victory for the republican theory that individuals should choose their citizenship, sweeping away "the follies and errors of a bygone age." Yet part of its "modern" resolution rested on stripping married women of any choice whatsoever when it came to nationality. Marital denationalization for British women went hand in hand with the expansion of expatriation for men.[78]

As the naturalization treaties began to pile up, Nathaniel Banks rushed to declare victory, crediting his own Expatriation Act of 1868 for paving the way for the revolutionary conventions. "All questions . . . have been finally and satisfactorily settled," he crowed. He was sadly mistaken.[79]

Epilogue

Exits

JUST TWO years after he left on *Erin's Hope,* John Warren returned a hero. A throng of friends and well-wishers, including William Nagle, greeted Warren and his comrade Augustine Costello when they arrived in New York City on May 9, 1869, aboard SS *Nevada.* "A GRAND PUBLIC RECEPTION will be tendered to our lately released fellow-citizens," promised an advertisement in the *Brooklyn Daily Eagle,* adding that there would be speeches by the New York governor and the mayor of New York City, plus tunes by Connel's Brass Band. Warren even had an audience with President Ulysses S. Grant, where he was "received with marked courtesy" as he made a plea to free all remaining American Fenians imprisoned by Britain. Grant assured Warren of "his intention to protect at all hazards the rights of American citizens in all parts of the world." All in all, it was a fine homecoming.[1]

But tragedy, too, awaited Warren. If friends greeted his ship, his family did not. The long separation had not been easy on his family, who had had to rely on fund-raisers to provide much-needed money and on family for shelter (John's sister, Mary O'Leary, had taken them into her large household in Arlington, Massachusetts). But even that was not enough to sustain the family until Warren's return. His daughter Eliza Jane, only seven years old, had died of consumption in January 1868, while he was in prison. His son John would soon follow, dying also at the age of seven, in 1873. And, only two weeks before Warren was released from prison, his wife, Joanna Madigan Warren, died at Massachusetts General Hospital on February 18, 1869, at age thirty-three. The cause of death: "burned." How she sustained her injuries is not clear, but fires were common occurrences in Boston's immigrant neighborhoods. Dying five months after she was burned, Joanna likely endured a lingering, painful death.[2] Warren's thirteen-year-old son, Timothy, was the only one left of his immediate family.

Soon Warren would also lose his comrade on *Erin's Hope,* William Nagle. His cause of death: "temporary insanity."[3] Nagle had long struggled with dark moods, perhaps even before the Civil War. In 1858, unable to find work and living hand to mouth, Nagle wrote, "What will become of me and my family God only knows. . . . The present is all darkness and despair to me." The Civil War gave him a job and honor but thrust him into some of the bloodiest, most traumatic battles of the war, reducing his company "to *seven* effective men" and leaving him weakened by malaria and a "nervous condition"—a condition that Irish jails, with their rules of silence and solitary confinement, did nothing to help. By November 1867, Nagle's attorney worried that if Nagle was imprisoned much longer, his "constitution may be entirely broken." Back in the States, Nagle appeared to rebound, working as a clerk in the New York City Tax Office (a plum patronage job) and busily giving speeches denouncing British tyranny and demanding the release of American citizens.[4]

But a cloud hung over Nagle, as stories circulated of the confession he had made to secure his release from prison in 1868. Irish nationalists condemned any concessions made to British authorities as signs of cowardice, but Nagle's purported confession was worse, as it strengthened the British government's hold over Warren and Costello, who had continued to proclaim their innocence.[5] As rumors of his confession mounted, Nagle made a public denial: "To the false reports sent forth, and already widely circulated through the press, that I made terms with the British Government, or any admission whatever, I pronounce *utterly untrue.*"[6] Nagle continued to be popular on the Fenian lecture circuit, yet the story was true, and Nagle appears to have received a cool reception in some Fenian circles.[7] Then, too, he had his father's betrayal to deal with: did William ever confront David Nagle about the letter he sent to Irish officials, offering to inform on Fenians in exchange for his son's release?

Whatever the cause—a tendency toward depression, the traumatic experiences of war, guilt, or perhaps even an alcoholic rage—William Nagle jumped out of the attic window at his home in New York City on August 15, 1869, at 7:30 A.M., dying instantly upon impact. His father, in the room at the time, suspected "his intention" but "could not catch him in time." Nagle became part of an "epidemic of suicides" afflicting young veterans after the Civil War.

Warren and Costello, serving as pallbearers, carried their fallen colleague to his grave.[8]

WARREN's other "family"—the Fenian Brotherhood—also appeared to be in its death throes. Warren's homecoming was marred by a small dispute that revealed much larger fissures dividing the Fenians. Expecting a reception planned by public officials, Warren and Costello boycotted the event when circulars indicated that Anthony A. Griffin, "district centre" of the Fenian Brotherhood, was heading the Committee of Arrangements. "We will not recognize any faction or party," Warren and Costello pledged, holding out for an event sponsored by non-Fenians. They had not forsaken the Fenians. Warren "had devoted the best part of his life to the cause of Irish nationality," he told *Frank Leslie's Illustrated Newspaper,* and "has always been in the front rank when the tocsin-peal was sounded." But, as they had in their trials, the men worked hard to elevate the issue of expatriation as an American cause, not a Fenian one. And they insisted on their political independence. While Warren allied with the Republican Party, running (unsuccessfully) as its candidate for registrar of New York City in 1873, he also campaigned for Democrats loyal to the Fenian cause, saying "he was not committed to any party." But in the fractious political scene, it was impossible to remain neutral, and the Fenians, always divided over strategy, became even more splintered—and poorer, their treasury badly needing infusions—by 1870.[9]

The Fenians' last big hurrah, another invasion of Canada, this one on May 25, 1870, ended in humiliating defeat. On edge for years as rumors of possible Fenian raids circulated, the new Canadian Confederation was well prepared, thanks to a tip from the British spy, Henri Le Caron, who had wormed his way into General John O'Neill's confidence. A well-armed unit of the Canadian Volunteers waited on the border to greet an inexperienced and understaffed Fenian Army. Fewer than 200 of an expected 1,800 Fenians showed up for the fight at Eccles Hill in southern Quebec, and they "behaved badly," fleeing the minute their comrade John Rowe was shot and killed. Soon "the entire Fenian force . . . melted away, . . . utterly demoralized."[10] Canadians rejoiced, joking that "IRA" stood not for "Irish Republican Army" but for "I Ran Away."[11] John Boyle O'Reilly—the famous Fenian who escaped from an Australian prison and came to America, eventually taking over the Boston *Pilot*—was clearly disillusioned by the Fenian raid in 1870, reporting on it as a war correspondent for the *Pilot*. "I hate that infernal name—Fenianism," he wrote to another disenchanted Fenian, John Devoy, in 1871. "That meanly-sounding word, with its association of defeat, dissension, and trickery has been a millstone on the neck of our Nationality for years past."[12]

Losing the support of prominent members, the Fenians also could no longer depend on the U.S. government. Despite his politic and courteous reception of Warren and other released Fenian prisoners, Grant took a stern stance with those who broke the law and threatened international peace. Shortly before General O'Neill led his men into Canada, U.S. marshal George Foster arrived at the Fenian camp and read aloud President Grant's proclamation of neutrality, just published in newspapers throughout the country, warning that anyone who invaded Canada "will forfeit all right to the protection of this government." There would be no more diplomatic wrangling to free Fenians from their deserved fate. After the battle, Marshal Foster promptly arrested O'Neill for violating America's neutrality law, and U.S. officials seized thirty tons of Fenian munitions. While Johnson's administration had paid for the Fenians' transport home after the 1866 raids, Grant left the Fenians stranded, unassisted, in border towns, the men finally forcing their way en masse onto trains to get home, daring conductors to make them pay.[13] British and Canadian officials grumbled that the United States government could have done more to restrain the boisterous Fenians, but they had to admit it did much more than before. Grudgingly, they finally freed all remaining Fenian prisoners in Canada by 1872.[14] The Naturalization Treaty, with its promise of drawing brighter jurisdictional lines, appeared to be working.

The Department of State worked determinedly to shield American foreign policy from the shenanigans of the foreign-born. Finally the broken relationship between Britain and the United States appeared on the verge of repair, thanks, ironically, to the Fenians, who despite their best efforts to drive the two countries apart had wound up bringing the "transatlantic cousins" closer together. The Naturalization Treaty opened the door to further negotiations, the widely celebrated Treaty of Washington in 1871 providing for the arbitration of the San Juan boundary disputes, international fisheries, and especially the explosive *Alabama* claims. Hamilton Fish, a moving force behind the reconciliatory treaty, was not going to allow the Fenians or any other budding nationalist groups to derail American global interests. As the Fenian Brotherhood withered, new Irish nationalist groups arose: the Clan na Gael with its dynamite campaign, the Home Rule movement to restore the Irish Parliament, the Land League's efforts at sweeping Irish land reform.[15] Their members, like the Fenians, were often arrested, but with the expatriation issue resolved and diplomats anxious to contain disputes before they mushroomed, the political prisoners found it much more difficult to leverage their arrests into international controversies. American diplomats increasingly viewed naturalized Americans abroad with skepticism, Secretary of State Fish instructing his diplomatic agents to use "cautious scrutiny" when they asked for the government's protection.[16]

Congress—at least its Republican members—also lost patience with the foreign-born. As the 1870 Fenian raid came to its pitiful end, Congress took up bills to reform the naturalization process, determined to "purify the ballot box" after Tammany Hall's naturalization mill had churned out 41,112 new citizens just in time to help defeat New York Republicans in the 1868 election. The nation needed to be shielded from foreigners who "abuse our hospitality" by an "obstinate clinging to old nationalities" that dragged the United States into foreign questions, argued reformers, especially now that the 1868 Expatriation Act committed the government to protect naturalized citizens abroad.[17] Efforts to nationalize the naturalization process, stripping states and cities of the power to naturalize foreigners, failed. But Congress in the Naturalization Act of 1870 allowed federal judges significant oversight in federal elections and barred new citizens from voting until six months after their naturalization. The Enforcement Act of 1870 made false registration and repeat voting federal offenses and, most dramatically, empowered federal troops to patrol polling sites during federal elections in cities with more than 20,000 people. Democratic critics denounced the "federal invasion of New York" as 6,000 federal deputy marshals guarded ballot boxes in the New York election of 1870, but federal troops became a fixture in northern federal elections for more than twenty years.[18]

It was too much to claim, as House Speaker Thomas B. Reed did in the mid-1890s, that "the Irish in the United States are no longer a political force." Powerful Irish bosses ruled New York City almost uninterruptedly between 1871 and 1924, and Boston elected its first of several Irish Catholic mayors, Hugh O'Brien, in 1885.[19] But while Irish American politics continued to blossom, it did, perhaps, become domesticated. Patrick A. Collins, the up-and-coming Irish American politician in Boston who in 1901 would become the city's second Irish Catholic mayor, straddled Irish national and American identities in campaigning for the Democratic Party in 1876. A former Fenian, Collins did not hesitate to pull on Fenian strings, recalling the great expatriation fight of 1868: "Our protest thundered through the land. The halls of Congress trembled with it." But the "battle is over," Collins reminded his audience, England having "surrendered her doctrine of 'once a subject, always a subject." Now "Americans we are, Americans we remain," engaged in a "new agitation," not abroad but at home. There should be no "Irish vote," he urged, as he encouraged Irish Americans to shift their attention to domestic issues. "I am in the ranks," Collins thundered, speaking not of the Fenians but of the Democratic Party. Pushing the Democratic Party candidate for governor, Collins declared, "This is my general, and him I follow till the battle is done." The candidate he followed? None other than Charles Francis Adams, the nemesis of the Fenians.[20]

"THE CHAMPION of the Fenians" was how Thomas Nast gleefully entitled his cartoon of Adams, the Democratic nominee for governor of Massachusetts in 1876, fitting Adams out in full Irish nationalist gear with a shamrock between his teeth.[21] Adams was certainly aware of the irony. One of the founders of the Republican Party, he now was courted by the Democratic Party, home to the majority of Irish Americans in Massachusetts, who had bitterly denounced him in the 1860s. After arriving home in 1868, Adams looked forward to a quiet life in his Quincy home, editing his father's diaries for publication. He had been coaxed out of retirement only twice, to serve as the American arbitrator on the Geneva Tribunal, the multinational commission established in 1871 to settle the *Alabama* claims, and to deliver a eulogy for his colleague and lifelong friend William H. Seward, who died in 1872. The first task as arbitrator was a perfect assignment for the cool-tempered, experienced diplomat and brought a welcome sense of resolution for Adams, having been in the thick of the Anglo-American diplomatic storm for so long.

Honoring Seward also brought a sense of closure. Adams had despaired of Seward at times, confessing in July 1867 "to have lost all confidence in the wisdom or judgment of Mr. Seward." But in 1873, with the Fenian and *Alabama* crises over, Adams now credited Seward—not Lincoln—with saving the nation and praised him for placing duty above his own needs or ambitions, often with little appreciation by a critical public. Perhaps it gave Adams some personal solace to recognize in Seward the devotion to duty that he had been taught to cherish—to see reflected in Seward's career Adams's own sense of slugging away without proper recognition.[22]

Especially after his triumph as an arbitrator in Geneva, Adams's statesmanlike qualities drew attention, his cold demeanor and disdain for politicking making him appear trustworthy and all the more desirable as a candidate. Both Liberal Republicans and Democrats, encouraged by his criticism of the Radical Republican agenda, wooed Adams. But Adams resisted being tugged

"Champion of the Fenians." Cartoon by Thomas Nast, highlighting the irony of Charles Francis Adams being chosen as the Democratic candidate for governor of Massachusetts in 1876, especially in light of Irish Americans' bitter condemnation of Adams when he served as U.S. minister to Britain.

into the political sphere. When he found, to his dismay, that he had been nominated as the Democratic candidate for governor, Adams refused to attend any rallies or give any speeches. He consoled himself with the knowledge that he had little chance of winning, given Irish American hatred of him, whatever Patrick Collins said. To his great relief, he lost by a wide margin.

Adams returned to his scholarly endeavors, though those soon became unmanageable as his memory deteriorated rapidly. He lived out his remaining years until 1886 in relative obscurity and with few memories to trouble him.[23]

JOHN WARREN probably did not vote for Adams, though he remained passionate about politics, especially anything related to Ireland. He made at least one attempt to reconstruct a personal life, marrying a widow, Bridget Markey Smith, in New Jersey in 1873, but they soon became estranged as John returned to Boston.[24] There he enjoyed a certain local fame, frequently organizing events and speaking on the cause of the moment. But there was a sense, as one obituary concluded, that the major event of his life was behind him. "Since his return to Boston," concluded the *Irish American,* Colonel Warren took "no prominent part in public affairs."[25] Warren kept busy, starting a new newspaper, the *Irish Republican and Free Lance,* and becoming somewhat of a jack-of-all-trades: his business card from 1892 advertised him as "Real estate and insurance broker, auctioneer and justice of the peace. General agency. Rents collected, property taken care of, government claims secured." Warren had mixed experience with his own government claims. Finally, after thirty years of petitioning, Warren cleared his Civil War conviction for being absent without leave, a "gross outrage" that had weighed heavily upon him. By special legislation, Congress in 1892 vacated the charge and ordered the secretary of war to grant him an honorable discharge.[26] Warren had less success applying for a disability pension offered to Civil War veterans the same year. After poking and prodding, the doctor dismissed Warren's complaints of "deafness in both ears" and impaired eyesight, concluding that Warren, at 262 pounds, was a "large, heavy, well nourished" man, "well preserved for his age."[27]

Warren might have lived for years, perhaps even witnessing the creation of the independent Irish Free State in 1922, if not for an unfortunate accident. On September 10, 1895, Warren was strolling past the Masonic Temple, the "masterpiece of gothic architecture" opposite the Boston Common, which had been gutted by fire only a week earlier. A block of granite broke loose from the ruins and struck Warren on his head, fracturing his skull. Taken to a nearby drugstore and then to Massachusetts General Hospital, Warren—the man who had survived the Famine, the Civil War, and British prisons—died on September 13 at the age of sixty. Representatives from every imaginable Irish patriotic association turned out for Colonel Warren's funeral, and Augustine Costello, his still youthful companion from *Erin's Hope,* delivered a stirring eulogy. As obituaries summed up Warren's life, it was the voyage of *Erin's Hope* that stood out as his major achievement. By asserting his rights as an American citizen, Warren "woke up the American people." It was he who had finally secured the "sacred" right of expatriation for all Americans to enjoy.[28]

OF COURSE, Warren had not acted alone, nor was the right of expatriation secured by the Expatriation Act of 1868 and the Naturalization Treaties. Even when expatriation reached its highest recognition, individuals' right to leave their native land and choose their nationality had been yoked to the interests of states, determined to manage their mobile populations. Far from settling the right of expatriation, the Naturalization Treaties opened up new questions about who could exit—and enter—the polity, laying the seeds for future policies that would make a mockery of the right of expatriation.

By the 1890s, the right of expatriation had become strained by the tremendous surge of immigration in the late nineteenth and early twentieth centuries, and the gatekeeping regime that soon followed. As the United States rapidly emerged as the world's leading industrial power, it drew migrants from around the world, especially from southern and eastern Europe, to toil in its factories and fields. Almost 13 million immigrants arrived in the United States between 1868 and 1900; another 14.5 million followed between 1901 and 1920.[29] Immigrants built industrial America, but they also encountered a revived nativist movement, stirred by fears that America was under siege by foreign forces.

Chinese became the first targets, despite the Burlingame Treaty's eager encouragement of Chinese immigration. Francis Lieber, the eloquent defender of the natural right of migration and expatriation, drew the line at Chinese "who invade our country similar to the Norway rat" and advised Secretary of State Fish in 1870 that the United States should adopt a constitutional amendment "to bar entrance to all nonwhite peoples." For Lieber and many other "liberal internationalists" of the era, it was the "Cis-Caucasian race"—the French, the English, the German, the Americans—which "drew the chariot of civilization abreast," and it was primarily among those people that subjects and citizens could be exchanged among nations with ease.[30]

If Lieber's proposed amendment did not materialize, Congress did bar entrance to many "nonwhite people," first forbidding the immigration of Chinese laborers and the naturalization of all Chinese in the Exclusion Act of 1882, then expanding the ban on entry and citizenship to all Asians by 1924. The principle of racial exclusion—and the administrative mechanisms created to enforce it—migrated to other countries as a global color line was drawn to keep Chinese out of most of the Western Hemisphere and white settler nations. By 1924, southern and eastern Europeans, deemed a threat to the white "Nordic" stock, also fell victim to restriction, their immigration drastically slashed by the Quota Act of 1924.[31] Controlling entry rather than exit became the key focus of modern nation-states, their inherent sovereign power to police their territorial borders viewed as essential to what it meant to be a modern state. With entry and naturalization so restricted, observed Edwin Borchard in 1931, the right of expatriation "becomes rather an empty formula."[32]

Even the right to leave was far from secure by the twentieth century. Some countries—Russia and Turkey in particular—never recognized a right of exit, making emigration dangerous and costly, as emigrants had to be smuggled out of the country with dire consequences should they be caught.[33] After the burst of treaty-making ended in 1873, the United States failed to secure naturalization treaties with other key emigrant countries and faced backtracking from Germany as it began to regret loosening its hold on valuable expatriates. "I am not in favor of emigration," Bismarck said in 1884, nor of "a German who discards his fatherland like an old coat." As early as 1871, Germany tried again to stem the tide of migration, forbidding the emigration of men under the age of twenty-five and subject to military service.[34] And in the major world wars of the twentieth century, states returned to aggressive citizenship policies to poach potential military recruits and to lure their emigrants home. By the mid-twentieth century, Communist states in eastern Europe forbade emigration, portraying emigrants as dangerous and worthless defectors from a noble cause.[35]

International conventions to make nationality rules more uniform and secure recognition of expatriation faltered, revealing persistent divisions between "emigrant" and "immigrant" states. The Hague Convention on Nationality in 1930 ended with a compromise that satisfied few. Insisting that state sovereignty took precedence over individual rights, the convention allowed expatriation only for those who had obtained dual nationality "involuntarily"—that is, through birth, not naturalization—and even then only with the government's consent. The United States refused to sign the convention, its delegate Richard Flournoy protesting that under the American law, "the right of expatriation is a natural and inherent right of all people," to be exercised at the will of the individual.[36]

But in fact, even the United States had retreated from its commitment to voluntary expatriation. The ink was barely dry on the naturalization treaties before the State Department started worrying about what they and the Expatriation Act of 1868 would mean in practice. President Grant surveyed his cabinet on a range of perplexing questions in 1873, focusing especially on how individuals exercised their right to expatriation. Was naturalization, and perhaps the swearing of an oath, required to transfer one's political allegiance from one country to another, or could certain acts—especially residency abroad—be sufficient for the government to decide a citizen had expatriated? Could the United States impose different rules for naturalized citizens, given their presumed attachment to their homelands? Called upon to provide protection to the nation's far-flung citizens, American diplomats grew increasingly wary of those who sought the "cloak" of American citizenship "merely as a shield for nefarious practices," showing little true allegiance or attachment except to their own self-interest.[37] So, too, the United States still faced the ongoing dilemma of sorting out "who was who" in its international relations, constantly searching for ways to eliminate dual nationality.[38]

After decades of dithering, Congress finally responded to pleas from administrative officials for clearer rules, but in the process it gave the government powerful new weapons to police citizens, especially naturalized Americans. Cracking down on what it perceived to be a broken and fraudulent naturalization system that "trafficked" in citizenship, Congress in the Naturalization Act of 1906 centralized the control of naturalization and provided, for the first time, for the denaturalization of Americans who had gained naturalization certificates fraudulently or illegally or who left to take up permanent residence abroad. Under the Expatriation Act of 1907, the government could strip Americans of their citizenship for a variety of actions construed as acts of "voluntary" expatriation, regardless of the citizen's actual intent.[39]

When suffragist Ethel Mackenzie tried to exercise her newly granted right to vote in California, her native state, in 1913, the state registrar turned her away, saying her marriage to Gordon Mackenzie, a British subject, had turned her into an alien. With the Act of 1907, the United States joined the modern international trend in providing that married women take the nationality of their husbands. "No act of the legislature can denationalize a citizen without his [or her] concurrence," protested Mackenzie before the U.S. Supreme Court, but to no avail.

Ethel had chosen to marry Gordon, and having made that voluntary decision, the judges ruled, "she must bow to the will of the nation" to avoid "international complications" that frequently arose over families with divided nationalities. Similarly, the act created the presumption that naturalized Americans who lived in their native land for more than two years had made a "choice" to give up their American citizenship, though native-born Americans remained free to live in other countries with their citizenship intact. By 1954, American law declared that citizens (both native-born and naturalized) had "voluntarily" relinquished their citizenship if they served in foreign armies or foreign offices, voted in a foreign election, deserted the military in wartime, bore arms against the United States or advocated overthrowing it, or were convicted of treason. Zealous administrative officials used their considerable discretion under the new regime to scrutinize the allegiance of the foreign-born and radicals in times of war, punishing those perceived as disloyal by disowning them through denaturalization procedures.[40]

Once praised as a natural right wielded by the individual, expatriation by the twentieth century had become the tool of the state, used by totalitarian and democratic governments alike (though not to the same degree) to prune and manage their citizenry. Expatriation increasingly referred to losing, rather than choosing, citizenship—often with disastrous consequences. In 1922, the new Soviet Union denationalized 2 million Russians who had fled during the Russian Revolution, rendering them stateless. More chillingly, the Nazi government in 1935 took citizenship away from German Jews, the crucial first step in its evolving campaign to eradicate Jews. And without citizenship, the political theorist Hannah Arendt famously declared, people had no rights and no government to provide protection in a hostile world. By war's end, over 5 million Jews had been killed and millions of European refugees were left homeless and, often, stateless.[41]

In the wake of the Second World War and its massive destruction, the United Nations adopted the Universal Declaration of Human Rights on December 10, 1948, embracing the rights to migrate and expatriate as fundamental freedoms deserving international recognition. "Everyone has the right to leave any country, including his own, and to return to his country," the declaration insisted. Further, "everyone has a right to a nationality," including the "right to change his nationality." But the Universal Declaration of Human Rights was a nonbinding agreement, its framers knowing that they would be unable to persuade countries to sign it if they actually had to afford all the rights it laid out. It served as a "common standard of achievement for all peoples and all nations"—a statement of the rights that should be recognized.[42]

By the late 1950s, the hopeful principles laid out in the declaration began to percolate. The balance between state sovereignty and individual rights once again became recalibrated as the United States Supreme Court embarked on what many called a "rights revolution."[43] In 1958, when Clemente Martinez Perez challenged his expatriation for voting in Mexico, Chief Justice Earl Warren channeled Arendt when he delivered his stirring dissent: "Citizenship *is* man's basic right for it is nothing less than the right to have rights. Remove this priceless possession and there remains a stateless person, disgraced and degraded in the eyes of his countrymen. He has no lawful claim to protection from any nation, and no nation may assert rights on his behalf."[44]

In a companion case decided the same day, Warren swayed a bare majority in striking down the involuntary expatriation of a soldier convicted of desertion, declaring the government could not use denationalization as a "weapon . . . to express its displeasure at a citizen's conduct."[45] In 1964, the Supreme Court—still divided—overturned the 1952 law providing for the automatic expatriation of naturalized citizens who lived in their native countries for more than three years. "Living abroad, whether the citizen be naturalized or native born, is no badge of allegiance," the Court concluded, "and in no way evidences a voluntary renunciation of nationality and allegiance."[46] Finally, in 1967, when striking down the law that expatriated naturalized citizens who voted in a foreign election, Justice Hugo Black returned to the Expatriation Act of 1868 to declare that "the only way" citizenship could be lost "was by the voluntary renunciation or abandonment by the citizen himself." The Constitution "grants Congress no express power to strip people of their citizenship," Black lectured. "In our country the people are sovereign." It was a sentiment the Fenians would have embraced.[47]

IT IS TEMPTING to end on a note of triumph. The right to choose—and keep—one's nationality prevailed in Supreme Court opinions, and Congress soon followed the Court's lead and repealed most of its laws providing for involuntary expatriation. In 1980 the United States abrogated the Bancroft treaties, signed with such self-congratulatory glee over a hundred years earlier but now seen, in light of Supreme Court rulings, as embracing an unconstitutional discrimination against naturalized citizens.[48] Internationally, nations have again loosened their hold on citizens. In November 1989, crowds of East Berliners joyously scaled the Berlin Wall, the most visible symbol of Communist policies forbidding emigration, and defiantly streamed out of the Communist bloc. All sorts of walls seemed to be tumbling down by the 1980s and 1990s as Communist states crumbled, globalized economies flourished, and migration surged. Borders softened as the newly created European Union embraced the free flow of people and goods and championed the emerging human rights regime.[49]

Just as the spread of global capitalism and mass migration provoked deep questioning about membership and belonging in the mid-nineteenth century, so, too, citizenship studies is again a booming field as scholars—the descendants of Lieber and the "publicists"—ponder the impact of globalization and human rights on citizenship. Some look hopefully to a dawning "international law on citizenship," in which individual rights trump state sovereignty. They point to rapidly expanding access to citizenship as nations increasingly abandon discriminatory policies that imposed racial and gender restrictions on naturalization.

The United States, for example, not only repealed the Chinese exclusion laws and other immigration laws that prevented entry based on race or ethnicity but also dropped its racial requirement for naturalization in 1952. Dual and even multiple nationalities—the "barbarous" practice so condemned by nineteenth-century policymakers—is now unremarkable, the European Union explicitly allowing, and the United States tolerating, multiple citizenships. Perhaps the right to expatriation has become invisible in the modern era because the right to choose one's nationality seems so obvious and uncontroversial.[50]

Yet both the long view of history and current politics caution against triumphant tales, as migrants continue to become ensnared in domestic and international disputes. Britain's decision on June 23, 2016, to exit the European Union, primarily in response to what some portrayed as a "migration crisis," sharply checked expectations of generous international policies on citizenship.[51] "Homelanders" in the United States and elsewhere again throw up walls and demand policing of borders; Muslims have become the "new Chinese," warns one scholar, a suspect group viewed as dangerous and incapable of assimilation; and by the end of 2016 a total of 22.5 million refugees—the largest number of refugees since World War II—had been displaced from their homes by violence and persecution, with a mere 189,300 resettled in new countries in that year.[52] If the right to choose one's home and nationality has been secured in law, the right of expatriation remains, in practice, "an aspiration," not an accomplished fact.[53]

NOTES

ACKNOWLEDGMENTS

CREDITS

INDEX

Notes

Abbreviations

BP	George Bancroft Papers, Massachusetts Historical Society
CFA Diary	Charles Francis Adams Diaries, 1823–1880, Charles Adams Papers, Massachusetts Historical Society
CFA LB	Charles Francis Adams Papers, Letterbooks, Massachusetts Historical Society
CPR	Catholic Parish Registers, NLI (originals of all Catholic parish records available to view at http://registers.nli.ie; for digitized details, see https://churchrecords.irishgenealogy.ie/churchrecords)
DD	Despatches from U.S. Consul in Dublin, Ireland, 1790–1906, microfilm reel T199, entry 85, Central Files of the Department of State, RG 59, U.S. National Archives and Record Administration
DG	Despatches from U.S. Ministers to the German States and Germany, M44, entry 13, Central Files of the Department of State, RG 59, U.S. National Archives and Record Administration
FBR / CUA	Fenian Brotherhood Records and O'Donovan Rossa Personal Papers, Catholic University of America, http://archives.lib.cua.edu/findingaid/fenian.cfm
FO	Foreign Office, National Archives, Great Britain
FRUS	U.S. Department of State, *Papers Relating to Foreign Affairs*
FS	*Fenian Spirit* (Boston)
HO	Home Office, National Archives, Great Britain
ILN	*Illustrated London News*
Larcom Papers	Papers of Sir Thomas Larcom, 1820–1870, Department of Manuscripts, National Library of Ireland
LC	Library of Congress

Mayo Papers	Richard Bourke, 6th Earl of Mayo Papers, 1822–1873, Department of Manuscripts, National Library of Ireland
MHS	Massachusetts Historical Society
NA	National Archives (UK)
NAI	National Archives of Ireland
NARA	National Archives and Records Administration (US)
NLI	National Library of Ireland
NYH	*New York Herald*
NYT	*New York Times*
Pilot	*The Pilot* (Boston)
Times	*Times* (London)
Trials of American Citizens in Great Britain	*U.S. Senate, Message of the President of the United States, Communicating, in Compliance with a Resolution of the Senate of the 27th of January Last, Information in Relation to the Arrest and Trial of Rev. John McMahon, Robert B. Lynch and John Warren, by the Government of Great Britain, March 16, 1868, Senate Executive Document 42, 40th Congress, 2nd Session*

Prologue

1. "Captain John F. Kavanagh," *Brooklyn Eagle*, June 11, 1880, 4; *Report of the Trial of John Warren, for Treason-Felony at the County Dublin Commission* (Dublin, 1867), 39–40.

2. *Report of the Trial of John Warren*, 32.

3. The information on the occupations of the *Jacmel* men is gathered from testimony at the trials of Warren, Costello, and Nagle; from records compiled by the Irish government, found at INA, Chief Secretary's Office, Irish Crimes Records, Fenian Photographs 16; and from notes confiscated from William Nagle upon his arrest and presented at trial, "Copy Pencil Documents Found on the Person of the Prisoner Nagle on Arrest, by Constable Norris," *Queen v. Warren and Nagle*, 5–6, carton 10, Crown Briefs, 1865–1869, NAI.

4. On the origins of "Fenian," see Brian Jenkins, *Irish Nationalism and the British State: From Repeal to Revolutionary Nationalism* (Montreal, 2006), 104; Robert Kee, *The Green Flag: A History of Irish Nationalism* (New York, 2000), 310.

5. "Coming Back with a Vengeance," *FS*, Sept. 17, 1864, 2.

6. "Address of the New England Convention of the Fenian Brotherhood to Their Countrymen throughout the World," *FS*, Aug. 20, 1864, 1.

7. John Savage, *Fenian Heroes and Martyrs* (Boston, 1868), 448–449.

8. George Bancroft to W. B. Lawrence, Jan. 16, 1869, BP.

9. On being "shackled" as a British subject, see "Letter from Col. Warren," *The Nation* (Dublin), Apr. 3, 1869; Coke, 2 Inst. 121, quoted in William Blackstone, *Commentaries on the Laws of England* (Chicago, 1979), 1:357–358.

10. General Adam Badeau to Bancroft, April 24, 1868, BP; Charles Detmold to Bancroft, Mar. 8, 1868, BP; "Expatriation and Naturalization," *North American Review* 106 (Apr. 1868): 612–629; David Dudley Field, *An International Code. Address on This Subject, before the Social Science Association at Manchester, October 5, 1866* (New York, 1867), 7.

11. For contemporaries' commentary on the United States' growing international stature after the Civil War, see George Bancroft to Charles Sumner, Jan. 21, 1868, BP; Bancroft to President Johnson, Jan. 21, 1868, BP; Sir Frederick Bruce to Lord Stanley, Nov. 19, 1866, FO, 5 / 1340, NA.

12. The history of expatriation during Reconstruction has just begun to be written. See especially the important work of Christian G. Samito, *Becoming American under Fire: Irish Americans, African Americans, and the Politics of Citizenship during the Civil War Era* (Ithaca, NY, 2009), 172–216; David Sim, *A Union Forever: The Irish Question and U.S. Foreign Relations in the Victorian Age* (Ithaca, NY, 2013), 97–127; Peter J. Spiro, *At Home in Two Countries: The Past and Future of Dual Citizenship* (New York, 2016), 11–21; Nancy L. Green, "The Politics of Exit: Reversing the Immigration Paradigm," *Journal of Modern History* 77 (June 2005): 263–289; Nancy L. Green and Francois Weil, eds., *Citizenship and Those Who Leave: The Politics of Emigration and Expatriation* (Urbana, IL, 2007); Brian Jenkins, *Fenians and Anglo American Relations during Reconstruction* (Ithaca, NY, 1969). Most view Reconstruction as inaugurating a revolution in federal civil rights, even if that revolution was "unfinished." See, e.g., Eric Foner, *Reconstruction: America's Unfinished Revolution, 1863–1877* (New York, 1988); Robert Kaczorowski, "To Begin the Nation Anew: Congress, Citizenship, and Civil Rights after the Civil War," *American Historical Review* 92 (Feb. 1987): 45–68. Others call attention to the limits of Reconstruction. See especially Barbara Young Welke, *Law and the Borders of Belonging in the Long Nineteenth Century United States* (New York, 2010), esp. 113–144; Kunal M. Parker, *Making Foreigners: Immigration and Citizenship Law in America, 1600–2000* (New York, 2015), 116–147.

13. The number of naturalizations in the United States began to increase dramatically in the mid-1990s and remained high in the first decade of the twenty-first century. In 2008, naturalizations peaked at 1,046,539, declining to 753,060 in 2016. Katherine Witsman, "U.S. Naturalizations: 2016," *Annual Flow Report*, Nov. 2017, U.S. Department of Homeland Security, Office of Immigration Statistics, https://www.dhs.gov/sites/default/files/publications/Naturalizations_2016.pdf.

14. For an excellent analysis of shifting definitions of "expatriation" over time, see Nancy L. Green, "Expatriation, Expatriates, and Expats: The American Transformation of a Concept," *American Historical Review* 114 (April 2009): 307–328. On expatriation as a loss of citizenship, see Ben Herzog, *Revoking Citizenship: Expatriation in America from the Colonial Era to the War on Terror* (New York, 2015); Patrick Weil, *The Sovereign Citizen: Denaturalization and the Origins of the American Republic* (Philadelphia, 2013); John P. Roche, "Loss of American Nationality: The Years of Confusion," *Western Political Quarterly* 4 (June 1951): 268–294; John P. Roche, "The Expatriation Cases: 'Breathes There the Man

With Soul so Dead . . . ?,'" *Supreme Court Review*, 1963, 325–356; Elwin Griffith, "Expatriation and the American Citizen," *Howard Law Journal* 31 (1988): 453–496; T. Alexander Aleinikoff, "Theories of Loss of Citizenship," *Michigan Law Review* 84 (June 1986): 1471–1503.

15. Hannah Arendt, *The Origins of Totalitarianism* (New York, 1951), esp. 267–302. See also Linda K. Kerber, "Toward a History of Statelessness in America," *American Quarterly* 57 (Sept. 2005): 727–749; Kerber, "The Stateless as the Citizen's Other: A View from the United States," *American Historical Review* 112 (Feb. 2007): 1–34.

16. H.R. 3166, 112th Cong., 1st sess., introduced by Representatives Charles Dent (R-PA) and Jason Altmire (D-PA), cosponsored by Robert Latta (R-OH) and Frank Wolf (R-VA); S.B. 1698, 112th Cong., 1st sess., introduced by Senators Joseph Lieberman (I-CT) and Scott Brown (R-MA). The proposed legislation was similar to bills proposed by the same congressional sponsors in May 2010 (H.R. 5237 and S.B. 3327, 111th Cong.). Charlie Savage and Carl Hulse, "Bill Targets Citizenship of Terrorists' Allies," *New York Times*, May 7, 2010; Farah Stockman and Matt Viser, "Brown Wants Citizenship Revoked for Terror Ties," *Boston Globe*, May 7, 2010; David Cole, "Lieberman's Anti-Terror Posturing," *Washington Post*, May 8, 2010; David Harsanyi, "Stripping Citizenship Is a Bad Idea," *Denver Post*, May 7, 2010. For more recent attempts to revive such a bill, see S. 361, "Expatriate Terrorist Act," 115th Cong., introduced by Senator Ted Cruz (R-TX) on Feb. 13, 2017.

17. See, e.g., "Debate of Mr. Adam's Motion Respecting the Trials of Mr. Muir and Mr. Palmer," Mar. 10, 1794, in *The Parliamentary History of England: From the Earliest Period to the Year 1803* (London, 1817), 30:1498–1499, for definition of banishment as expatriation; Green, "Expatriation, Expatriates, and Expats," 308; Rebecca Kingston, "Unmaking of Citizens: Banishment and the Modern Citizenship Regime in France," *Citizenship Studies* 9 (Feb. 2005): 23–40; Robert G. Caldwell, "Exile as an Institution," *Political Science Quarterly* 58 (June 1943): 239–62 (arguing that Hale's story appealed because Nolan's punishment was so unusual). "Expatriation" referred both to physical expulsion (or emigration) and the loss of nationality.

18. Edward Everett Hale, "The Man without a Country," *Atlantic*, Dec. 1863, 665–680, 667; Kerber, "Toward a History of Statelessness in America," 727–728; Melinda Lawson, *Patriot Fire: Forging a New American Nationalism in the Civil War North* (Lawrence, KS, 2002), 122–128.

19. Aristide R. Zolberg, "The Exit Revolution," in *Citizenship and Those Who Leave*, ed. Green and Weil, 33–60; Reed Ueda, *Postwar Immigrant America: A Social History* (Boston, 1994), 3, 11. For studies of modern states' use of emigration policies and exit rules, see Laurie A. Brand, *Citizens Abroad: Emigration and the State in the Middle East and North Africa* (New York, 2006); David FitzGerald, *A Nation of Emigrants: How Mexico Manages Its Migration* (Berkeley, CA, 2009).

20. I am borrowing the phrase from Welke, *The Borders of Belonging*, 4–6.

21. On challenges of mobility to state sovereignty, see Lauren Benton, *A Search for Sovereignty: Law and Geography in European Empires, 1400–1900* (Cambridge, 2010), esp. 279–299; Thomas Bender, *A Nation among Nations: America's Place in World History*

(New York, 2006), 150–164; Daniel S. Margolies, *Spaces of Law in American Foreign Relations: Extradition and Extraterritoriality in the Borderlands and Beyond, 1877–1898* (Athens, GA, 2011); Antony Anghie, *Imperialism, Sovereignty and the Making of International Law* (Cambridge, 2005); Donna R. Gabaccia, *Foreign Relations: American Immigration in Global Perspective* (Princeton, NJ, 2012); Katherine Unterman, *Uncle Sam's Policemen: The Pursuit of Fugitives Across Borders* (Cambridge, MA, 2015).

22. "Expatriation," *Annals of Congress*, 15th Cong., 1st sess., 1035, 1043.

23. Shamrock Society of New-York, *Hints to Emigrants from Europe* (New York, 1816), 3.

Chapter 1: Clonakilty, God Help Us!

1. Kerby A. Miller, *Emigrants and Exiles: Ireland and the Irish Exodus to North America* (New York, 1985), 280–344, esp. 291, 280, 294.

2. John Warren to President Johnson, Aug. 3, 1867, *FRUS* 1867, 136; Oliver Macdonagh, "Ireland and the Union, 1801–1870," in *Ireland under the Union, I: 1801–1870*, ed. W. E. Vaughan, vol. V of *A New History of Ireland* (Oxford, 1989), xlvii–lxv; R. V. Comerford, "Ireland 1850–70: Post-Famine and Mid-Victorian," in *Ireland under the Union*, ed. Vaughan, 372–395; James S. Donnelly Jr., *The Land and the People of Nineteenth-Century Cork: The Rural Economy and the Land Question* (London, 1975), 132–150; Patrick Lynch and John Vaizey, *Guinness's Brewery in the Irish Economy, 1759–1876* (Cambridge, 1960), 243.

3. "Chilled Clon Happy to 'Go Slow,'" *Cork Independent*, Jan. 12, 2011; "Laid-Back Clon Joins Global Go-Slow," *Irish Examiner*, Nov. 22, 2011.

4. Tomás Tuipéar, *Historical Walk of Clonakilty and Its Sea-Front* (Clonakilty, 1988). Warren was the first cousin of Maxwell Irwin, Mary Jane's father. Michael O'Mahony, "The Rise and Demise of the Irwins of Clonakilty," *Clonakilty Historical and Archaeological Journal* 2 (2017): 79–100, 80.

5. John Savage, *Fenian Heroes and Martyrs* (Boston, 1868); Donnelly, *Land and the People of Nineteenth-Century Cork*, 3; Cormac Ó Gráda, *Black '47 and Beyond: The Great Irish Famine in History, Economy, and Memory* (Princeton, NJ, 1999), 25.

6. Nicholas Canny, *Making Ireland British, 1580–1650* (Oxford, 2001); Nicholas Canny, *The Upstart Earl* (Cambridge, 1982), 19, 308–328; Kathleen M. Lynch, *Roger Boyle, First Earl of Orrery* (Knoxville, TN, 1965), 1–5, 43; George Bennett, *The History of Bandon, and the Principal Towns in the West Riding of County Cork* (Cork, 1869), 346–348; Tuipéar, *Historical Walk of Clonakilty*.

7. Jane H. Ohlmeyer, "A Laboratory for Empire? Early Modern Ireland and English Imperialism," in *Ireland and the British Empire*, ed. Kevin Kenny (New York, 2004), 26–60, 38–39; Canny, *Making Ireland British*, 301–401; R. F. Foster, *Modern Ireland, 1600–1972* (London, 1988), 13–14.

8. Samuel Lewis, *A Topographical Dictionary, or Parliamentary Gazetteer of Great Britain and Ireland*, vol. 2 (London, 1846); *Slater's Late Pigot & Co.'s Royal National Commercial Directory of Ireland* (Manchester, 1856), 196.

9. Bennett, *History of Bandon*, 349–351, 471–472; Canny, *Making Ireland British*, 542–546.

10. Bennett, *History of Bandon*, 471–472; 349. See also Canny, *Making Ireland British*, 548–549.

11. Jeremiah O'Donovan Rossa, *Rossa's Recollections, 1838–1898* (1898; Shannon, 1972), 16–17. See also Daniel O'Connell, *Memoir on Ireland Native and Saxon* (Dublin, 1843), ch. III, part II; Canny, *Making Ireland British*, 568–577.

12. D. George Boyce, *Nationalism in Ireland*, 3rd ed. (New York, 1995), 20; Miller, *Emigrants and Exiles*, 127; Canny, *Making Ireland British*, 572–578.

13. On the ambiguous status of Ireland as a colony of Great Britain, see Kevin Kenny, "Ireland and the British Empire: An Introduction," 1–25; Ohlmeyer, "A Laboratory for Empire," 26–60; and Stephen Howe, "Historiography," 220–250, all in *Ireland and the British Empire*, ed. Kevin Kenny (New York, 2004).

14. For texts of the Penal Laws and the references to "popish masses," see http://library.law.umn.edu/irishlaw. See also Miller, *Emigrants and Exiles*, 21–25; Foster, *Modern Ireland*, 153–157; Ohlmeyer, "A Laboratory for Empire," 50–51; Donnelly, *Land and the People of Nineteenth-Century Cork*, 11.

15. Miller, *Emigrants and Exiles*, 41

16. David Dickson, *Old World Colony: Cork and South Munster, 1630–1830* (Madison, WI, 2005), 470–471; Tuipéar, *Historical Walk of Clonakilty*, 5–8; R. B. McDowell, "The Age of the United Irishmen: Revolution and the Union, 1794–1800," in *Eighteenth-Century Ireland, 1691–1800*, ed. Theodore William Moody and William Edward Vaughan, vol. IV of *A New History of Ireland* (Oxford, 1986), 339–373, esp. 362–373.

17. Tuipéar, *Historical Walk*, 6–7.

18. Thomas Bartlett, "Ireland, Empire, and Union, 1690–1801," in *Ireland and the British Empire*, ed. Kevin Kenny (Oxford, 2004), 61–89, quote at 84; Dickson, *Old World Colony*, 476–482, quote at 476; Alvin Jackson, "Ireland, the Union, and the Empire, 1800–1960," in *Ireland and the British Empire*, ed. Kenny, 130; Foster, *Modern Ireland*, 282–285.

19. "Aristocracy of worsted workers" from J. L. Hammond and Barbara Hammond, *The Skilled Labourer* (London, 1919), 195, quoted in Joyce Burnett, *Gender, Work and Wages in Industrial Revolution Britain* (Cambridge, 2008), 268–269; L. M. Cullen, *An Economic History of Ireland since 1660* (London, 1972), 9, 11, 23–25, 64–66, 99, 106, 121; Miller, *Emigrants and Exiles*, 207. While no direct evidence exists that Timothy Warren was a wool comber, his wife, Mary, and his brother, Michael, are listed in *I. Slater's National Commercial Directory of Ireland* (Manchester, 1846), 175, as wool combers in Clonakilty. In England, the wool combers' guild strictly regulated entry into the trade to the sons of wool combers, but wives assisted their husbands in wool combing and most guilds allowed widows to continue in their husband's trade under the assumption that they had been trained by the husband; Burnett, *Gender, Work and Wages in Industrial Revolution Britain*, 269. Timothy and Mary Canty Warren (c. 1811–1885) were married in 1829; see Marriage of Timotheum Warren and Mariam Canty, Oct. 25, 1829, Clonakilty parish, microfilm 04772 / 03, p. 61,

CPR, NLI. John was baptized in Clonakilty on May 18, 1834 (Clonakilty parish, microfilm 04772 / 02, p. 47, CPR, NLI) but gave his birthdate as May 14, 1834, on his naturalization certificate. See Certificate of Naturalization for John Warren, Oct. 12, 1866, Superior Civil Court, Suffolk Co., Boston, 18. He had four sisters: Teresa (b. 1830), Mary Anne (1832), Anastatia (1836), and Eliza (1838).

20. *Slater's Commercial Directory of Ireland* (1846), 174; Cullen, *Economic History of Ireland*, 100–101; J. Pigot and Co., *Pigot and Co.'s City of Dublin and Hibernian Provincial Directory* (London, 1824) 234–236, www.corkpastandpresent.ie/places/streetandtradedirectories /1824pigotsdirectorycorkcityandcounty; Dickson, *Old World Colony*, 418–421; on the brewery, see Tuipéar, *Historical Walk of Clonakilty*.

21. Cullen, *Economic History of Ireland*, 53–64, 85–87; Bartlett, "Ireland, Empire and Union," 68; *Pigot and Co.'s City of Dublin and Hibernian Provincial Directory*, 234–236; Samuel Lewis, *A Topographical Dictionary of Ireland* (London, 1837), www.libraryireland.com/topog /C/Clonakilty-East-Carbery-Cork.php; Lewis, *Topographical Dictionary or Parliamentary Gazetteer of Great Britain and Ireland*, 7:422–24.

22. Cullen, *Economic History of Ireland*, 36–43, 106, 119–124; Lewis, *Topographical Dictionary or Parliamentary Gazetteer of Great Britain and Ireland*, 422–423; Miller, *Emigrants and Exiles*, 193–279, esp. 209; George O'Brien, *The Economic History of Ireland from the Union to the Famine* (London, 1921); Frank Geary, "The Act of Union, British-Irish Trade, and Pre-Famine Deindustrialization," *Economic History Review*, n.s., 48 (Feb. 1995): 68–88; L. A. Clarkson, "Ireland 1841: Pre-industrial or Proto-industrial; Industrializing or De-industrializing?," in *European Proto-Industrialization*, ed. Sheilagh C. Ogilvie and Markus Cerman (Cambridge, 1996), 67–84; Cormac Ó Gráda, "Industry and Communications, 1801–45," in *Ireland under the Union, I: 1801–1870*, ed. W. E. Vaughan, vol. V of *A New History of Ireland* (Oxford, 1989), 137–157; Bartlett, "Ireland, Empire and Union," 63–68. The population of Clonakilty dropped from 4,033 in 1821 to 3,297 in 1851, and to 3,108 in 1861. W. E. Vaughan and A. J. Fitzpatrick, ed., *Irish Historical Statistics: Population, 1821–1971* (Dublin, 1978), 3, 9, 32–33.

23. Liam Kennedy, "Population Explosion," *Encyclopedia of Irish History and Culture*, ed. James S. Donnelly, Jr. (Detroit, 2004), 2:572–574; Kevin Kenny, *The American Irish* (New York, 2000), 45–54; Miller, *Emigrants and Exiles*, 209–223.

24. Miller, *Emigrants and Exiles*, 212–217; Robert James Scally, *The End of Hidden Ireland: Rebellion, Famine and Emigration* (New York, 1995), 9–104.

25. Scally, *End of Hidden Ireland*, 136–58, quotes at 152, 156.

26. The 1846 *Slater's Directory* recorded schools of industry for Protestant and Catholic girls and a "free school for boys," 175. In 1837 Lewis's *Topographical Dictionary of Ireland* mentions a "classical school established in 1808" attended by "more than 60 boys." Neither records the existence of a national school in Clonakilty. Based on numbers provided by Samuel Lewis in 1846, of 1,612 males and 1,953 females over the age of five, 779 males could read and write (48.3%) compared to 563 females (28.8%), while 643 males (39.9%) and 1,056 females (54%) were completely illiterate. See Lewis, *Topographical Dictionary or Parliamentary Gazetteer of Great Britain and Ireland*, 423.

27. "Letter from Colonel Warren," *Nation*, Apr. 3, 1869.

28. Miller, *Emigrants and Exiles*, 60–69; Kevin Kenny, *Making Sense of the Molly Maguires* (New York, 1998), 13–44; James S. Donnelly Jr., *Captain Rock: The Irish Agrarian Rebellion of 1821–1824* (Madison, WI, 2009); Maurice T. Bric, "Priests, Parsons and Politics: The Rightboy Protest in County Cork 1785–1788," *Past and Present* 100 (Aug. 1983): 100–123.

29. Dickson, *Old World Colony*, 480–485, 491–492; Marie-Louise Legg, *Newspapers and Nationalism: The Irish Provincial Press, 1850–1892* (Dublin, 1999), 22–23, 58–66; Miller, *Emigrants and Exiles*, 96–101; Oliver Macdonagh, "The Age of O'Connell, 1830–45," in *Ireland under the Union, I: 1801–1870*, ed. W. E. Vaughan, vol. V of *A New History of Ireland* (Oxford, 1989), 158–168.

30. Quoted in David George Boyce, *Nationalism in Ireland*, 3rd ed. (London, 1995), 160.

31. Donnelly, *Captain Rock*, 4, 20–21.

32. "Tithe War (1830–38)," in *Encyclopedia of Irish History and Culture*, ed. Donnelly, 701–703.

33. *The Evidence Taken before the Select Committees of the Houses of Lords and Commons, Appointed in the Sessions of 1824 and 1825, to Inquire into the State of Ireland* (London, 1825), 53.

34. Boyce, *Nationalism in Ireland*, 155–161; James S. Donnelly Jr., "A Famine in Irish Politics," in *Ireland under the Union*, ed. Vaughan, 357–371. Warren's first cousins, Maxwell Irwin and Timothy Warren Anglin, were both active in the Young Ireland movement, Warren Anglin moving on to an illustrious political career in Canada, becoming Speaker of the Parliament. O'Mahony, "Rise and Demise of the Irwins in Clonakilty," 80; William M. Baker, *Timothy Warren Anglin, 1822–96: Irish Catholic Canadian* (Toronto, 1977).

35. "The Potato Murrain," *ILN*, Aug. 19, 1846, 133–134; James S. Donnelly Jr., *The Great Irish Potato Famine* (Gloucestershire, 2001), 41–47.

36. United Nations, Food and Agricultural Organization, "International Year of the Potato," http://www.fao.org/potato-2008/en/index.html, accessed July 19, 2016; John Reader, *Potato: A History of the Propitious Esculent* (New Haven, CT, 2011); Líam Kennedy, Paul S. Ell, E. M. Crawford, and L. A. Clarkson, *Mapping the Great Irish Famine: A Survey of the Famine Decades* (Dublin, 1999), 65–69; Kenny, *The American Irish*, 89–91; Ó Gráda, *Black '47 and Beyond*, 16–18; John Feehan, "The Potato: The Root of the Famine," in *Atlas of the Great Irish Famine*, ed. John Crowley, William J. Smyth, and Mike Murphy (New York, 2012), 28–37; William J. Smyth, "'Mapping the People': The Growth and Distribution of the Population," in *Atlas of the Great Irish Famine*, ed. Crowley, Smyth, and Murphy, 13–22.

37. Asenath Nicolson, *Lights and Shades of Ireland* (London, 1850), 330, excerpted in Colm Tóibín and Diarmaid Ferriter, *The Irish Famine: A Documentary* (London, 1999), 132; Kerby A. Miller, "Emigration to North America in the Era of the Great Famine, 1845–55," in *Atlas of the Great Irish Famine*, ed. Crowley, Smyth, and Murphy, 214–227; "Population by Counties, 1821–1911," in *Irish Historical Statistics: Population, 1821–1971*, ed. W. E. Vaughan and A. J. Fitzpatrick (Dublin, 1978), 9; S. H. Cousens, "The Regional Variation in Mortality during the Great Irish Famine," *Proceedings of the Royal Irish Academy* 63 (Feb. 8,

1963): 127–149; Kennedy et al., *Mapping the Great Irish Famine*, 26–29, 104–124; Scally, *End of Hidden Ireland*, 109–115; Donnelly, *Great Irish Potato Famine*, 169–186. Smyth says 1.2 million emigrated, but all the other major sources put the number at 2.1 million; Smyth, "'Mapping the People,'" 13.

38. James Mahony, "Sketches in the West of Ireland," *ILN*, Feb. 13, 1847, 100; Donnelly, *Land and the People of Nineteenth-Century Cork*, 89–91; Paul Clements, "That Beats Banagher—An Irishman's Diary on Catchphrases and Towns," *Irish Times*, June 25, 2016. James Joyce included the line in *Finnegan's Wake*, (London, 1939), Book 1, 57.

39. Mitchel quoted in Tóibín and Ferriter, *Irish Famine*, 41, and Ó Gráda, *Black '47 and Beyond*, 6; "Depopulation of Great Britain," *New York Times*, Nov. 28, 1851, 2, makes a similar critique.

40. Quoted in Kennedy et al., *Mapping the Great Irish Famine*, 106.

41. Ó Gráda, *Black '47 and Beyond*, 6–10, 77–83; letter from Sir Charles Trevelyan, assistant secretary to the treasury to Sir Randolph Routh, Feb. 3, 1846, reprinted in Tóibín and Ferriter, *Irish Famine*, 70–71; letter to London *Times*, Sept. 1, 1846, in Tóibín and Ferriter, *Irish Famine*, 179–180; James S. Donnelly Jr., "'Irish Property Must Pay for Irish Poverty': British Public Opinion and the Great Irish Famine," in *Fearful Realities: New Perspectives on the Famine*, ed. Chris Morash and Richard Hayes (Dublin, 1996), 60–76.

42. T. H. Marmion in the *Cork Constitution*, Dec. 17, 1846, quoted in Ó Gráda, *Black '47 and Beyond*, 68; Donnelly, *Land and People of Nineteenth-Century Cork*, 85; Donnelly, *Great Irish Potato Famine*, 70–92.

43. Donnelly, *Great Irish Potato Famine*, 102, 94–116.

44. "Fenianism; and the Irish at Home and Abroad," *Blackwood's Edinburgh Magazine* 103 (Feb. 1868): 221–241; Donnelly, *Great Irish Potato Famine*, 132–168.

45. Ó Gráda, *Black '47 and Beyond*, 44–46, 69–73; Scally, *End of Hidden Ireland*, 5–6, 95–100, 105–129; Donnelly, "'Irish Property Must Pay for Irish Poverty,'" 76.

Chapter 2: Exiles and Expatriates

1. Warren to Fernando Wood, Aug. 2, 1867, reprinted in *Congressional Globe*, 40th Cong., 2nd sess., Jan. 9, 1868, 318; "Letter from Colonel Warren," *The Nation* (Dublin), Apr. 3, 1869.

2. Miller, *Emigrants and Exiles*, 193–223, 291–300; Ó Gráda, *Black '47 and Beyond*, 104–114; "The Tide of Emigration to the United States and to the British Colonies," *ILN*, July 6, 1850, 1; "The Depopulation of Ireland," *ILN*, May 10, 1851, 1.

3. "The Depopulation of Ireland"; Vere Foster, *Work and Wages; or, the Penny Emigrant's Guide to the United States and Canada for Female Servants, Laborers, Mechanics, Farmers*, 5th ed. (London, 1855), 5, 7, 8; Maldwyn A. Jones, *Destination America* (London, 1976), 24–32; Edward E. Hale, *Letters on Irish Emigration* (Boston, 1852), 7.

4. Reed Ueda, *Postwar Immigrant America: A Social History* (Boston, 1994), 3, 11; "Table Ad106–120: Immigrants, by Country of Their Last Residence—Europe, 1820–1997,"

Historical Statistics of the United States, Millennial Edition Online, ed. Susan B. Carter et. al. (Cambridge, 2006); Aristide R. Zolberg, "The Exit Revolution," in *Citizenship and Those Who Leave: The Politics of Emigration and Expatriation,* ed. Nancy L. Green and François Weil (Urbana, IL, 2007), 33–60.

5. Roger Daniels, *Coming to America: A History of Immigration and Ethnicity in American Life,* 2nd ed. (Princeton, NJ, 2002), 124–125; Ueda, *Postwar Immigrant America,* 3, 11, fig. 1 and fig. 2.

6. Bruce Levine, *The Spirit of 1848: German Immigrants, Labor Conflict and the Coming of the Civil War* (Urbana, IL, 1992), 12–16; Daniels, *Coming to America,* 145–152.

7. Thomas H. O'Connor, *The Boston Irish: A Political History* (Boston, 1995), 60–61; Oscar Handlin, *Boston's Immigrants: A Study in Acculturation* (New York, 1968), table VII: "Nativity of Bostonians, 1855."

8. W. E. Vaughan and A. J. Fitzpatrick, eds., *Irish Historical Statistics: Population, 1821–1971* (Dublin: Royal Irish Academy, 1978), 3, 9, 32–33; Handlin, *Boston's Immigrants,* table II: "Population of Boston and Its Environs" (Handlin gives 126,296 as the population for "Boston proper" but 247,606 when including surrounding neighborhoods, such as Charlestown, Cambridge, Somerville, etc.); Kenny, *The American Irish,* 104–107. Boston ranked the highest in terms of the Irish-born percentage of the total urban population, constituting 22.7 percent of Boston's population in 1870–1871; William Jenkins, *Between Raid and Rebellion: The Irish in Buffalo and Toronto, 1867–1916* (Montreal, 2013), appendix A. On "chain migration" and importance of Irish county in American residence patterns, see David W. Emmons, *Beyond the American Pale: The Irish in the West, 1845–1910* (Norman, OK, 2010), 25; Tyler Anbinder, *Five Points: The 19th-Century New York City Neighborhood That Invented Tap Dance, Stole Elections, and Became the World's Most Notorious Slums* (New York, 2001), 42–50.

9. *Report of the Committee of Internal Health on the Asiatic Cholera* (Boston, 1849), 13, quoted in Handlin, *Boston's Immigrants,* 113. On conditions, see Handlin, *Boston's Immigrants,* 54–123; Kenny, *The American Irish,* 109–111; Anbinder, *Five Points,* 72–140; Joseph P. Ferrie, *Yankeys Now: Immigrants in the Antebellum U.S. 1840–1860* (New York, 1999), 71–100.

10. Advertisements in *Boston Daily Globe,* Oct. 27, 1877, 3; *Boston Evening Transcript,* Dec. 5, 1868.

11. Advertisement for "John Warren, Grocer and Provision Dealer," *FS,* Aug. 20, 1864; John Bodnar, *The Transplanted: A History of Immigrants in Urban America* (Bloomington, IN, 1985), 131–138; Handlin, *Boston's Immigrants,* 64–67; Dennis P. Ryan, *Beyond the Ballot Box: A Social History of the Boston Irish, 1845–1917* (Rutherford, NJ, 1983), 83–85.

12. Warren's sister Mary Ann O'Leary (1832–1903) and her husband, Dennis, appear in the 1855 Massachusetts state census (as "O Lary"), reel 18, vol. 25, and in the 1860, 1870, 1880, and 1900 federal census records, which reveal she eventually owned a house in Arlington and took in two of John's children, who lived with her in 1870. Another sister, Anastatia Warren (1836–1904), appears on the 1860 federal census in Saugus, working as a

cigar maker; Mary Warren (1811–1885) was living with John and Joanna in Charlestown in 1860 (*1860 United States Federal Census*, microfilm publication M653, Washington, DC, NARA, Schedule I: Free Inhabitants in Charlestown in the County of Middlesex, State of Massachusetts, 39, 32). Mary Warren was living with Mary O'Leary in 1865 (Massachusetts state census 1865), and with Anastatia in 1880 (Federal census). Warren had five children: Timothy (1856–1906), George (1858–?); Eliza Jane (1861–1868), Robert Emmett (1863–1865), and John (1865–1873). Information from Massachusetts State Archives, Death Records and Birth Records.

13. "1864," *FS*, Aug. 27, 1864, 4–5. Warren was a captain in Company B of the 63rd New York regiment. On Irish in Civil War, see Susannah Ural Bruce, *The Harp and the Eagle: Irish-American Volunteers and the Union Army, 1861–1865* (New York, 2006). On Irish in the Confederate Army, see David T. Gleeson, "Irish Rebels, Southern Rebels: The Irish Confederates," in *Civil War Citizens: Race, Ethnicity, and Identity in America's Bloodiest Conflict*, ed. Susannah J. Ural (New York, 2010), 133–155.

14. Naturalization Act of April 14, 1802; John Warren, Certificate of Naturalization, Superior Civil Court, Suffolk Co., Boston, Dec. 12, 1866, 189; Dorothee Schneider, *Crossing Borders: Migration and Citizenship in the Twentieth-Century United States* (Cambridge, MA, 2011), 196–201.

15. Warren to Fernando Wood, Aug. 2, 1867.

16. Warren claimed to be a pioneering member of the Fenian Brotherhood, created as the Irish Republican Brotherhood in Ireland in 1858 and as the Fenian Brotherhood in the United States in 1859. Examples of oaths for the Fenian Brotherhood include "Obligation" (a printed form) and the handwritten oath of Timothy Sullivan, both in box 2, folder 5, FBR / CUA.

17. For general histories of the Fenian Brotherhood, see William D'Arcy, *The Fenian Movement in the United States: 1858–1886* (New York, 1947); W. S. Neidhardt, *Fenianism in North America* (University Park, PA, 1974); Leon Ó Broin, *Fenian Fever: An Anglo-American Dilemma* (New York, 1971); R. V. Comerford, *Fenians in Context: Irish Politics and Society, 1848–82* (Dublin, 1985); Oliver P. Rafferty, *The Church, the State and the Fenian Threat, 1861–1875* (London, 1999); Patrick Steward and Bryan McGovern, *The Fenians: Irish Rebellion in the North Atlantic World, 1858–1876* (Knoxville, TN, 2013); Mitchell Snay, *Fenians, Freedmen and Southern Whites: Race and Nationality in the Era of Reconstruction* (Baton Rouge, LA, 2007).

18. *Proceedings of the First National Convention of the Fenian Brotherhood Held in Chicago, Illinois, November 1863* (Philadelphia, 1863), 28; "Prospectus. The Fenian Spirit," *FS*, Aug. 27, 1864, 4. The *Fenian Spirit*'s first issue was Aug. 20, 1864, and the last issue I have found is Oct. 22, 1864. Western Reserve Historical Society Library and Archives has the only extant copy that I have been able to locate in the United States, the issue for Aug. 20, 1864. The Irish National Archives has the fullest—and perhaps the complete—run of the newspaper. See E. M. Archibald to T. H. Burmley, File A2, Fenian Papers, "A" Series, "Reports from America," NAI. Scholars' numerical estimates of the Fenian membership vary

widely, from 45,000 to 250,000; Samito, *Becoming American under Fire*, 120–121, and Kenny, *The American Irish*, 128. On Fenianism as an Irish American organization, see also Samito, *Becoming American under Fire*, 120–125.

19. See, e.g., the comments by John Arthur Roebuck in the House of Commons, "Habeas Corpus Suspension (Ireland) Act Continuance (No. 2) Bill," May 23, 1867, vol. 187, cc. 942–991, http://hansard.millbanksystems.com/commons/1867/may/23/habeas -corpus-suspension-ireland-act. For British bafflement over Fenians, see John Stuart Mill, *England and Ireland* (London, 1868), 6; Karl Marx, "Outline of a Report on the Irish Question to the Communist Educational Association of German Workers in London," Dec. 16, 1867, in *Marx and Engels on Ireland* (Moscow, 1971), 126–139.

20. "The Fenian Fever at Home and Abroad," *NYH*, Apr. 16, 1866, 4.

21. "The Fenian Movement," *ILN*, Sept. 23, 1865, 1335. See also "Fenianism; and the Irish at Home and Abroad," *Blackwood's Edinburgh Magazine* 103 (Feb. 1868): 222; "State of England—Panic in Ireland," *Pilot*, Nov. 16, 1867, 3; "The Irish Utopia," *Living Age* 92 (Jan. 12, 1867): 99 (reprint from the *Spectator*, Dec. 8, 1866); *Irish Rebellions, No. 3: The Fenians of 1866* (London, n.d.).

22. Seward to Charles Francis Adams, Mar. 10, 1866, *FRUS 1866*, 78. For a similar opinion, see "Official Correspondence re Fenianism in Ireland and America," MS 7517, Larcom Papers.

23. "Letter from Colonel Warren," *The Nation*, Apr. 3, 1869; "The Fenian Sisterhood of Quincy, Ill.: To Irishwomen in America," *FS*, Aug. 20, 1864, 1; *Fenianism, or the Irish Republic; Its Origin and Progress* (New York, 1865), which described the movement as both Irish and American; Miller, *Emigrants and Exiles*, 335–344.

24. Boston Board of Health, *The Sanitary Condition of Boston: The Report of a Medical Commission* (1875), reprinted in Edith Abbott, *Historical Aspects of the Immigration Problem* (1926; New York, 1969), 664–671. See Death Records, Massachusetts, 1865, vol. 184, p. 144 (Robert Emmett); 1868, vol. 212, p. 79 (Eliza Jane); 1973, vol. 247, p. 2 (John junior). George Warren, born 1858 and appearing in the 1860 federal census, appears to have died as well, though no death record could be located. Timothy, the eldest, died in 1906 at the age of fifty.

25. On Irish poverty and sickness, see Kenny, *The American Irish*, 107–108; Handlin, *Boston's Immigrants*, 114–117; Rev. W. H. Lord, *A Tract for the Times: National Hospitality* (Montpelier, 1855), reprinted in Abbott, *Historical Aspects of the Immigration Problem*, 805.

26. "Inaugural Address of His Excellency Henry J. Gardner," in *Acts and Resolves Passed by the General Court of Massachusetts in the Year 1854–1855* (Boston, 1855), 977–1000, quotes at 978–980, 982, 984; Tyler Anbinder, *Nativism and Slavery: The Northern Know-Nothings and the Politics of the 1850s* (New York, 1992), 92, 127, 135–139; John R. Mulkern, *The Know-Nothing Party in Massachusetts: The Rise and Fall of a People's Movement* (Boston, 1990), 91–95.

27. "Thirty-Third Congress, First Session," *NYT*, July 13, 1854, 8; see also Edward Everett Hale, *Letters on Irish Emigration* (Boston, 1852).

28. U.S. Constitution, Art. II, sec. 1; Kettner, *Development of American Citizenship*, 236–246; "An Irishman's Letter to Governor Gardner," reprinted in James Bernard Cullen, ed., *The Irish in Boston* (Boston, 1889), 435; "America for the Americans," *Putnam's Monthly*, May 1855, 531–540.

29. "Inaugural Address of His Excellency Henry J. Gardner," 979.

30. Kenny, *The American Irish*, 118–119, 124–125; Albert J. Von Frank, *The Trials of Anthony Burns: Freedom and Slavery in Emerson's Boston* (Cambridge, 1998), 136–137, 242–253, 286–287; John T. McGreevy, *Catholicism and American Freedom: A History* (New York, 2003), 43–67.

31. Charles Francis Adams Jr., *Richard Henry Dana: A Biography* (Boston, 1891), 280–281. On the "Know-Nothing" dual platform, see Anbinder, *Nativism and Slavery*.

32. Letter to the editor, Dec. 12, 1851, *NYT;* Dale T. Knobel, *Paddy and the Republic: Ethnicity and Nationality in Antebellum America* (Middletown, CT, 1986); Ray Allen Billington, *The Protestant Crusade, 1800–1860: A Study of the Origins of American Nativism* (New York 1938); Kenny, *The American Irish*, 112–115; John Higham, *Strangers in the Land: Patterns in American Nativism* (New Brunswick, NJ, 1955).

33. Steven P. Erie, *Rainbow's End: Irish-Americans and the Dilemmas of Urban Machine Politics, 1840–1985* (Berkeley, CA, 1988), 25–34; Kenny, *The American Irish*, 120–121; O'Connor, *The Boston Irish*, 69–75.

34. Hidetaka Hirota, *Expelling the Poor: Atlantic Seaboard States and the Nineteenth-Century Origins of American Immigration Policy* (New York, 2017), 100–128, appendices B–D, 215–218.

35. "Street Preaching in Brooklyn. Serious Riot," *NYT,* June 5, 1854, 8; "Inaugural Address of His Excellency Henry J. Gardner," 981–982, 986–989; Anbinder, *Nativism and Slavery*, 135–142.

36. Anbinder, *Nativism and Slavery*, 140–142; Martin Duberman, *Charles Francis Adams, 1807–1886* (Stanford, CA, 1960), 213; Mulkern, *The Know-Nothing Party in Massachusetts*, 94–95, 157, 211.

37. Levine, *The Spirit of 1848*, 241–244; Alison Clark Efford, *German Immigrants, Race, and Citizenship in the Civil War Era* (New York, 2013), 53; Carl Schurz, *Speeches, Correspondence and Political Papers of Carl Schurz*, ed. Frederic Bancroft (New York, 1913), 1:48–72, quote at 59; "Inaugural Address of His Excellency Henry J. Gardner," 980, 990; "Know-Nothing Demonstration," *NYT*, Nov. 10, 1854, 8; "America for Americans!," *The Wide-Awake Gift: A Know-Nothing Token for 1855* (New York, 1855), reprinted in Abbott, *Historical Aspects of the Immigration Problem*, 789–791.

38. "Letter from Colonel Warren"; Thomas Colley Grattan, *Civilized America* (London, 1859), 2:2–6, quotes at 2, 5.

39. "Letter from Col. Warren"; see also Jon Gjerde, *The Minds of the West: Ethnocultural Evolution in the Rural Middle West, 1830–1917* (Chapel Hill, NC, 1997), 58–59, on naturalization as "rebirth."

40. John Warren to Fernando Wood, Aug. 2, 1867; "Letter from Colonel Warren"; "A Plea for the Celtic Race," *Brooklyn Eagle*, Feb. 1, 1868, 2.

41. *Citizen* (New York), Oct. 28, 1854, 681, reprinted in Abbott, *Historical Aspects of the Immigration Problem*, 466–467; Grattan, *Civilized America*, 9–10; Brian Jenkins, *Irish Nationalism and the British State: From Repeal to Revolutionary Nationalism* (Montreal, 2006), 225–254. For varied interpretations of American roots of Irish American nationalism, see David Brundage, "Recent Directions in the History of Irish American Nationalism," *Journal of American Ethnic History* 28 (Summer 2009), 82–89.

42. "Concerning Skedaddling," *NYT*, Aug. 10, 1862, 1; Don H. Doyle, *The Cause of All Nations: An International History of the American Civil War* (New York, 2015), 158–182; William L. Burton, *Melting Pot Soldiers: The Union's Ethnic Regiments* (New York, 1998); Ural, ed., *Civil War Citizens*; Bruce, *The Harp and the Eagle*, 42–81.

43. Quote of Meagher from *Boston Morning Journal*, Sept. 24, 1861, in Samito, *Becoming American under Fire*, 32; "The Sixty-Third N.Y.S.V.," *NYT*, Nov. 19, 1861, 8. Massachusetts also repealed the "two-year" amendment in 1863; Samito, *Becoming American under Fire*, 102–108.

44. "Look Out for the Registered Aliens," *NYT*, Nov. 3, 1863, 1; "The Conscription—Grievances of the Inchoate Citizens," *NYT*, May 24, 1863, 4. The conscription act exempted aliens only if they agreed to leave the United States within sixty-five days. Eugene H. Berwanger, *The British Foreign Service and the American Civil War* (Lexington, 1994), 126–144; Candice Bredbenner, "A Duty to Defend? The Evolution of Aliens' Military Obligations to the United States, 1792 to 1946," *Journal of Policy History* 24 (2012): 230–234.

45. Quoted in Bruce, *The Harp and the Eagle*, 183; "The Raging Riot," *NYT*, July 15, 1863. On the riot, see Bruce, *The Harp and the Eagle*, 178–184; Iver Bernstein, *The New York City Draft Riots: Their Significance in American Society and Politics in the Age of the Civil War* (New York, 1991).

46. M. Keane, Nashville, TN, to the editors of the *Fenian Spirit*, Oct. 9, 1864, in *FS*, Oct. 22, 1864, 6.

47. Bruce, *The Harp and the Eagle*, 153–156; Nagle quoted in Craig A. Warren, "'Oh, God, What a Pity!': The Irish Brigade at Fredericksburg and the Creation of a Myth," in *Civil War History* 47 (2001): 193–221, 194; John Warren to J. Holt, Judge Advocate General, June 8, 1863, file 17289, Office of the Adjutant General, Volunteer Service Branch, 1886, RG 94, NARA. Warren claimed his commanding officer, Colonel John Burke, sought revenge for Warren's charges against him for cowardice, which ultimately led to Burke's dishonorable discharge in October 1862. It probably did not help Warren's case that he had been dishonorably discharged on Feb. 28, 1862, for being intoxicated on duty, but was mustered in again in April. John Warren, General Orders no. 79, Feb. 28, 1862, Army of the Potomac, File II761, Court-Martial Case Files, Records of the Office of the Judge Advocate General, RG 153, Entry 15, NARA.

48. "A Warning," *FS*, Sept. 17, 1864, 8. See also Bruce, *The Harp and the Eagle*, 143–149, 174–178; Doyle, *The Cause of All Nations*, 178–180.

49. Bruce, *The Harp and the Eagle*, 136–189.

50. "The Sixty-Third N.Y.S.V."; Nagle's letter to father, in *Pilot*, May 30, 1863, quoted in Bruce, *The Harp and the Eagle*, 159.

51. "Address of the New England Convention of the Fenian Brotherhood," *FS*, Aug. 20, 1864, 1.

Chapter 3: The Fenian Pest

1. "The Fenian Brothers," *NYT*, July 26, 1865, 8; "The Orphan's Fair," *Boston Daily Advertiser*, Nov. 2.

2. "Artemus Ward among the Fenians," in Charles F. Brown, *The Complete Works of Artemus Ward* (New York, 1882); Robert Rowlette, "'Mark Ward on Artemus Twain': Twain's Literary Debt to Ward," *American Literary Realism* 6 (Winter 1973): 12–25.

3. R. V. Comerford, "Patriotism as Pastime: The Appeal of Fenianism in the Mid-1860s," *Irish Historical Studies* 22, no. 86 (Sept. 1980): 239–250. See also Comerford, *Fenians in Context: Irish Politics and Society 1848–82* (Dublin, 1985). For criticism of Comerford's thesis, see Mary Burgess's review of the reprint of Comerford's book *Fenians in Context* in *History Ireland*, Spring 1999, 49–52.

4. On informants, see, e.g., E. Archibald, Consul at New York, to Earl Russell, Mar. 18, 1865, HO 45 / 7799; Brown, Superintendent of U.S. Telegraph Company, to Sir George Grey, Home Department, Mar. 3, 1866, HO 45 / 7799; Pierrepont Edwards, Acting Consul, New York, to Lord Stanley, Nov. 6, 1866, FO 5 / 1340 (re information from a *New York Herald* reporter). See also correspondence and newspaper clippings in Fenian Papers, "A" Series: "Reports from America," NAI; Breandán Mac Giolla Choille, "Fenian Documents in the State Department Office," *Irish Historical Studies* 16 (1969): 258–284.

5. E. M. Archibald to T. H. Burmley, File A2, Fenian Papers, "A" Series, "Reports from America," NAI.

6. D'Arcy, *Fenian Movement in the United States*, 72, 120. Both the Fenians and the British government tended to exaggerate the numbers of Americans arriving in Ireland, making it difficult to discern how many actually went to Ireland.

7. Report of Daniel Ryan, Superintendent of Police, Dublin, March 17, 1866, HO, 7799 / 79; Daniel Ryan to Commissioner of Police, Feb. 26, 1866, HO, 45 / 7799.

8. "Memorial to His Excellency the most Noble the Marquis of Abercom Lord Lieutenant General and General Governor of Ireland," from Fermoy, Chairman, HM Lieutenant of the County of Cork, Magistrates of the County of Cork, n.d. (ca. Dec. 1866), HO, 45 / 7799; Sir Thomas Larcom to H. Waddington, Jan. 22, 1866, HO, 45 / 7799; letter to Lord Naas, Dec. 1, 1866, about "*panic* which has seised the public mind," ms. 11,189, folder 2, Mayo Papers; F. Hutchinson Synce, Ennis, County Clare, to Lord Mayo, Dec. 8, 1866, ms. 11,189, folder 5, Mayo Papers; "Fenian Weapons Seized at Cork," *ILN*, Sept. 30, 1865, 322.

9. Adams to Seward, Jan. 18, 1866, CFA LB.

10. D'Arcy, *Fenian Movement in the United States*, 47–51.

11. John O'Mahony, "Special Order No. 9," Aug. 31, 1864, reprinted in *FS*, Oct. 8, 1864, 5; Warren to J. O'Mahony, Oct. 18, 1864, FBR / CUA.

12. "Head-quarters of the Fenians at New York," *ILN*, Dec. 16, 1865, 589; "The Constitution of the Fenian Brotherhood, 1865," reproduced in *The Fenians Progress: A Vision* (New York, 1865), 68–91; D'Arcy, *Fenian Movement in the United States*, 81.

13. "The Fenian Brothers," *NYT*, July 26, 1865, 8; "Song of the Brother-Fenians," words by Jonathan Cain, pub. H. De Marsan (New York, n.d.).

14. Robert E. May, "Young American Males and Filibustering in the Age of Manifest Destiny: The United States Army as a Cultural Mirror," *Journal of American History* 78 (Dec. 1991): 857–886.

15. Garth Stevenson, *Ex Uno Plures: Federal-Provincial Relations in Canada, 1867–1896* (Montreal, 1993), 3–22; W. S. Neihardt, *Fenianism in North America* (University Park, PA, 1975), 16–21, 109–111.

16. Quoted in D'Arcy, *Fenian Movement in the United States*, 111, 114. On ongoing annexation debates, see Neihardt, *Fenianism in North America*, 16–23; Alan Taylor, *The Civil War of 1812: American Citizens, British Subjects, Irish Rebels, & Indian Allies* (New York, 2010), 137–138; Glyndon G. Van Deusen, *William Henry Seward* (New York, 1967), 535–537; Robert E. May, *Manifest Destiny's Underworld: Filibustering in Antebellum America* (Chapel Hill, NC, 2003), 4, 10–13, 55, 286–287.

17. Consul Kortright, Philadelphia, to Earl of Clarendon, March 12, 1866, HO, 7799 / 79.

18. P. H. Casey, "The Fenian's Native Land," Air: 69th Regiment, pub. H. De Marsan (New York, n.d.), in "America Singing: Nineteenth-Century Song Sheets," American Memory Collection, Library of Congress, http://memory.loc.gov/ammem/amsshtml /amsshome.html.

19. Ronald Hyam, *Britain's Imperial Century, 1815–1914: A Study of Empire and Expansion* (London, 1976), 70–77, 206–229; Philippa Levine, *The British Empire: Sunrise to Sunset* (London, 2007), 61–81; Jill C. Bender, *The 1857 Indian Uprising and the British Empire* (Cambridge, 2016).

20. "Erin's Little Difficulty," *Punch*, Sept. 30, 1865.

21. On the ambiguous status of Ireland as a colony, see the essays in Kenny, ed. *Ireland and the British Empire*.

22. "The Fenian-Pest," *Punch*, March 3, 1866, 230; "Physic for Fenians," *Punch*, Dec. 8, 1866, 46; "Rebellion Had Bad Luck," *Punch*, Dec. 16, 1865;"The Fenian Movement," *ILN*, Sept. 13, 1865, 1335; "Fenian Conspiracy," *Times*, Oct. 13, 1865, 8.

23. House of Commons, May 23, 1867, vol. 187, cc. 942–991, http://hansard.mill banksystems.com/commons/1867/may/23/habeas-corpus-suspension-ireland-act.

24. Bender, *The 1857 Indian Uprising*; Brian Jenkins, *The Fenian Problem: Insurgency and Terrorism in a Liberal State, 1858–1874* (Montreal, 2008), 3–7; Jonathan Parry, *The Rise and Fall of Liberal Government in Victorian Britain* (New Haven, CT, 1993); Lauren Benton

and Lisa Ford, *Rage for Order: The British Empire and the Origins of International Law, 1800–1850* (Cambridge, MA, 2016), 182–188.

25. Denis McCarthy, *Dublin Castle at the Heart of Irish History* (Dublin, 1997); R. F. Foster, *Modern Ireland, 1600–1972* (London, 1988), 59–78, 117–137.

26. Thomas E. Jordan, "Two Thomases: Dublin Castle and the Quality of Life in Victorian Ireland," *Social Indicators Research* 64 (Nov. 2003): 257–291, esp. 281–288; Jenkins, *Fenian Problem*, 34–39, 50–52, 66–67; R. B. McDowell, *The Irish Administration, 1801–1914* (London, 1964), 52–77.

27. Louis Paul-DuBois, *Contemporary Ireland* (Dublin, 1908), 187,

28. Kieran Flanagan, "The Chief Secretary's Office, 1853–1914: A Bureaucratic Enigma," 24 *Irish Historical Studies* (Nov. 1984), 210.

29. Larcom Papers, ms. 11191 / 5, quoted in Leon Ó Broin, *Fenian Fever: An Anglo-American Dilemma* (New York, 1971), 165.

30. CFA to Seward, Sept. 22, 1865, Despatches from Great Britain, RG59: General Records of the Department of State, NARA, M30.

31. McDowell, *The Irish Administration*, 135–145; Levine, *The British Empire: Sunrise to Sunset*, 117; Parliament, House of Commons, June 15, 1865, vol. 180, cc. 319–325, http://hansard.millbanksystems.com/commons/1865/jun/15/adjourned-debate. For Irish districts proclaimed as disturbed in August 1865, see "Peace Preservation Act: Districts Proclaimed," folder 10, file 11,188, Mayo Papers.

32. Henry J. Rae to Consul William West, Nov. 24, 1865, DD; John Fanning to Seward, Nov. 11, 1865, *FRUS 1866*, 29–30.

33. Byron to West, Mar. 19, 1866, DD.

34. Treason Felony Act 1848 c. 12 (Regnal. 11 and 12 Vict.), www.legislation.gov.uk/ukpga/Vict/11-12/12/contents; Sean McConville, *Irish Political Prisoners, 1848–1922: Theatres of War* (London, 2003), 25–30; Crown Security Bill, House of Commons, April 7, 1848, vol. 98, cc. 20–59 (see esp. Prime Minister Lord Russell's explanation of act as "mitigating" the severity of the treason act and why it was needed at 38–39, 55–56, 122–128).

35. Jenkins, *Fenian Problem*, 28–30, 36–37, 41–42; McConville, *Irish Political Prisoners*, 123–124.

36. Habeas Corpus Suspension (Ireland) Act, 29 and 30 Vict., c. 1; "Suspension of the Habeas Corpus Act in Ireland," *Times*, Feb. 19, 1866, 5; editorial, *Times*, Feb. 17, 1866; "The Habeas Corpus," *Times*, Feb. 19, 1866, 7; "The Fenian Conspiracy in Ireland," *ILN*, Mar. 3, 1866, 214; "Ireland," *Times*, Feb. 19, 1866, 9.

37. "Parliamentary Intelligence," *Times*, Feb. 19, 1866, 5.

38. Editorial, *Times*, Nov. 5, 1867, 8; "The Fenian Trials," *Illustrated London News*, May 11, 1867, 453.

39. *Irish American Weekly*, Nov. 2, 1867, 2.

40. "Fenian Conspiracy," *Times*, Oct. 13, 1865, 8.

41. Of the initial ninety-one arrested, thirty-eight were listed as Irish Americans. The others, presumably Irish, included publicans, skilled artisans, millworkers, and even a schoolteacher. "List of Prisoners," Ryan to Commissioners of Police, Feb. 18, 1866, HO 45 / 7799.

42. Daniel Ryan to Commissioners of Police, Feb. 18, 1866, HO 45 / 7799; "The Fenian Conspiracy in Ireland;" "Ireland." For a personal account from a prisoner, see *Frank Roney, Irish Rebel and California Labor Leader: An Autobiography,* ed. Ira Cross (Berkeley, CA, 1931), 136–167.

43. Neihardt, *Fenianism in North America,* 43–52.

44. Quoted in Neihardt, *Fenianism in North America,* 62.

45. *Battle of Ridgeway, C.W.* (Buffalo, N.Y.: Sage, Sons and Co., ca. 1869), Library of Congress, https://www.loc.gov/item/2006677453.

46. *Trials of American Citizens in Great Britain,* 59; see also Neihardt, *Fenianism in North America,* 60; Peter Vronsky, *Ridgeway: The American Fenian Invasion and the 1866 Battle That Made Canada* (Toronto, 2011).

47. Neihardt, *Fenianism in North America,* 59–75.

48. Neihardt, *Fenianism in North America,* 30–31, 43–45.

49. Neihardt, *Fenianism in North America,* 71, 76–84. On Fenians' beliefs that the government secretly supported the Canadian invasion, see Bruce to Stanley, Nov. 19, 1866, FO 5 / 1340.

50. Neihardt, *Fenianism in North America,* 73, 149 n. 38; Vronsky, *Ridgway.* Nine Canadians died in the battle, but as many as twenty-three died from causes related to the conflict. A total of nine Fenians were killed in action or died from wounds sustained in battle. "Fenian Raid 1866 Canadian Casualties Master List" and "Known Fenian Brotherhood Casualties Killed in Action or Died of Wounds 1866," http://www.ridgeway battle.ca.

51. "Fate of the Fenian Prisoners," *Pilot,* June 30, 1866, 3; Brian Jenkins, *Irish Nationalism and the British State: From Repeal to Revolutionary Nationalism* (Montreal, 2006), 207–208.

52. Quoting author of bill, Chief Justice Robinson, in Rainer Baehre, "Trying the Rebels: Emergency Legislation and the Colonial Executive's Overall Legal Strategy in the Upper Canadian Rebellion," in *Canada State Trials,* vol. II, *Rebellion and Invasion in the Canadas, 1837–1839* (Toronto, 2002), 44–45; Neihardt, *Fenianism in North America,* 95, 99; F. N. Blake, U.S. Consul at Fort Erie, to F. W. Seward, Aug. 6, 1866, in *Trials of American Citizens in Great Britain,* 29–30; "The Fenian Prisoners in Canada—How They Are to Be Tried," in *Trials of American Citizens in Great Britain,* 151–152.

53. Neihardt, *Fenianism in North America,* 99–107. For summaries of trials of Lynch and McMahon, see *Trials of American Citizens in Great Britain,* 53–74 (quote at 73), 131–141. Neihardt says 25 Fenians were convicted (107), but the defense attorney reports 21 convictions and 22 acquittals of the 96–97 Fenians imprisoned. Mackenzie to Mr. Thurston, Mar. 11, 1867, *Trials of American Citizens in Great Britain,* 149.

54. "Fenianism in Ireland," *ILN*, Dec. 1, 1866, 517.

55. On divisions within Fenian Brotherhood, see "The Fenian Congress," *New York Tribune*, Sept. 11, 1867, 1; "The Irish Question in Its Present Phase," *Pilot*, June 11, 1867; Thomas to Wood, Dec. 14, 1867, File A66, Fenian Papers, NAI; Archibald to Clarendon, Dec. 29, 1865, File A72, Fenian Papers, NAI.

56. The *New York Times* referred to the Fenians' invasion of Canada as the "Fenian Fiasco" (June 8, 1866, 1) and the "Fenian Folly" (June 5, 1866, 1). See also "The Lesson of the Hour," *Pilot*, June 16, 1866, 1.

57. "The Fenian Men," pub. H. De Marsan (New York, n.d.), Library of Congress, https://www.loc.gov/item/amss.as201000.

Chapter 4: *Civis Americanus Sum*

1. Adams to J. L. Motley, U.S. Envoy to Vienna, Sept. 22, 1865, CFA LB.

2. CFA Diary, May 13, 1864.

3. CFA Diary, Jan. 4, 1865.

4. CFA Diary, Jan. 16, 1865, Feb. 5, 1865.

5. Doris Kearns Goodwin, *Team of Rivals: The Political Genius of Abraham Lincoln* (New York, 2005), 735–737.

6. CFA Diary, Apr. 26, 1865; Adams to John Palfrey, Feb. 8, 1866, CFA LB.

7. CFA Diary, Jan. 2, 1866; Adams to John Palfrey, Jan. 9, 1866, CFA LB.

8. Henry Adams, *The Education of Henry Adams*, ed. Ira B. Nadel (New York, 1999), 99.

9. Adams, *Education of Henry Adams*, 98; Martin Duberman, *Charles Francis Adams, 1807–1886* (Stanford, CA, 1960), 1–12.

10. Duberman, *Charles Francis Adams*, 258–262; George Bemis, "British Neutrality," letter to the editor, *NYT*, Mar. 16, 1868; George Bemis, *Hasty Recognition of Rebel Belligerency and Our Right to Complain of It* (Boston, 1865). Howard Jones, *Blue and Gray Diplomacy: A History of Union and Confederate Relations* (Chapel Hill, NC, 2010), 9–81, argues the United States misread the British position.

11. Adams to William Hunter, July 13, 1865, CFA LB; Adams to Seward, Oct. 19, 1865, CFA LB; Adams, *Education of Henry Adams*, 117, 106–107; Ronald Hyman, *Britain's Imperial Century, 1815–1914: A Study of Empire and Expansion* (New York, 1976), 165, 173–180, quotes at 179; Duberman, *Charles Francis Adams*, 258–314, esp. 263–267; David Brown, *Palmerston: A Biography* (New Haven, CT, 2010), 59–96, 451–454; Richard J. M. Blackett, *Divided Hearts: Britain and the American Civil War* (Baton Rouge, LA, 2000); Don H. Doyle, *The Cause of All Nations: An International History of the American Civil War* (New York, 2015); Jones, *Blue and Gray Diplomacy*, 31–38.

12. Adams, *Education of Henry Adams*, 107.

13. Robert Ralph Davis Jr., "Diplomatic Plumage: American Court Dress in the Early National Period," *American Quarterly* 20 (Summer 1968): 164–179; Duberman, *Charles*

Francis Adams, 262–263, quote from the queen is from 471 n. 11 and is taken from Benjamin Moran's diary, Nov. 18, 1861.

14. Adams, *Education of Henry Adams*, 100.

15. Charles Francis Adams, "Tribute to Wm H. Seward by Mr. Adams," *Proceedings of the Massachusetts Historical Society* 12 (1871–1873): 305; Duberman, *Charles Francis Adams*, 267–269, 329–330; Amanda Foreman, *A World on Fire: Britain's Crucial Role in the American Civil War* (New York, 2010), 190–191; Doyle, *Cause of All Nations*, 50–65.

16. Duberman, *Charles Francis Adams*, 278–284; Jones, *Blue and Gray Diplomacy*, 83–111; W. W. Story to George Bemis, Mar. 1, 1867, George Bemis Papers, MHS.

17. Duberman, *Charles Francis Adams*, 293–295, 300–314, 323–324; Adrian Cook, *The Alabama Claims: American Politics and Anglo-American Relations, 1865–1872* (Ithaca, NY, 1975), 31–32; Jones, *Blue and Gray Diplomacy*, 192–201.

18. "Great Britain and the United States—Our Feeling toward England," *NYT*, May 20, 1865, 4; "America and England," *NYT*, Sept. 7, 1865, 4; "A Just Claim upon British Sympathy," *NYT*, May 14, 1865, 4.

19. CFA Diary, Feb. 15, 1865.

20. Editorial, *Times*, Mar. 14, 1865, 9; CFA Diary, Jan. 31, 1865; Debate on Increasing Canadian Defence, House of Commons, March 13, 1865, vol. 177, cc. 1539–1637; "The Coming War," *NYT*, March 31, 1865, 5; "England and America," *Times*, July 10, 1865; "War between England and America," *NYT*, Jan. 14, 1856.

21. Adams to Seward, Dec. 21, 1865, CFA LB; "Great Britain and the United States—Our Feeling toward England"; Adams to Lord Russell, Sept. 18, 1865, CFA LB.

22. Adams to Seward, Jan. 4, 1866, CFA LB; Adams to Motley, Sept. 22, 1865, CFA LB.

23. Henry J. Rae to Consul William West, Nov. 24, 1865, DD; John Fanning to Seward, Nov. 11, 1865, *FRUS 1866*, 29–30.

24. Henry T. Tuckerman, "American Diplomacy," *Atlantic Monthly*, Sept. 1868, 352. On American consuls in Ireland, see Bernadette Whelan, *American Government in Ireland 1790–1913: A History of the US Consular Service* (Manchester, 2010), 54–104.

25. On obligation as a key aspect of citizenship in the nineteenth century, see Linda Kerber, *No Constitutional Right to Be Ladies: Women and the Obligations of Citizenship* (New York, 1998); Christopher Capozzola, *Uncle Sam Wants You: World War I and the Making of the Modern American Citizen* (New York, 2008), 1–17. On the limits of modern concepts of citizenship in understanding nineteenth-century citizenship, see William J. Novak, "The Legal Transformation of Citizenship in Nineteenth-Century America," in Meg Jacobs, William J. Novak, Julian E. Zelizer, eds., *The Democratic Experiment: New Directions in American Political History* (Princeton, NJ, 2003), 85–119.

26. M. Kerwin to West, Feb. 21, 1866, and March 20, 1866; see also Denis F. Burke to West, Feb. 21, 1866; John H. Gleeson to West, March 20, 1866; and J. O'Carroll to West, March 23, 1866; all DD. On military service as a claim to citizenship, see Christian Samito, *Becoming American under Fire: Irish Americans, African Americans and the Politics of Citizenship during the Civil War Era* (Ithaca, NY 2009). For other scholarly treatments of habeas corpus

arrests and diplomatic disputes, see David Sim, *A Union Forever: The Irish Question and U.S. Foreign Relations in the Victorian Era* (New York, 2013), 97–109; Brian Jenkins, *Fenians and Anglo-American Relations during Reconstruction* (Ithaca, NY, 1969), 70–102.

27. West to Adams, Sept. 22, 1865, DD; West to Adams, Nov. 6, 1865, DD; Whelan, *American Government in Ireland*, 167.

28. On greater mobility and Americans living abroad, see John Westlake, comments during "Discussion of Change of Nationality," *Transactions of the National Association for the Promotion of Social Science, Birmingham Meeting, 1868* (London, 1869), 179; John Westlake, "On Naturalisation and Expatriation; or, On Change of Nationality," *The Law Magazine and Law Review, or Quarterly Journal of Jurisprudence*, vol. 25 (Mar.-Aug. 1868): 125–126; Detmold to Bancroft, Mar. 8, 1868, BP; John Bigelow to Bancroft, May 5, 1868, BP; F. W. Sargent to Bemis, Nice, Jan. 10, 1866, Bemis Papers, MHS. Moran quoted in Whelan, *American Government in Ireland*, 55. See also Nancy L. Green, "Americans Abroad and the Uses of Citizenship: Paris, 1914–1940," *Journal of American Ethnic History* 31 (Spring 2012): 5–32.

29. Austin's position, as restated by Sir William Vernon Harcourt, "International Law," *Transactions of the National Association for the Promotion of Social Sciences, Birmingham Meeting, 1868*, 137; Richard Pankhurst, "Change of Nationality," *Transactions . . .* , 160; W. David Clinton, *Tocqueville, Lieber, and Bagehot: Liberalism Confronts the World* (New York, 2003); Marti Koskenniemi, *The Gentle Civilizer of Nations: The Rise and Fall of International Law, 1870–1960*, 11–97; Antony Anghie, *Imperialism, Sovereignty and the Making of International Law* (Cambridge, 2005), esp. 44–47, 67–68; Mark Mazower, *Governing the World: The History of an Idea, 1815 to the Present* (New York, 2012), 38–48.

30. Historicus [William Harcourt], "The Status of Aliens," *Times*, Feb. 6, 1868, 6; Anghie, *Imperialism, Sovereignty and the Making of International Law*, 57–58; Edwin M. Borchard, "Basic Elements of Diplomatic Protection of Citizens Abroad," *American Journal of International Law* 7 (1913): 497–500.

31. Mary Ann Glendon, *Rights Talk: The Impoverishment of Political Discourse* (New York, 1991); Dennis Nolan, "Sir William Blackstone and the New Republic: A Study of Intellectual Impact," *Political Science Reviewer* 6 (Fall 1976): 283–322; Daniel Boorstin, *The Mysterious Science of the Law* (Cambridge, MA, 1941).

32. William Blackstone, *Commentaries on the Laws of England*, facsimile ed. (1765; Chicago, 1979), 1:354–359; Daniel Webster, "The Case of Thrasher," *The Works of Daniel Webster* (Boston, 1890), VI:526; Borchard, "Basic Elements of Diplomatic Protection of Citizens Abroad," 504–506; J. Mervyn Jones, *British Nationality Law and Practice* (Oxford, 1947), 1–69.

33. West to Adams, Feb. 18, 1866, DD.

34. Blackstone, *Commentaries*, vol. I, 358.

35. On the strategic use of "protection" claims, wielded both by individuals seeking aid from powerful countries and by the British Empire seeking to extend its power over foreign territories, see Lauren A. Benton and Lisa Ford, *Rage for Order: The British Empire*

and the Origins of International Law, 1800–1850 (Cambridge, MA, 2016), 85–116; Sarah Abrevaya Stein, "Protected Persons? The Baghdadi Jewish Diaspora, the British State, and the Persistence of Empire," *American Historical Review* 116 (Feb. 2011): 80–108.

36. Henry John Temple, 3rd Viscount Palmerston, "On Affairs in Greece," *The World's Famous Orations. Great Britain: II (1780–1861)*, 1906, www.bartleby.com/268/4/18. For earlier examples of British protection of subjects abroad, see Jordana Dym, "Citizen of Which Republic? Foreigners and the Construction of National Citizenship in Central America, 1823–1845," *The Americas* 64 (Apr. 2008): 497–498. On the "portability of subjecthood and allegiance" in the nineteenth century, see Lauren A. Benton, *A Search for Sovereignty: Law and Geography in European Empires, 1400–1900* (New York, 2010), esp. 279–299.

37. Historicus, "The Status of Aliens," 8.

38. Fanning to Seward, Nov. 11, 1865, *FRUS 1866;* George H. Yeaman, *Allegiance and Citizenship* (Copenhagen, 1867), 25–26.

39. Historicus, "The Status of Aliens"; Emer de Vattel, *Law of Nations* (1758), Book I, §14–16.

40. Thomas Larcom to H. Waddington, Oct. 25, 1866, FO 5 / 1340.

41. Blackstone, *Commentaries,* 1:357–358 (Blackstone quoted Sir Edward Coke, 2 Inst. 121); James H. Kettner, *The Development of American Citizenship, 1608–1870,* 7–8, 13–28; on tensions between voluntary and involuntary allegiance in Blackstone, see Kunal Parker, *Making Foreigners: Immigration and Citizenship Law in America, 1600–2000* (New York, 2015), 22–28.

42. West to Adams, Feb. 18, 1866, DD.

43. Eneas Dougherty to West, March 20, 1866, DD.

44. Kettner, *Development of American Citizenship,* 173–209.

45. Nancy L. Green, "The Politics of Exit: Reversing the Immigration Paradigm," *Journal of Modern History* 77 (June 2005): 263–289; Mack W. Walker, *Germany and the Emigration, 1816–1885* (Cambridge, 1964), 74–96; Andreas Fahrmeir, *Citizenship: The Rise and Fall of a Modern Concept* (New Haven, CT, 2007), 56–88; Torpey, *Invention of the Passport,* 58–91; Green and Weil, ed., *Citizenship and Those Who Leave;* Andreas Fahrmeir, Olivier Faron, and Patrick Weil, eds., *Migration Control in the North Atlantic World: The Evolution of State Practices in Europe and the United States from the French Revolution to the Inter-War Period* (New York, 2003).

46. John Torpey, *The Invention of the Passport* (Cambridge, 2000), 79–91; David Feldman and M. Page Baldwin, "Emigration and the British State, ca. 1815–1925," in *Citizenship and Those Who Leave,* ed. Green and Weil, 135–155; François Weil, "The French State and Transoceanic Emigration," in *Citizenship and Those Who Leave,* ed. Green and Weil, 114–131.

47. George Jabet, "Discussion: Change of Nationality," *Transactions of the National Association for the Promotion of Social Science, Birmingham Meeting, 1868,* 182–183. France allowed expatriation, in theory, but discouraged it through onerous requirements—the consent of its government and a steep fee. Expatriation without the government's consent could result

in the loss of property, the inability to inherit French estates, and arrest and imprisonment, should unlawful expatriates return. Alexander Cockburn, *Nationality: or the Law Relating to Subjects and Aliens* (London, 1869), 53–55. See also Fahrmeir, *Citizenship*, 70; Patrick Weil, *How to Be French: Nationality in the Making since 1789* (Durham, NC, 2008), 30–42.

48. Borchard, "Basic Elements of Diplomatic Protection of Citizens Abroad," 519.

49. Alan Taylor, *The Civil War of 1812* (New York, 2010), 3–5, 101–124, 358–379; Donald R. Hickey, *The War of 1812: A Forgotten Conflict* (Urbana-Champaign, IL, 2012); Cockburn, *Nationality*, 75–78; John Adams, "The Inadmissible Principles of the King of England's Proclamation," in *The Works of John Adams*, ed. Charles Francis Adams (Boston, 1854), 9:315–316.

50. John Quincy Adams to John Adams, Dec. 27, 1807 in *Writings of John Quincy Adams*, ed. Worthington Chauncey Ford (New York, 1914), 3:166–173; Taylor, *Civil War of 1812*, 409–440; Hickey, *War of 1812*, 2–3, 287–307; Steven Watts, *The Republic Reborn: War and the Making of Liberal America, 1789–1820* (Baltimore, 1989), 204–206.

51. U.S. Congress, House of Representatives, "American Citizens Imprisoned in Ireland," H.R. ex. doc. 19, 30th Cong., 2nd sess., Dec. 28, 1848. See also the controversy over the "Patriot Rebellion" in Canada, in Taylor, *Civil War of 1812*, 441–458, and Cassandra Pybus, *American Citizens, British Slaves: Yankee Political Prisoners in an Australian Penal Colony, 1839–50* (East Lansing, MI, 2002).

52. 13 Stat. L. 490, sec. 21. The provision also applied to those who left the United States to avoid conscription and barred declarants who violated the law from completing their naturalization. See Harcourt's criticism of American hypocrisy in "British Citizenship," *Times*, Jan. 10, 1868, 10.

53. Tsiang, *The Question of Expatriation in America*, 29–70; Kettner, *Development of American Citizenship*, 173–209; Parker, *Making Foreigners*, 50–80; Welke, *Law and the Borders of Belonging*, 63–93; Martha S. Jones, *Birthright Citizens: A History of Race and Rights in Antebellum America* (New York, 2018); Elizabeth Stordeur Pryor, *Colored Travelers: Mobility and the Fight for Citizenship before the Civil War* (Chapel Hill, NC, 2016).

54. "Quit the country" quoted in Eric R. Schlereth, "Privileges of Locomotion: Expatriation and the Politics of Southwestern Border Crossing," *Journal of American History* 100 (Mar. 2014): 999; "Expatriation," *History of Congress*, House of Representatives, February 1818, 1046. For privateer cases, see Tsiang, *The Question of Expatriation*, 27–37.

55. *United States v. Isaac Williams*, quoted in Tsiang, *The Question of Expatriation*, 3 (citing "Trial of Isaac Williams," *State Trials of the United States*, ed. Francis Wharton [C.C.D. Conn. 1799], 653).

56. "Our Nationality and Naturalization," *NYT*, June 17, 1859, 4; "The Case Fairly Stated," *Federal Republican and Commercial Gazette*, Dec. 9, 1812, 3. On the law of expatriation before Civil War, see Kettner, *Development of American Citizenship*, 267–284; Nancy L. Green, "Expatriation, Expatriates, and Expats: The American Transformation of a Concept," *American Historical Review* 114 (Apr. 2009), 307–328; Schlereth, "Privileges of Locomotion," 995–1020; Richard J. Flournoy Jr., "Naturalization and Expatriation," *Yale Law Journal*

(May 1922): 702–719; Frank George Franklin, *Legislative History of Naturalization in the United States: From the Revolutionary War to 1861* (Chicago, 1906), 134–165; Rising Lake Morrow, "The Early American Attitude toward Naturalized Americans Abroad," *American Journal of International Law* 30 (1936): 647–663; John P. Roche, "Loss of American Nationality: The Years of Confusion," *Western Political Quarterly* 4 (June 1951): 268–294; Tsiang, *Question of Expatriation*, 25–70.

57. *Opinions of the Principal Officers of the Executive Officers of the Executive Departments and Other Papers Relating to Expatriation, Naturalization and Change of Allegiance* (Washington, DC, 1873), 125; Tsiang, *Question of Expatriation*, 71–72.

58. Tsiang, *Question of Expatriation*, 72–82; Jay Sexton, "Toward a Synthesis of Foreign Relations in the Civil War Era, 1848–1877," *American Nineteenth-Century History* 5 (Fall 2004): 53–55.

59. Marcy quickly backtracked on his claim that the United States would protect declarants; only those who could prove their American citizenship could demand the government's protection. "Rights of Americans Abroad," *NYT*, Aug. 18, 1853, 3; "American Protection to Naturalized Citizens," *NYT*, Aug. 25, 1853, 4; Andor Klay, *Daring Diplomacy: The Case of the First American Ultimatum* (Minneapolis, 1957); Cockburn, *Nationality*, 119–122; Craig Robertson, *The Passport in America* (New York, 2010), 134–142.

60. "The Naturalization Question," *Constitution* (Washington, DC), July 14, 1859, 3; "The King of Prussia and American Citizenship," *NYT*, Nov. 2, 1858, 5; "The Naturalization Question," *San Francisco Bulletin*, July 27, 1859, 2; *Opinions of the Principal Officers*, 127.

61. Kettner, *Development of American Citizenship*, 264–265, 287–333; Elizabeth Duquette, *Loyal Subjects: Bonds of Nation, Race, and Allegiance in Nineteenth-Century America* (New Brunswick, NJ, 2010), esp. 17–60; Jones, *Birthright Citizens*; Novak, "The Legal Transformation of Citizenship in Nineteenth-Century America," 91–93; Douglas Bradburn, *The Citizenship Revolution: Politics and the Creation of the American Union, 1774–1804* (Charlottesville, VA, 2009); Michael A. Schoeppner, "Status across Borders: Roger Taney, Black British Subjects, and a Diplomatic Antecedent to the Dred Scott Decision," *Journal of American History* 100 (June 2013): 46–67; Don E. Fehrenbacher, *The Dred Scott Case: Its Significance in American Law and Politics* (New York, 1978).

62. On triumph of national allegiance, see the proposed Constitutional Amendment XIII, Francis Lieber [Loyal Publication Society], *Amendments of the Constitution* (New York, 1865); Lawson, *Patriot Fire*, 179–186.

63. West to Adams, Feb. 17, 18, and 19, 1866, DD. For prisoners' demands, see Cleary to West, Feb. 1866, 5; O'Brien to West, Mar. 18, 1866, 12; Byron to West, Mar. 19, 1866, 12; Dougherty to West, Mar. 20, 1866, 13; Kirwin to West, Mar. 22, 1866, 15.

64. CFA Diary, Feb. 17, 1866.

65. Adams to Seward, Sept. 23, 1865, Oct. 5, 1865, Dec. 28, 1865, CFA LB; Adams to Seward, Feb. 22, 1866, *FRUS 1866*, 69; CFA Diary, Feb. 17, 19; Mar. 5, 1866; Adams to West, Feb. 19, 1866, CFA LB.

66. "Fenian Movements," *NYH*, Mar. 12, 1866, 5; "Fenian Mass Meeting," *NYT*, Mar. 19, 1866; "The Irish Republic," *NYH*, May 15, 1866, 10. For useful accounts of the habeas corpus dispute, see D'Arcy, *Fenian Movement*, 123–130; Jenkins, *Fenians and Anglo-American Relations during Reconstruction*, 88–102.

67. Seward to Adams, Mar. 10, 1866, 77; Mar. 22, 1866, 86, *FRUS 1866*.

68. Adams to West, Feb. 19, 1866, CFA LB; Adams to Young, Jan. 29, 1866, CFA LB; Adams to West, Mar. 7, 1866, CFA LB; CFA Diary, Mar. 1, 1866; Mar. 5, 1866.

69. Craig Robertson, *The Passport in America*, 4–7, 125–150. Births might be recorded in family Bibles or through baptismal records in churches, but not necessarily in city or state records.

70. See, e.g., letters to West in DD from Kerwin, Feb. 21, 1866, Byron, Mar. 19, 1866; Hefferman, Dec. 29, 1865; Lawlor, Feb. 24, 1866; Hugh Dennedy, Feb. 24, 1866; Dunne, Feb. 24, 1866; Burke, Feb. 21, 1866. Several prisoners thought their military service alone had turned them into American citizens, with no need to go through the naturalization process. For similar claims made in the twentieth century to U.S. consuls abroad, see Green, "Americans Abroad and the Uses of Citizenship."

71. Adams to Seward, Aug. 27, 1867; Adams to West, Feb. 28, 1866, CFA LB.

72. Law Officers' Report to Earl of Clarendon, Mar. 9, 1866, HO 45 / 7799, NA; Larcom to West, Feb. 21, 1866, Feb. 28, 1866, HO 45 / 7799, NA; Adams to Seward, June 14, 1866, *FRUS 1866*, 136–137; CFA Diary, Feb. 25, 1866, and Apr. 11, 1866; Adams to Seward, Mar. 2, 1866, *FRUS 1866*, 74. The dispute over documentation revealed another messy reality: the boundaries between aliens and citizen remained blurry in the mid-nineteenth century, as the Kostza case had revealed. During the Civil War, Britain had conceded a "qualified nationality" might exist, allowing the United States' conscription of British subjects who were on the path to American citizenship. Paul Quigley, "Civil War Conscription and the International Boundaries of Citizenship," *Journal of the Civil War Era* 4 (Sept. 2014): 373–397; Candice Bredbenner, "A Duty to Defend? The Evolution of Aliens' Military Obligations to the United States, 1792 to 1946," *The Journal of Policy History* 24 (2012): 224–262.

73. Larcom to West, Mar. 10, 1866, HO 45 / 7799; Seward to Adams, Mar. 22, 1866, *FRUS 1866*, 86; Seward to Adams, Mar. 31, 1866, *FRUS 1866*, 94; Bruce to Stanley, Nov. 21, 1866, FO 5 / 1340; CFA Diary, Mar. 5, 1866, and Apr. 11, 1866; Adams to West, Feb. 19, 1866, CFA LB; Adams to Seward, Mar. 15, 1866, *FRUS 1866*, 83–84; Adams to Seward, Apr. 12, 1866, *FRUS 1866*, 102–104.

74. Adams to Seward, Apr. 19, 1866, *FRUS 1866*, 106; Adams to Seward, May 10, 1866, *FRUS 1866*, 118–119; Adams to Seward, June 1, 1866, *FRUS 1866*, 124–125.

75. Neihardt, *Fenianism in North America*, 105–107; Bruce to Lord Stanley, Nov. 21, 1866, FO 5 / 1340, NA; Stanley to Colonia Office, Nov. 10, 1866, FO 5 / 1340; Lord Carnarvon to Governor Monck, Nov. 26, 1866, FO 5 / 1340.

76. Adams to Seward, June 1, 1866, *FRUS 1866*, 124–125.

77. Adams to Seward, Feb. 6, 1867, *FRUS 1867*, 62–63.

78. Larcom to Naas, Mar. 21, 1867, Mayo Papers, 11, 191 / 5.

Chapter 5: A Floating Rebellion

1. "Is Irish Freedom a Chimera?," *FS*, Sept. 3, 1864, 4; "Address of the New England Convention of the Fenian Brotherhood," *FS*, Aug. 20, 1864, 1; "The True Path," *FS*, Aug. 27, 1864, 4.

2. Brian Jenkins, *The Fenian Problem: Insurgency and Terrorism in a Liberal State, 1858–1874* (Montreal, 2008), 80–86; Leon Ó Broin, *Fenian Fever: An Anglo-American Dilemma* (New York, 1971), 96–99, 119–173; R. V. Comerford, *Fenians in Context: Irish Politics and Society, 1848–82* (Dublin, 1985), 134–139; E. G. Eastman, U.S. consul at Queenstown to Seward,, Nov. 24, 1866, *FRUS 1866*, 65; Eastman to Seward, Mar. 7, 1867, *FRUS 1867*, 66.

3. The excitement began soon after the *Herald* published news of the (failed) raid on Chester Castle to seize weapons on Feb. 15, 1867. "The Fenians in This City," *NYH*, Feb. 16, 1867; "Fenians in New York," *NYH*, Feb. 17, 1867, 5; "The Fenians in New York," *NYH*, Feb. 18, 1867, 8; "The Fenians," *NYH*, Mar. 3, 1867, 8; "The Fenians in New York," *NYH*, Mar. 10, 1867, 5; "The Fenians," *NYH*, Mar. 12, 1867, 10; "The Fenians: Grand Rally in Union Square," *NYH*, Mar. 14, 1867, 10; William D'Arcy, *The Fenian Movement in the United States: 1858–1886* (New York, 1947), 228–232.

4. "The Fenians in New York," *NYH*, Feb. 21, 1867, 10; "The Cable," *NYH*, Feb. 17, 1867, 5; "The Situation in Ireland," *New York Tribune*, Mar. 11, 1867, 1.

5. Thomas J. Kelly to "My Dear General," Mar. 15 and Mar. 19, 1867, box 2, folder 8, FBR / CUA.

6. "The Fenians," *NYH*, Mar. 19, 1867, 4.

7. "Meeting of Irish-American Officers," *Irishman*, Mar. 9, 1867, 580; "Meeting of Irish American Officers," *NYH*, Mar. 10, 1867, 5; D'Arcy, *The Fenian Movement*, 232.

8. "The Fenians: Another Fenian War Manifesto," *NYH*, Dec. 1, 1866, 8; "Meeting of Irish-American Officers," *NYH*, Mar. 10, 1867, 5; "The Fenians in New York," *NYH*, Feb. 20, 1867, 10. Warren identified himself as the "late Commandant Centre Column Fenian Army at Malone."

9. "The Fenians," *NYH*, Mar. 14, 1867, 10.

10. For the "letter of marque and reprisal" form, see "Blank Commission of a Naval Vessel of the Irish Republic," box 2, folder 9, FBR / CUA.

11. John Savage, *Fenian Heroes and Martyrs* (Boston, 1868), 448–449.

12. "The Fenians," *NYH*, Mar. 12, 1867, 10; "The Fenians in New York," *NYH*, Mar. 10, 1867, 5.

13. Kelly to "My Dear General," Mar. 15 and 19, 1867.

14. The following narrative about the *Erin's Hope* expedition is drawn from several primary and secondary sources, all of which have various biases. The most detailed firsthand

accounts come from the testimony of the informer Daniel J. Buckley and witness Michael Gallagher in the trials of John Warren and Augustine Costello in Dublin (See *Report of the Trial of John Warren*, 32–61, 88–95, and *Queen v. Costello*, Fenian Briefs, box 11, INA) and from the report made by Captain John Kavanagh, captain of the vessel, to the Fenian Brotherhood upon his return to the United States, which informs a 1916 pamphlet, M. J. O'Mullane, *The Cruise of the "Erin's Hope"; or Gun-running in '67* (Dublin, 1916). Several historians of the Fenian movement include discussion of the *Erin's Hope* expedition. See especially D'Arcy, *The Fenian Movement*, 228–278; Jenkins, *Fenians and Anglo-American Relations*, 236–241; Steward and McGovern, *The Fenians*, 162–175; Sim, *A Union Forever*, 109–118.

15. On the USS *Dunderberg*, see http://www.steelnavy.com/CombrigDunderberg .htm; see also Tony Gibbons, *Complete Encyclopedia of Battleships: A Technical Directory of Capital Ships from 1860 to the Present Day* (New York, 1983). For dimensions of *Jacmel Packet*, see "Copy Pencil Documents Found on the Person of the Prisoner Nagle," *Queen v. Warren and Nagle*, "Crown Briefs," 5, carton 10, NAI; D'Arcy, *Fenian Movement*, 244. Buckley estimated the *Jacmel* to be 115 tons, and O'Mullane, 200 tons. *Trial of John Warren*, 35; O'Mullane, *The Cruise of the "Erin's Hope,"* 7.

16. *The Jacmel Packet*, 13 F 264 (SDNY, 1868). For conflicting accounts of *Jacmel*'s history, see letter of U.S. Customs official in Colón, Dec. 21, 1866, reprinted in *Launceston Examiner* (Tasmania), Apr. 23, 1867, 4; "Marine Intelligence," *NYT*, Feb. 3, 1867, 8; D'Arcy, *The Fenian Movement*, 244; Steward and McGovern, *The Fenians*, 166.

17. Daniel Buckley testimony, *The Trial of John Warren*, 35–36; *The Jacmel Packet*, U.S. District Court of the Southern District of New York, in *Reports of Cases . . . in the District Courts of the United States within the Second Circuit*, II:107–111; O'Mullane, *The Cruise of the "Erin's Hope,"* 9.

18. D'Arcy, *The Fenian Movement*, 243–245; O'Mullane, *The Cruise of the "Erin's Hope,"* 7–8; "The Fenians," *NYH*, Mar. 19, 1867, 4; Steward and McGovern, *The Fenians*, 166.

19. See Costello and Tresilian speeches at "The Fenians," *NYH*, Mar. 14, 1867, 10. Tresilian, Daniel J. Buckley, and Warren had been among the men who participated in the earlier Canadian invasion. Buckley's testimony: *Report of the Trial of John Warren*, 33–34. For biographical details on *Jacmel* men, see Chief Secretary's Office, Irish Crimes Records, Fenian Photographs 16, NAI; notes confiscated from William Nagle in *Queen v. Warren and Nagle*, "Crown Briefs," 5–6, carton 10, NAI; "Roster of the Military Officers of the Fenian Brotherhood New York," box 2, folder 6, FBR / CUA; Steward and McGovern, *The Fenians*, 166–179.

20. Tyler Anbinder, *Five Points: The 19th-Century New York City Neighborhood That Invented Tap Dance, Stole Elections, and Became the World's Most Notorious Slum* (New York, 2001), 1, 274–302; D'Arcy, *The Fenian Movement*, 245.

21. O'Mullane in *The Cruise of the "Erin's Hope"* (14–15) reprints a letter or appreciation from the *Erin's Hope* men to Captain Kavanagh, dated May 24, 1867, and the signatures indicate that Nagle was second in command and Warren third in command.

22. Samuel L. Anderson, Memo on Fenianism, 433–435, Ms. 7517, Larcom Papers; Shunsuke Katsuta, "The Rockite Movement in County Cork in the Early 1820s," *Irish Historical Studies* 33 (May 2003): 278–296; James S. Donnelly Jr., *Captain Rock: The Irish Agrarian Rebellion of 1821–1824* (Madison, WI, 2009), esp. 106–108, 180–186, 316–317.

23. Census of 1860, Brooklyn, Ward 6, District 3, Kings, New York, Roll M653_766, Page 942, Image 508, Family History Library Film, 803766, AncestryLibrary.com; "Presentation of a Sword," *NYT*, Dec. 3, 1861, 8; Office of Military Personnel File, William J. Nagle, RG 319, Records of the Army Staff, NARA; "Death of General William J. Nagle," *NYH*, Aug. 16, 1869; Steward and McGovern, *The Fenians*, 167.

24. Kelly to "My Dear General," Mar. 19, 1867.

25. "Captain John F. Kavanagh," *Brooklyn Eagle*, June, 11, 1880, 4; see Steward and McGovern, *The Fenians*, 167–168, for a slightly different version.

26. Testimony of Daniel Buckley, *Report of the Trial of John Warren*, 36.

27. Edwards to Larcom, April 13, 1867, ms. 7517, Larcom Papers, and Larcom to Naas, May 19, 1867, ms. 11191, Mayo Papers, quoted in Padraic Cummins Kennedy, "Political Policing in a Liberal Age: Britain's Response to the Fenian Movement, 1858–1868," Ph.D. diss., Washington University, 1996, 335–336. On Tresilian, see "Roster of the Military Officers of the Fenian Brotherhood New York," 23–24, box 2, folder 6, FBR / CUA; Steward and McGovern, *The Fenians*, 167.

28. O'Mullane, *Cruise of the "Erin's Hope,"* 8.

29. Jenkins, *The Fenian Problem*, 80–87, 93–96; letter of Joseph Hertford, New York, Nov. 19, 1866, HO 45 / 7799; Superintendent Daniel Ryan to Commissioner of Police, Dublin Metropolitan Police, April 8, 1867, HO 45 / 7799; "The Fenian Insurrection in Ireland," *ILN*, Mar. 16, 1867, 262; "Fenian Trials at Dublin," Apr 27, 1867, *ILN*, 408; "Ireland," *Times*, May 27, 1867, 6; "The Dungarvan Invasion," *Irishman*, June 3, 1867, 792–793.

30. In various records, Doherty's name is also spelled "Dougherty" and "Dogherty."

31. O'Mullane, *The Cruise of the "Erin's Hope,"* 11–13. The population of Sligo is for the year 1871. See "Population and Demography," http://www.sligolibrary.ie/sligolibrary new/media/Population%20%283%29.pdf.

32. Gallagher's testimony in *Report of the Trial of John Warren*, 51–53.

33. *Report of the Trial of John Warren*, 40–44. Colonels James Pendergast, George Phelan, and Patrick Devine left with Burke. On Burke, see "Statement of William Million," June 14, 1867, folder 7, file 43,887, Mayo Papers; "Augustine Costello Dead," *Gaelic-American*, Nov. 20, 1909, 4.

34. *Trial of John Warren*, 43, 63–68.

35. "Statement of William Million" (on water rations); "Copy Pencil documents found on the person of the prisoner Nagle," *Queen v. Warren and Nagle*, "Crown Briefs," 5, carton 10, INA.

36. *Trial of John Warren*, 46–47; T. D. Sullivan, ed., *Speeches from the Dock; or, Protests of Irish Patriotism* (1868; New York, 1904), 297. Dismissed as a traitor to the Fenian cause in

most accounts, Buckley receives more sympathetic treatment in Steward and McGovern, *The Fenians*, 171.

37. P. J. Kain to Mr. O'Donovan Rossa, Nov. 20, 1909, folder 6, box 5, FBR / CUA; speech of Colonel S. R. Tresilian, quoted in Sullivan, ed., *Speeches from the Dock*, 297; "Statement of William Million."

38. Testimony of Daniel Buckley and Patrick Whelan, *Report of the Trial of John Warren*, 48–49, 68–70; Sylvester Murray, "The Fenian Landing at Helvic," Waterford County Museum, www.waterfordmuseum.ie/exhibit/web/Display/article/323/4/The _Fenian_Landing_At_Helvic_The_Erins_Hope_Arrives.html.

39. "Singular Affair near Sligo—Two Men Shot," *Pilot*, June 22, 1867, 3; "Ireland: Landing of Supposed Fenians in Dungarvan," *Pilot*, June 29, 1867, 1; *Queen v. Warren*, 74–77, 78–79; *Queen v. Costello*, 47–48; "Memorandum of the Constables by Whom the Different Prisoners Were Arrested on 1st June 1867," *Queen v. Warren and Nagle*, "Crown Briefs," carton 10, NAI.

40. Testimony of Patrick Browne, Daniel Collins, George Jones, Andrew Roche, Police Sergeant James Norris, *Report of the Trial of John Warren*, 68–79; "Statement of Patrick Whelan & Ptk Brown, Fishermen, Helvick Head, 1 June 1867," Fenian Files R / 1869 / 7042R, NAI.

41. H. E. Redmond to Larcom, June 2, 1867, HO 45 / 7799; "Memorandum of the Constables by Whom the Different Prisoners Were Arrested on the 1st June, 1867," *Queen v. Warren and Nagle*, 46–47; Memoranda in Fenian Files R / 1869 / 7042R, NAI.

42. "The Dungarvan Mystery," *Pilot*, June 29, 1867, 3 (reprinting *Cork Examiner* article).

43. H. E. Redmond to Larcom, June 2, 1867, HO 45 / 7799.

44. Bloomfield to Lord Naas, June 6, 1867, folder 10, ms 11,189, Mayo Papers; "Landing of Supposed Fenians in Dungarvan," *Pilot*, June 29, 1867, 5 (reprinting article from *Cork Examiner*, June 6); Goold to Lord Naas, June 7, 1867, file 7595, Larcom Papers.

45. Bloomfield to Larcom, June 7, 1867, File 7595, Larcom Papers; Goold to Naas, June 22, 1867, folder 7, File 43,887, Mayo Papers; Naas to Goold, [June 20, 1867?], folder 7, file 43,887, Mayo Papers; "A Police Outrage at Waterford," *Irishman*, June 22, 1867, 822; "Fatal Rioting in Waterford—Attack on the Police," *Irish Times*, June 15, 1867, 3; Goold to Larcom, June 14, 1867, folder 7, file 43,887, Mayo Papers; "Desperate Fenian Affray in Ireland," *Illustrated Police News*, June 22, 1867.

46. Bloomfield to Lord Naas, June 6, 1867, folder 10, ms 11,189, Mayo Papers.

47. Henry Redmund to Larcom, June 2, 1867, HO 45 / 7799.

48. Naas to Larcom, June 11, 1867, ms. 7595, Larcom Papers. Superintendent of Police Daniel Ryan reported that Colonel Kelly, the leader of the Fenian mission in Ireland, "is gone towards the South or West to see some of the men who escaped the fate of their companions at Dungarvan, & it is believed that many of the Prisoners as well as of those who escaped are very important personages in the conspiracy." Ryan to Commissioner of Police, June 10, 1867, HO 45 / 7799.

49. Jenkins, *Fenian Problem*, 206–208; "News Paragraphs," *Newark Advocate*, July 19, 1867.

50. "Statement of William Million."

51. "Statement of William Million"; Ryan to Commissioner of Police, June 18, 1867, HO 45 / 7799.

52. George Goold to Lord Mayo, June 19, 1867, folder 7, ms. 43,887, Mayo Papers.

53. "Strictly Confidential—for the Cabinet . . . Lord Strathnairn's Annual Confidential Report," folder 14, ms. 11,188, Mayo Papers.

54. On suspension of habeas corpus, see Habeas Corpus Suspension (Ireland) Act, House of Commons, May 23, 1867, vol. 187, cc. 942–991.

55. Samuel Lee Anderson to Larcom, June 14, 1867, File 7595, Larcom Papers.

56. *The Jacmel Packet*, 13 F 264 (SDNY 1868); O'Mullane, *Cruise of the Erin's Hope*, 28–32.

57. "Colonel Nagle," *Freeman's Journal*, Mar. 4, 1868.

58. "New York Affairs," *Milwaukee Daily Sentinel*, Jan. 27, 1868.

Chapter 6: The Voice from the Dungeon

1. Adams to Seward, Oct. 10, 1867, *FRUS 1867*, 157; Habeas Corpus Suspension (Ireland) Act Continuance (No. 2) Bill, House of Commons, May 23, 1867, vol. 187, cc. 942–991.

2. "Ireland," *Times*, Nov. 19, 1867, 12; Jeremy Bentham, *The Panopticon Writings*, ed. Miran Bozovic (London, 1995); Michel Foucault, *Discipline and Punish: The Birth of the Prison* (New York, 1977).

3. Kenneth C. Wenzer, *Henry George, the Transatlantic Irish and Their Times* (Bingley, UK, 2009), 115; "Irish Prisoners and Whitewashed Walls," House of Commons, August 1, 1889, vol. 339, cc. 66–67.

4. "Ireland," *Times*, Nov. 19, 1867, 12.

5. *A History of Kilmainham Gaol, 1796–1924* (Dublin, 2006); Seán McConville, *Irish Political Prisoners, 1848–1922: Theatres of War* (New York, 2003); "Ireland," *Times*, Nov. 19, 1867, 12; "Life in the Bastiles [*sic*]," *Irishman*, Oct. 26, 1867, 264–265.

6. *Forty-Sixth Report of the Inspector-General of the General State of the Prisons of Ireland, 1867* (Dublin, 1868), 493. See also John Warren, "A Voice from the Dungeon," *Dublin Weekly News*, Aug. 31, 1867, reprinted in *FRUS 1867*, 134–135.

7. McConville, *Irish Political Prisoners*, 149. On the Ladies' Committee, see Patrick Joseph Murray, Government Prisons Office, to Undersecretary Larcom, Oct. 3, 1866, FO 5 / 1340; Michael O'Brien, Mountjoy Prison, to Katie Smith, Oct. 1, 1866, FO 5 / 1340; Report of Superintendent of Police Daniel Ryan, Sept. 23, 1867, HO 7799 / 79; West to Adams, July 27, 1867, DD, 523–524.

8. *Forty-Sixth Report of the Inspectors-General of the General State of the Prisons of Ireland, 1867* (Dublin, 1868), 488, 491; *Thirteenth Annual Report of the Director of Convict*

Prisons in Ireland for the Year Ended 31st December, 1866 (Dublin, 1867), 10, 14; McConville, *Irish Political Prisoners*, 144–145; Ryan to Commissioner of Police, Dublin, May 27, 1867, HO 7799 / 79, 1407–1414.

9. Warren, "A Voice from the Dungeon."

· 10. "The Dungarvan Mystery—Important Particulars," *Irishman*, June 8, 1867, 360; Breandán Mac Suibhne and Amy Martin, "Fenians in the Frame: Photographing Irish Political Prisoners, 1865–1868," *Field Day Review* 1 (2005): 106.

11. West to Adams, July 27, 1867, DD, 523–524; see also West to Adams, Sept. 9, 1867, DD, 561–562. During the war, Nagle had received sick leave on numerous occasions due to the debilitating effects of the fever, including emaciation, weakness, and nervousness. Official Military Personnel File, William J. Nagle, RG 319, Records of the Army Staff, NARA. On mental and physical illnesses caused by the American Civil War, see R. Gregory Lande, "Felo de Se: Soldier Suicides in America's Civil War," *Military Medicine* 176 (May 2011): 531–536; E. T. Dean Jr., *Shook over Hell: Post-Traumatic Stress, Vietnam, and the Civil War* (Cambridge, MA, 1997); Frank R. Freeman, *Gangrene and Glory: Medical Care during the American Civil War* (Champagne, IL, 2001), 206–209; Andrew McIlwaine Bell, *Mosquito Soldiers: Malaria, Yellow Fever, and the Course of the American Civil War* (Baton Rouge, LA, 2010).

12. *Thirteenth Annual Report of the Director of Convict Prisons in Ireland for the Year Ended 31st December, 1866* (Dublin, 1867), 18, 21; McConville, *Irish Political Prisoners*, 150–153; Beverly A. Smith, "Irish Prison Doctors—Men in the Middle, 1865–90," *Medical History* 26 (1982): 371–394.

13. William C. Nugent to West, Dec. 13, 1867, 657–658, and John T. Scallan to West, Feb. 13, 1868, 708–712, in DD; Larcom to Mayo, "William C. Nugent 'Jackmel' Prisoner," folder 16, ms. 11,188, Mayo Papers; No. 3 in "Memoranda Respecting the Supposed Conspiracy by Colonel Nagle of the Jackmel Expedition to Assassinate William Million," ms. 7517, Larcom Papers.

14. Several letters written to families and friends are reprinted in *Papers Relating to Foreign Affairs*. See, for example, letter of William Nagle to his father, David Nagle, written from County Cork jail on June 14, 1867, reprinted in *FRUS 1867*, July 9, 1867.

15. "The Patriot," with the inscription "Kilmainham Gaol, Aug. 20, 1867," reprinted in *Irishman*, Oct. 5, 1867, 219.

16. No. 3 in "Memoranda Respecting the Supposed Conspiracy by Colonel Nagle of the Jackmel Expedition to Assassinate William Million," ms. 7517, Larcom Papers.

17. See, e.g., "A Voice from the Prison," *Irishman*, Oct. 19, 1867; "More Prison Voices," *Irishman*, Oct. 5, 1867, 219; "A Peep behind the Scenes: How Information Is Manufactured in Fenian Cases," letter to the editor, Oct. 11, 1867, printed in *Irishman*, Oct. 12, 1867, 237, reprinted in *Pilot*, Nov. 2, 1867, 1; Warren, "A Voice from the Dungeon."

18. Warren, "A Voice from the Dungeon," 136; *Forty-Sixth Report of the Inspectors-General of the General State of the Prisons of Ireland, 1867* (Dublin, 1868), 489.

19. "The New York Herald," *North American Review* 102 (April 1866): 377.

20. Richard A. Schwarzlose, *The Nation's Newsbrokers*, vol. 1 (Evanston, IL, 1989); Richard R. John, *Spreading the News* (Cambridge, MA, 1995), 31, 37; Marie-Louise Legg, *Newspapers and Nationalism: The Irish Provincial Press, 1850–1892* (Dublin, 1998), 45, 110; Thomas C. Leonard, *News for All: America's Coming-of-Age with the Press* (New York, 1995), 91; Cian McMahon, "Ireland and the Birth of the Irish-American Press, 1842–61," *American Periodicals* 19 (2009): 5–20.

21. Laura Murphy DeGrazia, *Irish Relatives and Friends: From the "Information Wanted" Ads in the* Irish-American, *1850–1871* (Baltimore, 2010).

22. "The New York Herald," 377; Benedict Anderson, *Imagined Communities: Reflections on the Origins and Spread of Nationalism* (London, 1983); Matthew Jacobson, *Special Sorrows: The Diasporic Imagination of Irish, Polish, and Jewish Immigrants in the United States* (Cambridge, MA, 1995), 57–64; Leonard, *News for All*, 28–32.

23. West to Adams, July 27, 1867, DD, 523–524.

24. Legg, *Newspapers and Nationalism*, 76, 109–115; Brian Jenkins, *The Fenian Problem: Insurgency and Terrorism in a Liberal State, 1858–1874* (Montreal, 2008), 27–30, 296.

25. Nos. 2 and 3 in "Memoranda Respecting the Supposed Conspiracy by Colonel Nagle of the Jackmel Expedition to Assassinate William Million," ms. 7517, Larcom Papers.

26. "Life in the Bastilles," *Irishman*, Oct. 26, 1867, 264–265; "Humiliation of the Stars and Stripes," *Pilot*, Aug. 3, 1867, 3; "News from a Fenian Martyr," *New York Tribune*, Sept. 3, 1867, 8.

27. Warren, "A Voice from the Dungeon," 134–135.

28. "The Dungarvan Invasion," *Irishman*, June 3, 1867, 793.

29. Warren to President Johnson, Aug. 3, 1867, *FRUS 1867*, 136.

30. William Nagle to Father, Co. Cork Jail, June 14, 1867, reprinted in *FRUS 1867*, 112–113; Patrick Kane claimed to be in Ireland to "visit friends." Hugh Dunigan to Seward, July 10, 1867, reprinted in *FRUS 1867*, 115; John Hart (alias William Halpin) to Bart, July 10, 1867, Fenian Files/R Series/1869/4934R, NAI.

31. "Trial of a New York Fenian in Ireland," Baltimore *Sun*, Mar. 8, 1867, 1; "Stephen Joseph Meany," *NYH*, Feb. 27, 1867, 4; "Fenian Movements," *NYH*, Mar. 12, 1866, 5; "Stephen Joseph Meany (1822–1888)," Fenian Graves: Ours to Honor and Remember, http://feniangraves.net/S.J.%20Meany/SJMeany.htm.

32. George Cornewall Lewis, *On Foreign Jurisdiction and the Extradition of Criminals* (London, 1859), 7–9; "Ireland," *Times*, Apr. 19, 1867, 6; "Ireland," *Times*, June 24, 1867, 10.

33. "Irish American Citizens Abroad: The Case of Stephen J. Meany," letter to the editor, *Pilot*, Aug. 24, 1867, 2; "Stephen Joseph Meany," in *Speeches from the Dock; or, Protests of Irish Patriotism*, ed. T. D. Sullivan (1868; New York, 1904), 206–307; Wm. J. Nagle to Father, Co. Cork Jail, June 14, 1867, reprinted in *FRUS 1867*, 112–113; Warren, "A Voice from the Dungeon," 134.

34. "Humiliation of the Stars and Stripes."

35. "Stephen Meany and Martin Koszta," *Irishman*, Oct. 26, 1867, 265.

36. "Irish American Citizens Abroad," *Pilot*, Aug. 24, 1867, 2.

37. "Our Diplomacy during the Rebellion," *North American Review* 102 (Apr. 1866): 447.

38. John Hart (alias William Halpin) to Bart, July 10, 1867, Fenian Files/R Series/1869/4934R, NAI.

39. Extract from article by "Tyrone" in the *Irish Republic* (Chicago), reprinted in *Irishman*, Nov. 16, 1867, 311; Warren, "A Voice from the Dungeon."

40. CFA Diary, entries for June 10, 1867; Aug. 12, 13, 18, 1867; Oct. 1, 3, 10, 1867. For Adams on the history of his mission, see entries for Aug. 30, 1867; Sept. 7, 9, 19, 1867.

41. Benjamin Moran Journal, Aug. 2, 1867 and Sat., Aug. 3, 1867, vol. 19, Benjamin Moran Journals, 1851–1875, Library of Congress.

42. Joseph J. McCadden, "Governor Seward's Friendship with Bishop Hughes," *New York History* 47 (Apr. 1966): 163–165; Walter Stahr, *Seward: Lincoln's Indispensable Man* (New York, 2012), 7–8, 38, 60–61, 68–70, 107, 134–135, 146–153, 187–191. Seward delivered an oration at the New York immigration station when the great Irish leader Daniel O'Connell died. William H. Seward, *An Oration on the Death of Daniel O'Connell: Delivered at Castle Garden, New York, September 22, 1847* (Auburn, NY, 1847).

43. Lynch to Seward, Dec. 6, 1866, *Trials of American Citizens in Great Britain*, 117.

44. David Nagle to Seward, Jan. 11, June 7, Oct. 25, Oct. 31, 1841; Feb. 26, 1849; William J. Nagle to Seward, Dec. 22, 1851, June 12, 1852, Dec. 29 1855, Aug. 26, 1856, June 8 and 29, 1858, Feb. 24, 1863; William Henry Seward Papers, University of Rochester; William Nagle to David Nagle, Sept. 30, 1867, in *Irish American Weekly*, Nov. 2, 1867, 1.

45. Jay Sexton, "William H. Seward in the World," *Journal of the Civil War Era* 4 (Sept. 2014): 398–430; Ernest N. Paolino, *The Foundations of the American Empire: William Henry Seward and U.S. Foreign Policy* (Ithaca, NY, 1973); Glyndon G. Van Deusen, *William Henry Seward* (New York, 1967), 432–485, 511–549.

46. On the interplay between domestic and foreign policy issues in the period between 1848 and 1877, see Jay Sexton, "Toward a Synthesis of Foreign Relations in the Civil War Era, 1848–1877," *American Nineteenth Century History* 5 (Fall 2004): 50–73, 68; Kinley J. Brauer, "Seward's 'Foreign War Panacea': An Interpretation," *New York History* 55 (Apr. 1974): esp. 136–138.

47. "The Fenian Congress," *New York Tribune*, Sept. 11, 1867, 1.

48. Jenkins, *Fenians and Anglo-American Relations*, 157–160, 177–179.

49. Extract from article by "Tyrone" in the *Irish Republic* (Chicago), reprinted in *Irishman*, Nov. 16, 1867, p. 311.

50. "Fenianism and English Rule in Ireland," *New York Tribune*, June 19, 1867.

51. "Fortieth Congress," *Daily Picayune*, July 16, 1867; *NYH*, July 11, 1867; *Philadelphia Inquirer*, July 11, 1867; "Release of American Fenian Prisoners," *Freeman's Journal*, Sept. 12, 1867.

52. Constitutional Union Association to Seward, July 23, 1867, *FRUS 1867*, 120–121. See also "Local Politics," *NYT*, Oct. 5, 1867. On New York Democratic platform, see *NYH*, Oct. 5, 1867, 8; *New Orleans Times*, Oct. 12, 1867, 3.

53. "Release of American Fenian Prisoners," *Freeman's Journal*, Sept. 12, 1867.

54. "Our Claims against England," *NYT*, Sept. 12, 1867, 1; "The Alabama Claims" and "The Fenian Congress," *New York Tribune*, Sept. 11, 1867, 1; Adrian Cook, *The Alabama Claims: American Politics and Anglo-American Relations, 1865–1872* (Ithaca, NY, 1975).

55. Jenkins, *Fenians and Anglo-American Relations*, 99–100, 130–231, 227–230, 259–262; Kori Schake, *Safe Passage: The Transition from British to American Hegemony* (Cambridge, MA, 2017); Kathleen Burk, *Old World, New World: Great Britain and America from the Beginning* (New York, 2007).

56. CFA Diary, Aug. 23, 1867; Nov. 29, 1867. Seward, in contrast, was an enthusiastic proponent of the telegraph and the Atlantic cable. *The Works of William H. Seward*, ed. George E. Baker (Boston, 1889), IV:45–46.

57. Henry Adams, *The Education of Henry Adams* (New York, 1999), 90–91; Amanda Forman, *A World on Fire: Britain's Crucial Role in the American Civil War* (New York, 2012), 156–157; CFA Diary, Nov. 23, 1865; Van Deusen, *William Henry Seward*, 549; Jenkins, *Fenians and Anglo-American Relations*, 253–254.

58. CFA Diary, July 10, 1867; "Tribute to Wm H. Seward by Mr. Adams," *Proceedings of the Massachusetts Historical Society* 12 (1871–73): 305.

59. Seward to Adams, Sept. 14, 1867, *FRUS 1867*, 142–143; Seward to Adams, Sept. 20, 1867, *FRUS 1867*, 144–145; Adams to Seward, Aug. 23, 1867, *FRUS 1867*, 128–129; Mayo to West, Sept. 11, 1867, DD, 566.

60. Costello to West, Sept. 14, 1867, DD, 571, and Sept. 16, 1867, DD, 573–574. See also Patrick Kane to West, Sept. 19, 1867, DD, 580–581; Warren to West, Sept. 26, 1867, DD, 585; William Nugent to West, Sept. 25, 1867, DD, 584.

61. Seward to Adams (telegram), Sept. 11, 1867, Diplomatic Instructions of the Department of State, vol. 21, M77, NARA; Seward to Adams, Sept. 20, 1867, *FRUS 1867*, 144–145; CFA Diary, Sept. 12 and 23, 1867; "Local Politics," *NYT*, Oct. 5, 1867; "Release of American Fenian Prisoners," *Freeman's Journal*, Sept. 12, 1867; E. C. Edgerton, Foreign Office, to Under Secretary of State, Home Department, Aug. 24, 1867, folder 19, file 11,188, Mayo Papers.

62. Adams to Seward, Sept. 3, 1867, *FRUS 1867*, 133.

63. Adams to Stanley, Sept. 11, 1867 and Sept. 13, 1867, *FRUS 1867*, 140–141; West to Adams, Sept. 9, 1867, DD, 561–562; Nagle to Father, Sept. 30, 1867, reprinted in *Freeman's Journal*, Nov. 5, 1867.

64. Adams to Stanley, Sept. 18, 1867, *FRUS 1867*, 141; Adams to Seward, Sept. 13, 1867, *FRUS 1867*, 140.

65. Stanley to Mayo, Sept. 13, 1867; Stanley to Mayo, Sept. 21, 1867; Stanley to Mayo, Sept. 23, 1867; folder 19, file 11,188, Mayo Papers.

66. Jenkins, *The Fenian Problem*, 93–96.

67. Lord Derby to Mayo, Aug. 28, 1867, folder 19, file 11,188, Mayo Papers.

68. Adams to Seward, Aug. 27, 1867, *FRUS 1867*, 131–132; Memorial of Warren and Nagle to the Lord Justices of Ireland, enclosure in letter from John Lawless, Esq., to West, July 30, 1867, DD, 526–527.

69. CFA Diary, June 10, 1867; Adams to Seward, Sept. 3, 1867, *FRUS 1867*, 133.

70. Nagle to Father, Sept. 30, 1867, reprinted in *Irish American Weekly*, Nov. 2, 1867, 1.

71. See DD: West to Adams, Sept. 9, 1867, 561–562; Nagle to West, Oct. 17, 1867, 598; Nagle to West, Oct. 19, 1867, 599; Costello to West, Sept. 14, 1867, 571; Oct. 16, 1867, 595. For Adams's responses, see CFA LB reel 175: Adams to Nagle and Warren, Oct. 12, 1867, 238; Adams to West, Oct. 12, 1867; Adams to West, Oct. 23, 1867, 250–251; Adams to J. F. Scallan, Esq., Oct. 28, 1867, 253.

72. Warren, "A Voice from the Dungeon," 135.

73. Nugent to West, Apr. 24, 1868, DD, 793.

74. West to Adams, Sept. 5, 1867, DD, 556.

75. Ryan to Commissioner of Police, June 18, 1867, HO 45 / 7799.

76. Mayo to Disraeli, Sept. 17, 1867, quoted in Brian Jenkins, *The Fenian Problem*, 105.

77. Gathorne Hardy to Fitzgerald, Sept. 19, 1867, HO 7799 / 79; Jenkins, *The Fenian Problem*, 104–117; Ó Broin, *Fenian Fever*, 192–200.

78. Gathorne Hardy to Fitzgerald, Sept. 19, 1867, HO 7799 / 79.

79. Adams to Seward, Sept. 21, 1867, *FRUS 1867*, 145.

80. "Americans in British Prisons," *Pilot*, Nov. 2, 1867, 4; Nagle to Father, Sept. 30, 1867, reprinted in *Irish American Weekly*, Nov. 2, 1867, 1.

81. Seward to Adams, Oct. 3, 1867, *FRUS 1867*, 156; extract from letter of Mr. Ford, Oct. 7, 1867, folder 19, file 11,188, Mayo Papers.

82. Robert Warren to Mayo, Sept. 27, 1867, folder 19, file 11,188, Mayo Papers; "A Peep behind the Scenes."

83. For Buckley's statement of September 12, see *Queen v. Warren and Nagle*, Crown Briefs, carton 10, 1–3, NAI; Forrester warned of Buckley's possible betrayal on Oct. 11, "Irish Fenian Prisoners," *Pilot*, Nov. 2, 1867, 1.

84. Anderson to Lord Mayo, Oct. 15, 1867, file 1867 / 18196, Chief Secretary's Office Registered Papers, NAI.

85. Robert Warren to Lord Mayo, Oct. 8, 1867, folder 11, file 11,189, Mayo Papers.

Chapter 7: All the World's a Stage

1. Costello to West, Oct. 25, 1867, DD, 608. On the public and political nature of trials, see Robert A. Ferguson, *The Trial in American Life* (Chicago, 2007), 1; Martha Merrill Umphrey, "Introduction," *Trials* (Aldershot, UK, 2008), xi. For other accounts of Warren's trial, see David Sim, *A Union Forever: The Irish Question and U.S. Foreign Relations in the Victorian Age* (Ithaca, NY, 2013), 111–118; Christian Samito, *Becoming American under Fire: Irish Americans, African Americans, and the Politics of Citizenship during the Civil War Era* (Ithaca, NY, 2009), 194–199.

2. "The Fenian Movement," *Freeman's Journal*, Oct. 26, 1867. On tensions between British liberalism and constitutionalism and Britain's control over Ireland, see Brian Jenkins, *The Fenian Problem: Insurgency and Terrorism in a Liberal State, 1858–1874* (Montreal, 2008),

esp. ix–xv, 3–60; Michael Brown and Seán Patrick Donlan, "The Laws in Ireland, 1689–1850: A Brief Introduction," in *The Laws and Other Legalities in Ireland*, ed. Michael Brown and Seán Patrick Donlan (Aldershot, UK, 2011), 1–32.

3. Dublin *Evening Mail*, Oct. 25, 1867; "The Fenian Movement," *Freeman's Journal*, Oct. 26, 1867; "Fenianism," *Evening Post* (New Zealand), Dec. 27, 1867, 2.

4. On Augustine Costello's remarks, see *Speeches from the Dock; or, Protests of Irish Patriotism*, ed. T. D. Sullivan, A. M. Sullivan, D. B. Sullivan (New York, 1904; 1st ed. 1867), 310, and for Emmet's speech, 37–51. Green Street Courthouse continued to be used to try political offenders well into the twentieth century, including famous trials of Irish Republican Army members in the 1970s. The building closed as a courthouse in 2009. For history of the courthouse, see Constantine Malloy, "A Central Criminal Court for the County and City of Dublin," *Journal of the Statistical and Social Inquiry Society of Ireland* XXIV (Jan. 1868); Mícheál Mac Donncha, "Remembering the Past: Green Street—Two Centuries of Political Trials," *An Phoblacht*, January 7, 2010.

5. For images of the courtroom, see "Fenian Trials at Dublin," *ILN*, Apr. 27, 1867, 408; "Trial of Mitchel," in John Mitchel, *Jail Journal* (Dublin, 1913); "The State Prosecutions in Ireland, the Scene in Green-Street Court House, Dublin, " *ILN*, Feb. 26, 1887; Ben Moore, "'Green Street'—Giving the Dublin Fringe Festival Justice," Beanmimo (blog), September 14, 2012, http://beanmimo.wordpress.com/2012/09/14/green-street-giving-the-dublin-fringe-festival-justice.

6. Chatterton to Lord Naas, Apr. 11, 1867, folder 4, file 43,885, Mayo Papers. In Special Commission trials, the Irish government could appoint the judges and bring cases to trial more quickly; see Jenkins, *The Fenian Problem*, 41.

7. "Judge Keogh Again," *Irishman*, Nov. 5, 1867, 281; "Judge William Nicholas Keogh," *Journal of the Galway Archaeological and Historical Society* 38 (1981 / 82): 8–9; Jenkins, *The Fenian Problem*, ix–xv, 41–42, 338–343; "Career of an Irish Judge," *NYT*, Sept. 5, 1878, 5; Jeremiah O'Donovan Rossa, *O'Donovan Rossa's Prison Life: Six Years in Six Prisons* (New York, 1874), 62, 65; John Finerty, *People's History of Ireland* (New York, 1904), 823–824; R. B. McDowell, "The Irish Courts of Law, 1801–1914," *Irish Historical Studies* 10 (1957): 368.

8. Finerty, *People's History of Ireland*, 823–824; Matthew Stradling, *The Bar Sinister* (Dublin, 1871), 32–33; *Speeches from the Dock*, ed. Sullivan et al., 205, 301; "Judge Keogh Again," *The Irishman*, Nov. 5, 1867.

9. David Johnson, "Trial by Jury in Ireland, 1860–1914," *Legal History* 17 (Dec. 1996): 273–281, 289; Sean McConville, *Irish Political Prisoners, 1848–1922: Theatres of War* (London, 2003): 25–30. Solicitor-general's memo on the use of the "stand-by" option: folder 4, file 43,885, Mayo Papers.

10. R. B. McDowell, "The Irish Courts of Law, 1801–1914," *Irish Historical Studies*, 10 (1957): 371; Johnson, "Trial by Jury in Ireland," 277–278, 285, 286. On the question of venue, see Robert Warren to Mayo, Sept. 27, 1867, folder 19, ms. 11,188, and Warren to Mayo, Oct. 8, 1867, folder 11, ms. 11,189, Mayo Papers. On the "superiority" of Dublin juries, see "Memo on Fenianism," ms. 7517, Larcom Papers.

11. "The Fenian Movement," *Freeman's Journal,* Oct. 31, 1867; Johnson, "Trial by Jury in Ireland," 277.

12. "Justice with Closed Doors," *Irishman,* Nov. 23, 1867, 329–330; "The Fenian Movement"; "Trial of Augustine E. Costello," *Freeman's Journal,* Nov. 8, 1867; *Belfast News-Letter,* Nov. 1, 1867. Re lack of interest in *Jacmel* trials, see also unsigned memo in folder 5, ms. 43,885, Mayo Papers.

13. West to Adams, Oct. 30, 1867, DD, 609–610.

14. "The State Trials," *Weekly News* (Dublin), Nov. 2, 1867; clipping in DD, v. 6.

15. Philip Schofield, "Heron, Denis Caulfield (1824–1881)," *Oxford Dictionary of National Biography* (Oxford, 2004); on Dowse, see John O'Leary, *Recollections of Fenians and Fenianism* (London, 1896), I:221; *ILN,* Oct. 21, 1867, 386; C. L. Falkiner, rev. by Peter Gray, "Dowse, Richard (1824–1890)," *Oxford Dictionary of National Biography* (2004).

16. Marianne Constable, *The Law of the Other: The Mixed Jury and Changing Conceptions of Citizenship, Law, and Knowledge* (Chicago, 1994), 9.

17. *Report of the Trial of John Warren, for Treason-Felony at the County Dublin Commission* (Dublin, 1867), 5–6. The case was *Reg. v. Manning and Manning.* See Constable, *The Law of the Other,* 134–137.

18. *Report of the Trial of John Warren,* 9.

19. Niamh Howlin, "Fenians, Foreigners and Jury Trials in Ireland, 1865–69," *Irish Jurist* 45 (2010): 51–81.

20. *Report of the Trial of John Warren,* 6–7, 9, 10, 12; *Freeman's Journal,* Oct. 31, 1867.

21. *Report of the Trial of John Warren,* 13, 14 (my emphasis). For Keogh's response, see *Freeman's Journal,* Oct. 31, 1867.

22. *Report of the Trial of John Warren,* 14–15.

23. *Report of the Trial of John Warren,* 17–20.

24. *Report of the Trial of John Warren,* 22.

25. *Report of the Trial of John Warren,* 20, 22. On O'Donovan Rossa, see *O'Donovan Rossa's Prison Life,* 49.

26. CFA LB, reel 175: Adams to West, Oct. 17, 1867, 242; Adams to West, Oct. 23, 1867, 250–251; Adams to Seward, Oct. 19, 1867, *FRUS 1867,* 159–160; DD: Warren to West, Oct. 16, 1867, 596; Nagle to West, Oct. 17, 1867, 598; West to Nagle, Oct. 19, 1867, 598–599; West to Adams, Oct. 23, 1867, 606.

27. Adams to Seward, Nov. 1, 1867, *FRUS 1867,* 165–166.

28. *Report of the Trial of John Warren,* 24; Treason-Felony Act of 1848, 11 Vict. c. 12, sec. III.

29. "Copy Pencil Documents Found on the Person of the Prisoner *Nagle* on Arrest, by Constable Norris," *Queen v. Warren and Nagle,* pp. 5–6, Crown Briefs, carton 10, NAI.

30. On statute's vagueness on "overt acts," see the House of Commons debate on the Treason-Felony Act of 1848 on April 7, 1848, v. 98, cc. 20–59.

31. *Reg. v. Meany,* 15 *Weekly Reporter* 1082 (1867), 1085.

32. *Reg. v. Meany,* 1084, 1089.

33. *Pinkerton v. United States*, 328 U.S. 640 (1946); George P. Fletcher, *Basic Concepts in Criminal Law* (New York, 1998), 191–194.

34. *Reg. v. Meany*, 1084.

35. "The Irish State Trials," *Freeman's Journal*, Aug. 19, 1867.

36. *Report of the Trial of John Warren*, 30–31; "The Irish State Trials."

37. *Report of the Trial of John Warren*, 101. The charge of being a co-conspirator in the March 5 Rising allowed the Crown to try the case in Dublin rather than Waterford. See Robert R. Warren to Mayo, Sept. 27, 1867, folder 19, file 11,188, Mayo Papers.

38. "Statement of William Million, Late Lieut. in the Federal Army, Now in Waterford Gaol," folder 7, file 43,887, Mayo Papers; Anderson to Mayo, Oct. 15, 1867, CSO / RP File 1867 / 18196, NAI. The informer's name is spelled as "Millen" in the Fenian Brotherhood documents, but as "Million" in the Irish government files. On the assassination of Millen, see "Memoranda Respecting the Supposed Conspiracy by Colonel Nagle of the Jackmel Expedition to Assassinate W. F. Million, One of His Companions," ms. 7517, Larcom Papers.

39. "Particulars Relating to Daniel J. Buckley," F.P. 37, Form K, Fenian Photographs, NAI.

40. County Dublin Commission, 1867, *Queen v. Augustine E. Costelloe*, 23, Crown Briefs, box 11, 9 / C, Fenian Briefs, Crime Special Branch, CSO, NAI (hereafter *Queen v. Costello*). For alternative (but unverified) explanations for Buckley's turning informer, see Sylvester Murray, "The Fenian Landing at Helvic," Waterford County Museum, 2003, http://www.waterfordmuseum.ie/exhibit/web/Display/article/323/5/The_Fenian _Landing_At_Helvic_Arrest_And_Trial.html; Patrick Steward and Bryan P. McGovern, *The Fenians: Irish Rebellion in the North Atlantic World, 1858–1876* (Knoxville, TN, 2013), 171.

41. *Trial of John Warren*, 32–49.

42. "Illustrious Visitors to Waterford: How Government Informers Are Honoured in That City," *Waterford Citizen*, June 10, 1867, reprinted in *The Irishman*, June 22, 1867, 822–823; "Ireland," *Times*, June 15, 1867, 8; Goold to Larcom, n.d., ms. 7595, Larcom Papers; Goold to Larcom, June 10, 1867, Fenian Files, R/1869/7042R, NAI.

43. *Queen v. Costelloe*, 9, 11.

44. *Trial of John Warren*, 79–86. The attorney general seemed unaware of other damning evidence against Warren—the complete run of Warren's *Fenian Spirit*—in the government's voluminous files on the Fenians. E. M. Archibald to T. H. Burmley, File A2, Fenian Papers, "A" Series, "Reports from America," NAI.

45. *Report of the Trial of John Warren*, 106.

46. *Queen v. Costelloe*, 32.

47. *Report of the Trial of John Warren*, 55.

48. *Report of the Trial of John Warren*, 55–58, 64–66.

49. *Report of the Trial of John Warren*, 49–55.

50. *Report of the Trial of John Warren*, 56.

51. *Report of the Trial of John Warren*, 89–90.

52. *Report of the Trial of John Warren*, 56, 61, 90, 121.

53. Robert R. Warren to Mayo, Sept. 27, 1867, folder 19, file 11,188, Mayo Papers.

54. *Report of the Trial of John Warren*, 63.

55. Warren to President Johnson, Aug. 3, 1867, *FRUS 1867*, 136.

56. *Report of the Trial of John Warren*, 68–71; *Freeman's Journal*, Nov. 1, 1867.

57. *Report of the Trial of John Warren*, 72–77, quotes at 75, 76.

58. *Report of the Trial of John Warren*, 100.

59. *Report of the Trial of John Warren*, 121.

60. John A. Walker, "The Jacknell Prisoners," letter to the editor, *Times*, Aug. 7, 1868, 8.

61. *Speeches from the Dock*, ed. Sullivan et al., 7–13.

62. Descriptions of Warren in "The Dungarvan Mystery," *Pilot*, June 29, 1867, 3; Fenian Photographs 16, p. 34, Irish Crimes Records, Chief Secretary's Office, NAI; *Report of the Trial of John Warren*, 127; "The Fenians in Dublin," *Trewman's Exeter Flying Post*, Nov. 20, 1867.

63. Bruce to Stanley, Mar. 19, 1867, FO 115:465, quoted in D'Arcy, *Fenian Movement*, 237–238.

64. *Report on the Trial of John Warren*, 126; Historicus [William Harcourt], "British Citizenship: Discussion of the Naturalization Question by the British Press," *NYT*, Jan. 27, 1868, 8.

65. *Report of the Trial of John Warren*, 128.

66. *Report of the Trial of John Warren*, 128.

67. *Report of the Trial of John Warren*, 129–133, quotes at 130, 131. William Halpin was sentenced at the same time for his part in the March 5 Rising. See *Report of the Trial of William Halpin* (Dublin, 1868).

68. *Report of the Trial of John Warren*, 133.

69. "The Fenian Movement: The Sentences," *Freeman's Journal*, Nov. 18, 1867.

70. Nagle to Adams, Nov. 22, 1867, *FRUS 1867*, 24–26.

71. "The Fenian Movement: The Sentences."

72. Adams to Seward, Nov. 5, 1867, *FRUS 1867*, 171; Nagle to Adams, Nov. 22, 1867, *FRUS 1867*, 24–25; "The Fenian Movement: The Sentences"; John Westlake, "On Naturalisation and Expatriation; or, on Change of Nationality," *Law Magazine and Law Review* 25 (Mar-Aug. 1868): 131, 140–143; "Sir R. Phillimore on the Law of Naturalisation," *ILN*, Jan. 18, 1868, 74.

73. Those to be tried at Sligo included both native-born Americans and naturalized Americans for whom there was insufficient evidence of participation in the Fenian Brotherhood. Robert Warren to Mayo, Nov. 10, 1867, folder 12, file 11,189, Mayo Papers; see also memo on William C. Nugent, file 11,188, folder 16, Mayo Papers.

74. John Savage, *Fenian Heroes and Martyrs* (Boston, 1868), 452–453.

75. Jenkins, *The Fenian Problem*, 141–145; Mervyn Busteed, "The Manchester Martyrs: A Victorian Melodrama," *History Ireland* 16 (Nov. / Dec. 2008): 35–37; *Pilot*, Dec. 7, 1867, 1.

76. Articles in *Pilot*: "Imprisoned American Fenians," Dec. 7, 1867, 5; "Rights of Naturalized Citizens," Dec. 28, 1867, 6; "Protection to American Citizens Abroad," Dec. 28,

1867, 4; "American Citizens Abroad," Jan. 4, 1868, 4; "Rights of Our Citizens Abroad," Jan. 11, 1868, 4; "Rights of Our Citizens Abroad," Jan. 18, 1868, 5; "American Citizenship," Jan. 25, 1868, 4.

77. Patrick A. Collins, *Charles Francis Adams as Minister to England and an Anti–Know Nothing* (Boston, 1876), 7.

Chapter 8: Are Naturalized Americans, Americans?

1. John Warren to the Honorable Members of the United States Congress in Session Assembled, Nov. 28, 1867, reprinted in *Congressional Globe*, 40th Cong., 2nd sess., Dec. 19, 1867, 270.

2. The following discussion of Sumner draws upon David Donald, *Charles Sumner and the Rights of Man* (New York, 1970); David Donald, *Charles Sumner and the Coming of the Civil War* (New York, 1960); Eric Foner, *Reconstruction: America's Unfinished Revolution, 1863–1877* (New York, 1988), 228–280.

3. "Intercede," *Pilot*, Feb. 1, 1868, 4.

4. Charles Sumner, *Are We a Nation? Address of Hon. Charles Sumner before the New York Young Man's Republican Union at Cooper Institute* (New York, 1867).

5. Sumner to Wendell Phillips, May 1, 1865, in *The Selected Letters of Charles Sumner*, ed. Beverly Wilson Palmer (Boston, 1990), 2:298; Williamjames Hull Hoffer, *The Caning of Charles Sumner: Honor, Idealism and the Origins of the Civil War* (Baltimore, 2010); David Donald, *Charles Sumner and the Rights of Man* (New York, 1970), 428–433; Donald, *Charles Sumner and the Coming of the Civil War*, 242–266; Sumner, "The Equal Rights of All: Speech of Hon. Charles Sumner of Massachusetts in the United States Senate, Feb. 6 and 7, 1866," *Congressional Globe*, (Washington, DC: Congressional Globe Office, 1866).

6. Michael Vorenberg, *Final Freedom: The Civil War, the Abolition of Slavery, and the Thirteenth Amendment* (New York, 2001).

7. Sumner to Duchess of Argyll, Apr. 24, 1865, 2:295; Sumner to John Bright, Apr. 24, 1865, 2:297; and Sumner to Salmon P. Chase, July 1, 1865, 2:313, in *Selected Letters*. See also Foner, *Reconstruction*, 176–227, 261–264.

8. Sumner, *Are We a Nation?*, 7; Sumner to Francis Lieber, Oct. 12, 1865, in *Selected Letters*, 2:337.

9. *Scott v. Sandford*, 60 U.S. 393 (1857), 406–407; "A Bust of Chief Justice Taney," *NYT*, Feb. 24, 1865, 5.

10. "The Dred Scott Case," *Harper's Weekly*, Mar. 28, 1857, 193.

11. Foner, *Reconstruction*, 18–34, 469–472; Sumner to the Duchess of Argyll, Apr. 3, 1866, in *Selected Letters*, 2:358–360; David Quigley, *Second Founding: New York City, Reconstruction, and the Making of Modern Democracy* (New York, 2004), 24–25.

12. Craig Robertson, *The Passport in America: The History of a Document* (New York, 2012), 131–133; Donald, *Charles Sumner and the Rights of Man*, 47; Elizabeth Stordeur Pryor, *Colored Travelers: Mobility and the Fight for Citizenship before the Civil War* (Chapel Hill, NC,

2016), 103–125; Martha S. Jones, *Birthright Citizens: A History of Race and Rights in Antebellum America* (New York, 2018).

13. Linda J. Kerber, "Toward a History of Statelessness in America," *American Quarterly* 57 (Sept. 2005): 733.

14. Foner, *Reconstruction*, 8, 195, 317; Christian G. Samito, *Becoming American under Fire: Irish Americans, African Americans, and the Politics of Citizenship during the Civil War Era* (Ithaca, NY, 2009), 45–76.

15. Frederick Douglass, *The Life and Times of Frederick Douglass* (1892; New York, 1962), 378.

16. "The Civil Rights Bill," *NYT*, Mar. 12, 1866, 1.

17. Michael Vorenberg, *Final Freedom: The Civil War, the Abolition of Slavery, and the Thirteenth Amendment* (New York, 2001); Harold M. Hyman and William M. Wiecek, *Equal Justice under Law: Constitutional Development, 1835–1875* (New York, 1982); Alexander Tsesis, ed., *The Promises of Liberty: The History and Contemporary Relevance of the Thirteenth Amendment* (New York, 2010).

18. Sumner to Carl Schurz, Oct. 20, 1865, in *Selected Letters*, 2:339.

19. The literature on the Fourteenth Amendment and its "revolutionary" character is substantial and contested. For a useful overview, see William E. Nelson, *The Fourteenth Amendment: From Political Principle to Judicial Doctrine* (Cambridge, MA, 1988), 1–12; Robert J. Kaczorowski, *The Nationalization of Civil Rights: Constitutional Theory and Practice in a Racist Society: 1866–1883* (New York, 1987); Foner, *Reconstruction*, 244–261, describing Reconstruction as an "unfinished revolution"; William J. Novak, "The Legal Transformation of Citizenship in Nineteenth-Century America," in Meg Jacobs, William J. Novak, and Julian Zelizer, eds., *The Democratic Experience: New Directions in Political History* (Princeton, NJ, 2003), 85–119; Barbara Welke, *Law and the Borders of Belonging in the Long Nineteenth Century United States* (New York, 2010), 113–117, 192–194, refuting its revolutionary impact. On African Americans' shaping of the Fourteenth Amendment, see Jones, *Birthright Citizens*.

20. Civil Rights Act of 1866, 14 Stat. 27–30; U.S. Constitution, Art. XIV, sec. 1.

21. Foner, *Reconstruction*, 232.

22. Francis Lieber, "Amendments to the Constitution," *Miscellaneous Writings* (Philadelphia, 1881), 167; Sumner, *Are We a Nation?*, 11; William L. Scruggs, "Ambiguous Citizenship," *Political Science Quarterly* 1 (June 1886): 199–200, 201–202. The foreign-born played on a key role of the naturalized citizen in reaffirming the American democratic regime as "choiceworthy"; Bonnie Honig, *Democracy and the Foreigner* (Princeton, NJ, 2001), 75.

23. Sumner, *Are We a Nation?*, 31.

24. Sumner, *Are We a Nation?*, 3; Foner, *Reconstruction*, 271–291; Donald, *Charles Sumner and the Rights of Man*, 310–312; Mitchell Snay, *Fenians, Freedmen, and Southern Whites: Race and Nationality in the Era of Reconstruction* (Baton Rouge, LA, 2007).

25. "Message from the President of the United States, Returning Bill (S. No. 61)," March 27, 1866, 39th Cong. 1st Sess., Sen. ex. doc. 31, quotes at 1, 2, 3, 8.

26. Foner, *Reconstruction*, 247–251.

27. "Hon. C. F. Adams and the Fenians," *Pilot*, Dec. 7, 1867; Foner, *Reconstruction*, 314–316.

28. "The Mississippi Legislature," *Harper's Weekly*, Nov. 3, 1866; "Southern Views of the Amendment," *Harper's Weekly*, Nov. 3, 1866; "Our New York Correspondence," Memphis *Daily Avalanche*, Feb. 8, 1866, 1; "The Fourteenth Amendment," *NYT*, July 31, 1868, 4; *Frank Roney, Irish Rebel and California Labor Leader: An Autobiography*, ed. Ira Cross (Berkeley, CA, 1931), 216.

29. "Centralization Not Essential to Nationality," *NYT*, Nov. 21, 1867, 4.

30. *Proceedings of the National Convention of Colored Men, Held in the City of Syracuse, N.Y., October 4, 5, 6, and 7, 1864* (Boston, 1864), quoted in Samito, *Becoming American under Fire*, 147–148. On "martial patriotism" as claim to citizenship, see Lucy E. Salyer, "Baptism by Fire: Race, Military Service, and U.S. Citizenship Policy, 1918–1935," *Journal of American History* 91, no. 3 (December 2004): 847–876.

31. Foner, *Reconstruction*, 255.

32. Kate Masur, *An Example for All the Land: Emancipation and the Struggle over Equality in Washington, D.C.* (Chapel Hill, NC, 2010), 7–11, 41–50, 87–126; Stephen Kantrowitz, *More Than Freedom: Fighting for Black Citizenship in a White Republic* (New York, 2012).

33. Elizabeth Cady Stanton, Susan B. Anthony, and Matilda Joslyn Gage, eds., *History of Woman Suffrage* (Rochester, NY, 1881), II:323–324.

34. Quoted in Ellen Carol DuBois, *Feminism and Suffrage: The Emergence of an Independent Women's Movement in America, 1848–1869* (Ithaca, NY, 1999), 59.

35. DuBois, *Feminism and Suffrage*, 63, 66.

36. DuBois, *Feminism and Suffrage*, 53–68, quotes at 63, 66; Stanton, Anthony, and Gage, eds., *History of Woman Suffrage*, II:324 (reprint of *The Revolution*, Dec. 10, 1868).

37. "The Most Interesting Book Ever Published," *Pilot*, Dec. 14, 1867, 4; John Savage, *Fenian Heroes and Martyrs* (Boston, 1868). The chapter on the *Jacmel* expedition focuses on Warren and Nagle and their imprisonment, so it appears that book was completed and in press before the trials of Warren and Costello took place.

38. "Great Demonstration in Boston," *Pilot*, Dec. 21, 1867, 3; "A Lecture by George Francis Train," *Pilot*, Dec. 21, 1867.

39. C. L. Vallandigham to Messrs. John O'Neil, M. M. Goulden, and P. H. Rice, Dec. 26, 1867, reprinted in "Rights of Foreign-Born Citizens," *NYT*, Jan. 1, 1868, 5 (the author was the controversial antiwar Democrat, convicted of treason by military tribunal in 1863 and exiled to the Confederacy; Lawson, *Patriot Fires*, 86–88); "Intercede," *Pilot*, Feb. 1, 1868, 4; Chris L. Nesmith, "'Slavery in Massachusetts' and Mitchel's 'Citizen': Rhetoric, Reform and Reprobates in 1854," *Concord Saunterer*, n.s., 9 (2001): 40–55; Bryan P. McGovern, *John Mitchel: Irish Nationalist, Southern Secessionist* (Knoxville, TN, 2009); Miller, *Emigrants and Exiles*, 338–340.

40. Jon Gjerde, *The Minds of the West: Ethnocultural Evolution in the Rural Middle West, 1830–1917* (Chapel Hill, NC, 1997), 103–107; Miller, *Emigrants and Exiles*, 520–522; David M. Emmons, *Beyond the American Pale: The Irish in the West, 1845–1910* (Norman, OK, 2010), 25.

41. Albert Augustin, Champaign, IL, to family, Aug. 21, 1861, in *Germans in the Civil War: The Letters They Wrote Home*, ed. Walter D. Kamphoefner and Wolfgang J. Helbich (Chapel Hill, NC, 2006), 77.

42. Martin Weitz to family, Rockville, CT, Aug. 23, 1857, in *News from the Land of Freedom: German Immigrants Write Home*, ed. Walter D. Kamphoefner and Wolfgang J. Helbich (Ithaca, NY, 1991), 356. On occupations of Germans and Irish, see Kamphoefner and Helbich, ed., *News from the Land of Freedom*, 288; Kevin Kenny, *The American Irish* (New York, 2000), 109; Joseph P. Ferrie, *Yankeys Now: Immigrants in Antebellum U.S. 1840–1860* (New York, 1999), 187–189. On conflicts, see Kenny, *American Irish*, 65; Gjerde, *Minds of the West*, 243; Kathleen Neils Conzen, *Immigrant Milwaukee, 1836–1860: Accommodation and Community in a Frontier City* (Cambridge, MA, 1976), 214.

43. Gjerde, *Minds of the West*, 112–113.

44. Keppler to family, Nov. 19, 1864, in *Germans in the Civil War*, ed. Kamphoefner and Helbich, 192; see also Richter to family, Mar. 2, 1863, 101. For anti-German sentiment, especially over the Chancellorsville battle, see Kamphoefner and Helbich, eds., *Germans in the Civil War*, 23–26; Stephen D. Engle, "Yankee Dutchmen: Germans, the Union, and the Construction of Wartime Identity," in *Civil War Citizens: Race, Ethnicity, and Identity in America's Bloodiest Conflict*, ed. Susannah J. Ural (New York, 2010), 24–31; Samito, *Becoming American Under Fire*, 110.

45. Keppler to family, Nov. 19, 1864, *Germans in the Civil War*, ed. Kamphoeffner and Helbich, 192.

46. *Toledo Blade*, Mar. 9, 1859, quoted in Bruce Levine, *The Spirit of 1848: German Immigrants, Labor Conflict, and the Coming of the Civil War* (Urbana, IL, 1992), 244. See also Levine, *Spirit of 1848*, 241; Alison Clark Efford, *German Immigrants, Race, and Citizenship in the Civil War Era* (New York, 2013), 53.

47. Otto von Rhein, "Rights of Naturalized American Citizens Abroad," letter to editor, *NYH*, Dec. 22, 1858, 8; "Value of an American Passport," *NYT*, Oct. 25, 1858, 4; "Spanish Subjects and American Citizens," *NYT*, Mar. 17, 1860.

48. Wright to Seward, Apr. 18, 1866, and Wright to Count Bismarck, Apr. 16, 1866, *FRUS*, 1866, part II (1867), 15–16.

49. Mr. Bigelow to Mr. Drouyn de Lhuys, April 13, 1866, *Correspondence between the Government of the United States and the Governments of France and Prussia, Touching the Claim of Military Service . . .* , 40th Cong., 1st sess., Sen. Ex. Doc. no. 4, 44–45.

50. Geo. F. W. Striebg to Seward, Feb. 1, 1866, in *FRUS*, 1866, part II (1867), 6–7.

51. On inequality of naturalized and native-born citizens and significance of oaths, see Sanford Levinson, "Symposium on Law and Community: Constituting Communities

through Words That Bind: Reflections on Loyalty Oaths," *Michigan Law Rev* 84 (June 1986): 1440.

52. Warren, "A Voice from the Dungeon," 136.

53. "Rights of Naturalized Citizens," *Pilot*, Dec. 28, 1867, 6; "Great Demonstration in Boston," *Pilot*, Dec. 21, 1867, 3.

54. Thomas Colley Grattan, *Civilized America* (London, 1859), II:6.

55. Though only 4 percent of the general population, German-born soldiers made up 10 percent of the Union Army. Levine, *The Spirit of 1848*, 256; Kathleen Neils Conzen, "Germans," in *Harvard Encyclopedia of American Ethnic Groups*, "Table 1. Germans in the U.S. Population, 1850–1970," 406. See also Alison Clark Efford, *German Immigrants, Race, and Citizenship in the Civil War Era* (New York, 2013); Engle, "Yankee Dutchmen." On the polyglot nature of the Union Army, see Don H. Doyle, *The Cause of All Nations: An International History of the American Civil War* (New York, 2015), 158–181. Not all fought willingly. One in six German-born soldiers was drafted. *Germans in the Civil War*, ed. Kamphoefner and Helbich, 20.

56. Joseph R. Reinhart, *August Willich's Gallant Dutchman: Civil War Letters from the 32nd Indiana Infantry* (Kent, OH, 2006), 141–144, quoted in Engle, "Yankee Dutchmen," 35.

57. "American Citizenship," letter to the editor, Dublin *Nation*, Dec. 7, 1867, reprinted in *Pilot*, Jan. 25, 1868, 3.

58. *Times*, Nov. 25, 1868, 4. The story may be apocryphal, but it is still telling.

59. "Who Are Americans?," *Pilot*, Nov. 28, 1868, 4. See also "'Irish Citizens,' Etc.," *Pilot*, Nov. 7, 1868, 1; "Are Foreigners Citizens," *Pilot*, Oct. 31, 1868, 4.

60. Harold Hyman, *To Try Men's Souls: Loyalty Tests in American History* (Berkeley, CA, 1959), 139–266; Anne Sarah Rubin, *A Shattered Nation: The Rise and Fall of the Confederacy, 1861–1868* (Chapel Hill, NC, 2005), 164–171; Elizabeth Duquette, *Loyal Subjects: Bonds of Nation, Race, and Allegiance in Nineteenth-Century America* (New Brunswick, NJ, 2010), 17–60.

61. See, e.g., the resolutions adopted in St. Joseph, Missouri ("Rights of Naturalized Citizens," *Pilot*, Dec. 28, 1867), and in Fitchburg, Massachusetts ("Our Citizens Abroad," *Pilot*, Feb. 8, 1868, 1); see also speech of John Savage, "Great Demonstration in Boston," *Pilot*, Dec. 21, 1867, 3.

62. "To Uncle Sam: A Cry from the American Soldiers in Mountjoy Prison, near Dublin," in "The American Fenians in England," *Pilot*, Dec. 2, 1867, 3; "American Citizens in British Prisons," Dublin *Weekly News*, Dec. 14, 1867; "Rights of Foreign-Born Citizens," *NYT*, Jan. 1, 1868, 5.

63. "Rights of Our Citizens Abroad," *Pilot*, Jan. 11, 1868, 4; "Rights of Our Citizens Abroad," *Pilot*, Jan. 18, 1868, 5;"Our Citizens Abroad," *Pilot*, Feb. 8, 1868, 1; "American Citizenship," *Pilot*, Jan. 25, 1868, 4. See also "The Naturalization Question—Meeting of Foreign-Born Citizens," *Philadelphia Inquirer*, Dec. 19, 1867, 4.

64. Charles Munde, *The Bancroft Naturalization Treaties* (Würzburg, 1868), 87.

Chapter 9: This Is a White Man's Government!

1. "This Is a White Man's Government," *Harper's Weekly*, Sept. 5, 1868, 568. For Irish American criticism of the cartoon, see "A Mean Caricature!," *Pilot*, Sept. 12, 1868, 4.

2. Warren, "A Voice from the Dungeon," *Dublin Weekly News*, Aug. 31, 1867, reprinted in *FRUS 1867*, 136.

3. "Rights of Our Citizens Abroad," *Pilot*, Jan. 25, 1868, 5 (see esp. report from Maine); Hasia Diner, *Erin's Daughters in America: Irish Immigrant Women in the Nineteenth Century* (Baltimore, 1983); Donna Gabaccia, *From the Other Side: Women, Gender, and Immigrant Life in the U.S., 1820–1990* (Bloomington, IN, 1995); Madeline Y. Hsu, *Dreaming of Gold, Dreaming of Home: Transnationalism and Migration between the United States and South China, 1882–1943* (Palo Alto, CA, 2000); Philip A. Kuhn, *Chinese among Others: Emigration in Modern Times* (New York, 2008).

4. Angelina Grimké, "Address to the Massachusetts Legislature," Feb. 1838, quoted in Kunal M. Parker, *Making Foreigners: Immigration and Citizenship Law in America, 1600–2000* (New York, 2015), 88. Coverture referred to women's loss of legal identity upon marriage, as her legal status became submerged under the husband's.

5. Stephen Kantrowitz, "'Not Quite Constitutionalized': The Meanings of 'Civilization' and the Limits of Native American Citizenship," in *The World the Civil War Made*, ed. Gregory P. Downs and Kate Masur (Chapel Hill, NC, 2015): 75–105, quote at 75; Parker, *Making Foreigners*, 89–92.

6. Elizabeth Stordeur Pryor, *Colored Travelers: Mobility and the Fight for Citizenship before the Civil War* (Chapel Hill, NC, 2016); Martha S. Jones, *Birthright Citizens: A History of Race and Rights in Antebellum America* (New York, 2018); Leon F. Litwack, *Been in the Storm So Long: The Aftermath of Slavery* (New York, 1979), 292–335; Nell Irvin Painter, *Exodusters: Black Migration to Kansas after Reconstruction* (New York, 1977); John Fabian Witt, *Patriots and Cosmopolitans: Hidden Histories of American Law* (Cambridge, MA, 2009), 83–154; Leslie A. Schwalm, *Emancipation's Diaspora: Race and Reconstruction in the Upper Midwest* (Chapel Hill, NC, 2009). Very few African Americans, only a thousand between 1872 and 1890, emigrated to Africa in the end; Parker, *Making Foreigners*, 93–99, 136–138.

7. President Abraham Lincoln, "The Gettysburg Address," Nov. 19, 1863, http://www.abrahamlincolnonline.org/lincoln/speeches/gettysburg.htm.

8. Colorado *Tribune*, Nov. 16, 1867, reprinted in George Francis Train, *An American Eagle in a British Cage; or Four Days in a Felon's Cell* (Cork, 1868), 13; A. D. Richardson, letter to *New York Tribune*, reprinted in San Francisco *Daily Evening Bulletin*, Feb. 12, 1867 ("eccentric genius"); William Lloyd Garrison, letter to *The Revolution*, Jan. 29, 1868 ("crack-brained harlequin and semi-lunatic"); Boston *Daily Advertiser*, Feb. 18, 1868, col. A ("superabundant vitality"); George Francis Train, *My Life in Many States and Foreign Lands* (New York, 1902), quotes at ix, x, xi, 7, 315; Willis Thornton, *The Nine Lives of Citizen Train* (New York, 1948); Francis B. C. Bradlee, "The Dreadnought of Newburyport," *Historical*

Collections of the Essex Institute 56 (Jan. 1920): 13–15; Richard White, *Railroaded: The Transcontinentals and the Making of Modern America* (New York, 2011), 20–21, 26–35.

9. Boston *Daily Advertiser,* Jan. 27, 1868.

10. Quoted in Thornton, *Nine Lives of Citizen Train,* 178, 131–132; Boston *Daily Advertiser,* Feb. 18, 1868, col. A; Stanton, Anthony, and Gage, eds., *History of Woman Suffrage* (Rochester, NY, 1881), II:243–246; Patricia Holland, "George Francis Train and the Woman Suffrage Movement, 1867–70," from *Books at Iowa* 46 (April 1987), http://www.lib.uiowa.edu/scua/bai/holland.htm; Ellen Carol DuBois, *Feminism and Suffrage: The Emergence of an Independent Women's Movement in America, 1848–1869* (Ithaca, NY, 1999), 93–104.

11. "A Lecture by George Francis Train," *Pilot,* Dec. 21, 1867.

12. Adams quote from Train's letter, read at Dec. 7 rally, "Great Demonstration in Boston," Dec. 21, 1867, *Pilot.*

13. "George F. Train's Great Speech," *Pilot,* Dec. 28, 1867, 1.

14. Train made these particular comments in a letter read at the first rally held for John Warren on Dec. 7, but they were similar in tone, substance, and style to those made in his speech on Dec. 21. "George F. Train's Great Speech," *Pilot,* Dec. 28, 1867, 1.

15. Quoted in Thornton, *Nine Lives of Citizen Train,* 236.

16. "Lecture by George Francis Train," Boston *Daily Advertiser,* Dec. 19, 1867.

17. William Lloyd Garrison to Susan B. Anthony, Jan. 4, 1868, in *The Selected Papers of Elizabeth Cady Stanton and Susan B. Anthony,* ed. Ann D. Gordon (New Brunswick, NJ, 2000), II:124.

18. David Quigley, *Second Founding: New York City, Reconstruction and the Making of American Democracy* (New York, 2004), 39–44, 59–65, quotes at 63; Lawrence Grossman, *The Democratic Party and the Negro: Northern and National Politics, 1868–92* (Urbana, IL, 1976), 1–14. New Democratic majorities in Ohio and New Jersey revoked their states' previous ratification of the Fourteenth Amendment; Grossman, *The Democratic Party and the Negro,* 1–2.

19. See, e.g., Warren's articles aligning the Fenian cause with other nationalist movements, including the Maoris in New Zealand ("The Maories Forever," *FS,* Aug. 27, 1864, 3); Bruce Nelson, *Irish Nationalists and the Making of the Irish Race* (Princeton, NJ, 2012), 61; Mitchell Snay, *Fenians, Freedmen, and Southern Whites: Race and Nationality in the Era of Reconstruction* (Baton Rouge, LA, 2007), 12–15. By the late nineteenth century, Irish nationalists increasingly identified with the "white colonizer." Cian T. McMahon, "Caricaturing Race and Nation in the Irish American Press, 1870–1880: A Transnational Perspective," *Journal of American Ethnic History* 33, no. 2 (2014): 33–56; Nelson, *Irish Nationalists,* 121–147; Kevin Kenny, "The Irish in the Empire," in *Ireland and the British Empire,* ed. Kevin Kenny (New York, 2004), 90–122.

20. Patrick Steward and Bryan McGovern, *The Fenians: Irish Rebellion in the North Atlantic World, 1858–1876* (Knoxville, TN, 2013), 207; "The First Victim," *NYH,* Nov. 10, 1871; "Irish Republicans," Boston *Daily Advertiser,* Oct. 1, 1884, 8. On Irish Americans

belonging to Republican Party, see "Appeal to Irish Citizens," *NYT*, Aug. 19, 1868, 2; "The New Movement Among the Irish-Americans," *NYT*, Sept. 29, 1868, 4; Kate Masur, *An Example for All the Land: Emancipation and the Struggle over Equality* (Chapel Hill, NC, 2010), 203–204; Christian G. Samito, *Becoming American under Fire: Irish Americans, African Americans, and the Politics of Citizenship during the Civil War Era* (Ithaca, NY, 2009), 116–118; Snay, *Fenians, Freedmen, and Southern Whites*, 13–14, 44–46. On African American and Irish American alliances, see Samito, *Becoming American under Fire*, 154–158, 185–187; Bruce Nelson, *Irish Nationalists*, 86–118; Arnold Shankman, "Black on Green: Afro-American Editors on Irish Independence, 1840–1921," *Phylon (1960–)* 41 (3rd qtr. 1980): 284–299.

21. William Nagle to Seward, Aug. 26, 1856 and Nov. 27 1860, Papers of William H. Seward, University of Rochester.

22. Alison Clark Efford, *German Immigrants, Race, and Citizenship in the Civil War Era* (New York, 2013), 53–85; Bruce C. Levine, *The Spirit of 1848: German Immigrants, Labor Conflict, and the Coming of the Civil War* (Urbana, IL, 1992), 217–219; Walter D. Kamphoefner and Wolfgang Helbich, eds., *Germans in the Civil War: The Letters They Wrote Home* (Chapel Hill, NC, 2006), 20, and letter of August Horstmann to parents, Sept. 18, 1863, 124.

23. Friedrich Kapp, *Immigration and the Commissioners of Emigration of the State of New York* (New York, 1870), 142–147; "About Immigration," *NYT*, Dec. 29, 1866, 4.

24. Hans L. Trefousse, *Carl Schurz: A Biography* (Knoxville, TN, 1982), esp. 92–94, 150–176.

25. Charles A. Page, *On the Naturalization Question* (Washington, DC, 1869), 5–8.

26. "How It Is Done," *New York Tribune*, Nov. 4, 1867, 4; "Appeal," *New York Tribune*, Nov. 4, 1867, 4; "Gigantic Fraud," *New York Tribune*, Oct. 31, 1867, 4; Page, *On the Naturalization Question*, 8; Quigley, *Second Founding*, 61–62, 74–75.

27. Steven P. Erie, *Rainbow's End: Irish-Americans and the Dilemmas of Urban Machine Politics, 1840–1985* (Berkeley, CA, 1988), 51.

28. Kathleen Neils Conzen, *Immigrant Milwaukee, 1836–1860: Accommodation and Community in a Frontier City* (Cambridge, MA, 1976), 154–191; Jon Gjerde, *Minds of the West: Ethnocultural Evolution in the Rural Middle West, 1830–1917* (Chapel Hill, NC, 1997), 61, 103–131; Efford, *German Immigrants, Race, and Citizenship in the Civil War Era*, 32–43; *NYT*, June 4, 1863, quoted in *Germans in the Civil War: The Letters They Wrote Home*, ed. Kamphoeffner and Helbich, 31.

29. Adams to West, Apr. 5, 1866, CFA LB; "Non-American Citizenship," *Harper's Weekly*, July 10, 1869, 435; "'Irish' Republicans," *Harper's Weekly*, Aug. 7, 1869, 499.

30. "A Letter to Irishmen," *Pilot*, Feb. 15, 1868, 4.

31. George Marsh, "Protection to Naturalized Citizens," *The Nation*, Aug. 9, 1866, 116.

32. "No More Sneers Against the Irish," *The Revolution*, April 23, 1868, 251; "A Mean Caricature," *Pilot*, Sept. 12, 1868, 4; "Nationality in the United States," *Pilot*, Aug. 3, 1867; "Are Irish-Americans Perjurers?," *Pilot*, Aug. 10, 1867; "A Novel Standard of Citizenship," *Pilot*, Aug. 17, 1867, 4.

33. "The Attempt at Blarneying," *Pilot*, July 28, 1866. See also "Ex-Governor Boutwell on the Irish American Citizens," *Pilot*, June 16, 1866, 4; "A Letter to Irishmen," *Pilot*, Feb. 15, 1868, 4; "Get Naturalized—the Blacks," *Pilot*, June 29, 1867, 2.

34. In addition to the examples above, several influential Irish nationalist leaders distanced themselves from the racism that seemed so pervasive among Irish Americans, including John Boyle O'Reilly, writer and editor of the Boston *Pilot* beginning in 1870, Michael Davitt, and Patrick Ford, editor of the *Irish World*, starting in 1870. Nelson, *Irish Nationalists and the Making of the Irish Race*, 125–127.

35. "Radical Attempt to Blarney the Irish American Vote," *Pilot*, July 14, 1866, 4. See also "Ex-Governor Boutwell on the Irish-American Citizens," *Pilot*, June 16, 1866, 4.

36. On economic and psychological "wages" of whiteness, see David R. Roediger, *The Wages of Whiteness: Race and the Making of the American Working Class* (London, 2007), 11–13, 144–145; Eric Arnesen, "Whiteness and the Historian's Imagination," *International Labor and Working Class History* 60 (Oct. 2001): 3–32. On "whiteness," see also Matthew Frye Jacobson, *Whiteness of a Different Color: European Immigrants and the Alchemy of Race* (Cambridge, MA, 1998); Alexander Saxton, *The Rise and Fall of the White Republic: Class Politics and Mass Culture in Nineteenth-Century America* (New York, 1990); Noel Ignatiev, *How the Irish Became White* (New York, 1995); Timothy J. Meagher, *The Columbia Guide to Irish American History* (New York, 2005), 214–233. For criticism of the "whiteness" studies in explaining Irish identity, see Kevin Kenny, *The American Irish: A History* (New York, 2000), 66–71.

37. On Irish Americans and patronage, see Erie, *Rainbow's End*, 32–45, 57–66. For a classic account, see William L. Riordon, *Plunkitt of Tammany Hall* (New York, 1905). On race and citizenship, see Ian F. Haney Lopez, *White by Law: The Legal Construction of Race* (New York, 1996); Rogers M. Smith, *Civic Ideals: Conflicting Visions of Citizenship in U.S. History* (New Haven, CT, 1997); Ariela Gross, *What Blood Won't Tell: A History of Race on Trial in America* (Cambridge, MA, 2008); Lucy E. Salyer, "Baptism by Fire: Race, Military Service, and U.S. Citizenship Policy, 1918–1935," *Journal of American History* 91 (Dec. 2004): 847–876.

38. George Francis Train, "Epigram on a National Sham," Boston, Dec. 1867, re-printed in George Francis Train, *The People's Candidate for President, 1872, George Francis Train* (New York, 1872), 8.

39. Efford, *German Immigrants, Race, and Citizenship in the Civil War Era*, 75–77, 115–142.

40. Charles Munde, *The Bancroft Naturalization Treaties* (Würzburg, 1868), 87.

41. Efford, *German Immigrants, Race, and Citizenship in the Civil War Era*, 108–111, 115–142.

42. *Speeches of Ex-Gov. Horatio Seymour and Hon. Samuel J. Tilden before the Democratic State Convention at Albany, March 11, 1868*, (New York: The World, [1868?]), 12–14; Grossman, *The Democratic Party and the Negro*, 3–4.

43. "Message from the President of the United States, Returning Bill (S. No. 61)," March 27, 1866, 39th Cong. 1st Sess., Sen. ex. doc. 31, quotes at 1, 2, 3, 8.

44. "*Only* an American Citizen?," *Irishman,* Nov. 2, 1867, 280.

45. Barbara Young Welke, *Law and the Borders of Belonging in the Long Nineteenth Century United States* (New York, 2010).

46. Efford, *German Immigrants, Race and Citizenship in the Civil War Era,* 19, 49–51.

47. Joanna Madigan was also known by the names Hannah and Johanna.

48. Act of February 10, 1855 (10 Stat. 604). American women, however, could not confer citizenship upon their foreign-born husbands, nor upon their children born abroad. Kristin A. Collins, "Illegitimate Borders: *Jus Sanguinis* Citizenship and the Legal Construction of Family, Race, and Nation," *Yale Law Journal* 123 (2014): 2134–2235, esp. 2155–2157. The following discussion of marital naturalization draws upon Candice Bredbenner, *A Nationality of Her Own: Women, Marriage, and the Law of Citizenship* (Berkeley, 1998), 15–44; Kerber, *No Constitutional Right to Be Ladies,* 3–46; Nancy F. Cott, "Marriage and Women's Citizenship in the United States, 1830–1934," *American Historical Review* 103 (Dec. 1998): 1440–1474; Virginia Sapiro, "Women, Citizenship, and Nationality: Immigration and Naturalization Policies in the United States," *Politics and Society* 13 (1994): 1–26.

49. *Jane L. Brand v. United States,* no. 180, Am. and Brit. Claims Com., and case of Elise Lebret, in John Bassett Moore, *History and Digest of the International Arbitrations to Which the United States Has Been a Party* (Washington, DC, 1898), 3:2487–2506, quote at 2487; Bredbenner, *A Nationality of Her Own,* 20–22; *Pequignot v. City of Detroit* 12 F. 211 (C.C.E.D. Mich. 1883), 216.

50. Helen Irving, *Citizenship, Alienage and the Modern Constitutional State: A Gendered History* (Cambridge, 2016).

51. *Report of the Woman's Rights Convention, Held at Seneca Falls, New York, July 19th and 20th, 1848. Proceedings and Declaration of Sentiments* (Rochester, NY: John Dick, 1848).

52. Bredbenner, *A Nationality of Her Own,* 19–21; Kerber, *No Constitutional Right to Be Ladies,* 11–29; Norma Basch, *In the Eyes of the Law: Women, Marriage and Property in Nineteenth-Century New York* (Ithaca, NY, 1982); Nancy F. Cott, *Public Vows: A History of Marriage and the Nation* (Cambridge, MA, 2000); Hendrik Hartog, *Man and Wife in America: A History* (Cambridge, MA, 2000).

53. See, e.g., *Shanks v. Dupont,* 3 Peters 242 (1830). However in 1869, Attorney General Hoar issued an opinion that an American woman married to a French citizen and living in France was *not* an "American citizen residing abroad." In *Pequignot v. City of Detroit* (1883), the Federal Circuit Court for the East District in Michigan decided that American women citizens lost their nationality when they married foreigners, but the law remained in flux until the Expatriation Act of 1907. Anastatia V. Warren, "Return of a Death," Aug. 30, 1904, Massachusetts Deaths and Burials, 1795–1910. On Mary Canty and Eliza Warren, see Chapter 2.

54. "1870 Census: Instructions to Assistant Marshals," Steven Ruggles, J. Trent Alexander, Katie Genadek, Ronald Goeken, Matthew B. Schroeder, and Matthew Sobek, Integrated Public Use Microdata Series: Version 5.0 (machine-readable database), University

of Minnesota, 2010; Marian L. Smith, "'Any Woman Who Is Now or May Hereafter Be Married . . .': Women and Naturalization, ca. 1802–1940," *Prologue Magazine* 30 (Summer 1998); Schneider, *Crossing Borders*, 195, 196–197. I thank Irene Bloemraad for the information regarding the 1870 census instructions for recording naturalization of only men.

55. "The Fenian Sisterhood," *NYH*, Dec. 29, 1865, 5; "The Servant Girls and the Fenians," *Pilot*, Sept. 21, 1867, 3; The *Irishman*'s critique is quoted in "Foreign Correspondence: Female Franchise," *The Revolution*, Apr. 16, 1868, 234. See also dispute between James Stephens and Ellen Mahony, in "The Fenian Sisterhood," *Daily Constitutional Union* (Washington, DC), Aug. 28, 1866, 1; Steward and McGovern, *The Fenians*, 103.

56. Efford, *German Immigrants*, 19, 23–25, 47–51, 81–82, 103–104, 140–141.

57. On gender relations during Reconstruction, see Peter W. Bardaglio, *Reconstructing the Household: Families, Sex and the Law in the Nineteenth-Century South* (Chapel Hill, NC, 1998); Laura F. Edwards, *Gendered Strife and Confusion: The Political Culture of Reconstruction* (Urbana, IL, 1997). "Manhood rights" was Train's phrase; Train, "Epigram on a National Sham," 8.

58. William H. Grace to Nathaniel Banks, Jan. 25, 1868, cont. 42, Banks Papers, LC (emphasis in original).

Chapter 10: The Politics of Expatriation

1. "Atrocious Fenian Outrage," *Times*, Dec. 14, 1867; "The Fenian Gunpowder Plot in Clerkenwell," *ILN*, Dec. 21, 1867, 663; "Affairs in England," *NYT*, Dec. 29, 1867, 1; "The Fenian Mode of Warfare," *NYT*, Dec. 29, 1867, 4; "Fenianism in England—the Clerkenwell Explosion," *NYH*, Dec. 15, 1867, 7; Brian Jenkins, *The Fenian Problem: Insurgency and Terrorism in a Liberal State, 1858–1874* (Montreal, 2008), 147–161.

2. Adams to Seward, Dec. 24, 1867, CFA LB; Report of Chief Inspector of Sewers Walker, Dec. 26, 1867, HO 7799 / 79.

3. "The Fenian Conspiracy," *ILN*, Jan. 18, 1868, 65; reprinted extracts of *The Nation*, folder 6, ms. 11,188, and A. [Brewster?] to Mayo, Nov. 5, 1867, folder 12, ms. 11,189, Mayo Papers; "Fenianism," *ILN*, Feb. 15, 1868, 151; Jenkins, *The Fenian Problem*, 174–175; Marie-Louise Legg, *Newspapers and Nationalism: The Irish Provincial Press, 1850–1892* (Dublin, 1999), 109–118.

4. Edward H. Cooper to Mayo, Dec. 26, 1867; Mayo to Dublin Castle, Dec. 25, 1867; Samuel Lee Anderson to Mayo, Dec. 25, 1867, folder 13, ms. 11,189, Mayo Papers.

5. Seward to Adams, Jan. 13, 1868, *FRUS 1868*, 142–143.

6. "England and America," *NYT*, Feb. 2, 1868, 4. See also *ILN*, Feb. 22, 1868, 174.

7. "Message of the President of the United States and Accompanying Documents to the Two Houses of Congress at the Commencement of the Second Session of the Fortieth Congress," Dec. 4, 1867, *FRUS 1868*, 1–21, quotes at 21.

8. "The Right of Self-Expatriation: A Proper Subject for Friendly Negotiation," *Frank Leslie's Illustrated Newspaper*, Jan. 11, 1868, col. A.

9. "Rights of American Citizens," *Pilot*, Feb. 1, 1868, 2; "Rights of American Citizens Abroad," *Pilot*, Feb. 15, 1868, 1.

10. See *Congressional Globe*, 40th Cong., 2nd sess.: the resolutions of Mr. Cullom, Dec. 4, 1867, 27; Mr. McCarthy, Jan. 14, 1868, 505; Mr. Van Horn, Jan. 20, 1868, 363; Sen. Conness, Jan. 21, 1868, 650; Mr. Griswold, Feb. 17, 1868, 1229; Mr. Price, Dec. 20, 1868, 309; Mr. Paine, Jan. 9, 1868, 417; Fernando Wood, Jan. 9, 1868, 417; William E. Robinson, Feb. 3, 1868, 945. Dawes's quote is from Jan. 14, 1868, 505.

11. James G. Hollandsworth, *Pretense of Glory: The Life of General Nathaniel P. Banks* (Baton Rouge, LA, 1998), 2, 11; Brian Jenkins, *Fenians and Anglo-American Relations during Reconstruction* (Ithaca, NY, 1969), 180. Also, B. R. Corlis to George Bemis, Dec. 22, 1866; John Appleton to Bemis, Dec. 23, 1866, Charles F. Blake to Bemis, Jan. 9, 1867; Francis Weyland to Bemis, Feb. 5, 1867; C. C. Washburn to Bemis, May 12, 1867; all in George Bemis Papers, 1794–1901, MHS.

12. William Makepeace Thayer, *The Bobbin Boy, or How Nat Got His Learning* (Boston, 1860), (on power of speech) 17–27, 183–195, 236–246; specific quotes at 21, 24, 244.

13. On Banks's pragmatism, see Hollandsworth, *Pretense of Glory*, 1–2, 8–44; Fred Harvey Harrington, "Nathaniel Prentiss Banks: A Study in Anti-Slavery Politics," *New England Quarterly* 9 (Dec. 1936): 626–654. On Lincoln's and Seward's support of Banks as a moderate, see *Diary of Gideon Welles, Secretary of Navy under Lincoln and Johnson* (Boston, 1911), II:26–27; Hollandsworth, *Pretense of Glory*, 214, 228–231. On objections to his working-class background: John R. Mulkern, *The Know-Nothing Party in Massachusetts: The Rise and Fall of a People's Movement* (Boston, 1990), 30–33.

14. Hollandsworth, *Pretense of Glory*, 22–25; "Speech of Hon. Nath. P. Banks," *Appendix to the Congressional Globe*, Dec. 18, 1854, 33d Cong., 2nd sess., 48–53; *Address of His Excellency Nathaniel P. Banks to the Two Branches of the Legislature of Massachusetts, January 7, 1858; Address of His Excellency Nathaniel P. Banks to the Two Branches of the Legislature of Massachusetts, January 6, 1860* (Boston, 1860), 8–11; Mulkern, *The Know-Nothing Party in Massachusetts*; Tyler Anbinder, *Nativism and Slavery: The Northern Know-Nothings and the Politics of the 1850s* (New York, 1992).

15. "A Bill More Effectually to Preserve the Neutral Relations of the United States," H.R. 806, 39th Cong., 1st sess., July 25, 1866; "Neutral Relations," H.R. Report No. 100, 39th Cong., 1st sess.; David Sim, *A Union Forever: The Irish Question and U.S. Foreign Relations in the Victorian Era* (Ithaca, NY, 2013), 69–96. For criticism of Banks's neutrality bill, see "Our Neutrality Laws," *NYT*, Jan. 4, 1867, 8; Sumner to Bemis, Dec. 23, 1866, John Appleton to Bemis, Dec. 23, 1866, G. S. Hillard to Bemis, Dec. 26, 1866, H. J. Raymond to Bemis, Dec. 31, 1866, Charles F. Blake to Bemis, Jan. 9, 1867, and Charles F. Adams to Bemis, Feb. 4, 1867, Bemis Papers, MHS; Charles Sumner to Moncure D. Conway, July 30, [1866], 2:374–375, Charles Sumner, *The Selected Letters of Charles Sumner*, ed. Beverly Wilson Palmer, v. 2 (Boston, 1990); Sumner to Bemis, Dec. 12, 1866, 2:384, and Sumner to Lieber, Dec. 29, 1866, 2:389, in *Selected Letters of Charles Sumner*, ed. Palmer.

16. In the Nathaniel Prentiss Banks Papers, 1829–1911, LC, see: David Nagle to Banks, Feb. 22, 1868; George Pepper to Banks, Jan. 8, 1868; Thomas Lavan, State Center, Fenian Brotherhood, Ohio, July 26, 1866, J. W. Fitzgerald, Centre Cincinnati Brotherhood, to Banks, July 27, 1866. Banks received numerous invitations to speak to Irish American audiences; see Thomas McGirr, Chicago, IL, July 11, 1866; Fenian Brotherhood of Newark, NJ, July 24, 1866; Lavelle Circle, Milford, MA; Jan. 7, 1868, from Washington, DC; Dec. 2, 1867, from Boston; Patrick Collins to Banks, Dec. 9, 1867; Thos. H. Conway to Banks, Dec. 9, 1867. See also William D'Arcy, *The Fenian Movement in the United States: 1858–1886* (New York, 1947), 280–281.

17. Banks, *Congressional Globe*, Jan. 29, 1868, 832; Orth, *Congressional Globe*, Feb. 11, 1868, 1103; Banks, *Congressional Globe*, Apr. 20, 1868, 2312. See also "The United States," *Times*, Feb. 21, 1868; "American Citizens Abroad," *Pilot*, Feb. 8, 1868, 1; "Rights of American Citizens," *Pilot*, Feb. 15, 1868, 4; "The Question of Citizenship," *NYT*, Feb. 1, 1868, 4.

18. "A Bill Concerning the Rights of American Citizens in Foreign States," 40th Cong., 2nd sess.; H.R. 584, Jan. 27, 1868, *Congressional Globe*, 783; Banks, *Congressional Globe*, Jan. 29, 1868, 832–833.

19. "Rights of Naturalized Citizens," *Pilot*, Dec. 28, 1867, 6; resolutions adopted in Kansas City, MO, in "Rights of Our Citizens Abroad," *Pilot*, Jan. 18, 1868, 5; resolutions adopted in Illinois, in "Protection to American Citizens Abroad," *Pilot*, Dec. 28, 1867, 4; "Rights of American Citizens," resolutions adopted in Allegany, NY, Jan. 9, 1868, *Pilot*, Feb. 1, 1868, 2; "The Naturalization Question," *Philadelphia Inquirer*, Dec. 19, 1867, 4.

20. Orth, *Congressional Globe*, Feb. 11, 1868, 1103. For legislators' criticisms, see *Congressional Globe*, statements by James Wilson, Jan. 29, 1868, 867–868; Bailey, Feb. 4, 1868, 967; George Woodward, 866–867; William Pile, 868, 1127; Norman Judd, 987; Jehu Baker, 110; James Ashley, 1101; Sidney Clark, 1107.

21. Letter quoted by Norman Judd, *Congressional Globe*, Feb. 5, 1868, 986; John E. Schuetze, St. Louis, MO, to Banks, Apr. 14, 1868, cont. 42, Banks Papers, LC; John Chanler, *Congressional Globe*, Feb. 6, 1868, 1015; Jehu Baker, *Congressional Globe*, Feb. 11, 1868, 1101.

22. Judd, *Congressional Globe*, Feb. 5, 1868, 986; William Pile, *Congressional Globe*, Jan. 30, 1868, 869; Sidney Clark, *Congressional Globe*, Feb. 11, 1868, 1106; Burton Cook, *Congressional Globe*, Feb. 11, 1868, 1099; Louis Schade, Washington, DC, to Banks, Jan. 29, 1868, cont. 41; H. Friedberger to Banks, Jan. 28, 1868, cont. 41, Banks Papers, LC.

23. Banks, *Congressional Globe*, Feb. 20, 1868, 1799; Orth, *Congressional Globe*, Feb. 11, 1868, 1103. For opposition to reprisals, see *Congressional Globe*, statements by Bingham, Feb. 3, 1868, 946; Pile, Jan. 30, 1868, 869; Judd, Feb. 5, 986; Cook, Feb. 11, 1868, 1099; Baker, 1100; Jenckes, 1158; Woodbridge, Feb. 12, 1868, 1131; Spalding, Jan. 29, 1868, 831; Donnelly, Jan. 30, 1868, 866. See also William Grace to Banks, June 25, 1868, cont. 42, Banks Papers, LC.

24. Pile, *Congressional Globe*, Jan. 30, 1868, 866; Higby, *Congressional Globe*, Feb. 4, 1868, 968; Jenckes, *Congressional Globe*, Feb. 13, 1868, 1159; Banks, *Congressional Globe*, Mar. 10, 1868, 1798.

25. The House sent the bill back to the Committee on Foreign Affairs on Feb. 13, 1868; *Congressional Globe*, 1159.

26. "Geo. Francis Train's Last Words," *The Revolution*, Jan. 22, 1868, 41; Willis Thornton, *The Nine Lives of Citizen Train* (New York, 1948), 143, 180–181. On Durant, see Richard White, *Railroaded: The Transcontinentals and the Making of Modern America* (New York, 2011), 19–22, 28.

27. Telegram to President Johnson, in George Francis Train, *An American Eagle in a British Cage; or Four Days in a Felon's Cell* (Cork, 1868), 7; telegram to the *Cork Examiner* and the *World*, reprinted in Train, *American Eagle*, 106; see also Train's telegram to the *Revolution*, Jan. 22, 1868, 40. For copies of telegrams forwarded to Dublin Castle, see folder 22, ms. 11,188, Mayo Papers.

28. "To the Editor of the Times, London," Jan. 19, 1868, in Train, *American Eagle*, 123–124; to Major-General Sir Thomas Aisken Larcom, in Train, *American Eagle*, 144.

29. The newspaper name is unclear, but the clipping is from New York, dated Jan. 22, 1868, and is reprinted in Train, *American Eagle*, 106.

30. "George Francis Train," Boston *Daily Advertiser*, Jan. 23, 1868, col. B; *New York World*, Jan. 20, 1868, reprinted in *American Eagle*, 109; "The Arrest of American Citizens in England," *NYT*, Jan. 20, 1868, 4; "A Matter That May Be Serious," *NYT*, Jan. 19, 1868, 4.

31. CFA Diary, Jan. 19 and Jan. 20, 1868.

32. Stanley to Mayo, Jan. 20, 1868, folder 14, file 11,189, Mayo Papers; CFA Diary, Jan. 21, 1868; *Cork Examiner*, Jan. 22, 1868, reprinted in Train, *American Eagle*, 31.

33. "To Whom It May Concern," Jan. 23, 1868, reprinted in Train, *American Eagle*, 63; memo from Resident Magistrate Hamilton to Dublin Castle, Jan. 23, 1868, folder 22, ms. 11,188, Mayo Papers; *Cork Examiner*, Jan. 22, 1868, in Train, *American Eagle*, 36.

34. *Irish Times*, Feb. 1, 1868, in Train, *American Eagle*, 56; *Morning Post*, Jan. 21, 1868, 93; Boston *Daily Advertiser*, Feb. 18, 1868, col. A; CFA Diary, Jan. 31, 1868 and Feb. 1, 1868; See correspondence in Mayo Papers, folder 22, ms. 11,188, especially letter of Feb. 14, 1868, revealing the government's dilemma.

35. Mayo to Attorney General, Feb. 29, 1868, folder 1, file 43,859, Mayo Papers. See Harcourt's *Times* articles (under the pen name Historicus): "British Citizenship," Jan. 10, 1868, 10; "The Status of Aliens," Feb. 6, 1868, 8; "The Law of Aliens," Feb. 12, 1868; editorial, Jan. 8, 1868, 4. On Nagle's trial, see "The Prosecution Opened," *Times*, Feb. 29, 1868, 8; "England and America," *NYT*, Feb. 2, 1868; "Expatriation and Naturalisation," *ILN*, Feb. 22, 1868, 174.

36. "The Fenian Trials in Sligo," *Irishman*, Mar. 7, 1868; "Nagle's Case," *Philadelphia Inquirer*, Mar. 4, 1868, 4; Michael Harrison (solicitor general) to Mayo, Feb. 29, 1868, folder 2, ms. 43,859, Mayo Papers.

37. Mayo to Attorney General, Feb. 29, 1868; Robert Warren to Mayo, Mar. 1, 1868 (emphasis in original); Solicitor General Michael Harrison to Mayo, Feb. 29, 1868; folder 2, ms. 43,859, Mayo Papers. See also "Ireland," *Times*, Mar. 4, 1868, 9.

38. "Ireland," *Times*, Mar. 5, 1868, 10; "The Trial of Patrick Nugent," *Irishman*, Mar. 7, 1868; R. Coulson to Chief Undersecretary, Mar. 4, 1868, Fenian Files/R Series/1634R, NAI; Christopher Hamlin, *Cholera: The Biography* (New York, 2009), 18–34.

39. "Ireland," *Times*, Mar. 5, 1868, 10; "Colonel Nagle," *Freeman's Journal*, Mar. 4, 1868.

40. [John Bull], *Philadelphia Inquirer*, Mar. 17, 1868, 4.

41. Adams to Seward, Mar. 11, 1868, *FRUS 1868*, 174.

42. CFA Diary, Jan. 8, 1868; Feb. 15, 1868; Feb. 25, 1868; Mar. 4, 1868. Also, Adams to Seward, Dec. 11, 1867, *FRUS 1868*, 38; Adams to Seward, Jan. 8, 1868, *FRUS 1868*, 135; Adams to Seward, Jan. 15, 1868, *FRUS 1868*, 143; Adams to Seward, Feb. 18, 1868, *FRUS 1868*, 155.

43. Jenkins, *Fenians and Anglo-American Relations*, 259–263; "The United States," *Times*, Feb. 27, 1868, 10; "The Question of Naturalization," *Times*, Jan. 9, 1868, 5.

44. Detmold to Bancroft, Mar. 8, 1868, box 1868, BP; CFA Diary, Mar. 2, 1868.

45. Seward to Adams, Mar. 7, 1868, *FRUS 1868*, 158–159; Thornton to Lord Stanley, Mar. 10, 1868, FO 5/1339; CFA Diary, Mar. 26, 1868; Jenkins, *Fenians and Anglo-American Relations*, 265–266.

46. Stanley to Thornton, Mar. 16, 1868, FO 5/1339; "Expatriation and Naturalisation," *ILN*, Feb. 22, 1868, 174; CFA Diary, Feb. 15, 1868. The House of Commons discussed the issue in early March; "Affairs in England," *NYT*, Mar. 6, 1868, 2. For disposition of each case, see "List of All the Jackmel Prisoners," folder 26, ms. 11,188, Mayo Papers. See also DD: letters of Michael O'Brien to West, Mar. 12, 1868; J. H. Lawlor to West, Apr. 8, 1868; Michael Green to West, Feb. 16, 1868.

47. Nagle to Adams, Apr. 6, 1868, *FRUS 1868*, 190–191. See also Nugent to Lord Lieutenant of Ireland, Mar. 18, 1868, and other requests for discharge, folder 16, ms. 11,188, Mayo Papers.

48. Confidential Memo on William C. Nugent, folder 16, ms. 11,188, Mayo Papers; Anderson, "Memo on Fenianism," 434–435, ms. 7517, Larcom Papers. On other prisoners' resistance, see DD: Nugent to West, Apr. 24, 1868, 793; Nugent to West, Apr. 10, 1868, 766; Apr. 11, 1868, 772; Apr. 14, 1868, 777; Larcom to West, Mar. 21, 1868, 748–750; Andrew Leonard to West, Apr. 8, 1868, 768; Denis O'Connor to West, Apr. 30, 1868, 801.

49. Confession of William Nagle, Mountjoy Prison, May 5, 1868, and letter of May 6, 1868, folder 24, ms. 11,188, Mayo Papers; Larcom to West, May 8, 1868, DD; Nagle to West, Apr. 18, 1868, 785, DD.

50. Anderson, "Memo on Fenianism," 434–435, ms. 7517, Larcom Papers; James S. Donnelly, *Captain Rock: The Irish Agrarian Rebellion of 1821–1824* (Madison, WI, 2009), 316–317.

51. West to Moran, May 21, 1868, DD, 811.

52. CFA Diary, Dec. 4, 1867, Nov. 21, 1867, Nov. 22, 1867 (on assassination threat), Jan. 31, 1868; Adams to Seward, Nov. 21, 1867, CFA LB, 280–281.

53. "Mr. Adams," *Saturday Review*, Feb. 29, 1868, reprinted in *Living Age* 97 (1868); CFA Diary, Apr. 8, 1868. See also clippings in CFA Diary, Feb. 5, 1868.

54. CFA Diary, Mar. 23 and 24, 1868 (on presidential prospects); CFA Diary, May 6, 1868 (on Nagle).

55. CFA Diary, May 13, 1868.

56. West to Adams, May 7, 1868, DD, 805–806; "Colonel William J. Nagle," *Irishman*, June 20, 1868; "Government Propaganda of Fenianism," *Evening Mail*, May 15, 1868; "George Francis Train and the Men of the Jacknell Expedition," *Evening Freeman*, June 3, 1868.

57. "'Squinting Justice' and a Dumb Defence," *Irishman*, June 6, 1868.

58. "Great Reception of Colonel Nagle by the Fenian Brotherhood," *Irishman*, June 27, 1868 (reprinting article from *New York Tribune*); David Quigley, *Second Founding: New York City, Reconstruction and the Making of American Democracy* (New York, 2004), 63–65, 94–96.

59. Republican Party platforms: "Republican Party Platform of 1868," May 20, 1868, online by Gerhard Peters and John T. Woolley, American Presidency Project, http://www.presidency.ucsb.edu/ws/?pid=29622; Democratic Party platforms: "Democratic Party Platform of 1868," July 4, 1868, online by Gerhard Peters and John T. Woolley, American Presidency Project, http://www.presidency.ucsb.edu/ws/?pid=29579.

60. H.R. 768, reported from Committee on Foreign Affairs, *Congressional Globe*, Feb. 20, 1868, 1294; introduced with remarks by Banks on Mar. 10, 1868, 1797–1805; H.R. 768, 40th Cong., 2nd sess., Feb. 20, 1868; passed Apr. 20, 1868, *Congressional Globe*, 2317.

61. "Banks' Buncombe," *NYT*, Apr. 22, 1868, 4; *Liverpool Mercury*, Apr. 23, 1868. See also "An Old Citizen," Brooklyn, to Banks, Jan. 30, 1868, cont. 41, Banks Papers, LC.

62. *Congressional Globe*, Dec. 19, 1867, 270.

63. *Congressional Globe*, July 18, 1868, 4204; *Selected Letters of Charles Sumner*, ed. Palmer, 2:4–5; David Herbert Donald, *Charles Sumner and the Rights of Man* (New York, 1970), 3–16, 99–100, 125–137, 369–370.

64. "The United States," *Times*, Aug. 4, 1868, 8; Glyndon G. Van Deusen, *William Henry Seward* (New York, 1967), 515.

65. Sumner to John Bright, Aug. 11, 1868, reel 82, Charles Sumner Correspondence, 1829–1874, Houghton Library, Harvard University.

66. "American Citizens Abroad," *Pilot*, Feb. 8, 1868, 1; "American Prisoners in Great Britain," *Congressional Globe*, 40th Cong., 2nd sess., June 15, 1868, 3175; "Imprisonment of Warren and Costello," House of Representatives, Ex. Doc. 312, 40th Cong., 2nd sess.

67. *Congressional Globe*, June 22, 1868, 3347.

68. *Times*, Aug. 4, 1868, 8; *Evening Star* (Washington, DC), July 16, 1868; *National Republican* (Washington, DC), July 18, 1868, 1; "Washington," *NYT*, July 26, 1868, 1.

69. Lieber to Sumner, June 27, 1868, reel 82, Sumner Correspondence, Harvard University.

70. Sumner, *Congressional Globe*, July 18, 1868, 4206.

71. H.R. 768 in the Senate of the United States, June 23, 1868, reported by Mr. Sumner with amendments, 40th Cong., 2nd sess.; Sumner to Duchess of Argyll, June 30, 1868, *Selected Letters of Charles Sumner*, ed. Palmer, 434.

72. Conness, *Congressional Globe*, July 22, 1868, 4332, and July 23, 1868, 4353. See also speeches of William Stewart, *Congressional Globe*, July 20, 1868, 4237, and William Sprague, *Congressional Globe*, July 23, 1868, 4349.

73. Conness, *Congressional Globe*, July 18, 1868, 4208; Charles D. Drake, *Congressional Globe*, July 18, 1868, 4212; Conness, *Congressional Globe*, July 22, 1868, 4331; Sumner, *Congressional Globe*, July 22, 1868, 4331–4332. On discriminatory treatment of Chinese in the news, see, e.g., "Facts for the Chinese Embassy," *NYT*, June 25, 1868, 4.

74. "An Act Concerning the Rights of American Citizens in Foreign States," July 27, 1868, 40th Cong., 2nd sess., 15 Stat. 223; *Congressional Globe*, July 25, 1868, 4446; Donald, *Charles Sumner and the Rights of Man*, 362–364; "Rights of American Citizens Abroad," *NYT*, July 23, 1868, 1; "The Close of the Session," *NYT*, July 28, 1868, 1. For examples of senators' impatience, see *Congressional Globe*, July 24, 1868, 4357, 4360.

75. Conness, *Congressional Globe*, 40th Cong., 2nd sess., July 18, 1868, 4207.

76. "Our Victory," *Irishman*, Aug. 1, 1868, 71, 89–90; "Banks' Buncombe," *NYT*, Apr. 22, 1868, 4; editorial, *Times*, July 29, 1868, 8; "The United States," *Times*, Aug. 10, 1868, 10.

77. Philadelph Van Trump, *Congressional Globe*, Mar. 10, 1868, 1801–1802; Woodbridge, *Congressional Globe*, Feb. 12, 1868, 1130; Alexander Cockburn, *Nationality, or, The Law Relating to Subjects and Aliens* (London, 1869), 91–106, quotes at 102, 91–92, 103; "British Citizenship," *Times*, Jan. 10, 1868, 10.

78. See *Congressional Globe*, remarks by: John Winthrop Chanler, Feb. 6, 1868, 1012; Banks, *ibid.*, Apr. 28, 1868, 2312; Ferry, July 25, 1868, 4446; Patterson, July 20, 1868, 4231; Sumner, July 22, 1868, 4331; Vickers and Buckalew, July 22, 1868, 4329.

79. "Topics of the Week," *Irishman*, Aug. 1, 1868, 80; "Our Victory," *Irishman*, 72; House of Commons, July 16, 1868, vol. 193, cc. 1282–1283; "The Question of Naturalization," *Times*, Aug. 24, 1868, 4; Moran to Seward, July 11, 1868, *FRUS 1868*, 323–324; Scallan to Editors, *Times*, July 31, 1868, and editorial, *Times*, Aug. 4, 1868; Reverdy Johnson to Seward, Sept. 3, 1868, *FRUS 1868*, 349–350; Johnson to Seward, Oct. 9, 1868, *FRUS 1868*, 358–359.

80. William Scruggs, "Ambiguous Citizenship," *Political Science Quarterly* 1 (June 1886): 204; John T. Maguire, "Naturalization of Aliens," *Harvard Law Review* 32 (Dec. 1918): 162; John Roche, "The Expatriation Cases," in *Supreme Court Review, 1963*, ed. Philip B. Kurland (Chicago, 1963), 330. Despite the critics' dismissal of the act as irrelevant, it had an unexpected role in the Iran hostage crisis more than a century later; Abner J. Mikva and Gerald L. Neuman, "The Hostage Crisis and the 'Hostage Act,'" *University of Chicago Law Review* 79 (Spring 1982): 292–354.

81. "The Rights of American Citizens Abroad," *NYT*, July 19, 1868, 4.

82. Judd, *Congressional Globe*, Feb. 4, 1868, 969; Sumner, *Congressional Globe*, July 22, 1868, 4332.

Chapter 11: Private Diplomatizing

1. Francis Lieber to Charles Sumner, Sept. 13, 1867, reel 81, Charles Sumner Correspondence, Houghton Library, Harvard University (in noting the changing times, Lieber highlighted negative events as well); J. A. S. Grenville, *Europe Reshaped, 1848–1878,* 2nd ed. (Oxford, 2000), 232–239, 241–279; "Irish Church and America," *Morning Star,* Apr. 13, 1868; David Feldman and M. Page Baldwin, "Emigration and the British State, ca. 1815–1925," in *Citizenship and Those Who Leave: The Politics of Emigration and Expatriation,* ed. Green and Weil, 146; C. A. Bayly, *The Birth of the Modern World, 1780–1914* (Malden, MA, 2004), 199–218, 234–242; Brian R. Hamnett, *A Concise History of Mexico* (New York, 1999), 160–204; Catherine Hall, Keith McClelland, and Jane Rendall, *Defining the Victorian Nation: Class, Race, Gender and the British Reform Act of 1867* (Cambridge, 2000).

2. John Lathrop Motley, *Historical Progress and American Democracy: An Address Delivered before the New-York Historical Society . . . Dec. 16, 1868* (New York, 1869), 6; Lieber, *Fragments of Political Science on Nationalism and Internationalism* (New York, 1868), 22.

3. Lieber to "All My Dear Ones," May 12, 1827, in *Life and Letters of Francis Lieber,* ed. Thomas Sergeant Perry (Boston, 1881), 69; Frank Freidel, *Francis Lieber, Nineteenth-Century Liberal,* (Baton Rouge, LA, 1948), 1–62, quote at 52.

4. Lieber to Ruggles, July 14, 1842, Francis Lieber Papers, LC.

5. Harmut Keil, "Francis Lieber's Attitudes on Race, Slavery and Abolition," *Journal of American Ethnic History* 28 (Fall 2008): 13–33, quotes at 20, 21; Francis Lieber to Oscar Lieber, Autumn 1860, in *Life and Letters of Francis Lieber,* 313–314; Freidel, *Francis Lieber,* 135–141, 223–258, 290–305.

6. Francis Lieber to Oscar Lieber, Autumn 1860, in *Life and Letters of Francis Lieber,* 313–314; Lieber to Ruggles, n.d., Lieber papers, LC; Freidel, *Francis Lieber,* 317–359; John Fabian Witt, *Lincoln's Code: The Laws of War in American History* (New York, 2012), 1–3, 177–196.

7. Lieber to Ruggles, Feb. 7, 1843, Lieber Papers, LC; Lieber to Oscar Lieber, Autumn 1860, in, *Life and Letters of Francis Lieber,* 313–314; Lieber to G. S. Hillard, Dec. 27, 1860, in *Life and Letters of Francis Lieber,* 316; Paul Lawrence Farber, *Finding Order in Nature: The Naturalist Tradition from Linnaeus to E. O. Wilson* (Baltimore, 2000); Lawrence Goldman, *Science, Reform and Politics in Victorian Britain: The Social Science Association 1857–1886* (New York, 2004).

8. Witt, *Lincoln's Code,* 170–219; Gary D. Solis, review of Witt's *Lincoln's Code, American Journal of International Law* 107 (Jan. 2013): 279–284.

9. Francis Lieber, "Amendments of the Constitution," in *Miscellaneous Writings,* II:138, 141; John R. Vile, "Francis Lieber and the Process of Constitutional Amendment," *Review of Politics* 60 (Summer 1998): 525–543; Michael Vorenberg, "Emancipating the Constitution," in *Francis Lieber and the Culture of the Mind,* ed. Charles R. Mack and Henry H. Lesesne (Columbia, SC, 2005), 23–29. See also Henry Sumner Maine, *Ancient Law: Its Connection with the Early History of Society and Its Relation to Modern Ideas* (London, 1861),

23, 74–75; Calvin Woodard, "A Wake (or Awakening?) for Historical Jurisprudence," in *The Victorian Achievement of Sir Henry Maine*, ed. Alan Diamond (Cambridge, 1991), 217–237.

10. Lieber to Ruggles, Apr. 23, 1847, and Lieber letter of Aug. 20, 1872 [recipient not listed], Lieber Papers, LC.

11. Lieber, "Amendments of the Constitution," 138, 169.

12. Francis Lieber, *Fragments of Political Science on Nationalism and Inter-nationalism* (New York, 1868), esp. 19–22; W. David Clinton, *Tocqueville, Lieber, and Bagehot: Liberalism Confronts the World* (New York, 2003), 46–50.

13. Lieber's wording was "exchange and colonization (emigration)." It's not clear whether he referred to imperialist colonization or used the phrase in a more informal way, as an equivalent to emigration. Lieber to Hamilton Fish, Aug. 28, 1863, box 26, Francis Lieber Papers, 1815–1888, Huntington Library, San Marino, CA; Lieber, *Notes on Fallacies Peculiar to American Protectionists, or Chiefly Resorted to in America* (New York, 1869), 6–7; Lieber to Franz von Holtzendorff, Aug. 11, 1872, in *Life and Letters of Francis Lieber*, 427–428.

14. Lieber, "Nationalism and Internationalism," 20–21; Lieber to Fish, Aug. 28, 1863, box 26, Lieber Papers, Huntington Library. See also David Dudley Field, *An International Code* (New York, 1867), 4–5.

15. Lieber to Fish, Sept. 1, 1869, box 64, Hamilton Fish Papers, LC. Liberal publicists advocated uniform monetary policies, standard weights and measures, rules of copyright, and the development of international infrastructure for speedier communication and transportation. Field, *An International Code*, 10; Lieber, "Nationalism and Internationalism," 21; Clinton, *Tocqueville, Lieber and Bagehot*, 55–56.

16. J. C. Bluntschli, "Lieber's Service to Political Science and International Law," in Lieber, *Miscellaneous Writings*, II:13–14; Betsy Baker Röben, "The Method behind Bluntschli's 'Modern' International Law," *Journal of the History of International Law* 4 (2002): 251. On Lieber as a prolific correspondent, see Witt, *Lincoln's Code*, 176–177. On Laboulaye and the Statue of Liberty, see Yasmin Sabina Khan, *Enlightening the World: The Creation of the Statue of Liberty* (Ithaca, NY, 2010), 37–47; Don H. Doyle, *The Cause of All Nations: An International History of the American Civil War* (New York, 2015), 284–285, 311–314.

17. Lieber, "Nationalism and Internationalism," 22–23; David Kennedy, "International Law and the Nineteenth Century: History of an Illusion," *Quinnipiac Law Review* 17 (Spring 1997): 105; Arthur Nussbaum, *A Concise History of the Law of Nations*, rev. ed. (New York, 1954), 202; Martti Koskenniemi, *The Gentle Civilizer of Nations: The Rise and Fall of International Law 1870–1960* (New York, 2002), 3–4; Mark Mazower, *Governing the World: The History of an Idea, 1815 to the Present* (New York, 2012), 38–54, 65–70; Edward Keene, "The Treaty-Making Revolution of the Nineteenth Century," *International History Review* 34 (Sept. 2012): 475–500; Wayne Sandholtz, *Prohibiting Plunder: How Norms Change* (New York, 2007), on "international law activists."

18. Adams to George Bemis, Feb. 4, 1867, George Bemis Papers, 1794–1901, MHS; Witt, *Lincoln's Code*, 149; Francis Lieber to Martin Thayer, Feb. 5, 1868, box 51, Lieber Papers, Huntington Library.

19. R. C. Waterston to Bemis, Dec. 22, 1866, Bemis Papers, MHS. On rise of professional international lawyers, see Koskenniemi, *The Gentle Civilizer of Nations*, 1–97.

20. Lieber to Bemis, Mar. 20, 1868, and Waterston to Bemis, Dec. 22, 1866, Bemis Papers, MHS.

21. Bancroft to Mrs. J. C. Bancroft Davis, Jan. 1868, in *The Life and Letters of George Bancroft*, ed. M. A. DeWolfe Howe (New York, 1908), 2:200–201; Bancroft to George Ripley, Jan. 17, 1868, in *Life and Letters of George Bancroft*, 188–194.

22. George Bemis to Charles Sumner, Aug. 26, 1869, Bemis Papers, MHS. On transatlantic intellectual networks, see Leslie Butler, *Critical Americans: Victorian Intellectuals and Transatlantic Liberal Reform* (Chapel Hill, NC, 2007).

23. A. G. Gardiner, *The Life of Sir William Harcourt* (New York, 1923), 1:129. For Harcourt's articles in U.S. government publications, see, e.g., "British Citizenship," *Times*, Jan. 10, 1868, reprinted in *FRUS 1868*, 137–141.

24. See, for example, Lieber to Sumner, Christmas 1866, reel 80, Lieber to Sumner, June 11, 1868, reel 82, and Lieber to Sumner, June 27, 1868, Sumner correspondence, Harvard University; Lieber to Secretary of State Hamilton Fish, Apr. 25, 1871, in *Life and Letters of Francis Lieber*, 410 (promoting international law on copyright); Lieber to General Garfield, Dec. 13, 1871, forwarding a proposed bill on naturalization, in *Life and Letters of Francis Lieber*, 417–419; Charles Sumner to George Bemis, Dec. 23, 1866, Bemis Papers, MHS; Secretary of State Seward to Bemis, Dec. 10, 1867 (begging Bemis to come to the District of Columbia to index *Alabama* claims correspondence), and Sumner to Bemis, Sept. 22, 1868, Bemis Papers, MHS.

25. Lieber to Dufour, Apr. 10, 1872, quoted in Clinton, *Tocqueville, Lieber, and Bagehot*, 73. See also Bemis, "British Neutrality," letter to editor, *NYT*, Mar. 16, 1868; Whitelaw Reid, *New York Tribune*, to Bemis, Jan. 21, 1870, Bemis Papers, MHS. Also, W. Vernon Harcourt, "Address on International Law," *Transactions of the National Association for the Promotion of Social Science, Birmingham Meeting, 1868*, ed. Andrew Edgar (London, 1869), 147. Grotius, in reality, was "deeply immersed in Dutch politics" as he helped to carve out a new law of the sea among competing imperial powers. Lauren Benton, *A Search for Sovereignty: Law and Geography in European Empires, 1400–1900* (New York, 2010), 120–148.

26. Even marriage linked the transatlantic intellectuals; Harcourt, who was English, wed the daughter of John Lothrop Motley, the American diplomat and historian. Peter Stansky, "Harcourt, Sir William George Granville Venables Vernon (1827–1904)," *Oxford Dictionary of National Biography*, online version.

27. Freidel, *Francis Lieber*, 225–227; Clinton, *Tocqueville, Lieber and Bagehot*, 56–58. Lieber to Sumner, June 25, 1868, Sumner Correspondence, Harvard University; Patrick Jackson, *Harcourt and Son: A Political Biography of Sir William Harcourt, 1827–1904*

(Madison, NJ, 2004), 9, 336, Harcourt's quote at 45; Irwin Abrams, "The Emergence of the International Law Societies," *Review of Politics* 19 (July 1957): 361–363.

28. Lieber to Fish, Mar. 29, 1871, box 26, Lieber Papers, Huntington Library; Lieber to Sumner, June 25, 1868, Sumner Papers, Harvard University.

29. Lieber to Fish, Aug. 28, 1863, box 26, Lieber Papers, Huntington Library; Jackson, *Harcourt and Son,* 9, 336, Harcourt's quote at 45. On limits of international law to Europeans, see Antony Anghie, *Imperialism, Sovereignty and the Making of International Law* (New York, 2005); Koskenniemi, *Gentle Civilizer of Nations,* 98–178.

30. Lieber to Bluntschli, Aug. 21, 1868, in Perry, *The Life and Letters of Francis Lieber,* 388–389; Koskenniemi, *The Gentle Civilizer of Nations,* 12–15; Bluntschli, "De la qualité de citoyen d'un état au point de vue des relations internationales," *Revue de droit international et de législation comparée* II (1870): 115. I am indebted to Janet Polasky for the translation of Bluntschli's article.

31. John Westlake, comments during "Discussion of Change of Nationality," *Transactions of the National Association for the Promotion of Social Science, Birmingham Meeting, 1868,* 179; John Westlake, "On Naturalisation and Expatriation; or, On Change of Nationality," *The Law Magazine and Law Review, or Quarterly Journal of Jurisprudence,* vol. 25 (Mar.-Aug. 1868): 125–126.

32. *Ancient Law,* 130–165, quote at 165; Woodard, "A Wake (or Awakening?) for Historical Jurisprudence," 217–237.

33. Historicus [William Harcourt], "Naturalization: Who Is a British Subject?," *Times,* Dec. 11, 1867, 6; George Yeaman, *Allegiance and Citizenship* (Copenhagen, 1867); Röben, "The Method behind Bluntschli's 'Modern' International Law," 257–258.

34. Yeaman, *Allegiance and Citizenship.* See also Amy Dru Stanley, *From Bondage to Contract: Wage Labor, Marriage, and the Market in the Age of Slave Emancipation* (New York, 1999); Eric Foner, *Free Soil, Free Labor, Free Men: The Ideology of the Republican Party before the Civil War* (New York, 1970).

35. Alexander Cockburn, *Nationality, or, The Law Relating to Subjects and Aliens* (London, 1869), 199.

36. Westlake, "On Naturalisation and Expatriation," 132–133; Harcourt, Discussion of "Change of Nationality," 184, 186; Cockburn, *Nationality,* 202.

37. "A Telegraph from Washington Informs Us," *Times,* Apr. 22, 1868, 9; Harcourt, "British Citizenship," *Times,* Jan. 10, 1868, 10; Jordana Dym, "Citizen of Which Republic? Foreigners and the Construction of National Citizenship in Central America, 1823–1845," *The Americas* 64 (Apr. 2008): 477–510; Tamar Herzog, *Defining Nations: Immigrants and Citizens in Early Modern Spain and Spanish America* (New Haven, CT, 2003).

38. Lieber, "Amendments of the Constitution," in *Miscellaneous Writings,* 167; Cockburn, *Nationality,* 183–185; Westlake, "On Naturalisation and Expatriation," 130.

39. Lieber, "Amendments to the Constitution," 167. Lieber spoke, here, of the divided allegiance between states and the federal government in the United States, but applied the same rationale to the question of expatriation.

40. Freidel, *Francis Lieber*, 1–23, 51–52, 231–232, 324–326; Lieber to Ruggles, Apr. 23, 1847, Lieber Papers, LC; Lieber to Sumner, June 25, 1868, Sumner Correspondence, Harvard University; Francis Lieber, *Amendments to the Constitution Submitted to the Consideration of the American People* (New York: Loyal Publication Society, 1865), [2–3], 36, 27; Historicus, "Who Is a British Subject?"; Yeaman, *Allegiance and Citizenship*, 20; "An International Congress," *Times*, Feb. 17, 1868, 6. See also Peter Spiro, "Dual Nationality and the Meaning of Citizenship," *Emory Law Journal* 46 (1997): 1411.

Chapter 12: Treating Expatriation

1. Bancroft to Seward, June 15, 1867, BP; Seward to Bancroft, May 20, 1867, BP; Seward to Bancroft, Aug. 22, 1867, *FRUS 1867*, 583 ("never-ending dispute"); Bancroft to Seward, Dec. 20, 1867, *FRUS 1867*, 40–41 ("long-vexed question"); Bancroft to Seward, Sept. 9, 1867, BP ("this troublesome question").

2. Bancroft to President Johnson, June 26, 1868, BP.

3. Edward Keene, "The Treaty-Making Revolution of the Nineteenth Century," *International History Review* 34 (Sept. 2012): 482; Arthur Nussbaum, *A Concise History of the Law of Nations* (New York, 1947), 196–204; William Starr, *Seward: Lincoln's Indispensable Man* (New York, 2012), 519. On the early history of using treaties to decide issues of naturalization, see Amanda Demmer, "Trick or Constitutional Treaty? The Jay Treaty and the Quarrel over the Diplomatic Separation of Powers," *Journal of the Early Republic* 35 (Winter 2015): 579–598.

4. Fessenden, *Congressional Globe*, 40th Cong., 2nd session, July 22, 1868, 4331. On ongoing ties of U.S. immigrants with homelands, see Donna R. Gabaccia, *Foreign Relations: American Immigration in Global Perspective* (Princeton, NJ, 2012).

5. Bancroft to Seward, Aug. 29, 1867, and Bancroft to Seward, Sept. 9, 1867, *FRUS 1867*, 584–585.

6. H. Villard, "Karl Otto von Bismarck-Schönhausen," *North American Review* 108 (Jan. 1869): 173; E. J. Feuchtwanger, *Bismarck* (London, 2002), 4, 27; John Lothrop Motley, *Historical Progress and American Democracy: An Address Delivered Before the New-York Historical Society, at Their Sixty-Fourth Anniversary, December 16, 1868* (New York, 1869), 44; John T. Walker, "John Lothrop Motley: Boston Brahmin and Transatlantic Man," in *Traveling between Worlds: German-American Encounters*, ed. Thomas Adam and Ruth Gross (College Station, TX, 2006), 66–67; Gordon Alexander Craig, *Germany, 1866–1945* (New York, 1978), 2.

7. Count Otto zu Stolberg-Wernigerode, *Germany and the United States of America during the Era of Bismarck* (Reading, PA, 1937), 86–94; John Torpey, *The Invention of the Passport* (Cambridge, 2000), 58–66, 71–92; Andreas Fahrmeir, *Citizens and Aliens: Foreigners and the Law in Britain and the German States, 1789–1870* (New York, 2000), 19–43; Eli Nathans, *The Politics of Citizenship in Germany: Ethnicity, Utility and Nationalism* (New York, 2004), 17–107.

8. Henry Blumenthal, "George Bancroft in Berlin: 1867–1874," *New England Quarterly* 37 (June 1964): 226–227; Lilian Handlin, *George Bancroft: The Intellectual as Democrat* (New York, 1984), 300–301; Stolberg-Wernigerode, *Germany and the United States*, 86–100. The literature on Bismarck is considerable. In addition to the primary sources cited, my discussion of Bismarck draws most heavily on Feuchtwanger, *Bismarck;* J.A.S. Grenville, *Europe Reshaped, 1848–1878*, 2nd ed. (Oxford, 2000), esp. 241–263; Craig, *Germany;* Jonathan Steinberg, *Bismarck: A Life* (New York, 2011).

9. Bancroft to Seward, Oct. 22, 1867, *FRUS 1867*, 592–593.

10. Ute Frevert, *A Nation in Barracks: Modern Germany, Military Conscription and Civil Society* (New York, 2004), 150–157; Feuchtwanger, *Bismarck*, 84, 79–82; Grenville, *Europe Reshaped*, 127–128, 138–140; Joseph Wright to Seward, Mar. 18, 1867 and Apr. 1, 1867, DG.

11. Wright to Seward, Feb. 18, 1867, DG.

12. Thile to Wright, Sept. 23, 1866, *Message of the President of the United States Communicating in Compliance with a Resolution of the Senate of July 28, 1866, Correspondence between the Government of the United States and the Governments of France and Prussia*, Sen. Ex. Doc. 4, 40th Cong., 1st sess., 141–142.

13. Herman Raster to Bancroft, Aug. 5, 1869, BP; Wright to Seward, Mar. 18, 1867, DG.

14. See correspondence between Bancroft and Seward, and between Bancroft and Prince Hohenlohe, the Bavarian foreign minister, in the fall of 1867, *FRUS 1867*, 589–593.

15. Bancroft to Seward, Jan. 21, 1868, *FRUS 1868*, 41–42; Bancroft to Gerolt, Jan. 31, 1868, BP; Bancroft to Seward, Feb. 14, 1868, *FRUS 1868*, 44–46; Bancroft to Seward, Feb. 22, 1868, *FRUS 1868*, 47–49; Bancroft to König, Feb. 18, 1868, DG; German (North German Confederation) Naturalization Convention, Feb. 22, 1868, 15 Stat. 615, Treaty Series 261.

16. Bancroft to Seward, Feb. 22, 1868, *FRUS 1868*, 47–49; Bancroft to Seward, Feb. 21, 1868, DG.

17. General Adam Badeau to Bancroft, Apr. 24, 1868, BP; "Our New German Treaty—American Rights Abroad," *NYT*, Mar. 1, 1868, 4; John T. Morse, "Allegiance and Citizenship," *North American Review* 106 (Apr. 1868): 613–614; Otto Freiherr von Völerndorff to Charles Munde, June 29, 1868, reprinted in Charles Munde, *The Bancroft Naturalization Treaties with the German States* (Würzburg, 1868), 79; C. E. Detmold to Bancroft, Mar. 8 and Oct. 4, 1868, BP; "The Right of Expatriation," *Philadelphia Inquirer*, July 20, 1868, 4; Samuel Williams to Seward, Apr. 10, 1868, William Henry Seward Papers, University of Rochester; Charles Hale to Bancroft, Aug. 29, 1868, BP; "The Treaty with Prussia," *NYT*, Mar. 13, 1868, 1. See also letters to Bancroft from John Bigelow, May 5, 1868, Friedrich Kapp, Dec. 31, 1868, and Ripley, Dec. 24, 1868, BP.

18. B. Roelker to Bemis, [Mar. / Apr. 1868], George Bemis Papers, 1794–1901, MHS; Munde, *Bancroft Naturalization Treaties*, 96, 158; "A German-American on Mr. Bancroft's Treaty," Fuerth, Bavaria, April 1868, encl. in G. Blumenthal to Bancroft, May 8, 1868, BP.

19. See BP: W. H. Davidge to Bancroft, Apr. 8, 1868; Julius Oberndorft, Stuttgart, to Bancroft, Apr. 8, 1868; G. Blumenthal, Bavaria, to Bancroft, May 8, 1868; Th. Hilgard, Heidelberg, to Bancroft, May 18, 1868; Charles Munde, Würzburg, to Bancroft, June 24,

1868; Baron Gerolt to Bancroft, Mar. 2, 1868; Detmold to Bancroft, Oct. 4, 1868; Kapp to Bancroft, Dec. 31, 1868; Seward to Bancroft, Mar. 23, 1868 (on German American opposition). See also John E. Schuetze to Nathaniel Banks, Apr. 14, 1868, Nathaniel Prentiss Banks Papers, 1829–1911, LC; Henry Seligman, Apr. 21, 1868, Charles Sumner Correspondence, 1829–1874, Houghton Library, Harvard University; "The Treaty with Prussia and the North-German States," *The World*, Mar. 31, 1868; "The Treaty with North Germany," *Philadelphia Inquirer*, Mar. 16, 1868;

20. Bancroft to Seward, Apr. 3, 1868, *FRUS 1868*, 50–52; *Harper's Weekly*, Aug. 1, 1868; Thornton to Stanley, Mar. 30, 1868; Apr. 13, 1868, FO 5 / 1339, on Seward's explanation of Art. IV.

21. Charles Sumner to Dr. Charles Munde, July 8, 1868, in Munde, *Bancroft Naturalization Treaties*, 89.

22. Paul F. Munde, "The Munde Water Cure," in Charles Arthur Sheffeld, ed., *The History of Florence, Massachusetts* (Florence, MA, 1895), 190–193, quote at 193; *Registers of Vessels Arriving at the Port of New York from Foreign Ports, 1789–1919*, M237, NARA; Charles Munde, *Passport Applications, 1795–1905*, roll 137: Mar. 1, 1866–Mar. 31, 1866, NARA; Charles Munde, *U.S. Naturalization Record Indexes, 1791–1992*; U.S. Census Records for 1850 (Massachusetts) and 1880 (New York); Paul F. Munde, *U.S. Naturalization Record Indexes, 1791–1992*; Paul F. Munde, New York, Military Service Cards, 1816–1979; Paul Fortunatus Mundé, *The National Cyclopaedia of American Biography* (New York, 1904), 12:272. Technically, Paul Munde became a naturalized citizen for a second time, first becoming an American citizen as a minor by virtue of his father's naturalization.

23. See Detmold to Bancroft, Mar. 8, 1868, BP; John Bigelow, to Bancroft, May 5, 1868, BP; and F. W. Sargent to Bemis, Nice, Jan. 10, 1866, in Bemis Papers, MHS, for examples of Americans who resided abroad.

24. "The Würzburg Protest," June 20, 1868, in Munde, *Bancroft Naturalization Treaties*, 67–68; for copy in Nathaniel Banks papers, LC, see cont. 42; Munde to Sumner, June 17, 1868, and July 28, 1868, reprinted in Munde, *Bancroft Naturalization Treaties*, 85, 87, 90. See also Charles St. Clair to Sumner, Apr. 6, 1868, Sumner Correspondence, warning of loss of German American vote.

25. Bancroft to W. B. Lawrence, Jan. 16, 1869, BP. See also Bancroft to Kapp, Jan. 20, 1868, on issue of domicile, and Kapp's response to watch out for Prussian trickery, Feb. 12, 1868. Bancroft raised the issue during negotiations, explaining that he hoped the treaty "might *empower* but not *compel*" the returning emigrant to resume his previous nationality, but he did not appear to insist upon that interpretation; Bancroft to König, Feb. 18, 1868, DG. In future treaties with German states, Bancroft inserted "a full & clear Protocol" to guide interpretation of Articles II and IV. Bancroft to Seward, May 20 and May 29, 1868, BP; Seward to Bancroft, June 22, 1868, BP.

26. Bancroft to Sumner, Mar. 12, 1869, BP. See also Bancroft to Seward, Aug. 11, 1868; Aug. 25, 1868; Mar. 2, 1869; Bancroft to W. H. Hunter, Aug. 28, 1868, BP. The treaties were finally ratified; Bancroft to Fish, Aug. 27, 1869, BP.

27. Munde, *Bancroft Naturalization Treaties*, 120–123, 147, 158–159.

28. Zhang Deyi, *Diary of a Chinese Diplomat*, trans. Simon Johnstone (Beijing, 1992), entries for Mar. 12–16, 1868, 39–43.

29. Zhang, *Diary of a Chinese Diplomat*, Mar. 31, 1868, 46–47.

30. Elizabeth Sinn, *Pacific Crossing: California Gold, Chinese Migration, and the Making of Hong Kong* (Hong Kong, 2013), 3–8, 43–73, app. 2, 312.

31. Knight Biggerstaff, "The Official Chinese Attitude toward the Burlingame Mission," *American Historical Review* 41 (Jul. 1936): 682–702; Ernest N. Paolino, *The Foundations of the American Empire: William Henry Seward and U.S. Foreign Policy* (Ithaca, NY, 1973), 152–163; Gordon H. Chang, *Fateful Ties: A History of America's Preoccupation with China* (Cambridge, MA, 2015), 92–96; Gordon H. Chang, "China and the Pursuit of America's Destiny: Nineteenth-Century Imagining and Why Immigration Restriction Took So Long," *Journal of Asian American Studies* 15 (June 2012): esp. 158, 162–163.

32. Guofu Liu, *The Right to Leave and Return and Chinese Migration Law* (Leiden, 2007), 131–132; Philip A. Kuhn, *Chinese among Others: Emigration in Modern Times* (Lanham, MD, 2008), 18–25.

33. On the "Old China Trade," see Chang, *Fateful Ties*, 14–29; John Kuo Wei Tchen, *New York before Chinatown: Orientalism and the Shaping of American Culture, 1776–1882* (Baltimore, 1999), 1–38; Dael A. Norwood, "Trading in Liberty: The Politics of the American China Trade, c. 1784–1862," Ph.D. diss., Princeton University, 2012.

34. "Lin Tse-Hsü's Moral Advice to Queen Victoria, 1839," in Ssu-yü Teng and John K. Fairbank, *China's Response to the West: A Documentary Survey, 1839–1923* (Cambridge, MA, 1954), 24–27; Arthur Waley, *The Opium War through Chinese Eyes* (Stanford, CA, 1958), 28–31, 34, 37, 56–57; Lydia H. Liu, "Legislating the Universal: The Circulation of International Law in the Nineteenth Century," in *Tokens of Exchange: The Problem of Translation in Global Circulations* (Durham, NC, 1999), 140–142; Wang Tieya, "International Law in China: Historical and Contemporary Perspectives," *Académie du droit international, recueil de cours* 221, no. II (1990): 228–230.

35. Emer de Vattel, *The Law of Nations, or, Principles of the Law of Nature, Applied to the Conduct and Affairs of Nations and Sovereigns, with Three Early Essays on the Origin and Nature of Natural Law and on Luxury,* ed. Béla Kapossy and Richard Whitmore (Indianapolis, IN, 2008). A nod to George Orwell's classic line "All animals are equal, but some animals are more equal than others"; George Orwell, *Animal Farm* (New York, 1946), 123.

36. Chang, *Fateful Ties*, 31–35; Adam McKeown, *Melancholy Order: Asian Migration and the Globalization of Borders* (New York, 2008), 152–157; Antony Anghie, *Imperialism, Sovereignty and the Making of International Law* (New York, 2005), 32–114; Gerrit Gong, *The Standard of "Civilization" in International Society* (New York, 1984). The last sentence is a paraphrase of Anson Burlingame's speech in New York on Burlingame's tour of the United States, in which he compared the status of China in relation to the Western treaty powers with that of Dred Scott. John Schrecker, "'For the Equality of Men—For the Equality of Nations': Anson Burlingame and China's First Embassy to the United States, 1868,"

Journal of American–East Asian Relations 17 (2010): 20. On importance of international law to recognition of state sovereignty and the "legal geography" of the law of nations, see Eliga H. Gould, *Among the Powers of the Earth: The American Revolution and the Making of a New World Empire* (Cambridge, MA, 2012); Eliga H. Gould, "Zones of Law, Zones of Violence: The Legal Geography of the British Atlantic, circa 1772," *William and Mary Quarterly*, 3rd ser., 60, no. 3 (2003); Lauren Benton, *A Search for Sovereignty: Law and Geography in European Empires, 1400–1900* (Cambridge, MA, 2010) 32–33.

37. Wang, "International Law in China," 237–259; Eileen Scully, "Historical Wrongs and Human Rights in Sino-Foreign Relations: The Legacy of Extraterritoriality," *Journal of American–East Asian Relations* 9 (Spring–Summer 2000): 129–146, 134; Pär Kristoffer Cassel, *Grounds of Judgment: Extraterritoriality and Imperial Power in Nineteenth-Century China and Japan* (New York, 2012), 1–29, 46–62; McKeown, *Melancholy Order*, 149–152.

38. McKeown, *Melancholy Order*, 66–89; Moon-Ho Jung, *Coolies and Cane: Race, Labor, and Sugar in the Age of Emancipation* (Baltimore, 2006); Elliot Young, *Alien Nation: Chinese Migration in the Americas from the Coolie Era through World War II* (Chapel Hill, NC, 2014), 21–94; Sinn, *Pacific Crossing*, 14–15, 51–53.

39. Frederic E. Wakeman, *The Fall of Imperial China* (New York, 1975), 163–185; Wang, "International Law in China," 230–237.

40. Xu Guoqi, *Chinese and Americans: A Shared History* (Cambridge, MA, 2014), 36; "The Celestial Embassy," *Harper's Weekly*, July 18, 1868; "The Chinese Embassy," *NYT*, Oct. 24, 1868, 4. On the Burlingame Mission, see Xu, *Chinese and Americans*, 25–73; S. S. Kim, "Burlingame and the Inauguration of the Co-Operative Policy," *Modern Asian Studies* 5 (1971): 337–354; Biggerstaff, "The Official Chinese Attitude toward the Burlingame Mission," 682–702; Frederick Wells Williams, *Anson Burlingame and the First Chinese Mission to Foreign Powers* (New York, 1912); Schrecker, "'For the Equality of Men'"; Chang, *Fateful Ties*, 92–99.

41. "The Celestial Embassy," *Harper's Weekly*, July 18, 1868; Thomas Nast, "The Youngest Introducing the Oldest," *Harper's Weekly*, July 18, 1868, 460.

42. "Washington: The Chinese Embassy Presented to the President," *NYT*, June 6, 1868, 1; "The Chinese Embassy," *NYT*, June 10, 1868, 1; "The Chinese Embassy," *NYT*, Aug. 24, 1868, 1.

43. *Journal of the House of Representatives*, June 9, 1868, 40th Cong., 2nd sess., 823–824; "The Chinese Embassy," June 24, 1868, *NYT*, 8; "China and America," *NYT*, May 18, 1868, 8.

44. Zhang, *Diary of a Chinese Diplomat*, June 5, 1868, 75–80; Xu, *Chinese and Americans*, 57–58, on Seward's role; Walter LaFeber, *The New Empire: An Interpretation of American Expansion, 1860–1898* (Ithaca, NY, 1963); Michael H. Hunt, *The Making of a Special Relationship: The United States and China to 1914* (New York, 1983); Warren I. Cohen, *America's Response to China: An Interpretive History of Sino-American Relations* (New York, 1971).

45. "American Supremacy in Asia," *NYT*, Oct. 6, 1868, 6.

46. Treaty of Peace, Amity and Commerce with China, July 28, 1868, 16 Stat. 739, Treaty Series 48; "The Chinese Embassy," June 24, 1868, *NYT*, 8; Chang, *Fateful Ties*, 96;

Schrecker, "'For the Equality of Men,'" 11, 26–31. Xu, *Chinese and Americans*, 25–26, 58, 60, notes that the Chinese government failed to abide by the free migration principle. On the treaty's challenge to discriminatory laws, see Yucheng Qin, *Diplomacy of Nationalism: The Chinese Six Companies and China's Policy toward Exclusion* (Honolulu, 2009), 51–55; Charles J. McClain, *In Search of Equality: The Chinese Struggle against Discrimination in Nineteenth-Century America* (Berkeley, CA, 1994); "The Chinese Treaty," *New York Tribune*, Aug. 4, 1868, 2; "Facts for the Chinese Embassy," *NYT*, June 25, 1868, 4.

47. Quoted in Xu, *Chinese and Americans*, 60. The treaty forbade "coolie labor," tapping into a volatile debate about free labor and Chinese immigration. See Jung, *Coolies and Cane*, 13–38; Young, *Alien Nation*, 63–73, 90–93; McKeown, *Melancholy Order*, 68–89.

48. Act of Mar. 26, 1790, 1 Stat. 103; U.S. Congress, *Senate Exec. Journal*, 40th Cong., 2nd sess., July 24, 1868, 355.

49. "Message of the President of the United States Returning Bill (S. No. 61)," Senate Ex. Doc. No. 31, 39th Cong., 1st sess.

50. "John Bull in Trouble," *Pilot*, Oct. 10, 1868, 4.

51. Hunk E. Doré, "The Coming Man—John Chinaman," *Harper's Weekly*, Aug. 28, 1869, 560; Najia Aarim-Heriot, *Chinese Immigrants, African Americans, and Racial Anxiety in the United States, 1848–82* (Urbana, IL, 2003), 104–108; Kevin Kenny, *The American Irish* (New York, 2000), 68–69, 157–158; Alexander Saxton, *Indispensable Enemy: Labor and the Anti-Chinese Movement in California* (Berkeley, CA, 1971). But see Andrew Gyory, *Closing the Gate: Race, Politics and the Chinese Exclusion Act* (Chapel Hill, NC, 1998).

52. "The Celestial Embassy," *Harper's Weekly*, July 18, 1868; Tchen, *New York before Chinatown*, 97–130; Lucretia Bancroft Farnum to George Bancroft, June 30, 1865, box 1865, BP. See also Charles Francis Adams Jr., "Protecting the Ballot Box," *Journal of Social Science* 1 (June 1869): 107–110.

53. Morse, "Allegiance and Citizenship," 621, 625. See also George H. Yeaman, *Allegiance and Citizenship* (Copenhagen, 1867), 5–6; Thomas Kleven, "Why International Law Favors Emigration over Immigration," *University of Miami Inter-American Law Review* (Spring 2002): 69–100.

54. Seward to Johnson, July 20, 1868, in *The Works of William H. Seward*, ed. George E. Baker (New York, 1884), 477–480; Seward to Johnson, Sept. 23, 1868, 354–356, and Seward to Johnson, Sept. 14, 1868, 351, *FRUS 1868*. Bancroft shared the Prussian treaty with British diplomats as a model for the Anglo-American Treaty, but the Crown's law officers found faults with it, especially Article IV. Bancroft to Seward, Mar. 10, 1868, BP; D. to Thornton [British minister to U.S.] on Law Officers' Report, Mar. 14, 1868, FO 5 / 1339. On the treaty negotiations, see Rising Lake Morrow, "The Negotiation of the Anglo-American Treaty of 1870," *American Historical Review* 39 (1934): 663–681; Brian Jenkins, *Fenians and Anglo-American Relations during Reconstruction* (Ithaca, NY, 1969), 248–281; David Sim, *A Union Forever: The Irish Question and U.S. Foreign Relations in the Victorian Age* (Ithaca, NY, 2013), 118–127; Christian G. Samito, *Becoming American under Fire: Irish Americans, African Americans, and the Politics of Citizenship during the Civil War Era* (Ithaca, NY, 2009), 212–214.

55. "British Citizenship," *Times,* Jan. 10, 1868, 10; "England and America," *Times,* Feb. 28, 1868, 4; Alexander Cockburn, *Nationality: or, The Law relating to Subjects and Aliens* (London, 1869), 106; "The Law of Aliens," *Times,* Feb. 12, 1868, 5.

56. Stanley to Thornton, June 16, 1868, FO 5 / 1339; Johnson to Seward, Sept. 12, 1868, *FRUS 1868,* 350.

57. This was Seward's proposal, reported by Thornton to Stanley, Apr. 13, 1868, FO 5 / 1339, renewed by Johnson. Johnson to Seward, Sept. 12, 1868, *FRUS 1868,* 350.

58. Johnson to Seward, Sept. 25, Oct. 7, and Oct. 9, 1868, *FRUS 1868,* 356–360.

59. For the protocol provisions, see "Protocol Showing the Principles Agreed upon by the United States and British Governments on the Question of Naturalization," *FRUS 1868,* 359–360.

60. "Colonel Warren's Reception in the South," *Irish Times,* Mar. 18, 1869. On receptions, see newspaper clippings forwarded by William West to Secretary of State, Mar. 19 and Mar. 20, 1869, DD. "Whilom" is an old English word, meaning "formerly" or "in the past."

61. Johnson to Seward, Feb. 23, 1869, U.S. House of Representatives, *American Citizens Prisoners in Great Britain,* 6, 41st Cong., 2nd sess., H. R. Ex. Doc. No. 170.

62. C.P.J., "The State of the Country as to Fenianism," Feb. 2, 1869, Fenian Files / R Series / 1869 / 5129R, NAI.

63. "Address in Answer to Her Majesty on Her Most Gracious Speech," Feb. 8, 1870, HC Debate, v. 199, cc. 58–109; Jenkins, *Fenians and Anglo-American Relations,* 283–284.

64. "Unconquered Still!," *Weekly News,* Apr. 3, 1868, 1; West to Fish, Mar. 19 and 20, 1869, DD; editorial, *Daily Express,* Mar. 19, 1869; "The Fenian Meeting at Cork," *Leeds Mercury,* May 1, 1869; Warren's letter to the editor, *The Nation* (Dublin), Apr. 3, 1869; on "The Sword of Bunker Hill," see http://www.drjosephwarren.com/2015/07/the-sword -of-bunker-hill.

65. Editorial, *Daily Express,* Mar. 19, 1869; "From Our London Correspondent," *Dublin Evening Post,* Mar. 19, 1869; "The Fruits of the Fenian Amnesty," *Dublin Express,* Mar. 27, 1869; "House of Commons: Recent Events in Ireland," *ILN,* May 8, 1869, 462; *Brooklyn Eagle,* July 22, 1869, 2. In Reverdy Johnson to Washburne, Mar. 24, 1869, *American Citizens Prisoners in Great Britain,* 10–11; Fish to Johnson, Apr. 13, 1869, 11; Motley to Fish, Oct. 5, 1869, 33; Motley to Fish, Oct. 19, 1869, 36–37. Also, Motley to Fish, Sept. 27, 1869, container 65, Hamilton Fish Papers, 1732–1914, LC.

66. David Herbert Donald, *Charles Sumner and the Rights of Man* (New York, 1970), 374–385, quotes at 376, 379; Jenkins, *Fenians and Anglo-American Relations,* 282–292; Fish to Motley, May 17, 1869, Fish Papers, LC.

67. "Nationality," *Times,* Jan. 15, 1870, 4; Cockburn, *Nationality,* 185–186, 199; *Report of the Royal Commissioners for Inquiring into the Laws of Naturalization and Allegiance* (London, 1869), v. On difficulties in resolving issues, see Stanley to Thornton, June 16, 1868, FO 5 / 1339; "Parliamentary Intelligence," *Times,* Mar. 11, 1870; "Memorandum: Note on the Difficulties in Preparing an Act of Parliament to Carry out Lord Stanley's Naturalization Protocol," FO 5 / 1356; Lord Clarendon, Second Reading of Naturalization Bill, Mar. 3,

1870, House of Lords, v. 199, cc. 1118–1136; Jenkins, *Fenians and Anglo-American Relations*, 280–281; Morrow, "Negotiation of the Anglo-American Treaty," 679.

68. Earl of Carnavan, Mar. 10, 1870, House of Commons; Comments of Lord Westbury and Lord Chancellor, Mar. 10, 1870, House of Lords; Mr. Buxton, Mar. 20, 1870, House of Commons; Lord Stanley, Mar. 20, 1868, House of Commons.

69. Lord Chancellor, Mar. 3, 1870, House of Lords; Report of W. Vernon Harcourt, *Report of the Royal Commissioners*, xii–xv; remarks of Vernon Harcourt and Sir Roundell Palmer, House of Commons, Apr. 28, 1870, vol. 200 cc. 2020–2025; "The Naturalization Bill: E. C. Clark, to the Editor of the Times," *Times*, Apr. 14, 1870, 4; "The Naturalization Bill: Cosmopolite to the Editor of the Times," *Times*, Apr. 25, 1870, 6.

70. An Act to Amend the Law Relating to the Legal Condition of Aliens and British Subjects, sec. 10; comments of W. Lawrence, Mr. Kinnaird, and Attorney General, April 25, 1870, House of Commons; Helen Irving, *Citizenship, Alienage and the Modern Constitutional State: A Gendered History* (Cambridge, 2016); Laura Tabili, "Outsiders in the Land of Their Birth: Exogamy, Citizenship, and Identity in War and Peace," *Journal of British Studies* 44 (Oct. 2005): 796–815; M. Page Baldwin, "Married Women and the British Nationality and Status of Aliens Act," *Journal of British Studies* 40 (Oct. 2001): 522–556; Married Women's Property Act of 1870: 33, 34 Victoria c. 93: An Act to Amend the Law Relating to the Property of Married Women; Frances Power Cobbe, *Criminals, Idiots, Women and Minors: Is the Classification Sound? Concerning the Property of Married Women* (Manchester, 1869).

71. An Act to Amend the Law Relating to the Legal Condition of Aliens and British Subjects, 12th May, 1870: 33, 34 Victoria c. 14 (see sec. 17 for limits on married women); Lord Penzance, House of Lords, Mar. 10, 1870, vol. 199, cc. 1604–1618; *Morning Post*, Feb. 28, 1868 (on mixed jury).

72. U.S. Senate, 41st Cong., 2nd sess., "Petition of John Warren Praying for Redress for His Arrest and Imprisonment . . . ," Misc. Doc. No. 141, quotes at 1, 4. Warren apparently asked for $500,000 compensation. "A Fenian Case in the House," *Pilot*, Apr. 4, 1870.

73. Benjamin Disraeli called Warren an "able writer," in "Address in Answer to Her Majesty on Her Most Gracious Speech," Feb. 8, 1870, House of Commons.

74. Naturalization Convention with United Kingdom, May 13, 1870, 16 Stat. 775, Treaty Series 130; "Tenth Ward Democratic Party Mass Meeting," *Brooklyn Eagle*, June 17, 1870, 3.

75. The United States made naturalization treaties with (in order of signing): North German Confederation (Feb. 2, 1868), Bavaria (May 26, 1868), Mexico (July 10, 1868), Baden (July 19, 1868), Württemberg (July 27, 1868), Hesse (Aug. 1, 1868), Belgium (Nov. 16, 1868), Sweden and Norway (May 26, 1869), Great Britain (May 13, 1870), Austria-Hungary (Sept. 20, 1870), Ecuador (May 6, 1872), and Denmark (July 20, 1872). Copies can be found in *Treaties and Other International Agreements of the United States of America, 1776–1949*, compiled under the direction of Charles I. Bevans (Washington, DC, 1968–1976), http://www.loc.gov/law/help/us-treaties/bevans.php.

76. Emer de Vattel, *Law of Nations* (1758), §125 ("every man has a right to dwell some-where upon the earth"); §223 ("a citizen has an absolute right to renounce his country, and abandon it entirely"); §15–20 (on sovereignty of nations).

77. Alfred Erbe memo, Oct. 2, 1867, enclosed in Kapp to Bancroft, Oct. 4, 1867, BP.

78. *NYH*, Apr. 21, 1869.

79. "Arrest of American Citizens in Great Britain, Report of the Committee on Foreign Affairs," House of Representatives, 40th Cong., 3rd sess., H. R. Rept. No. 44, 6.

Epilogue

1. "Arrival of the Released Fenians Warren and Costello from England—Their Reception in This City," *NYT*, May 10, 1869, 1; "The Famous Fenians, John Warren and Augustine E. Costello," *Brooklyn Daily Eagle*, May 10, 1869, 2; "The Proposed Reception of Warren and Costello," *NYT*, May 15, 1869, 5; "American Citizens in British Prisons" (advertisement), *Brooklyn Daily Eagle*, May 13, 1869, 1; "Colonel Warren's Interview with the President," *NYH*, July 9, 1869, 4.

2. Massachusetts Death Records, 1841–1915: Eliza Jane Warren, died Jan. 8, 1868, vol. 212, 9; John Warren, died June 22, 1873, vol. 257, 2; Joanna Warren, died Feb. 18, 1868, vol. 222, 28. For examples of fires, see *Charlestown Advertiser*, Oct. 24, 1868, 1. For Timothy and John Warren living with Mary and Dennis O'Leary and their six children: U.S. Federal Census, 1870, Town of Arlington, 75 (Eliza died in Arlington, suggesting she was also living with the O'Learys); Timothy Irwin to Mary Jane Irwin O'Donovan Rossa, Jan. 22, 1868, FBR / CUA. On benefits to aid Warren's family, see "The Colonel in Boston," *Pilot*, June 20, 1868, 4.

3. U.S. Census Mortality Schedules, New York, 1850–1880: Year: 1870; Roll: M5; Line Number: 6.

4. William Nagle to Seward, June 29, 1858, and Feb. 24, 1863, William Henry Seward Papers, University of Rochester; Official Military Personnel File, Nagle, William J., Nov. 18, 1863, "Surgeon's Certificate for Sick Leave," RG 319, Records of the Army Staff, NARA; John T. Scallan to William B. West, Nov. 16, 1867, DD, 629–630.

5. Patrick Joseph Murray, Government Prisons Office, Dublin Castle, to Under-secretary, Oct. 3, 1866, FO 5 / 1340; "'Squinting Justice' and a Dumb Defence," *Irishman*, June 6, 1868; "Release of Fenian Prisoners," *NYT*, May 11, 1868, 1.

6. *Pilot*, May 29, 1868. See also letter of Denis O'Connor to George Francis Train, May 29, 1868, denying his confession, reprinted in *Evening Freeman*, June 3, 1868.

7. On popularity as a speaker, see "The Colonel in Boston," *Pilot*, June 20, 1868, 4; "The White Boys in Blue," *Brooklyn Daily Eagle*, Aug. 29, 1868; "Col. Nagle on the Subject," *Pilot*, July 11, 1868, 1; "Great Reception of Col. Nagle by the Fenian Brotherhood," *Irishman*, June 27, 1868. On cool reception, see "The Return of the Fenian General Nagle," *NYH*, Apr. 18, 1868, 7; "Reception to Colonel Nagle," *NYH*, June 20, 1868, 4.

8. "Death of General William J. Nagle," *NYH*, Aug. 16, 1869, 6; "Suicide of Colonel William J. Nagle, the Well-Known Fenian," *New York World*, Aug. 16, 1869; "Suicide of a Fenian Leader," *NYT*, Aug. 16, 1869, 8; R. Gregory Lande, "Felo De Se: Soldier Suicides in America's Civil War," *Military Medicine* 176 (May 2011): 531; Patrick Steward and Bryan P. McGovern, *The Fenians: Irish Rebellion in the North Atlantic World, 1868–1876* (Knoxville, TN, 2014), 198.

9. "Card from Warren and Costello," *NYT*, May 14, 1869, 1; "The Proposed Reception of Warren and Costello," *NYT*, May 15, 1869, 5; "Colonel John Warren," *Frank Leslie's Illustrated Newspaper*, May 29, 1869, 163; "W. E. Robinson for Mayor," *Brooklyn Daily Eagle*, Sept. 18, 1871; "Tenth Ward Democratic Mass Meeting," *Brooklyn Daily Eagle*, June 17, 1870; "The First Victim," *NYH*, Nov. 10, 1871; Steward and McGovern, *The Fenians*, 207; Brian Jenkins, *Fenians and Anglo-American Relations during Reconstruction* (Ithaca, NY, 1969), 292–293; William D'Arcy, *The Fenian Movement in the United States: 1858–1886* (New York, 1947), 370–411.

10. *Official Report of General John O'Neill* (New York, 1870), 15–21; "The Fenian Campaign Explained," *Pilot*, July 9, 1870; "The Fenians on the Warpath," *Pilot*, June 4, 1870; Jenkins, *Fenians and Anglo-American Relations*, 269–273, 276–277, 292–306.

11. D'Arcy, *The Fenian Movement*, 356 n. 88.

12. Quoted in Jenkins, *Fenians and Anglo-American Relations*, 317; James Jeffrey Roche, *Life of John Boyle O'Reilly* (New York, 1891), 107–108; *Official Report of General John O'Neill*, 20–21, 25.

13. Jenkins, *Fenians and Anglo-American Relations*, 303–308; Wilfried Neidhardt, *Fenianism in North America* (University Park, PA, 1975), 118–126; "The Fenians on the Warpath," *Pilot*, June 4, 1870. D'Arcy suggests that William M. Tweed paid for their passage home. D'Arcy, *The Fenian Movement*, 356.

14. Jenkins, *Fenians and Anglo-American Relations*, 316.

15. "Our Transatlantic Cousins," *NYT*, Dec. 17, 1867; David Sim, *A Union Forever: The Irish Question and U.S. Foreign Relations in the Victorian Age* (Ithaca, NY, 2013), 138–142, 153–162; M. J. Sewell, "Rebels or Revolutionaries? Irish-American Nationalism and American Diplomacy, 1865–1885," *Historical Journal* 29 (Sept. 1986): 723–733; Allan Nevins, *Hamilton Fish: The Inner History of the Grant Administration* (New York, 1936), II:470–493; Kevin Kenny, "American-Irish Nationalism," in *Making the Irish American: History and Heritage of the Irish in the United States*, ed. J. J. Lee and Marion R. Casey (New York, 2006), 289–301; David Brundage, "Recent Directions in the History of Irish American Nationalism," *Journal of American Ethnic History* 28 (Summer 2009): 82–89.

16. Sim, *A Union Forever*, 142–151, 165–173; Jonathan W. Gantt, "Irish-American Terrorism and Anglo-American Relations, 1881–1885," *Journal of the Gilded Age and Progressive Era* 5 (Oct. 2006): 325–357; Charles A. Page, *On the Naturalization Question* (Washington, DC, 1869), 16–19; *Regulations Prescribed for Use of the Consular Service of the United States*, Article XI, "Passports and Protection of Citizens of the United States," sec. 110, 111 (Washington, DC, 1870).

17. Steven P. Erie, *Rainbow's End: Irish-Americans and the Dilemmas of Urban Machine Politics, 1840–1985* (Berkeley, 1988), 51; "Fraudulent Naturalization," *NYT*, Nov. 4, 1868, 4; "The Naturalization Problem," *NYT*, June 20, 1870, 4; "Naturalization," *NYT*, Oct. 23, 1868; "Our Naturalization Laws," *NYT*, July 7, 1868, 4; Page, *On the Naturalization Question*, 4, 7.

18. David Quigley, "Acts of Enforcement: The New York City Election of 1870," *New York History*, Summer 2002, 271–292, quote at 288; Erie, *Rainbow's End*, 36; Kevin Kenny, *The American Irish* (New York, 2000), 158–159.

19. Reed quoted in Sim, *A Union Forever*, 172; Kenny, *The American Irish*, 160–163; Erie, *Rainbow's End*, 39–45, 74–79, table 2 (20–21).

20. Patrick A. Collins, *"Irish Voters": No Distinction of Creed or Race in American Politics* (Boston, 1876), 4, 7–8, 9; Lawrence W. Kennedy, "Young Patrick A. Collins and Boston Politics after the Civil War," *Historical Journal of Massachusetts* (Spring 2010): 38–59.

21. Thomas Nast, "The Champion of the Fenians," *Harper's Weekly*, Oct. 21, 1876. See also "Mr. Adams and the Fenians," *Times*, Oct. 3, 1876, 8.

22. Martin B. Duberman, *Charles Francis Adams, 1807–1886* (Stanford, CA, 1960), 334–389; CFA Diary, July 3, 1867; Charles Francis Adams, *An Address on the Life, Character and Services of William Henry Seward* (Albany, NY, 1873); "Tribute to William H. Seward by Mr. Adams," *Proceedings of the Massachusetts Historical Society* 12 (Dec. 1872): 296–308; Henry Adams, *Education of Henry Adams* (New York, 1999), 90.

23. Duberman, *Charles Francis Adams*, 352–372, 389–398.

24. Though Timothy Warren declared in probate records that his father left no widow, Bridget Warren was very much alive, filing for benefits as a widow of a Civil War veteran in 1895. Widow Application no. 621.156, Sept. 30, 1895, Federal Military Pension Applications, NARA; Suffolk County, Massachusetts, Probate Records, "Petition for Administration of Probate by Timothy Warren," decree of May 12, 1898, 2nd ser., vol. 745, 247.

25. "Colonel John Warren," *Irish American*, Sept. 23, 1895; "Irish Republicans: An Enthusiastic Indorsement of Blaine and Logan," Boston *Daily Advertiser*, Oct 1, 1884, 8; "The Irish Republicans," *Boston Daily Globe*, Oct. 1, 1884, 2; "Ireland's Martyr Hero," *Boston Daily Globe*, Mar. 5, 1886, 2; "McCarthy Bides a Wee," Boston *Daily Globe*, June 7, 1889, 2; "All Express Sorrow," Oct. 8, 1891, *North American*, col. A; "Col. Warren Will Protest," *Boston Daily Globe*, Nov. 26, 1893, 6.

26. "A Bill for the Relief of John Warren," Jan. 21, 1892, H. R. 4489, 52nd Cong., 1st sess., and other papers in Accompanying Paper Files of Petition of John Warren, Records of the House of Representatives, RG 233, NARA; business card attached to letter of Warren to Secretary of War, July 1, 1892.

27. Declaration for an Original Disability Pension, application no. 1123.327, Federal Military Pension Applications, NARA.

28. "Magnificent Masonic Temple in the City of Boston," *Boston Daily Globe*, Aug. 25, 1895, SM38; "Temple in Ruins," Boston *Daily Advertiser*, Sept. 9, 1895, 6; "Colonel John Warren," *Irish American*, Sept. 23, 1895; "Col. John Warren Dead," *Boston Herald*, Sept. 15, 1895; "The Late Colonel Warren," *Boston Post*, Sept. 15, 1895; "Death of a Famous

Fenian," *Pilot*, Sept. 21, 1895; "Honored as a Patriot," *Boston Daily Globe*, Sept. 16, 1895; "Col. John Warren Dying," *Boston Daily Globe*, Sept. 14, 1895; "Death of Col. John Warren," *Boston Daily Globe*, Sept. 15, 1895, 20; "Col. John Warren Dies at Boston," *NYT*, Sept. 15, 1895, 13; "Irishmen's 'New Movement,'" *Boston Daily Globe*, Sept. 14, 1895, 7; Massachusetts Record of Death, "Deaths Registered in the City of Boston," 1891–1895, vol. 456, 365.

29. Reed Ueda, *Postwar Immigrant America: A Social History* (Boston, 1994), 156, table A.1; Erika Lee, "The Chinese Exclusion Example: Race, Immigration, and American Gatekeeping, 1882–1924," *Journal of American Ethnic History* 21 (Spring 2002): 36–62.

30. Frank Freidel, *Francis Lieber, Nineteenth-Century Liberal* (Baton Rouge, LA, 1947), 393–394; Francis Lieber, *Fragments of Political Science on Nationalism and Inter-nationalism* (New York, 1868), 22. Lieber created the term "Cis-Caucasian" because he believed "we stood in need of a name for the European part of the Caucasian race and its descendants in America and elsewhere." Lieber to Fish, Sept. 1, 1869, Francis Lieber Papers, 1815–1888, Huntington Library, San Marino, CA.

31. Elliott Young, *Alien Nation: Chinese Migration in the Americas from the Coolie Era through World War II* (Chapel Hill, NC, 2014), 103–128, 197–247; Marilyn Lake and Henry Reynolds, *Drawing the Global Colour Line: White Men's Countries and the International Challenge of Racial Equality* (Cambridge, 2008); Mae M. Ngai, *Impossible Subjects: Illegal Aliens and the Making of Modern America* (Princeton, NJ, 2004), 17–55; Adam M. McKeown, *Melancholy Order: Asian Migration and the Globalization of Borders* (New York, 2008), 149–184; John Higham, *Strangers in the Land: Patterns of American Nativism: 1860–1825* (New Brunswick, NJ, 1955).

32. Edwin Borchard, "The Decadence of the American Doctrine of Voluntary Expatriation," *American Journal of International Law* 25 (Aug. 1931): 314; McKeown, *Melancholy Order*, 6–7, 318–322; Frederick G. Whelan, "Citizenship and the Right to Leave," *American Political Science Review* 75 (Sept. 1981): 638–640.

33. David Edward Gutman, "Travel Documents, Mobility Control, and the Ottoman State in an Age of Global Migration, 1880–1915," *Journal of the Ottoman and Turkish Studies Association* 3 (Nov. 2016): 347–368; U.S. House of Representatives, *Citizenship of the United States, Expatriation, and Protection Abroad*, 59th Cong., 2nd sess., H. R. Doc. 326, 12–13; Eugene M. Avrutin, *Jews and the Imperial State: Identification Politics in Tsarist Russia* (Ithaca, NY, 2010), 53–115.

34. Count Otto zu Stolberg-Wernigerode, *Germany and the United States of America during the Era of Bismarck* (Reading, PA, 1937), 182–186. The United States signed a multilateral agreement with Central and South American states in 1906 that incorporated the earlier Bancroft treaty clause, presuming that naturalized citizens who resume residence in their native land had resumed their original citizenship. "Status of Naturalized Citizens Who Return to Country of Origin (Inter-American)," 37 Stat. 1653.

35. Alan Dowty, *Closed Borders: The Contemporary Assault on Freedom of Movement* (New Haven, CT, 1987); on threat posed by French nationality laws of 1889, see Marshall B. Woodworth, "Citizenship under the Fourteenth Amendment," *American Law Review* 30

(July–Aug. 1896): 552–554; Patrick Weil, *How to Be French: Nationality in the Making since 1789* (Durham, NC, 2008); John H. Wigmore, "Domicile, Double Allegiance, and World Citizenship," *University of Illinois Law Review* 21 (1927): 761; Andreas Fahrmeir, "From Economics to Ethnicity and Back: Reflections on Emigration Control in Germany, 1800–2000," in *Citizenship and Those Who Leave: The Politics of Emigration and Expatriation*, ed. Nancy L. Green and François Weil (Urbana, IL, 2007), 184–187; Ben Herzog, *Revoking Citizenship: Expatriation in America from the Colonial Era to the War on Terror* (New York, 2015), 61–62, 64–65.

36. Convention on Certain Questions Relating to the Conflict of Nationality Laws, The Hague, April 12, 1930; R. S. Fraser, "Expatriation as Practised in Great Britain," *Transactions of the Grotius Society* 16 (1930): 73–91; Peter Spiro, "A New International Law of Citizenship," *American Journal of International Law* 105 (Oct. 2011): 700–703, 707–709; Richard W. Flournoy Jr., "Nationality Convention," *American Journal of International Law* 24 (July 1930): 473–474.

37. *Opinions of the Principal Officers of the Executive Departments and Other Papers Relating to Expatriation, Naturalization, and Change of Allegiance* (Washington, DC, 1873), 10; Ulysses S. Grant, "Fifth Annual Message," December 1, 1873, online by Gerhard Peters and John T. Woolley, American Presidency Project, http://www.presidency.ucsb.edu/ws/?pid=29514; "Passports for Persons Residing or Sojourning Abroad," circular from Secretary of State John Hay, Mar. 27, 1899, in *FRUS*, 1902, pt. 1, 1–4; U.S. House of Representatives, Citizenship of the United States, Expatriation, and Protection Abroad, 59th Cong., 2nd sess., H. R. Doc. 326, 18; John P. Roche, "Loss of American Nationality: The Years of Confusion," *Western Political Quarterly* 4 (June 1951): 284–294.

38. Peter J. Spiro, "Dual Nationality and the Meaning of Citizenship," *Emory Law Journal* 46 (Fall 1997): 1411–1485; U.S. House of Representatives, Citizenship of the United States, Expatriation, and Protection Abroad, 59th Cong., 2nd sess., H. R. Doc. 326, 12–13; Herzog, *Revoking Citizenship*, 56–65.

39. Act of June 29, 1906; Act of March 2, 1907.

40. *Mackenzie v. Hare*, 168 Cal. 776 (1913); *Mackenzie v. Hare*, 239 U.S. 299 (1915); Candice Lewis Bredbenner, *A Nationality of Her Own: Women, Marriage and the Law of Citizenship* (Berkeley, CA, 1998), 45–112; Herzog, *Revoking Citizenship*, 43–55, 70–77; Patrick Weil, *The Sovereign Citizen: Denaturalization and the Origins of the American Republic* (Philadelphia, 2013), 15–43; Dorothee Schneider, *Crossing Borders: Migration and Citizenship in the Twentieth-Century United States* (Cambridge, MA, 2011), 134–149, 156–163, 211–241.

41. T. Alexander Aleinikoff, "Theories of Loss of Citizenship," *Michigan Law Review* 84 (June 1986): 1474–1475; Hannah Arendt, *Origins of Totalitarianism* (New York, 1966), 267–302; Gerald Daniel Cohen, *In War's Wake: Europe's Displaced Persons in the Postwar Order* (New York, 2012), 4–7; "Documenting Numbers of Victims of the Holocaust and Nazi Persecution," *Holocaust Encyclopedia*, United States Holocaust Memorial Museum, https://www.ushmm.org/wlc/en/article.php?ModuleId=10008193. On the shifting meaning of "expatriation," see Nancy L. Green, "Expatriation, Expatriates, and Expats: The

American Transformation of a Concept," *American Historical Review* 114 (Apr. 2009): 307–328.

42. Universal Declaration of Human Rights, Dec. 10, 1948, Articles 13 and 15, Preamble; Christopher Roberts, *The Contentious History of the International Bill of Rights* (Cambridge, 2015); Mary Ann Glendon, *A World Made New: Eleanor Roosevelt and the Universal Declaration of Human Rights* (New York, 2001); Frederick G. Whelan, "Citizenship and the Right to Leave," *American Political Science Review* 75 (Sept. 1981): 636–653.

43. See, e.g., Morton J. Horowitz, *The Warren Court and the Pursuit of Justice* (New York, 1999); Charles R. Epp, *The Rights Revolution: Lawyers, Activists and Supreme Courts in Comparative Perspective* (Chicago, 1998).

44. *Perez v. Brownell,* 356 U.S. 44 (1958), 64–65.

45. *Trop v. Dulles,* 356 U.S. 86 (1958), 92.

46. *Schneider v. Rusk,* 377 U.S. 163 (1964), 168–169.

47. *Afroyim v. Rusk,* 387 U.S. 253 (1967), 266, 257. For an excellent analysis of the Supreme Court's evolving position on the cases, see Weil, *The Sovereign Citizen,* 111–175. I differ with Weil in seeing *Afroyim* as a return to mid-nineteenth-century views (albeit altered by twentieth-century experiences with World War II, the Holocaust, and the emerging "human rights revolution"), whereas Weil sees *Afroyim* as evidence of a new view of the citizen (as opposed to the state) as sovereign. See also John P. Roche, "The Expatriation Cases: 'Breathes There the Man, With Soul so Dead . . . ?" *Supreme Court Review* v. 1963 (1963): 325–356; Aleinikoff, "Theories of Loss of Citizenship"; Herzog, *Revoking Citizenship,* 78–89.

48. Michael Walter, "The Bancroft Conventions: Second-Class Citizenship for Naturalized Americans," *International Lawyer* 12 (Fall 1978): 825–833; Herzog, *Revoking Citizenship,* 58–59.

49. Mary Elise Sarotte, *Collapse: The Accidental Opening of the Berlin Wall* (New York, 2014); Raymond Pearson, *The Rise and Fall of the Soviet Empire* (New York, 1998); Herzog, *Revoking Citizenship,* 65–69.

50. See, e.g., the Comparative Citizenship Project, created by the International Migration Policy Program of the Carnegie Endowment for International Peace in 1997. Several volumes have been published under its auspices, edited by T. Alexander Aleinikoff and Douglas Klusmeyer, including: *Citizenship Policies for an Age of Migration* (Washington, DC, 2002); *From Migrants to Citizens: Membership in a Changing World* (Washington, DC, 2000); *Citizenship Today: Global Perspectives and Practices* (Washington, DC, 2001). On the possibility of an individual-rights-oriented international law of citizenship, see Spiro, "A New International Law of Citizenship"; on prevalence of dual nationality, see Peter J. Spiro, *At Home in Two Countries: The Past and Future of Dual Citizenship* (New York, 2016). The Chinese Exclusion Act was repealed in 1943 (57 Stat. 600), the race requirement for naturalization abolished in 1952 (Immigration and Nationality Act of 1952, 66 Stat. 163, §403.1), and the national origins quota repealed in the Immigration and Nationality Act of 1965, which also declared unlawful any admission preferences based on race, sex, or nationality (79 Stat. 911, §2).

51. Will Somerville, "When the Dust Settles: Migration Policy after Brexit," June 2016, Migration Policy Institute, http://www.migrationpolicy.org/news/when-dust-settles-migration-policy-after-brexit.

52. Mark Nestmann, "'Homelanders' to U.S. Expatriates: Don't Come Back . . . Ever," June 23, 2013, https://www.nestmann.com/homelanders-to-u-s-expatriates-dont-come-back-ever; Mae Ngai, "Why Trump is Making Muslims the New Chinese," CNN, January 30, 2017; President of the United States, Executive Order 13769, Protecting the Nation from Foreign Terrorist Entry into the United States, January 27, 2017; United Nations High Commissioner on Refugees, *Global Trends: Forced Displacement in 2016*, June 21, 2017, 2–3 (the number displaced—including those designated as "refugees"—is much higher, reaching 65.6 million); Alexander Betts and Paul Collier, *Refuge: Transforming a Broken Refugee System* (London, 2017).

53. Borchard, "The Decadence of the American Doctrine of Voluntary Expatriation," 316.

Acknowledgments

This book has taken me on a long journey, much longer than I expected. I would like to thank the many people who have accompanied me along the way, lightening the load, relieving the tedium, buoying my spirits, and helping me steer a true course to the destination. Years ago, when I pondered jumping ship on the project I was working on to try my hand at writing narrative history, my friend and colleague Jeff Bolster said, "Go for it!" Since then, he has provided invaluable advice, from commenting on countless drafts to explaining how to identify a brigantine. Bill Harris has also been generous with his time and comments, assuring me that "this is a book" when it seemed more like a jumble of words. I am fortunate, indeed, to be in a department of stellar scholars and generous colleagues who asked sharp questions at seminars and provided unflagging support. Thanks especially to Nicoletta Gullace, Jessica Lepler, Janet Polasky, Julia Rodriguez, and Sara Wolper for their help on particular aspects of the project. The chairs of the History Department at the University of New Hampshire, Jan Golinski and Eliga Gould, provided vital support at critical junctures. So, too, have students at UNH. I have enjoyed superb research assistance over the years from Benjamin Bertrand, Joseph Juknievich, Molly Gallaher Boddy, Anna Brown, Jill Silos, and Linda Upham-Bornstein. Amanda Demmer read the entire manuscript with a keen eye, even though she had more than enough to do in her first year of teaching. My Justice Studies students never let me have *too* much fun while we were in Budapest, asking frequently, "How's the book coming?"

Colleagues in immigration and legal history have been incredibly supportive. I thank Dirk Hartog, Mae Ngai, and Barbara Welke, in particular, for their steadfast support of the project. My graduate school mentor,

Harry N. Scheiber, and Jane Scheiber have provided unflagging encouragement over many years. For their comments and questions, thanks to the faculty and students at the History Workshop at Boston College History Department; the Legal History Workshop at the University of Minnesota Law School; the Global Race, Ethnicity, and Migration Lecture Series at the Immigration History Research Center, University of Minnesota; the Legal History Seminar at Boston University School of Law; the Law and History Workshop at Columbia Law School; the American Bar Foundation; the Law and History Workshop at Harvard Law School; the Political Science Department at the University of Denver; and the Program in Legal Studies at the University of Massachusetts, Amherst. I am grateful for input from many scholars, including Susanna Blumenthal, Candice Bredbenner, Kristin Collins, Lynn Johnson, Dan Kanstroom, Kate Masur, José Moya, Gerald Neumann, Christina Duffy Ponsa-Kraus, Eric Schlereth, Brook Thomas, Leti Volpp, Michael Vorenberg, John Witt, and Vicky Saker Woeste. Kevin Kenny and Hidetaka Hirota offered very helpful advice on navigating Irish records as I embarked on several research trips to Ireland. A million thanks to Clonakilty historians Tomás Tuipéar, Clíodhna O'Leary, and Michael O'Mahony—and to Shane Kenna in Dublin—for helping me uncover the history of John Warren. Audra Wolfe provided invaluable editorial guidance at a critical point of the project. Kathleen McDermott, my editor at Harvard University Press, has been patient and judicious in helping to bring this project to fruition, for which I am most thankful. Finally, I am deeply grateful to Kunal Parker and Kevin Kenny for their critical interventions in the last stages of revisions.

Research and writing takes a lot of time, and this book would not have been possible without the generous aid of the Radcliffe Institute for Advanced Study at Harvard University, the William Nelson Cromwell Foundation, the National Endowment for the Humanities, the American Philosophical Foundation, the Law and Social Sciences Program at the National Science Foundation, and the American Council for Learned Societies. The University of New Hampshire generously granted leave and financial support through the Faculty Scholars Program, the Center for the Humanities, the Center for International Education, and the Graduate School Summer Fellowship Program. Thank you to Judith Vichniac, John Gordan, Sarah Barringer Gordon, Scott Barclay, Susan Sterett, and, at UNH, Dean Ken Fuld, Burt Feintuch, Ellen Cohn, Angele Cook, and Susan Sosa, for their assistance with the grants. The transatlantic research project was daunting at times but made much easier with the help of knowledgeable staff at the National Archives of Ireland, the National

Library of Ireland, the National Archives in England, the National Archives and Records Administration in Washington, D.C., and in Waltham, Massachusetts, the Massachusetts Historical Society, the Massachusetts State Archives, the Library of Congress, and the Huntington Library. Finally, every day and in every way, Laura Simard and Lara Demarest of the UNH History Department provided unfailing professional support.

Most especially, I thank my wonderful friends and family. For the walks and talks that helped keep me sane, thanks to Nicky Gullace, Sara Wolper, Anath Golomb, Ruth Wharton-McDonald, Julia O'Connell, Jeff and Molly Bolster, Sue Richmond, Malcolm Beaudett, Linda and Peter Bornstein, Rosann Greenspan, and Vicky Woeste; to my "bookies," Donna Bethke-Borg, Nancy Sell, Nancy Maiello, and Christine Duprez-Young; and to the "Milvia House alum": Cathy Kudlick, Mary Odem, Susan Sterett, and most especially, my "gsb," Marianne Constable, who has always been my rock.

Families know better than anyone the toll that a book can take. To my brothers and their families, to Penny and Shayla, to my in-laws, especially my late mother-in-law, Bea, thank you! I am deeply indebted to my husband, Lee, for his love and support and for putting up with my long absences, both physical and mental, as I worked on the book. Now that the book is done, I look forward to new joint adventures. My dear son, Nate, was a wonderful companion as we traveled together to Ireland in pursuit of the Fenians and was unfailing in his optimism about the project. Finally, while this is a book largely about men, I dedicate it to the two most important women in my life: to my mother, who taught me how to write, and my daughter, who was only six when I started this project. Now all grown up, she has taught me more than I could ever convey.

Credits

158   *Harper's Weekly*, Sept. 17, 1859. Widener Library, Harvard University.

163   *Harper's Weekly*, Apr. 14, 1866, 233. Widener Library, Harvard University.

179   Library of Congress, LC-DIG-cwpbh-01400.

199   Library of Congress, LC-DIG-ds-06802.

202   *Frank Leslie's Illustrated Newspaper*, Apr. 1, 1882, 96. Library of Congress, LC-USZC2-780.

204   *The Weekly News* (Dublin), Apr. 3, 1869, 1. National Library of Ireland.

217   *Harper's Weekly*, Oct. 21, 1876. Widener Library, Harvard University.

Index